D1454337

A Gap Year or Two

Adventures in Europe between
1970 and 1974

A Gap Year or Two

*Adventures in Europe between
1970 and 1974*

Jeremy Macdonogh

ATHENA PRESS
LONDON

A GAP YEAR OR TWO
Adventures in Europe between 1970 and 1974
Copyright © Jeremy Macdonogh 2007

ISBN 10-digit: 1 84401 987 X
ISBN 13-digit: 978 1 84401 987 8

First Published 2007 by
ATHENA PRESS
Queen's House, 2 Holly Road
Twickenham TW1 4EG
United Kingdom

Printed for Athena Press

Contents

Foreword

Thoughts on *A Gap Year or Two*

This is a curiously beguiling, even rather extraordinary book. I suspect, from my response to it, that I must have been expecting something else, a collection of comedy capers perhaps, or a straightforward travelogue. Well, in a way it is both of these but neither term gives one much of a flavour of what lies within. It belongs alongside *Tristram Shandy* or something similar, a journey not just through countries but through customs and history and whole civilisations and philosophies that have either vanished or been obscured within my lifetime. Presumably the publisher agrees with my assessment as he has allowed short introductory paragraphs, as well as a title, for every chapter ('A Holy Day of Obligation' *in which the author learns a little more about why the French are what they are, this time in a private chapel*), that would place it firmly in this tradition.

A Gap Year or Two gives a truthful and vivid account of how the author spent the years between university and the start of real life – I was going to say 'eking out his living' but the existence described here is anything but 'eked'. One early encounter with a rich, widowed aristocrat takes him to Switzerland, ostensibly to play bridge with her guests, in fact to learn to ski like a champion. Another piece of serendipitous timing finds him at the receiving end of a superb, free dinner at Tivoli in honour of Lord Palmerston's contribution to Italian unity. But what marks this book apart from any other pleasant, chatty memoir is the level of scholarship. Every country, every city, almost every church and even building, is given its own story and, in these anecdotes and incidents, is the history of Europe to be found. As all schoolchildren know, it is the detail of history, the loves, hates and rivalries that make us feel that the inhabitants of the past are connected to us. In fact, as this book makes clear, they *are* us, in different clothes maybe, but the same people as we are. If you want to know about the D-Day Landings or the Risorgimento, the burial place of the kings of France or the fate of the Crown of Greece, then read on. Nor is it necessarily always long ago. If you never knew that Glenn Close's first cousin was the immensely grand Italian Prince Torlonia, then this book will tell you all about it. But Macdonogh's skill is to keep it light, never too long on one subject, never too deep in politics or dates; he delivers the facts, making them entertaining and, more usefully, comprehensible, but never lingering long enough to bore.

Of course one of the reasons I loved the book was that it reminded me of how things were when I too left Cambridge in 1970. We did not know it then (at least I didn't) but we were in fact witnessing the end of the Old World. Those values that had obtained across society from the Battle of Hastings to the twentieth century, which had been challenged by the First World War and essentially doomed by the Second, were still in their dying fall. The last aristocratic government in Britain was really that of Harold Macmillan until the Profumo scandal of 1963 finished it, barely seven years before the start of this story. Those landowners who had attempted to make things work again after the war were, many of them, only then throwing in the towel. Presentation had finished just a few years before, in the 1950s, while divorcees were still forbidden entry to the Royal Enclosure at Ascot. In France, in the 1960s, it was considered odd, not to say eccentric (as the book makes wonderfully clear), for anyone with pretensions to birth to be waited on at table by maids instead of footmen. I loved Macdonogh's stuttering attempt to explain to his French hostess that his parents didn't have any servants *at all*. They were, as they would be, amazed. And in case you are wondering, this was all true. Like the author, I knew Peter Townend and was a member of his stable of eligible *partis* (God knows why, in my case). I also spent my nights at soirées, the grandeur of which, and at houses, the discomfort of which, still shocks me thirty-five years later. If some of his experiences of sharing jokes with Princess Margaret read as rather grander than most of mine, nevertheless I can vouch for their authenticity.

A French episode, where Macdonogh's hosts sit on gilded

thrones to hear Mass, high above the heads of their own peasantry, and turn their backs on the French Pretender as the descendant of a regicide, was curiously similar to my own time spent with a *Faubourg* family in order to learn my vowels. Once I ventured to discuss the merits of the British system of constitutional monarchy to be met with a blank stare. *'Julian,'* said my hostess in a pained voice, *'ici, on ne crois qu'un roi absolu.'* And another time, when I was spotted dancing with a certain Mademoiselle de Montebello at a *Rallye* ball: *'Julian, nous ne connaissons les familles Napoléoniques.'* The point is that this was all still going on at the start of the 1970s and yet, by the early '80s, one might have been describing life on Mars. Despite being less than forty years ago, most of the world Macdonogh describes seems as distant from Blair's Britain as the Chartists or the Great Exhibition. What little remains of it has gone into hiding now and is largely forbidden to the outsider; but still, if anyone out there is curious about the fading of those, to me, rather dear if sometimes ridiculous days, then this is the book for them.

Julian Fellowes,
July 2006

Preface

Before you read my adventures, you might want to know who I am or, better yet, who I was, way back in 1970; all critical research if you are to select a comfortable armchair, turn on the lamp, pour a drink and settle down to digest this history.

I was a very lucky and privileged fellow, just down from Cambridge. Not privileged in that easy way of being heir to a ducal fortune; quite the contrary. My privilege lay more in a good education, a certain amount of innocent charm and a taste for adventure. That, plus an apparent ability to remain unruffled; the 'swan syndrome' some call it. The French say *sans six sous et sans souci*.

I needed to stay calm. The unalloyed truth is that I, together with all but the brightest of my fellow graduates, was unable to land a job in early 1970s Britain. The country was tipping into a catastrophic economic recession where it would crash and burn for some years. The secondary banking system was on the verge of collapse. The country's greatest ever property crash was on its way, bringing with it a terrible 'winter of discontent'. 'Oil shock' and the terrifying 1973 stock market nosedive, when the SE30 index fell from 500 to below 200, had only been seen before in 1929. The sounds off were of three-day weeks and talk of an IMF rescue. There were even whispers of a coup d'état. In short, the lunatics were running the asylum.

And, if that weren't bad enough, there were rumours of the imminent dissolution of the Beatles.

I thought it best to cast off, drift around for a month or two and wait for the coast to clear. The tide took me, like driftwood, to Ireland, to Scotland and to that place we then called 'the Continent'. It turned out to be a Grand Tour of Europe (mostly) at other people's expense, though never (I hope) at their cost.

The expression 'gap year' had yet to be invented, and in the event my attempt at this now familiar institution was to last for around four years. I travelled alone, was open to every suggestion and new adventure, and had experience after life-enhancing experience. They were mostly funny or touching. One in particular was life-threatening, and yet another very sad.

This period was my gap between student and employee and saw me change, as Bernard Shaw would have it, 'from old boy to young man'. Each of my experiences gave me a slightly broader mind, and the effect was cumulative. My perspective gradually shifted from a pinhole view of the immediate towards a panorama of the eternal.

Kultur has more than a walk-on part in my adventures. When I started out, I knew a little about art, history, architecture and music. Apart from some basic French, however, I had no modern languages. All of this would radically change.

In my story comes great music, fine art, beautiful landscapes and consummate architecture, and me with my insatiable appetite for it all. If you travel with me you will share the awe I experienced, for example, on hearing Bach's *B minor Mass* for the first time. You will enjoy both social and gastronomic flavours of France and Italy, of Germany and Switzerland, of Ireland and Scotland. If you share a love of cooking you must let me share my first hamburger with you, as well as a *magret de pigeon*.

Come with me to Sicily and visit a feral taxidermist. Stay with me in a Marseilles brothel and meet the girls. Get arrested by an aggressive gendarme when we try to sleep rough under a bridge in Le Mans, or join me and an ex-convict in Rome's Caffé Greco. Narrowly avoid being kidnapped by Sardinian bandits.

One small reason why this account is a rare alternative to the more generally published memoirs from the early seventies, so inevitably set in a hell of horrific hardship, or on the golden hippy trail to Samarkand, is that you will meet the great and good of nearly half a century ago: Princess Margaret, Reginald Bosanquet, Diana Dors, Lady Sarah Coke, Lord Goodman and Lady Diana Cooper are a sample of the distinguished Brits who play cameo roles in this memoir. The names of those I met on my travels – royal, famous, peasants, or fellow flotsam – have usually been given. Where they have been withheld reflects my publisher's fear of a lawsuit or, perhaps, some vestigial chivalry of my own. That said, no further attempt has been made to spare my or anyone else's blushes.

Thoughts, opinions and observations on everything – starlets, politicians and their groupies, girls and bandits – pepper my story. Inevitably, they reflect an era before political correctness. There may still be a reader or two left out there who agrees with me – or more who profoundly disagree.

My tale reflects a youth with all the usual vices, and in my determination to tell the truth, I have included some embarrassing episodes. My excuse? I was a very young man feeling my way.

In presenting the process of growing up as a continuum of brief memoirs, I have tried to be other than a common retailer of traveller's tales and something more than a smug autobiographer. My experiences were rich and varied, and my plan is that you journey with me. By the time we finish, we shall have become childhood friends.

Today, as I sit in my house in Suffolk, about to lay my pen to rest, I think of my son Felix, already past my age in this chronicle, and how times have changed. But man has not. Pleasure and Principle still dance as partners through the fabric of our lives, just as they did when I was a coltish sybarite, as happy as the day was long.

I would urge anyone who might be musing on whether to take their life in their hands and take a 'gap year' in Europe, no matter how old they are, to gird their loins, sharpen their wits and do just that. This account of those eternal Golden Years, *Wanderjahren* perhaps, when an optimist can make his way around the world with little but charm, an open mind and a reasonable education to his name, may possibly help.

Jeremy Macdonogh,
Hoxne, Suffolk,
2006

Acknowledgements

I should like to thank David Mountford, Jane Ratcliffe, Pat Reeve, John Bawtree, Michael Culver-James, Tev Chaldecott, Gervas Douglas and Paul Hrynaszkiewitcz for their many suggestions and tireless proofreading. The text is both more accurate and vastly less prolix as a result of their efforts. Andrew Meredith-Davies actually appears in the Greek episode. Tim Hillyar, particularly, provided invaluable logistical help.

I should be nowhere without the conspiracy of the characters in the narrative; their contribution will be all too obvious. In this light, perhaps my sister Katharine should be singled out, while the late Johnnie FitzHerbert deservedly steals a lot of the thunder.

Long-suffering friends, such as George (who wants to keep his surname to himself), Piers de la Force, Colin Swan and Caroline Swan are yet to discover that the memories they had surely tried to suppress have been brought back to life by this unscrupulous author.

Charles-Henri de Bartillat, Olivier de Caumont la Force and Emmanuel de Bodard have been especially helpful in the exhumation of these traveller's tales.

So too have Lanfranco Secco-Suardo, Sandro Ridomi, Paola Igliori and Violante Gaetani.

But, saving the best till last, I need to pay a particular tribute to the unswerving and constant encouragement of my steadfast wife, Helen Kelsey.

Matins or Prologue
1970: Fisher House, Cambridge

Where do the Roman gods live these days? Can they really be cosying up to their Greek cousins on Mount Olympus? More likely, they prefer to infest the pantheons built for them in Rome and Paris, and nurse a grudge against the faithless they used to tease so many centuries ago... Or perhaps they are all around us, most of their awesome powers long dissipated, mostly looking like distinguished old men but with a mischievous twinkle in their eyes.

In 1970, I was about to find out. But before I could abandon myself to their strange games, I would have to sit my 'final final', the last hurdle of my degree. Probably I would scrape through. Most of us did. But for me it was going to be a close-run thing.

Cambridge that May was a joyless kindergarten, its students grey and unkempt, and would remain that way until all the faculties completed their own exams. The whole place already smelled of coffee and fear, everyone in a hurry and with no time to laugh. If you had finished, courtesy would require you to avoid smiling until the last of your fellow graduates had given this degree thing their best shot.

Then would come the oddly named 'May Week', those twelve days in June, when the gods in their capricious and pagan ways would sport with us. They would come in disguise to our last ever parties as students, marking our cards and playing games with our destinies. Saturnalia, their favourite season, would flourish until our results were published on a vast notice board, attached to the Senate House; the 'weeping wall', we called it. And then it would end. Comedy or tragedy, we'd sober up, get a haircut, remind our parents what we looked like, put on a suit and tie and go to an office for the rest of our allocated span – if (of course) that was what the gods had planned for us.

Ours had surely been the most exciting generation of students ever. Beatles, Kinks and Rolling Stones had serenaded us throughout. Our government had declined American invitations to send us to Vietnam. Christian innocence and the pagan Pill had combined in a luxurious way and the self-pitying strains of ultra-feminism were yet to be heard. And despite the fleshly tempta-tions, Cambridge still provided more Nobel Prize laureates than Harvard, and scholarship pervaded every conversation. Who could give such parties when we had gone?

Even by the surreal standards of the season, the day had started oddly.

Having failed to get to sleep for most of the night, at dawn I had finally sailed off into a dream-filled ocean. All too soon came the shock of the alarm clock, rude and unwelcome. Struggling to my feet I peered morosely at an unshaven face in the mirror over the fireplace and counted spots. Far too many; I was not eating properly. A card on the mantelshelf caught my eye, sent by some well-organised fellow sufferer, announcing his intentions for May Week. *Partir, c'est sourir un peu*, it read.[1] I had accepted that one. Another, on stiff board, had a coat of arms with what looked like dinner on it. It's a long time ago, but Coquilles St Jacques quartered with Turkey Rampant sticks in the mind. It was from Fr Richard Incledon, incumbent at Fisher House, the Cambridge University Catholic Chaplaincy. It was an invitation to lunch – for today. It was far too late for breakfast and my exam was not until the afternoon. I would ring and accept. It was a bit late but I was sure they wouldn't mind. Priests don't have to balance numbers, after all.

Fisher House had been founded by papal indult in 1895. After a disgracefully long injustice, the 'Test Acts' had finally been repealed and Catholics were again allowed to read for degrees at Oxford and Cambridge. By 1970 Fisher House had enjoyed about half a century in a seventeenth-century pub, an oxymoronic building that was grand, shabby, old-fashioned and modern in every ghastly permutation.

I knew a little about the saintly Dr John Fisher, after whom

---

[1] The French saying, from which this is adapted, is *Partir, c'est mourir un peu*, and is usually translated with Romeo's lovely line, 'Parting is such sweet sorrow'.

the Chaplaincy was named. He was the ultimate Cambridge man. He had a hand in the foundation of two of our loveliest colleges, Christ's and St John's. According to Erasmus, this was primarily in order to churn out yet more priests.

The main man, John Fisher, started out as a level-headed chap – in fact, his early and sound decision that all students at St John's should speak only in Greek, Latin or Hebrew certainly supports his claims to common sense. Judging by the nonsense they utter in English, it is a great shame this edict has elapsed.

But after this promising start he grew ambitious, even reckless, and it proved his undoing. When he saw a chance to cultivate Lady Margaret Beaufort (Henry VII's mother, whose Plantagenet blood was so important for the legitimacy of the first of the Tudor kleptocrats), he leapt at it. At first it paid off handsomely and he progressed to become, first, Bishop of Rochester, then Professor of Theology at Cambridge and finally Chancellor of the University.

The expression 'timing is everything' can also apply to university chancellors. Unfortunately for this clever and saintly cleric, King Henry VIII opted for total control of the Church just as everything was going so well. Fisher had to choose between his standing at court and his commitment to his Catholic faith. Becoming the private chaplain to Catherine of Aragon had been, perhaps, an appointment too far. Influenced by the saintly example of Thomas More, he thenceforward backed all the wrong horses.

He opposed the royal marriage to Anne Boleyn, rejected the King's authority over the Ecclesia Anglicana and railed against the Court's rejection of the Pope as St Peter's successor. It was not long before the Yeomen of the Guard arrived to march him off to the Tower. In June 1535, just sixty-six years old but so weak and gaunt that he needed to be carried to Tower Hill in a chair, John Fisher climbed the scaffold, slipped off his gown, pardoned the executioner, recited the Te Deum, was blindfolded and then beheaded.

Of course the story did not end there. Fisher arrived in a sunlit Elysium, his infirmities stripped away, to a Palladian pavilion somewhat resembling Chiswick House, where Jesus himself presented him with his martyr's crown to the sounds of Mozart's Flute and Harp Concerto, performed by the heavenly host.

In the circumstances, therefore, both from a respect for history and from the perspective of one's immortal soul, it seemed doubly unwise to decline an invitation from Fisher House, and at the stroke of noon I duly presented myself, properly clad in suit and gown.

Lunch proved to be a grand affair. The dining room was simply decorated with prints and etchings, all no doubt on high-minded matters. Around a groaning oak refectory table were a small number of dons and a couple of elderly clerics. Standing out was the diminutive figure of Monsignor Alfred Gilbey, already known to me as the patron saint of the recusant English Catholic upper class. The Monsignor was in familiar territory. He had been Chaplain here himself from 1932 to 1965. He was a 'Protonotary Apostolic', a distinction normally accorded to a priest of the chief college of the Papal Curia. Such men are tasked with recording consistories and canonisations and are permitted to sign papal bulls. Mgr Gilbey was an honorary member of this college, in effect a 'flying bishop', and Fr Incledon interrupted his twinkling but quiet chinwag with Fr Alfonso de Zulueta, a towering figure uniting Spanish nobleman and English gentleman, and formerly Chaplain at the Other Place. Gilbey was to say Grace.

I was the only undergraduate there; if any others had been invited they must have had more important things to do. Every so often the Chaplain rang a little electric bell under his place at table and a uniformed lackey swapped the empty plates for something even more delicious than before. So masterly was the badinage that I remember every word.

As a conversational gambit, I complimented Fr Incledon on his celebrated founding father.

'St John Fisher, you mean?'

'Certainly,' I said. 'Stout fellow. An example to us all.'

A murmur of agreement from the table meant that my wicket was not as sticky as it rightly should have been.

'I agree,' said Fr Incledon. 'I have always had a soft spot for martyrs, though had I lived in ancient Rome I would almost certainly have remained a good pagan. The early church, with its secret meetings in gloomy caves and its lurid taste for confessing the most banal of sins in public – my dear, it's simply not on. The old Roman pantheon has been over-severely maligned down the ages.'

I found this line slightly surprising.

'Still,' said Mgr Gilbey, taking up the theme, 'on the walls of one of the early necropoleis, under Santa Maria in Agone in Piazza Navona, there is a moving fresco,[2] dating from the time of that rascal Diocletian. It shows some poor Christian sap being torn apart by four chariots. The evil centurion is shouting at his men, and his words are written above him, as in a newspaper cartoon. They read, *Trahi, fili di puti!*

'Really?' said Fr de Zulueta. 'That sounds rather like Italian.'

'Precisely,' said Mgr Gilbey. 'It's the first example of Italian in written form, which makes it easily the oldest modern European language. English is almost the youngest.'

It was glaringly obvious I could not speak a word of Italian or, much worse, Latin. Mgr Gilbey put me out of my misery. 'The Italian means, "Pull, you sons of bitches". A wonderful phrase with which to kick off such a literary tradition.'

'My favourite martyr,' said Fr Incledon, 'while we're on this subject, has always been St Adauctus. Your "friend" Diocletian had ordered the paleo-Christian priest, St Felix, to be beheaded for his irreverence (as the Emperor saw it). He ordered the saint to be taken through the streets of Rome to keep his appointment with his Maker.

'While the crowds variously cheered and jeered, according to taste, another Christian had been watching the sad procession and could stand it no longer.

' "Why is he to be executed?" he demanded of anyone who would listen.

' "Because he's a Christian," came the answer.

' "Well, so am I!" insisted this holy fellow. He burst through the crowds and, despite the efforts of the citizens, people and soldiers alike to stop him, he leapt aboard the tumbrel, knelt beside the priest and joined him in prayer.

'The Romans begged him to get down and leg it. They wouldn't stop him, they told him. But he was adamant. "I want to go where this fellow is going. If his only crime is to believe in God, then I'm as much a criminal as he."

'So, inevitably, the poor fellow was beheaded alongside the

---

[2] A predecessor of the moving picture?

priest, and from that moment he was added to the long list of saints who fell in those early days. Trouble is, they never did find out his name. So they called him 'Adauctus', which simply means 'added to'... added to St Felix, of course.'

A natural pause in the conversation allowed the Chaplain's retainers to swap our Coquilles St Jacques for a plate of roast turkey. There was a little polite conversation about Mgr Gilbey's London arrangements – he seemed to spend six months of the year at the Travellers' Club in St James's, and the other six at the Athenaeum. Apparently he had converted a cupboard in the Travellers' into a private chapel so that he could celebrate Mass every day (as a priest must).

I had recently discovered that Fr de Zulueta was my father's parish priest, in Chelsea, and I wanted to ask him something significant. I waited until I had caught his eye.

'Have you ever met General Franco?' I asked the old Spaniard.

He might have done, after all. But it was best to keep the question open. You never know, he might easily have been a dyed-in-the-wool *franquista*.

'Yes I have, actually, but a long time ago. Shortly after the war broke out. Frightful little man, then and now, even if he did protect the Church.'

'I thought you were in England during the war?' Fr Incledon observed.

'Yes, I was. But I had offered my services as a native Spanish speaker to the denizens of the corridors of power, and the Prime Minister eventually called on them. My services, I mean.'

'Winston Churchill?' I asked. Mgr Gilbey looked at me sharply. The idiocy of youth, I could see he was thinking. Actually, I was wondering if he had meant Chamberlain.

'Yes, Churchill. He was our prime minister during the war, you know.'

It seemed that directly after Churchill had taken over from Chamberlain, the Great Man had summoned the Anglo-Spaniard to Downing Street. Zulu (as he hated being called) found himself in camera with Anthony Eden and the Prime Minister.

'I am sending you both to Madrid,' Churchill told them. 'Eden, you're to call on this *Caudillo* chappie' – pronouncing the Spanish word for dictator with a theatrical Spanish accent – 'and find out whether neutral means neutral for the Nazis' – *narzies*, he pronounced it – 'or neutral for us. Zulu, you're there to interpret. All right, that's enough, pack your bags and get going. I have other fish to fry.'

General Franco duly received the two envoys with great style at the Zarzuela Palace, where he offered them local delicacies and plied them with wine. Fr de Zulueta noticed that the generalissimo himself did not touch a drop. Franco addressed all his remarks to the priest, with the elaborate courtesy befitting a great nobleman, who duly translated for the Foreign Secretary.

'He says he is "neutral-neutral". He is not coming into the war on either side. And he will no longer permit the Germans, or us, access to his country except at diplomatic level.'

'Well, the Prime Minister will be greatly relieved,' said His Majesty's Secretary of State for Foreign Affairs. 'We had better head home and report the good news.'

'Would you mind if I see the Primate before we leave?' Zulueta was obviously suspicious.

'No, not at all,' said Eden. 'And I'll tag along too.'

The two men were admitted the same day to a palace that made the Zarzuela look modest. Priests scuttled through endless barrel-vaulted corridors. Their personal *vade mecum*, a purple-sashed monsignor, took them up great flights of marble and porphyry stairs, past portraits of Spanish cardinals, sinister princes and Renaissance popes until they were issued into the Presence.

In pole position was the most senior Catholic of Spain, enthroned and resplendent in his robes as a Prince of the Church. He waved a beringed finger at them, which Zulu kissed and over which the Foreign Secretary shifted uneasily.

'Your Eminence,' began de Zulueta, 'we are here to determine whether the Dictator will put any of Spain's military resource at the disposition of the gangsters currently in power in Berlin.' No point in mincing words.

'Fr de Zulueta,' pronounced the Cardinal, 'I have already raised this issue with the Holy Father in Rome. Between us, we have determined that Spain will remain neutral in this war, whatever our idiot-in-chief wants. You may sleep peacefully in your beds tonight.'

And with that reassurance the two flew back to Britain. The Dictator might propose, but the Cardinal would dispose.

What an extraordinary tale. I looked at my empty port glass and then realised, with a jolt, what the time was.

'Excuse me, Father,' I said. 'I hope you will not condemn me as irredeemably rude, but I've just remembered I have to take the last of my finals.'

Fr Incledon looked at me approvingly. 'No, dear boy, think nothing of it. Of course you must go. I wish you Godspeed.' And turning to Mgr Gilbey on his left, he said, within earshot but wholly enigmatically, 'You see, Father, there are still some of us left.'

'Unless he gets to Rome, Dawkins or Darwin will undo him. Mark my words,' replied the Protonotary Apostolic in a resigned tone. 'And Dawkins is an Oxford man.'

I had no time to consider this strange fragment of conversation. I ran to the examination hall. I was twenty-nine and a half minutes late and had worked up a muck sweat. I sat down and stared at the questions, blinking and uncomprehending. But just as I was beginning to fear the worst, a fellow victim on my right stacked his papers together, replaced his pen in his pocket and headed for the door.

'Nothing for me here,' he said quite loudly to a startled invigilator. That was it; off he went. A moment or two later I thought I heard the sound of a sports car pulling away from the hall and heading for Newmarket, perhaps. As there were just fifty of us in the faculty, and only half a per cent ever failed, that had to be him. Statistically speaking, I was home and dry, and with one and a half per cent to spare.

Hardly survival of the fittest, though.

Chapter the First

1970: 'Doxbridge'

In which the author, having taken his finals at Cambridge, decides to give Ireland a quick visit while awaiting his results, encounters poteen and West Coast skulduggery, and wins a small fortune at the races, before coming home to face the music.

My Cambridge education was now over. Standing in the dim Cambridge sunshine outside the examination hall, I wondered what I should do next. There was little point in hanging about, for at least a week. A friend of mine, over the Irish Sea at Trinity College, Dublin, would be in much the same position. Except that they had their May Week *before* their exams, as only the Irish would.

I had first been to Ireland as a very small boy but remembered little about it, apart from a large red setter called Oonagh. It was time to go there as a graduand. No, it was a duty. Too few of us Cambridge men even knew that it had been Doxbridge, not Oxbridge, before Eire had extricated herself from the United Kingdom.

My old friend Colin Swan had arranged for me to stay with Diana Pickersgill at her superb house in Ballsbridge, an unspoilt 1830s quarter of South Dublin. I had the idea that I would sneak into Trinity College's May Ball under cover of darkness. It was then, as now, the largest ball in Europe and world famous for its shenanigans. Just a couple of years before, a radical student, who may have disapproved of so many people in evening dress when so many Dubliners could still not afford shoes, admitted a flock of sheep to the great college. Each of them had a makeshift bow tie tied around its neck; this time, I did not expect to be disappointed.

I took the train and then caught the ferry from Holyhead to Dun Laoghaire.

The ancient ferry was an adventure in itself. The latest ferries have stabilisers.

Even before we had set sail, everyone had already made straight for the bar, some ordering several rounds at one go. There were all manner of people jockeying for position and trying to catch the steward's eye. Of course the Irish occasionally like a noggin. It does you a power of good and it keeps you warm at night, they say. Not that there's much of a choice. It's either stout or whiskey. Everything else is for cissies. The fuel I favoured was Guinness.

But no sooner had we pulled out of the picturesque Welsh harbour than the swell of the Irish Sea began to hurl the boat around like a little cork with sublime indifference to the stomachs of the passengers.

As the waves rose and fell, the valiant little ship steered straight for the salty mountains ahead. We seafarers duly crested them and plunged down into the cavernous briny canyons beyond. The wind blew off the tops of the waves and hosed our ship with spray. And one by one, braver men and women than I abandoned their hard won posts beside the bar and headed for the rails. Half an hour later, I was there too, though my Guinness was not. But beside the bar, still serving all comers as if we were crossing a millpond, the remaining topers were all in holy orders.

A convent's worth of nuns were knocking away the black stuff as if there were no tomorrow. And chatting with them easily was a party of priests, equally unruffled in their soutanes. Queasily, I stared at them. They were all in black, with hints of white towards the top. Was one of the great mysteries trying to unfold itself to me?

Once on Ireland's dry land, I was easily recognised by Diana and Colin. They were there to meet me and they had plans. Next day, Colin would show me round the great Elizabethan foundation of Trinity College (TCD), that vast Palladian end to Dame Street, enclosing a campus in the very heart of Dublin.

In 1970, Dublin was not the prosperous metropolis it has become today. There were still barefooted children and wild beggar women to be seen in her streets. It was said that there were students at Trinity College who kept warm in winter by staying in bed, saving the cost of fuel. But on the other hand the terrible despoliation of Dublin's magnificent Georgian heritage had not yet started. Nelson's Pillar had only recently succumbed to dynamite in O'Connell Street. The venerable Kildare Street Club and the Royal Hibernian, with its faded grandeur, were still the residences of the Irish Ascendancy when in town.

And boy did the Guinness flow! One way of imbibing a complete skinful in those days was to attempt the 'Stations of the Cross'. Fourteen pubs lie around the perimeter of TCD and the object is to down a pint in each and every one of them.

I can just about remember starting at Mulligan's but I have no idea whether I finished the course. Colin tells me I came a poor second, but how would he know? One day I'll try again with a more reliable witness.

Life in Dublin is a fine thing. It was party time there – isn't it always? – and I passed a few very jolly days with Diana before going to the west of Ireland with Colin, and to his family's house near Tralee (where the Rose comes from, as he informed me repeatedly).

I enjoyed the train journey. Irish trains sold packets of playing cards on board at the buffet, and we whiled away the long hours playing, of all things, canasta.

I had barely unpacked at Colin's when the telephone rang. Colin answered it. 'Righto,' he said, and explained, 'we're having dinner at my fiancée's and we're staying the night. Chez the lovely Judith. So get your glad rags on, it's black tie. And I have to be the handsome boatman.' He was quoting 'Carrickfergus', the most wonderful of the Irish ballads, but at the time I had no idea what he was talking about.

That evening, Colin took me down a very long drive to an important-looking ashlar-fronted Georgian house in County Limerick. Slightly to my surprise, I was ejected from his car under the porte cochère. Colin had still to fetch some people who lived some way away. Apparently their ancient car had finally curled up and died.

I waved him 'safe wheels' and rang the front doorbell. Answer came there none. I rang again and again.

The house seemed empty and I looked at my watch. It had turned eight o'clock. When was dinner? Somebody ought to be here.

Wandering around the house to see if there were any signs of life, it was not until I came to the stables that I found anyone capable of help. Here I met a man in his middle years, performing some arcane task with large copper pots that people who roll up their sleeves do in stables at eight o'clock at night.

'You'll be here for dinner,' he said, glancing at my dinner jacket. 'Well, I'll take you in and get you a drink.'

He led me back to the front door and opened it. It had not been locked. A great plastered hall stretched out in front of us, with a fine cantilevered staircase that flowed down, unsupported, from the floor above and contained its customers with barley sugar twists of mahogany banister.

The hall had a sylvan theme: herons and babbling brooks, nymphs and lusty shepherds, that sort of thing. And a pair of marvellously ornate doors led off to either side.

My 'Virgil' opened the door to my right. 'Come in here, will you, sir.' I found myself in the sort of drawing room you see in *Country Life*, four window bays long, and rising a good sixteen feet to its heavily stuccoed ceiling. At one end of the room, in a vast marble fireplace, a peat fire glowed softly, throwing out little heat but a very pleasant odour.

He opened a cupboard door to reveal a number of bottles. 'What will you have while you wait? I'm sure you'll not be kept waiting too long.'

I asked for an Irish whiskey, as you should in this excellent country. He brought a Collins glass filled almost to the brim with the pale liquor. It was quite the largest whiskey I had ever seen. I sat down with it, was left alone and I stared at the glass. If I drank this much whiskey I would end up as plastered as the ceiling.

Could an hour have passed before the fellow came back in?

I got to my feet, a little unsteadily. Yes, it was nine o'clock. I had read almost an entire Dick Francis novel, and it was brilliant. I had to know how it ended.

'Let me refill that glass,' said my man, who had now put on a white jacket, as he took the empty glass away. Had I really drunk that whiskey? The thriller must have been truly gripping. He pressed the refill on me. 'There you go, now. That'll work its magic, all right.'

With that he vanished and I stood up to stretch my legs. I could hear a car drawing up outside and I went to the window. It was indeed Colin, and this time he was with a couple of female passengers, dressed to kill.

They burst into the drawing room, apologising for having left me alone. Colin glanced at my refilled whiskey and raised an eyebrow. 'Glad to see you haven't drunk too much of that. It's deadly stuff. Seán here,' – he indicated the butler – 'distils it himself.'

Our host and hostess now came down the great staircase and two or three more cars drew up outside. The room filled with people, laughing brightly and complimenting each other on their finery. Seán did his stuff with the drinks, but everyone declined his 'whiskey' in favour of something more house-trained. Colin introduced me to a colleen of breathtaking beauty, who looked at me curiously when I tried to make small talk.

'Have you been sabotaged, old man?' Colin whispered to me solicitously. 'Happens here all the time. I'll look after you.'

The guests traipsed across the hall into the dining room but Colin held me back. 'Let's get rid of that glass, shall we,' he said. 'If you drink that you've no chance at all of lasting to midnight.'

'But what shall I do with it?' I asked pathetically.

'Just toss it on the fire,' said Colin in a practical way.

The room was now empty, and anyway this was the time to take all advice unquestioningly. I threw the entire contents of the glass on the red-hot peat.

Perhaps, had I been entirely sober, I would not have done that. I would have left it on a side table. Yes, that would have been the sensible thing to do.

Instead, the whole thing seemed to unravel in slow motion. My 'whiskey' – or whatever it was – travelled through the air from my glass to the fire. On touching the peat it exploded into a ball of flame a yard across, which threw out a fierce white light as bright as limelight. The room was lit as for a photo shoot.

The fireball itself 'pushed' past Colin and me and flew slowly towards the ceiling, hissing as it went. When it reached the plasterwork, it moved around like an art critic, seeking out the best of the ornamentation up there and hiding it from everyone else.

An age seemed to pass, but even though the doors were open, creating a short enfilade between the drawing room and the dining room, no one either noticed or came back to see what on earth was happening.

And then, just as suddenly, the fireball burnt itself out.

Colin and I were too dazzled at first to see if the thing had done any damage. I heard Judith's mother shout for us, and we hurried through, taking our places at the dining table, still blinking a little.

I shall leave the dinner that followed out of this narrative. All I need say is that it was hard work.

When we returned to the drawing room after the last course, I was even 'worser' for wear and made my excuses as soon as I decently could. As we were staying the night, my hostess showed me to my room, shaking her head slightly, I thought. Colin came up to say goodnight.

'Pity you've run out of steam,' he said. 'My brother and I are going into the village. Something there we've always wanted to do.'

'At this time of night?' I asked.

'Has to be, old man. No better time for it.' And with that he was gone, leaving me to the gentle arms of Morpheus.

I woke the next morning at about nine o'clock. My head felt as though someone had been playing football with it. I got dressed very slowly and carefully and made my way downstairs to see if there was any chance of breakfast.

The only person I met was Seán, who wondered if I needed a hair of the dog.

'I believe I need the whole pelt, Seán,' I told him reproachfully, 'after that moonshine of yours...' But whatever I might have been about to say to the blackguard, a furious knocking at the front door thwarted me. Seán disappeared like a wanted criminal through the back door – to his stables, most likely – so I went to the front door and threw it open. I was rather startled to see three uniformed Gardai, or policemen, plus a fourth in plain clothes.

'Were you in the village at all around midnight last night?' asked the one without the uniform.

'No, I was not.'

'Can you tell me where you were at all?'

'I was fast asleep. I had a glass of Seán's whiskey and needed an early night.' Oddly, this seemed to satisfy them.

Now it was my turn to ask the questions.

'What is all this about, officer?' I asked.

'Two people were observed near the crossroads at approximately the middle of the night. They've dug up part of a person that had been buried there, and that is quite totally against the law. Whoever they might be, we would be much obliged if they would pay us a visit at the police station and do some explaining. The villagers are too superstitious to have done it, so it seems to me it must have been someone from this house. Perhaps when you see the other house guests you might ask if any of them might consider a trip into town to enlighten us.'

And with that they were gone. Relieved that I at least had nothing to worry about, I had a coffee and retired to the drawing room to finish my excellent book about skulduggery among racing folk.

Colin and his brother were down very late that morning. I told them what had happened and they laughed.

'A highwayman was hanged and buried in the village in the 1750s,' explained Colin. 'His name was Swan. No idea if he was a relation, but we wanted to take a look. Come and see.'

We went to the workshops outside and there was a skull, quite white, which had been boiling in bleach for most of the night.

'It will look good on the chimneypiece,' said Colin. 'What do you think?'

I approved.

Those days passed as if jet propelled, and all too soon we were back in Dublin. Summer rained down on us while we journeyed from gallery openings to parties of all kinds. Colin, anticipating the racing season, was quite excited. So was everyone else in Dublin. From here on, the national equine fever would build up to its climax, via the races to the Royal Dublin Horse Show.

When I thought of my other life, in Cambridge, I gloomily supposed there would be little for me to celebrate.

'Come on,' said Colin, 'there's always your May Week. That

should be still going on. And you may even have fluked a degree.'

Yes, our homespun Cambridge May Week was worth the candle. But there were still some things to do in Dublin before the sand ran out.

I was back in Ballsbridge, on the southern side of the Grand Union Canal, and in that same delightful early nineteenth-century townhouse where I had started this trip. I had had a grand time and thought myself a very spoilt young fellow.

Now Colin drove me out to Co. Kildare and to the Curragh. Colin is one of life's natural racing men. There isn't much he doesn't know about horses and there's even less about racing.

The Curragh is a clockwise course, like Newmarket, the race-course nearest to Cambridge. I felt quite at home. Funds were low, unsurprisingly, though no one ever seemed to want me to spend any money. I checked my pockets, just in case I had absently shoved a ten-shilling note anywhere but my wallet.

My net asset value was down to five or six pounds, perhaps. I decided that the race should make or break me. It was time for The Bet.

Colin and I walked around the paddock where he appraised the beasts with his trained eye.

'Now that's a fine horse,' he observed, as a trainer led a good-looking and stately gelding around the little ring. 'Let's have a look now. Here we are. "Blue Grass". Could win. Let's check the form.'

The true racing man, as far as I can see, believes in breeding and form above everything else. In this he resembles an old school army general, or possibly a deb's mother. The point of the paddock, if any, is only to see if the horse is ill, or bruised, or in any way likely to disappoint.

Colin was impressed by Blue Grass's steady demeanour. He had been looking for nerves, or the barely suppressed excitement that might undermine the vital authority of the jockey. I thought he was about to recommend this nag, but when he read the sporting page in the *Irish Independent* he shook his head.

'No Irish form. One race in England. All the rest in Kentucky. The going will be unfamiliar. He'll get no support from the crowd. He's never run a clockwise track. Forget it.'

I looked down towards my elbow where an Irish lad was pressing a form sheet on me. He wanted a shilling for it. I took a chance. Colin had gone off to place a bet or two and I read the flyer I had just acquired. Blue Grass had run in England – at Newmarket, no less – where he had come second. In Kentucky, he had won a dozen races of around the same length. He should be good for an each-way bet. What were the odds?

I wandered over to the rail where the bookies were. The horse was quoted at five to one. Not a bad price.

I met up with Colin.

'Why are the odds so long on this Blue Grass creature?' I asked him. I told him about the form in detail.

Colin was thoughtful. 'You may be on to something. Sometimes we Irish can be a little nationalistic. Maybe the punters simply don't want to bet on a foreign horse. Try the tote. If I'm right, the odds will end up much longer there.'

So I went over to the tote. Blue Grass was not attracting much money. The clerk supposed it would fetch up at eight to one.

I would put five pounds on to win, I thought. If he wins, I have £45. That's easily enough money to stay on in Ireland for a few more days. It took the average man weeks to earn that much in 1970. And if Blue Grass lost? I'd have to go straight back to England.

But he led from the start. As that strange primordial sound of cavalry grew in our ears it was obvious that Blue Grass was going to win. And with a great cheer from Colin and me and all the American tourists, he won by a couple of lengths.

Diana was the kindliest of hostesses. Thanks to my huge win, I took her and Colin to dinner and, over a linen cloth in the Royal Hibernian, she asked me how I was getting on 'in my own country', as she put it.

'I'm having a ball,' I replied. Despite my name and ancestry, at this time I still considered myself very much an Englishman. 'It's not difficult. Everything here seems rather English,' I said, 'yet the country overall is still one of the poorest in Europe. Is there no anti-British feeling still about?'

'Well, perhaps a bit,' I was told patiently, 'but not in South Dublin. There are a few places, but neither Colin nor I will be taking you there quite yet. You have a lot to learn about Irish history and our way of life. Your education should start with the Horse Show. You promise you'll come back one August?'

And promise I did. Nothing ever again would keep me from Dublin for too long.

First Sunday After Trinity
Christ Church Cathedral, Dublin

A Sunday came along as predictably as a number eleven bus and I decided to climb on board.

Diana and Colin were Church of Ireland, of course, so they could not officially accompany me to Mass. I set off by myself, but in the event I rejected the neoclassical blandishments of Dublin's Catholic Pro-cathedral in favour of the great Norman pile of Christ Church.

I was drawn there by a curious fact. This is one of the very few ancient churches in the British Isles to have been given the chance to celebrate the Old Rite since Henry VIII severed the Roman moorings and its bloody retethering under his daughter Mary Tudor.

About a century and a half after the dissolution of the monasteries and the establishment of an 'English' church, in 1689 the cathedral was seized by Catholic troops serving King James II. For a few days, the rites of its pre-Reformation faith were again restored. On an extraordinary Sunday a fully Tredentine Holy Mass was celebrated in the King's presence. This was the strange fact that led me though the small doors into the vast Anglican church.

Sitric Silkenbeard, the Viking, had actually founded Christ Church as early as 1038. Donatus, the Bishop of Dublin, helped him build a great stave church, which must have looked something like a pagoda, as they still do in Norway. But between them they failed to consider that wood could never have lasted long in the soft Irish climate. The Normans, in the twelfth century, wisely elected to demolish the weather-beaten pile and took the next fifty years to rebuild it in stone.

Work began under the patronage of Robert de Clare, or Strongbow, the Norman prince who brought his invading

'Geraldines'[1] to Ireland in 1169, and who is buried here. This was the man who defeated Brian Boru and took Dublin for King Henry II, the English Pope[2] and for England. His monument also depicts his son, whom he cut in half for cowardice in battle. Those early knights were made of epic stuff.

Christ Church had already been incorporated into the 'Irish' church, so that Cashel and not Canterbury would consecrate its bishops. That decision was not reversed until 1395, when King Richard II sat in state in the cathedral and received homage from the kings of the four Irish provinces – O'Neill of Ulster, McMurrough of Leinster, O'Brien of Munster and O'Connor of Connacht. From then on, Canterbury ruled.

Christ Church is almost the only site of an English king's coronation outside England.[3] In 1487 Lambert Simnel, pretender to Henry VII's English throne, was 'crowned' here as King Edward VI.

When Henry VIII broke with Rome, the cathedral was already in ruins. The king ordered temporary repairs to take place immediately. As is so often the case, these 'temporary' repairs remained in place until the 1870s.

The patched-up church was at the heart of Reformation Dublin's business and social life, well into the seventeenth century. Its crypt has housed a market, a primitive business centre and a pub.

I am of Irish ancestry, of course. While the details were still somewhat hazy to me, I felt the need to venerate such history.

If today the cathedral looks to be in fine structural condition, this is mainly due to the enthusiastic – some would say excessive – renovations carried out by the great Victorian architect, G E Street.[4] Henry Roe, distiller of Jamieson's whiskey, gave £230,000 of his personal fortune to save the cathedral.

All in all, the Church of Ireland has not been such a bad caretaker, I considered. Nor, from what I could see, were the

---

[1] 'Geraldines' were so called after Maurice Fitzgerald de Windsor, the 'Invader of Ireland', Strongbow's principal leader in the Anglo-Norman invasion of Ireland of 1169.

[2] In 1155 Hadrian IV (Nicolas Breakspear) had granted the King of England the hereditary lordship of Ireland.

[3] Henry VI was famously crowned in Notre Dame in Paris.

[4] Known to Londoners for the Law Courts in the Strand.

differences in worship from the Old Faith so very marked. True, there was the famous difference of opinion over transubstantiation and on the elevation of the Host. The veneration of the saints had largely been retained, however, and the temptations of full-scale Protestantism (such as Calvinism) had mainly been resisted. Indeed, returning victorious from the Battle of the Boyne on 6 July 1690, King William III gave regal thanks here for his victory over King James II and presented the cathedral with a set of gold communion plate.

Other key dates include 1742, when the cathedral choir sang at the world's premiere performance of Handel's *Messiah*, and 1970, when I went there.

The service was far more 'Catholic' than my own church was then delivering. I should have expected something out of the ordinary from the strangely worded historical note in the doorway, which informed the curious that 'following the Reformation in England, the church in Ireland was regrettably [sic] obliged to follow suit.'

As it turned out, Mass was concelebrated. The three celebrants, clad in marvellous vestments, spent most of their time with their backs to the congregation, like priests, and not facing the audience, like opera singers.

While the Host was not elevated, as it is in my church, wine was offered to the faithful, which is not the case where I usually go.

The most astonishing thing (to me) was the use of Latin for some of the great prayers, and the wonderful English, when it was not. *Et cum spiritu tuo*, for example, was translated as 'and with thy spirit', which is a whole lot better than the frightful 'and also with you' which we Catholics are supposed to tolerate. *Credo in unum Deum* was 'I believe in one God', and not the patronising campfire togetherness of 'We believe...' These Anglicans were not afraid to use the expression 'Holy Ghost'. In my church, the word 'ghost' has been universally removed to stop kiddies' minds being directed to spooks.

All told, the service was far closer to our pre-Vatican II rite, and I envied the Church of Ireland, especially Tyndale's and Cranmer's English. By 1970 I had already endured seven long years of a travesty of a liturgy that had been written by the semi-literate for the benefit of the educationally subnormal.

As I thanked the priests and stepped out of Christ Church into secular Dublin, I felt as the congregation must have felt during those first few days in 1689 when, after an age, they were able again to experience the real thing.

Chapter the Second
1970: A Drone's Progress in London

In which the author, now based in Sloane Street, discovers how best to eat cheaply in London and, despite having no visible means of support, throws himself a twenty-first birthday dance. He meets the social 'fixer' Peter Townend, wears some frightful clothes and is arrested for discharging a firearm in Knightsbridge. Continuing to ignore all advice as to his future (scarcely needing any money of his own) he regards his failing as unimportant.

I had met Peter Townend while I was still an undergraduate, and it was undoubtedly one of my greatest strokes of luck.

Peter was an extraordinary man, blessed with an encyclopedic memory for people, their families and their faces. I had been at a party in Chelsea. Johnnie FitzHerbert was there and the two of us were talking schoolboy stuff. Fitz had just bought a starting pistol, which looked exactly like an old service revolver – a huge thing, replete with a ring on the grip to secure it to a Sam Browne.

He was desperately keen to take it out of his pocket and fire a few rounds in the air, when Peter came over.

'You are Johnnie FitzHerbert, aren't you?' Johnnie nodded. 'And your father, Colonel FitzHerbert, was decorated for his part in D-Day?'

Johnnie nodded again. 'You're Peter Townend,' he said. 'I've heard of you. Oh yes, and this is Jeremy Macdonogh.'

'Only good things, I hope,' said Peter, absently shaking my hand. There was a distinctly northern timbre in his voice, which had been at first disguised by his quiet speech and his slightly camp manner.

'I've been asked to put together a list for this year's season. I need some good-looking young men who can dance and who possess their own dinner jackets. There is a shortage of men again. Are either of you up for it?'

'Why don't we both do it?' Johnnie asked me with surprising enthusiasm. 'It could be a laugh!'

'I don't know,' I said. 'It's my finals next term. They are going to be hard enough without any distractions.'

But just then a very pretty girl came shyly up to us, an address book in hand. 'I'm Lizzie McPherson. I don't suppose I can take your address?' she asked. 'I'm giving a dance in August and I'd like you both to come.'

I looked at her carefully.

'Well, why not?' I had no plans for August, and Johnnie and I wrote our details in Lizzie's little pigskin address book and did the same in Peter's.

That was three months before.

Now it was summer, I was a graduate and I'd turned twenty-one.

Just back from my trip to Ireland, I was vaguely looking for a serious job. There seemed to be none around. None of my friends seemed to have found one, even those who had done rather better than me in their degrees. Except for George, of course, who had sailed into a promising number with a City stockbroking firm.

I didn't really need any money, most of the time. Peter Townend's list was providing me with a weekend away every week of the year. Great stacks of 'alabaster' cards were arranged on my mantelpiece in the flat I shared with some girls in Sloane Street. Around a third of the invitations were for dances, complete with house parties, and the rest were for cocktail parties and dinners in London.

I, with some equally impecunious friends, had completed some extremely useful research on staff canteens. We would put on our suits and queue up with our trays in many of the better company restaurants in London. What a strange sight we must have been, and to this day I don't really know how we got away with it. BEA's staff restaurant in their terminal building off Gloucester Road was one of our favourites. They were generally free, or occasionally needed a single 1/6d luncheon voucher.[1] These were easy to buy for around 1/3d in the nearest pub.

---

[1] 7.5 pence.

A little money was needed for taxis, and one had to take a girl out to dinner from time to time, particularly if one wanted more than dinner. But the dole was up for this, provided that we stuck to such restaurants as the Stock Pot in Basil Street. In the matter of restaurants, like so much else, think location, location and location. I liked wine, though I knew almost nothing about it, but I was a fast learner. The girls were very impressed that I would always order a white to go with the fish.

But suddenly I needed rather more than the pittance I was husbanding so adroitly. I had put off my twenty-first birthday party with the excuse of my impending exams, but they were over and people who mattered were beginning to comment on my niggardly contribution to their own freeloading agendas.

My mother listened to my request with indifference.

'Get a job,' she said.

That was no way to talk.

But then a *deus ex machina* moment happened, in the unlikely shape of my Great-aunt Joan. She lived in Boulder, Colorado, with a vast collection of paintings, children and horses, and had worked out for herself, without any prompting, that I had reached the age of adulthood and was now allowed to vote. A cheque had arrived in the post.

It was comfortably enough for a small dinner party.

I rang around my closest mates, suggesting a dinner in the Little French Club, off St James's Street. This was a handsome little dining club, in what had once been the London residence of General de Gaulle. The dining room was panelled with a pale and intricate Georgian fruitwood and hung with yellow silk curtains. Its cooking was celebrated. I was thrilled when they took my booking for twelve.

The next challenge was the party proper. A twenty-first means a dance. This would be more difficult, but I had had an idea.

At that time I had a friend called Peter. He had read Mathematics at Cambridge with me, and was the son of a wildly successful and famous osteopath who was lucky enough to own one of the larger villas in Park Village West. He was one of the few people I knew with a private ballroom. More than that, his downstairs loo was a replica of the blue grotto at Amalfi.

The bizarre thing was that while Peter was heir to a vast fortune and had a drawing room lit by chandeliers designed to resemble miniature Montgolfier balloons, he had very few friends. My situation was the exact opposite. A marriage made in heaven, so to speak, as he too needed to celebrate his coming of age. So the deal was done. It would be a joint twenty-first, with his name and mine on the invitation. He would provide the house, the wine, the catering and so on, and I would provide a cast of bright young things selected with care from the year's supply of glittering youth.

It would be an early dinner, following a few drinks, in St James's. Three taxis would be booked to take us on to Regent's Park, and there we would dance the night away.

I found myself one night at dinner in the Nash mansion with the doctor, his wife and my Cambridge chum. The doctor's wife, who had pretensions as an interior decorator, had created a lavish dining room. She had laboriously cut from gold and silver foil an enormous number of 'tesserae' – little tiles of about one square inch – and painstakingly glued them to the walls, to the extent that we felt that the room was a survivor from a recently unearthed Romano-British villa.

A long, seventeenth-century dining table, capable of seating perhaps eighteen people in comfort, had been set for the four of us. And around it were the most curious and ancient chairs.

'They are odd, aren't they?' agreed the doctor. 'I could tell what they were when I saw them at auction. It's the paler colour of the feet that gives it away.'

'So, excuse my ignorance, but I haven't got it. They are clearly very elaborate. Are they English?'

'No, dear boy, they are Spanish. These chairs have been recovered from the Spanish galleons that foundered off the coast during the Armada.'

'Oh, my! But what about the feet?'

'Exactly, that's how I knew. That is because the salt water they used to swab the decks has bleached the wood. Nothing else would have had that effect.'

The conversation turned to the forthcoming dance and it seemed there were no obstacles to my plan. Cognac was produced, and in the warm afterglow of a fine dinner and good company, I did a very stupid thing.

I leant back in my chair.

There was a petrifying crack, and the whole back of my chair fell away, to lie on the Syriac Kelim and point at me accusingly.

Silence fell in Regent's Park.

Finally, the doctor spoke.

'Damn silly chairs, far too fragile. Most of them have been repaired at some time or other. Think nothing of it.'

As a lesson in perfect manners this will remain with me all my days.

As it turned out, the party was a wild success. A school friend, Oswald Hotz de Baar, starting out for himself in business as a disc jockey, had volunteered to do the slot for nothing but a copy of the guest list. I hope he did well out of it. The guests certainly enjoyed his music.

Mind you, the music was good in 1970. the Beatles had just released *Abbey Road*, their finest album. T-Rex, Roy Orbison, Jimi Hendrix, Joni Mitchell, Simon and Garfunkel, Pink Floyd, Cream, Bob Dylan – the list was endless. And they were all in their prime. This was the music of our privileged generation, and if the Beatles could just stop quarrelling and stay together we would none of us grow old.

Eventually the party ended, a little after dawn. And from then on, if possible, the invitations fell thicker and faster on to my Sloane Street door mat.

I was losing touch with George, due to the pressure his company saw fit to impose on him, so I rang him up to suggest a drink.

When we met up, George and I discussed the way forward. His company was keeping him just too busy. So much so, he told me, that he wondered why he had ever joined the fashionable nightclub, Raffles, in the King's Road. He was always too tired to go there.

This little piece of information was valuable to me. The very next evening found me at Raffles, a young lady draped elegantly over my arm. I signed in as George, of course, and nobody turned a hair.

I have turned to my photograph album to get an idea of what we all looked like. The girls divided into two camps – Jean Shrimpton and Twiggy. In 1964, Barbara Hulanicki had opened a shop called Biba that, by 1970, had turned out to be a way of life. Every girl in London went there, when not in Kensington Market hunting for Afghan coats and velvet loons. Biba's '30s look was 'retro-chic'. It meant lots of satin, ostrich feathers and long dresses. The effect was moody and nostalgic, and the girls draped themselves in brown, plum, grey and pink scarves, feather boas, belts, hats and spangled handbags.

Fashion in the early 1970s had little to do with reason. 'Unisex' was all – and for men, the ghastly Jason King seemed to set the standard. We wore bell-bottoms and second-hand American military clothes, bought from Millet's in Oxford Street, or from Granny Takes a Trip in the King's Road. This was supposedly a British comment on the Vietnam War. Long live irony.

Both sexes wore tie-dyed shirts, and the girls wore mid-calf hemlines and granny dresses. The more daring of the fair sex began to wear hot pants and ra-ra skirts. Common ground was the bra, or more precisely, its absence. It was the big no-no of high fashion. Watching some girls as they ran for a bus could make your eyes water.

Some of the most dedicated followers of fashion, who, I hasten to add, did not include me, grew sideburns (as we called them) and Zapata moustaches. Even City suits had flares, and all our shirts sported serious collars. Every rule of good taste was broken.

Our evening wear was a riot.

White silk polo necks went under our dinner jackets, or white shirts with long collars, whose buttons were obscured by elaborate ruffles. Our women copied Michelle Dotrice and her friends in *Man About the House*. Particularly bizarre was that they wore thigh-high boots – to dance in.

Hats had one of their periodic revivals, and I bought myself a trilby. I had my fair share of crushed velvet flares, but I also favoured the '30s revival, down to its tweed jackets and fawn waistcoats, or its pinstripe suits with stripes so wide they would have embarrassed a Chicago bootlegger.

We all smoked, of course, and cigarette holders and their silver cases had re-emerged from our grandparents' attics.

What a sight we must have been.

One of my prize possessions was a threadbare bottle-green velvet smoking jacket. When I grew out of it, I sold it to George. Many years later, when he married, it was one of the first articles of clothing his new wife made him burn.

Around this time I met a role model for our epoch, a certain Tarquin de la Force, and his younger brother Piers. Names to conjure with, I think you will agree. Tarquin worked for de Beers, the diamond people, and Piers was with the major City reinsurance broker, C T Bowring. Piers still lived in his mother's flat in Knightsbridge.

Tarquin knew how to dress. He favoured high-waisted suits, extraordinarily polished black Oxford shoes, and was occasionally to be seen in spats. Braces always held his trousers aloft and all his suits had the regulation three pieces. He affected a grey Fedora and a pearl tiepin. To seal the whole thing he wore a monocle that he could pop out of his eye whenever he needed to express astonishment. He made Steed in *The Avengers* appear underdressed.

Piers, who was only a year or so older than me, was slightly less of a fashion template. He, with his mother, was part of the Arts Club set in Chelsea. So too was my mother, and we often used to meet there. I used to believe that in all this crazy world of ours, Piers was the nearest thing to sanity I knew. He had masses of what I now realise was good advice for me, but at that time I was too headstrong or wilful to pay any attention. This didn't offend Piers in the least.

'There's something you have to get out of your system,' he said to me one day, at his flat in Knightsbridge. 'After that you'll go far. Here, take my copy of *The Origin of Species*. Darwin will cure you of too much Catholicism.'

Curious advice.

At one of these London parties I met an adorable and very bright girl, the daughter of a High Court Judge. She seemed to find my fustian persiflage charming. She had a very distinctive and frequent laugh, which I found galvanisingly attractive. I asked her out to dinner.

We went to the Hungry Horse in the Fulham Road and had the bottle we had brought with us opened for a trivial fee.

It took less than a minute to realise that this girl wasn't merely beautiful, in a sexy and curvaceous way, but that she was seriously bright. I can't recall what we talked about after all these years, but I do remember that she let me take her hand, somewhere between the pudding and the coffee.

We went on to Raffles and we danced the night away.

Even Raffles had to close that night, but I was not in such a good position. For various reasons I couldn't take anyone back to Sloane Street, and my mother had already given me a lambasting for treating her flat as a hotel. As we stepped into the cool air of the small hours in the King's Road, my companion solved the problem for me.

'You could come back to my place,' she said. 'My parents are away and I do know how to make a decent cup of coffee.'

We did have coffee, as it turned out, and I realised that, bright as she was, she was still very young. But my conscience, never my long suit, did not trouble me for long, and we soon slipped between the covers of her single bed.

She was so sweet and generous. If I had been planning to go home at all, the idea faded quickly from my mind. Eventually, we curled up together like spoons and went to sleep in each other's arms.

At 6 a.m. I woke with a start. Someone was in the flat. I woke up my young friend, who said, 'Oh my God, it's my parents! We must get you out.'

But it was too late.

Her father's footsteps came towards our bedroom along the corridor, stopped outside the door. He knocked quietly.

I was very skinny then and, pulling the blankets over my head, I pressed myself into her back and contrived to disappear. When her father came in, and sat at the foot of her bed, I tried not to breathe.

'We decided to come back a day early. The weather on Skye had begun to close in.'

'That's nice, Daddy. Promise you'll tell me everything at breakfast. I got to bed rather late and I'm still a little sleepy.'

Had he seen me? The legal mind is a curious thing. Had he perhaps deemed me not to exist? Maybe my shoes, obvious to me as I dressed a few moments later, were somehow inadmissible evidence?

My young friend, now in her dressing gown, made her way noisily towards the kitchen, as I slipped discreetly away into the early morning through the front door.

Johnnie Fitz rang me up a little later.

'I thought we could all go to The Cod for lunch.' The Admiral Codrington was one of our favourite pubs. 'Are you on for it?'

'Why not? Can you pick me up in Sloane Street?'

'I'm on my way,' he said, and he was.

A furious car horn alerted me to his arrival and I made my way downstairs to join him. He had Lizzie, Bronwen and Philippa in the car already.

'Come on,' he said, waving his fake revolver at me menacingly, 'get in the car – and that's an order.'

I did as I was told.

We drove up Sloane Street and turned left into Knightsbridge. I don't know what madness possessed me, but I took Johnnie's gun off him and pointed it out of my window at an innocent passer-by. I know I shouldn't have done it, but I pulled the trigger.

It was a very lifelike starting pistol. A great sheet of flame came out of the barrel and the most convincing sound of gunshot accompanied it. The pedestrian, not unnaturally, dived for cover.

I had 'shot' another two or three before the police got to us.

A police motorcyclist drew level with the car and, reaching in through the open window, removed Johnnie's keys. Our car duly came to a halt.

Police cars, three behind us and one in front, now blocked the carriageway.

'Give me the weapon,' said the police officer who had appeared by my side. I handed it over. 'And get out of the car, all of you…'

The officer looked at the 'weapon'. It took him all of two seconds to see it was not the real thing.

'Do you realise how extraordinarily irresponsible you are?' he asked, and, unbelievably, handed the gun back to me. 'What would your parents say if I told them? You are very lucky to be in England. In most countries the police would have opened fire first and asked the questions later.'

And with that they were gone, leaving an embarrassed and rather excited group of young people beside a stationary motor car. Johnnie had his keys again, so we drove the remaining few hundred yards to The Cod. How we laughed! And how England has changed over the intervening years. In modern Britain we would have all been raked to death with machine-gun fire.

Several weeks later I got a call from George.

'What have you been up to?' he asked, an aggrieved timbre to his voice. 'I tried to get into Raffles last night and they wouldn't let me in. "You're not George," they told me. "We know him. Life and soul of the place. Skinny bloke. Looks a bit like Christopher Lee. So, on your bike, mate." '

Only strong friendships survive this sort of contretemps. It's a forgiveness thing.

Chapter the Third
1970: Loch Ness

In which the author, realising that the United Kingdom is made up of many parts, decides to accept a number of invitations to stay in Scotland and to turn the adventure into a Caledonian grand tour. He contrives to arrive in an ancient Rolls-Royce, narrowly avoids death in a foursome reel and watches the Highland Games in the long Scottish evening.

I was brought up, for the most part, in a country that has many names. It is correctly called England, though that brand is currently well out of fashion. More formally, it is called the United Kingdom of Great Britain and Northern Ireland, which at best is a bit of a mouthful. Or more plainly, Great Britain. It seems as though these three titles take it in turn.

The reason for the revolving name change is of course political. The kingdoms that form the British Isles (damn, there's another one) are, as everybody knows, England and Scotland. Then there is the Principality of Wales, which has a Welsh office in Westminster, an Eisteddfod and (these days) some sort of an Assembly. There is the Province of Northern Ireland, usually though incorrectly known as Ulster. There is the Isle of Man, with its tail-less cats, its public floggings and incredibly ancient parliament. There are the Channel Islands, ruled by Governors General, Constables and Seigneurs (or their Dames). Her Majesty, in these fortress islands, is still referred to as the Duke of Normandy, and their rulers refuse to have anything to do with the Mother of Parliaments, the UK, or the Common Market. Ireland is split into two unequal parts: the Republic versus the six most Protestant of Ulster's nine counties. There is the Duchy of Cornwall, with its defunct parliament – the Stanneries – which my old friend Richard Ford strives valiantly to revive. There's the Duchy of Lancaster, which has a Chancellor and nobody else. There's a County Palatine of Chester. The ancient town of Berwick, bestride the river Tweed, is still at war with Russia (it got missed out of the Treaty which concluded the Crimean War), but presumably the Russians don't believe it worth nuking. Lindisfarne is part of the mainland every so often and is an island in the North Sea the rest of the time. To the west there are the Outer Hebrides, where some of the natives speak pure Gaelic and have never heard of the Reformation. To the north lie the Shetlands where the natives communicate in a mysterious tongue called 'Norn' and are under the mistaken or simply stubborn impression that they are still under Danish rule. I have only ever met one person, Cherry Farrow, who has ever seen the Orkneys, and she contrived to bump into the Duke of Edinburgh while she was there. So they must still be on an important map somewhere.

In a more confident, more imperial age, the wise of Westminster decided that it would be easier for us all if the country were called Great Britain, tout court. Anyone wanting further refinement could have North Britain (where they play bagpipes), and West Britain (where they hurl and curl). The more ancient names of Caledonia and Hibernia were respectively brought back into temporary fashion for those of a more scholarly disposition.

The Irish thought this wholly absurd, though a look of Celtic merriment crosses their faces when they refer to those English who have settled in Ireland as 'West Brits'. It baffles most Anglo-Saxons who cannot get the joke.

Some Scots seem to quite enjoy their designation as North Brits, or at least they take it on the chin.

I had replied to a stiff piece of alabaster card that was trying to persuade me to attend a ball celebrating a daughter, no further explanation given, somewhere north of the Great Glen, in North Britain. I had quite a few such cards and I put a selection in the breast pocket of my best Harris tweed jacket. With a good and only slightly foxed leather suitcase I had bought from a stall in the Portobello Road, I headed towards Heathrow and on to a short but expensive flight to Aberdeen.

Aberdeen Airport in 1970 was not the gleaming hub of the global oil and gas industry it is today. These days the air is thick with helicopters, private jets, expensive cigar smoke (if they haven't banned it yet) and, well, the smell of money.

Back then it was rather different. Long before North Sea Oil was even heard of, Aberdeen seemed like a reasonable enough place to lay down a landing strip. We needed one to keep the Luftwaffe out and there were not too many stretches of level ground in the Scottish Highlands where one could safely put down a plane.

My airliner landed on the damp Scottish soil and we passengers carefully descended the wheeled ladder the airport staff had thoughtfully brought to the rear door.

Most of my fellow passengers were met by their families or friends, or by local taxis, which had driven out on to the runway to meet the incoming flight. An official, leaning against his bicycle, raised a loudhailer and directed a message at us.

'Would all those passengers who have not been met please proceed with haste and in an orderly way to Shack Number Nine.'

Think ahead, I told myself. I must learn a lesson here concerning taxis.

There were no taxis to be had, not even for ready money. They had been booked days, even months, before. This was 1970 and mobile phones were scarcely a twinkle in an inventor's eye. In fact, there were precious few telephones of any kind, so the bookings would have been done by letter. That sort of deal is difficult for either party to undo.

I did not have far to go, as the crow flies. My first stop was to be near Inverness, the 'Capital of the Highlands'; for the dance to be given by Mrs Ian McPherson of that Ilk for her striking eighteen-year-old daughter, Elizabeth. Its purpose was to allow every eligible man in the United Kingdom of Scotland and England to see just how fine a lassie she was in her white finery and pink sash, worn from right shoulder to left hip as befits the daughter of a chief.

Gentlemen, the instructions had stated, would wear Highland evening dress or white tie, with decorations. I had a tailcoat, bought second-hand from my very useful place in Notting Hill. Alas, I was not in a position to sport any decorations.

In those far-off days, the dinner jacket was still standard evening clobber for a house party, unless we were being extraordinarily grand, when evening tails were in order. I thought it was marvellous. About half of us had top hats, and one or two had evening cloaks, where two little lion heads at the front could be fastened with a gilt chain. For the more theatrical, opportunities existed for silver-topped canes, monocles and white kid gloves. Our shoes were of patent leather, and those who were out to impress wore them cut low along the top, over the thinnest of grey silk socks. I imagine there were some who wore these socks but once.

My Scottish tour was to start in a superb baronial pile, a turret or two or a tower at every corner and with the ghost of the Queen of Scots thrown in for free.

James and Gervas Sholto Douglas had prepared me for my journey north. These two brothers are 'Black' Douglases, Perthshire Highlanders to their last drop of ancient blood. Gervas particularly had patiently explained the hard times his tribe had had to endure over the last few centuries.

The bleak truth is there are precious few Catholic Highlanders left, and those few remaining are an unhappy lot. According to Gervas, Edinburgh had never understood them, with its Whiggish ways, its courts filled with lawyers and brokers and jobbers of all sorts. Indeed, it does not understand them now.

Highlanders, Protestant or Catholic, as Gervas made clear, are countrymen, with a particular way. They are still a very feudal breed and a number of them are fiercely aristocratic, with stained glass windows and great rolls of parchment that show their ancient lineage back and back to a Celtic twilight when Macbeth was king, perhaps, or Fingal was in his cave. But all of them, from belted earl to humble crofter, share more than separates them.

Gervas imparted the benefit of his wisdom. 'Sheep, ghosts, peat fires – whether rich or poor, Protestant or Catholic, the cold and damp depresses us all quite equally. It takes our music and whisky to lift our spirits above adversity and depression, so as to grasp that shining ambition from which we never relent – be it conquest, loot and rape or "merely" spiritual fulfilment. But,' he admitted soberly, 'we have also an interesting turn in technical innovation and metalwork, albeit when the *Usquebeath*[1] grabs our brain in the dead of night.'

When the Union of the Crowns occurred in the seventeenth century, James VI of Scotland accepted the throne of England, allowing himself to be known in more southern climes as James I. The Stuart house had supported the Highlanders and promised to tolerate the Old Faith. There were plenty of English Catholics who hoped he would end the bitter conflict the Tudors had provoked and fostered. In the event, the King hedged his bets and became ferociously Church of England, if you can imagine such a thing. Charles I, his son, also sought to tread the same ecumenical tightrope his father had negotiated with such self-confidence. Regrettably, he slipped. Fierce Protestants – Covenanters – sprang up in Scotland. In England, Puritans grasped the moment. And Britain slid into civil war.

A period of prolonged gloom settled over Britain; its name was Commonwealth. It was in reality a period of unremitting militant Puritanism, headed up by a cruel dictator. Happily for the Highlanders, Cromwell's murderous attentions were directed elsewhere – to the Irish, in fact, who reciprocated with enthusiasm the Lord Protector's loathing. Even today, people in Ireland still pause to abuse his memory, whether or not he is part of the conversation.

But eventually, even the easy-going English became fed up with a government that outlawed all they enjoyed. Cromwell banned foxhunting, music in church, alehouses, dancing, lace and even Christmas. Funny how dictators like to ban foxhunting.

'May the English and Scottish parliaments of today please take note,' pronounced Gervas, warming to his subject, the story of the Stuarts.

The restored monarch, Charles II, was a heaven-sent relief, though he provoked ambitious and rebellious grandees to folly, most notably his son, the Duke of Monmouth. But it was his younger brother, James II and VII, the last of the Stuart kings, who really let his side down when he fled England for France, effectively handing over the throne to the Dutchman, King William, who had no sympathy for Scots of any kind.

---

[1] 'Water of life' in Gaelic. Its pronunciation is something like 'whisky'.

The Stuarts had not completely finished their monarchical run, however. It was now the time for Stuart queens. James II's eldest daughter, Mary, married the Dutchman William of Orange and was crowned queen in a joint monarchy (incidentally 'legitimating' the position of her husband). The very last monarch of the ancient Stuart dynasty was Queen Anne. Born in 1665, she was the second daughter of James II and Anne Hyde. She played no part in her father's reign, and sided against him during the Glorious Revolution. She and her husband, George, Prince of Denmark, failed to produce an heir. And at just forty-nine she died, after a long battle with porphyria.

Overall (in terms of years enthroned) the Stuarts remain Europe's most successful European royal house, just ahead of the House of Savoy.

'In 1715,' Gervas explained, 'as is engraved on the heart of everyone in the Highlands of Scotland, James II's heir – James III or "the Old Pretender" as he is better known to history – plotted a rebellion against the usurper Hanoverian monarchy in London. He had support from the Scottish nobility, most of whom were highlanders. But it was not to be a success.

'And in 1745, James III's son, Bonnie Prince Charlie, invaded Scotland with his Men of Moidart, raising the clans on his way, retaking first Edinburgh and soon all of Scotland. He continued his march south until he reached Derby, where with a combination of indecision and poor advice, his seemingly inevitable takeover petered out.

'The final battle took place at Culloden, on 16 April 1746, in which 'Butcher' Cumberland defeated the Stuart pretender to the throne. Cumberland's victorious troops did not rest on their laurels. They scoured the Highlands and systematically murdered the surviving remnants of the uprising.'

The Scots adapted, as peoples do. They never could stand their Dutch king but they learned to deal with his successors. With the Industrial Revolution, they saw they had the running water and cheap land needed by iron foundries and distilleries alike. There was by now a plentiful supply of Protestant labour in the Lowlands, which was more amenable to discipline and the new, long hours than the recalcitrant, and often Catholic, warrior stock of the North.

Protestants had no religious holidays, after all. Only bank holidays.

But the new machines were of little use in the Highlands. In the glens and mountains the cruel economic reality was that sheep were worth more than crofters and the Highlands were largely cleared of their ancient populations, driven off to Canada or anywhere else to make do as best they could.

With fewer people, the country became safer and the industrialists grew richer. The old nobility now found that they had coal – masses of it – as well as rights to rivers and deer-filled mountains; their castles were repaired and became yet larger and grander. Every honest ruin became a wing of a vast pile that claimed to date from the thirteenth century.

'And the Catholics?' I asked my learned friend.

'Well, mostly they died out or sold up and went away, except where their land was entirely inhospitable. Many resisted the blandishments of the Presbyterians or the Church of England, but equally many jumped the fence. Highland families often had members of both confessions. In some ways what took place in 1745 had more in common with a civil war than a rebellion, except that it happened in slow motion.

'The Lowland Jacobites, often Protestant, were joined by two or three hundred thousand Lancastrians, and they combined with the Bonnie Prince's army as it marched on its way to Derby. These Lancastrians, while English, would almost certainly have been Catholic.'

Gervas's potted history was ringing in my ears as the light wind lashed the rain across my face. It was time to find a way out of this damned airport. I went to the front of Shack Number Nine to see if there were a bus to take me to the centre of town and I found a shop – or rather, a car-hire company. Here might be a solution to my problem, barring the minor detail that I had taken no driving test and possessed no licence.

'Not to worry, son,' parried the affable owner, feeling that any deal was better than none. 'I'll drive you myself.'

'In this?' I asked, pointing at the solitary car, a 1936 drophead coupé Rolls-Royce Phantom III.

'Aye, in this. No one is getting married today as I know. And how much will you be willing to pay?'

Well, he had a soft spot, or perhaps he simply guessed that this twenty-one-year-old could not possibly make a realistic offer. In the end he settled for ten shillings and he took me all the way to my destination, a great fortified mansion set on the banks of Loch Ness, home not to the famous monster but to the Urquhart family. Yes, it had its thirteenth-century wing. I was glad to have arrived in style.

Even after all these years I remember that house party remarkably well. Willy Peto was one of the guests, an amusing and generous spirit. He was already a captain in a fashionable regiment. He'll be a general by now. Johnnie FitzHerbert was there, talking cars and films as ever. Piers de la Force brought some worldly wisdom to the affair. As for the girls, they were simply beautiful, with that pale colour and glowing cheek that marks out the Scottish race, and in my view further improved with a light dusting of freckles to celebrate the season. Kirsty Nelson was about as pretty as they come.

At a marvellous dinner, me in my full gala (English) togs, I asked about something that had been troubling me. Why (with the exception of my 'taxi' driver) did no one in Scotland have a Scottish accent?

My hostess glanced around the room before looking at me with a slight sense of pity.

'Well, Jeremy,' she told me, gently, 'here in Scotland we regard anyone with a Scottish accent as a wee bit suspicious.'

I am happy to say that everyone laughed at this faintly improbable reply. But they had concluded, I am sure, that I had spent my time up to then consorting with proles.

Lizzie's ball was at the modern and purpose-built Caledonian Hotel, Inverness, and it was simply thrilling. I had prepared for my Scottish excursion at Cambridge (though not as thoroughly as Johnson, when Boswell persuaded the good doctor he needed to get out of London for a while) by going to 'muckleflugging' classes, and I could dance a 'Duke and Duchess of Perth' with the best of them. Or so I thought.

When our party arrived, we entered rooms that were decorated with hangings in dark red. The older women wore tiaras, those that had them. The whole place was ablaze with jewellery. But the sartorial winners were the men.

In velvet doublets and scarlet waistcoats, with precious lace cuffs and jabots, the Highlanders sported buttons of gold and silver, their filibegs (kilts) of every colour and shade; and in their cairngorms (buckle shoes) they were resplendence itself.

The pipes began to play, and continued to play till the sun forced its presence upon us through the drawn curtains.

The eightsomes were easy and most of the others could be approached with a mixture of sheer unbridled terror plus an indifference to physical pain. The sword dancing was diverting but not for novices. But it was the foursome reels that the Health and Safety Executive really needs to take a closer look at.

The floor of the Caledonian is sprung. This means that, before a dance, a team of hotel staff go into the basement and remove a large number of wooden blocks, normally used to separate the floorboards from the beams below. These blocks are six or seven inches thick. In their place are put a number of enormous springs.

The dance, therefore, takes place on a form of wooden trampoline. Anyone reckless enough to find themselves at the centre of the room should ensure that he, or she, is not out of step. The whole floor at this point can move by as much as a foot. Get caught out and it will break your leg, as surely as if it were made of glass.

The dance that really gets it going is the foursome reel. Most people discover that they have to be at the bar or make an urgent phone call whenever the dance is called. In the foursome reel, four-strong clusters of dancers interlock their arms and turn like a top before dissolving and reassembling with other dancers, into new spinning stars. The girls' ball gowns flare as they turn and their Highland escorts flash light from their polished silver dirks and buckles and from the square and precious metal buttons on their dress coats. These last items are as lethal as the floor; be in the wrong place at the wrong time and an armed cuff will cut through your clothes and flesh as would a claymore.

Dawn had risen when we were on the road for home.

The next day we were taken to see the oldest kirk in Scotland. Over the years that have followed, I have arrived at the conclusion that there are many such churches north of the border. This one, on the shores of the loch, was certainly very old. We paid our respects to the preacher, a member of the Free Church, who did indeed have a Scottish accent. He thought us English, or Sassenach, profoundly irreligious and waved a newspaper at us. He had proof. Some idiot had named a child Fifi Trixabelle or some such.

'Just what sort of a Christian name is that?' he fulminated. 'You might as well call a child Alpha or Beta.'

Back to the house, bags packed and into Johnnie FitzHerbert's car for the next destination on our lists. Around Loch Ness we went, on our way to yet another house party and ball. This was the world we lived in then, and it seemed some sort of antediluvian paradise. Even then we were asking ourselves how long it could last.

Cutty Sark, the whisky, was on every advertising hoarding that we passed, with a picture of the monster and the caption, 'Submit a photo of Nessie and win a million pounds'.

Piers de la Force had a real job. He was at Lloyd's, the vast insurance market in the City of London.

'Do you know how they can do that?' he said. None of us did.

'It's easy. They insure themselves against anyone actually taking a photo of the monster. One of our brokers did it for them. Trudged round Lloyd's until he found an underwriter who didn't believe in the Beastie. Asked him how much premium he'd want. Answer: £100 should cover the paperwork. And lo! An advertising campaign is born.'

'You're just in time for the Games,' said our hostess when we arrived. 'Luckily for you they're here, otherwise there would be no time for you to see them.'

We whiled away the sunny afternoon before we dressed for dinner by watching huge men toss the caber and small girls dance for us. We smoked cigarettes and (when the time was right) drank whisky.

Early that very evening I saw a hyperbolic item on the Six O'Clock News that implied that Cutty Sark was providing (at huge expense) a scientific and public-spirited motive for serious proof to be found, once and for all, of the monster's existence.

And still later, as we stretched our legs in the Scottish gloaming, on lawns that stretched forever towards the dark and sinister loch, we looked beyond, where the hills rose again, and patches of crepuscular sunlight chased each other like African game across the green and purple slopes.

And lurking beneath the gloomy, haunted waters, the Beastie was preparing for the night.

Chapter the Fourth
1970: Life is a Game of Cards in London

In which the author shares a flat in Piccadilly and learns to play bridge. It is a wise decision: he wins a holiday in Switzerland and before he knows it, he is in Geneva.

When I graduated from Cambridge in the summer of 1970 I had no idea at all where I wanted my career to take me. True, I had been considering Lloyd's, but I hadn't a clue how to set about it. I attended a number of interviews, with insurance companies, banks, marketing companies, but I received no job offers.

'Yes, yes, a Cambridge degree, that's all very well, but what do you know that is any use to us? Do you speak any languages, for instance?' I supposed I could muddle through across the Channel with my schoolboy French.

I might have found all these rejections dispiriting, but my life was wonderful and you could not have met a chirpier fellow in London.

A girl I knew, Sian Rhys by name, had found a flat to rent in Piccadilly itself, in an Edwardian block of flats opposite the great gates to Green Park, formerly the gates to Devonshire House, and invited me to share it with her. I moved in like a shot.

That summer I had seen a little of Ireland and Scotland. Courtesy of Peter Townend's lists, I was still on the country house circuit, spending most weekends as a guest in the better country mansions of England. As I saw it, the sun was shining non-stop and all was right with the world – apart from the fact that I was at a loss as to my future and not exactly rolling in the folding stuff.

But I was reckoning without the gods, who had decided to step into my little world and invest it with a little merriment all of their own.

At some social event, I had met the Hon. Mrs Doussa Hazlerigg, a diamond-encrusted widow from the very rafters of London's social fabric. By way of small talk she asked me if I played bridge. I told her I did. In fact, I went on, warming incautiously to the subject, I played rather well.

This, as it turned out, was the right answer. It transpired that she wanted a bridge player to come with her to Switzerland, from the early New Year until around Easter, to make up an occasional fourth for her house guests in Klosters. She would pick up any expenses I incurred on the slopes. Could I just possibly be tempted?

The only fly in the ointment was that my bridge was execrable. I had never played Duplicate and had never even heard of Chicago. The leading conventions – Acol, Precision, Standard American, Culbertson – were simply unknown to me.

'You will enjoy Klosters,' my new friend told me, 'it's frightfully smart. Lots of young people will stay at the chalet and the après-ski is justifiably famous. Prince Charles likes it better than Zermatt and the snow is the finest powder known to pharmaceutical science.'

Despite this odd metaphor, it was obvious that I would have a ball, all found, and when the time came I would depart this life a great skier and a better bridge player.

But there was an entry test. She had found another young chap who would do just as well, though he admitted to being only average at cards. We would all meet at her London flat that November and play a few rubbers. After that she would decide which one of us would accompany her.

The luckiness of the break and the scale of the challenge struck me next morning. How on earth was I to learn bridge to an adequate standard in four short months?

Then I remembered that a friend from Cambridge, Tim Coleman, was a keen player. Hadn't he told me that he had been Jersey's Under-25 Champion? I wondered if he too wanted to share a flat in Piccadilly for the summer.

As it turned out, he was keen as mustard. Of course, when he actually saw the flat, he pretended it wasn't an untidy student tip and claimed to be as happy as Larry. I know he was lying through his teeth because his rooms in college had always been meticulous. His sense of order had allowed him to place a pair of Dresden shepherdesses on his mantelshelf. In our Piccadilly residence, a rugby ball would have been more appropriate.

But Tim was a game fellow and we sat down together. He played three hands to my one, five nights a week, in exchange for his lodging.

Boy, could the man teach! Just four short weeks later we were into forcing and non-forcing Stamens, sliding Gerber and ROPI and DOPI bidding conventions.

He drilled me into remembering the cards in play, at first by remembering the court majors, and later knowing the numbers outstanding in every suit.

And I loved it. Five nights a week with such a star player was sheer magic. Except it played merry hell with my social life, and there were times when I made my excuses and skipped class. But, as exculpation, I would take Tim along to whatever cotillion the social whirl of those days was hosting, and he was as happy as a pig in clover.

Inevitably, the great day in November arrived and Tim wished me well as he set me off on the road to Mayfair to keep my appointment with destiny.

Doussa's duplex – it seems wrong to call such a place a mere flat – was everything you would expect. Once disgorged from her private lift, the first thing I saw was a framed ballerina hanging in her hall. Is this a Degas that I see before me? I wondered in the manner of Macbeth.

I played opposite Doussa, and my rival for the appointment sat on my right, pairing an elderly gentleman with gimlet eyes. The old boy looked at me suspiciously, but I was more interested in my real opponent, the slim and suntanned young fellow with the charming smile. I complimented him on his healthy appearance. Ah yes, he told us, he was just back from a two-week break on Guadeloupe, where he had found time to get in a little bridge. He had also landed a manta ray. Had I ever done that?

Doussa looked at him, well satisfied. I could see he would be an ornament to her gathering in the Swiss Alps.

I dealt, after the cards were cut to me, and found myself

looking at some very good cards. Sixteen points and, if I remember the evening as I should, no less than six spades. I had never played with Doussa before and, when we had briefly discussed conventions, all she had admitted was a weak no-trump and a taste for Blackwood if the cards were really astounding.

Here goes, I thought. I opened. 'Two spades.'

The elderly gentleman said 'No bid' in a clipped and military manner.

Doussa glanced at her cards and looked sharply up at me. Her eyes narrowed. The silence was tangible. And then she said, 'Four hearts.'

The rules of bridge allow you to ask your opponents at table what they understand by a bid. The only person you may not ask is your partner. I glanced at the gallant old boy, whom I had decided was a retired officer. The tanned fellow on my right wasn't going to help. But then, why should I have to ask? Particularly so early in the evening. I decided to brave the consequences and play by ear. There were lots of places in the world to see other than Switzerland. London, for instance. I could stay at home and get myself a 'real job', as my mother would call work in the City. Yes, a life in some counting house beckoned. That was where my future lay.

'Four spades,' I said, after the young, sun-kissed Adonis had said, 'No bid.' The general said, 'No bid', and the bidding was with Doussa.

She was looking at me as if I were psychologically impaired. My military friend let a smile play across his lips. To my right, the chap with the olive tint leaned back and stretched. He was thinking, I was sure, that he would need to work out a little before he went skiing that winter.

Doussa, her eyes not leaving mine, now spoke. 'Four no trumps,' she said quietly, but very firmly.

Had I missed the point? I was sure we could make four spades. That was a game call, and I had a powerful hand. I would take out trumps and still have enough to ruff any key cards the opposition might throw at me. And Doussa had bid in a way that suggested she had a strong hand, too, plus some good hearts, probably four of them. But my spade suit was long and I didn't want to play in no trumps. Or was Doussa playing this convention – 'Blackwood' – which she had mentioned in the chit-chat before we dealt? But I had opened, and by the rules of the convention it should have been me to see whether we could go for a slam.

'Five hearts,' I said, which is the way Blackwood lets you tell your opponents you have two aces. I had the ace of spades and the ace of diamonds, though that was my only diamond.

'No bid,' said the field marshal; and 'Five no trumps,' said Doussa.

'Double,' came the unexpected bid from my tanned rival.

Thanks to that double, I could leave her in her suit. If I said 'No bid', and the chap with the Queen's Commission said the same, Doussa could still bid. Perhaps she would reclaim her hearts suit and bid the mini-slam. Or I could reply to her, telling her how many kings I had. I would say 'six clubs' if I had none, 'six diamonds' for one, 'six hearts' for two, and so on. Or I could redouble my bronzed neighbour.

I said, 'Six hearts.'

'No bid,' came from the Chief of the Imperial General Staff.

'Six no trumps,' from Doussa.

'Double,' from the suntan department.

And feeling somewhat faint, I murmured, 'Seven spades.'

Another confident double from my right ended the bidding. At least I knew where the missing court card had to be.

The gallant veteran irritably flicked a small diamond on to the table and Doussa laid down her hand. We were playing my suit and she was 'dummy'. I looked at her cards with relief. She had a long run in diamonds and her hearts were magnificent. Eighteen points. No wonder she had wanted to play them herself. And the fit was perfect.

I felt I could have laid out my hand there and then but I wasn't sure of the form. Some people do that, but it seemed a bit against the spirit of the thing, somehow. Anyhow, that excellent youth, who under his tan now looked a little green, had doubled us twice. Let's eke it out, I thought.

The cards fell as they were bound to, and Doussa and I scored a doubled grand slam in spades on the first deal of the evening.

It was, for me, a triumph. And while no other hand that night came anywhere close, I knew from that moment it was in the bag. When my rival doubled me, he nearly caused the old soldier to declare war. If he were to be one of Doussa's house guests, he would never permit that whippersnapper to play.

And so it was an excellent evening, and when I left Doussa said she would be in touch about travel plans.

I stopped at an off-licence on the way home. A bottle of champagne for Tim was called for, both to celebrate victory and the fact that I would not have to play bridge again until the New Year.

Doussa was Egyptian by birth and had residences everywhere: in Cairo, Klosters, London and Geneva, and probably New York and Paris as well. We travelled out to Geneva together; she at the front of the plane, and me at the back. I was content with this arrangement. I was still unspoilt and did not then consider economy seats as cattle class. Maybe there was more legroom then? Anyway, I was obviously not there for my conversational skills.

We landed at Geneva, where Doussa needed to buy victuals for her chalet in the rue de la Croix d'Or, and to call on some of her friends. At a loose end, I set off to explore this bastion of Calvin and I started, naturally, with the Old Town.

It is a very old town. Its first inhabitants were a Celtic tribe, the Helvetii. Its slightly Latinised name, Geneva, can mean 'knee', as in 'genuflect' and reflect perhaps a bend in a river. More plausibly, it can also mean 'birth', as in 'genesis', and Lake Geneva gives birth to two mighty rivers, the Rhône and the Arve.

In 58 BC, Julius Caesar surrounded the place, incorporating it in his Gallia Narbonensis on that long westward march of his that ended in Britain; but after the fall of the Empire, Geneva declined. The Dukes of Burgundy made it their capital, but the Franks and the Holy Roman Emperors fought them for it. In practice its bishops ruled it.

In the Reformation, Geneva came to embrace Protestantism, and successfully resisted the northerly march of the Counter-Reformation under De Salis. The burghers of Evian, from their Catholic fastness on the other side of the lake they insist on calling Léman, still look resentfully at their Calvinist neighbour.

For several centuries Geneva stood alone as a stubborn and self-righteous republic, until the city fathers, in 1815, finally invited the protection of the Helvetic Confederation. There were many who opposed – most Swiss cantons were insufficiently Protestant for the Calvinists of Geneva.

If a modern visitor imagines he will find a central European Paris he will be cruelly disappointed. The town is ferociously clean and well organised. Fun, in the main, has been exorcised. There really isn't that much to do there, other than buy a watch. Zurich, for example, is far more relaxed. And be warned, nothing in Geneva looks particularly old to the casual glance. In fact, the town – even the Old Town – is in such perfect condition that only the occasional medieval twist to its streets betrays its age. Even the cathedral has a nice, tasteful and classical portico added on to disguise its Gothic mass.

Despite its great antiquity, it seems to me that Geneva does not really want everyone to know that it has not always been the earnest and dour citadel – the 'Protestant Rome' – it is today.

An Extraordinary Sunday
Cathédrale de St Pierre, Geneva

My first impressions of Geneva include taking a pint of Guinness in an Irish bar near the top of the hill. It was shockingly expensive. Rather than buy a second and risk an unseasonable bankruptcy, I decided to put my head around the door of the cathedral. Happily for me, it was open. I wandered inside.

St Pierre's was begun in the twelfth century, as a Catholic church of course, and is in a mixture of Romanesque and Gothic styles. It would probably have stayed that way, frescoed and filled with statues and reliquaries, but for the arch-Protestant Jean Calvin, who sequestered it and reordered it, removing its altars, side chapels and all traces of the eponymous saint, whose powerful intercession had been granted freely to the faithful of old. In the eighteenth century its rather modern classical front, emphasising reason, I suppose, was added. To my eye it looked grotesquely out of place. Still, Calvin did promise that he would return the church to the Catholic rite if those of the Roman confession ever came to outnumber those of the Protestant. Even in 1971 it was touch and go, and in 1974 the Catholics were to become the de facto majority in Geneva. But as far as I know the Calvinists have still to honour their founder's word.

Not a few English Protestants, perhaps wanting to avoid the 'bloody' attentions of Queen Mary (Tudor), settled in the 'Protestant Rome'. Among them was William Whittingham, who supervised the translation of the famous Geneva Bible. His collaborators were all Englishmen – Miles Coverdale, Christopher Goodman, Anthony Gilbey, Thomas Sampson and William Cole. Their purpose was to limit the use of the word 'kingdom', which for reasons of spin was used too freely in the King James translation.

I looked around the handsome interior, trying to get my bearings. The nave had long been stripped of its Catholic iconography. It looked more like a lecture or concert hall; not inappropriately, however, as an orchestra and choir were taking out their music and setting up their music stands.

That curious electric sound musicians emit just before they play began to fill the cathedral. They were talking and checking their instruments were in tune, but the anarchic sound beguiled me. It has never failed to do so since. I sat down near the back of what had been the nave.

After many rumours, no one could pretend any longer that the Beatles had not broken up. I was in mourning for the pop music of my youth. The Beatles had kept me – kept us all – young while they were together. If I were now doomed to grow old, then I would set out on the grown-up road of discovery that is Great Music.

I realise now, having done my research, that it was Nicholas Harnoncourt who was rehearsing that day his choir and orchestra one last time before a public performance. Leaning forward, I rested my head on my hands and waited to hear what would transpire.

In the years that have passed since then, I have learned that Bach's finest choral works are the *St Matthew's Passion* and the *B minor Mass*. OK, I know the cantatas are unbeatable. But the *B minor Mass* is the greatest of all sacred works by any composer. But that may be because I heard it here first, in St Pierre's impeccable acoustic.

The *St Matthew's Passion*, while it is intensely dramatic, works well in the devotional context of a church. The *Mass*, on the other hand, is so long and so complicated, so pious and so Catholic, that one wonders just where in Leipzig, where in the whole of Germany even, the old man ever thought it would be played. It was astonishing to hear it in Geneva.

It is perfect music, however; perhaps its one fault is that it can give even more joy to the musician than the audience – except when the audience, or congregation, is one solitary Englishman a long way from home. Since then I have heard almost everything by Tallis. Byrd's *Four Part Mass* has moved me close to tears, as has Mozart's *Requiem* and Haydn's *Mass in Times of War*. But the Bach?

The *B minor Mass* alone would be enough for J S Bach to be considered the greatest composer of all time. He is the only essential musician; if we lost all the rest, the talented of the future could mine Bach and start to rebuild the canon of Western music. A friend of mine overheard Isaiah Berlin call Bach the 'only necessary composer', which must mean the same thing.[1] But if you believe I exaggerate or if you want to try a little bit, but are daunted by the thought of listening to the whole caboodle, try an extract; I advise the 'Agnus Dei', in the Kathleen Ferrier/Elizabeth Schwarzkopf recording.

That evening I stayed there mesmerised while Harnoncourt put his people through their paces. They had it perfectly – he did not need to interrupt or urge them on. And two hours or so later, I returned home on a baroque cloud.

Was it a Protestant or Catholic baroque cloud, I hear you ask?

That question may be too theological for me to answer. Protestantism is after all a broad church. But it very definitely was not a Calvinist cloud. Bach's breathtaking ornamentation of the music of the Church would have had the sanctimonious old fraud (Jean Calvin, that is) revolving in his grave.

---

[1] According to Michael Evans, then at the British Academy.

Chapter the Fifth
1971: A Lotus in Klosters

In which the author meets the legendary Lord Lovat – erstwhile leader of the ill-starred 1940 British Expeditionary Force – and, washing down filets of perch with Swiss wine, convinces himself to stay in the skiing resort of Klosters for a little while.

The next day, Doussa and I travelled from Geneva by train. The last part of the journey was on the little narrow gauge railway that takes you to 2,000 metres above sea level, and the town of Klosters. The Swiss have trains on terrain where no railways can possibly be. They are, and have every right to be, extremely proud of them.

Klosters is both tremendously fashionable and totally discreet, quite unlike flashy St Moritz or Gstaad. It is German-speaking, so the place is not overrun with Italian millionaires and their bodyguards, like Cortina d'Ampezzo. The French won't go – they have their own resorts and they don't approve of the food. Instead, there is a sprinkling of European royals, both ruling and deposed, in more or less permanent residence; the rich of the southern hemisphere collect here – especially the South Americans – and so does a surprisingly large representation of the British upper class. But this is not Val d'Isère – 'Val de Sloane Square'; this is the real thing.

From Klosters, you can ski down into neighbouring Davos, where American billionaires are wont to hang out. On the longest pistes it is possible to ski downhill for almost fifteen kilometres without ever needing to walk or take a lift – arguably the finest downhill run in the world.

I should mention the Walserhof. This is the great hotel of Klosters and pivotal to its social whirl. For the young at Klosters, this was our rendezvous every night, when we were tired but overexcited and thrilled by our reckless adventures on the slopes. It was here that I met Peruvian Suzie, a model whose likeness illuminated every garage and workshop in South America, and with whom every instructor in Switzerland had fallen in love.

There are other great places for après-ski, and restaurants galore, but it is in the nature of things that society meets in their fine chalets. While everyone knows that kidnapping a tourist at random could probably guarantee a seven-figure ransom, the Swiss police monitor the place carefully and discreetly and are very keen to interview shifty characters, especially Italians. The Swiss are deeply suspicious of the Italians.

Klosters is Switzerland at its very best. True, the Swiss are the only nation capable of beating the Germans to the ski lifts in the morning, a fact that our Teutonic friends deeply resent. It's curious to realise the Swiss are of Celtic stock. Few Irishmen would be so energetic, but some energetic Englishmen would set their alarm clocks for a truly ungodly hour. Not me, though.

I loved skiing and the Alps. And I loved Peruvian Suzie.

The French are wrong about Swiss food. I came to appreciate it; rösti, filets of perch, both cheese and 'Chinese' fondues, not forgetting their superb raclette, and I washed them all down with their first-rate though expensive Dole and Johannisberger wines. I also recommend Glühwein on the slopes and chocolate, especially champagne truffles, whenever and wherever.

As for Swiss beer, I got quite used to it during the months that followed. For a long time only Swiss beers were available in Switzerland and even these did not always travel from one canton to another. But then Kronenbourg found the way in and the others followed. The Swiss also pioneered alcohol-free beers, bless their little cotton socks, but they are more famous for the world's strongest beer in regular production, made by their leading brewery, Hürlimann of Zurich. It is called Samichlaus, and it's a reddish-brown widow-maker of a beer, boasting a staggering 14 per cent alcohol. Two of those and you don't get up in a hurry. But it's seasonal. They only make it on 6 December every year, and then they age it for a year. By the end of January the shops have generally sold out.

During my three and a half months in Switzerland the sun

shone during the day and snow fell during the night, as befits an Alpine Camelot. I spent my days on the pistes, and my nights on the town, when not asked to help out at the bridge table. I occasionally helped out in the kitchen, where Doussa taught me how to cook rice to perfection.

In fact I was never needed as a 'fourth' more than three or four times a week. So by the end, I was getting quite good on my skis. I even tried some ski jumping.

I remember some of the house guests in Doussa's huge and exquisite wooden chalet, with its early eighteenth-century carved balconies. Lord Lovat with his attractive wife – the handsome old soldier who had taken the Lovat Scouts into occupied France in 1940, and whom Churchill had named the 'most elegant hand ever to have slit a throat'. He gave me some advice as well as an immense tip. 'Buy trees, dear boy,' he encouraged me. 'The future is in forestry.'

And I recall Sacheverell Sitwell, who told me that his impossibly ancient family was the only Saxon noble family still on the land they had owned 200 years before the Battle of Hastings. The incoming Normans catalogued their landholding in their Domesday Book of 1086. The Sitwells are still there, at Renishaw Hall. Nor will I ever forget his gorgeous granddaughter, Alexandra.

Then there were the Grantleys. Lord G was a dour city peer who underwrote vast risks at Lloyd's for his own account and for his Japanese paymasters.

Other guests included the Farquhars, who reminded me of Lord and Lady Metroland of Evelyn Waugh fame, and who owned oil wells in Venezuela. They were capable of complaining volubly; on one occasion their beef was that servants were, well, unobtainable in Dorset (where they kept a 'small' country house surrounded by lakes), even if you were prepared to pay them hotel wages. Despite my thinking I would want double the going rate to work for them, their son Francis and I became friends over the years ahead.

Doussa's visitors' book must be an autograph hunter's wet dream.

Many of these social lions seemed to be on a grand tour of Switzerland, stopping for a week or two here or there, like a succession of medieval princes on their respective progresses.

The months merged into a congenial haze, a tapestry of elegant nothings, of charm, of high courtesy and that affable *lenteur* which betokens earthly contentment. If ever I felt low, a mere glimpse at Peruvian Suzie's show-stopping face would carry me back from the brink. In short, as Doussa had implied, this was the land of Cockaigne.

As spring arrived and the snow on the lower slopes began to melt, the resort began to echo to the clatter of helicopters, looking for ever higher pistes or depositing their expensively clad passengers on the glaciers. As for me, even Doussa's generous hospitality did not extend to those rarefied tastes and my services were no longer required. In early April, she called for me and handed me a train and plane ticket back to London.

Now it was I who was tanned and fit and looked a million dollars. True, appearances can be deceiving. But I was not totally potless. Doussa's guests had tipped very generously, especially when we had won at cards. And I had scarcely a chance to spend any money.

But it was not to London that I went. I took the train back to Geneva and stayed for a few days with a young Neapolitan lady called Tiziana I had met at the Walserhof. Then, at the airport, and on the strangest of whims, I thought about Tiziana's Bay of Naples and its steep, cypress-bestrewn slopes that fell into the deep blue sea. Mozart, looking for an earthly paradise, had set his *Così Fan Tutte* there. What was good enough for Wolfie was good enough for me…

I swapped my air ticket to London for one for Naples, calculating that this chaotic Italian port and its Elysian bay would be the antidote to the perfectly managed idyll in which I had been so fully immersed.

An unrest cure, so to speak.

Chapter the Sixth
1971: Up Pompeii

In which the author arrives in Naples during Holy Week and sets off for the Bay, stopping in Pompeii to see the ruins and get a job, reflecting on the political situation and coming to the conclusion that since he has inadvertently found himself in paradise he might as well learn Italian and lie low for a while.

Holy Week in Naples is an ear-opener, and my plane chose to arrive on Good Friday.

At Naples airport the noise, the heat and the sheer numbers of people were daunting – especially after Switzerland. No one merely spoke; if they weren't shouting it was because they were bellowing. The airport tannoys had the volume turned to max, so that travellers might be distracted from their children, pets, *mutilés de guerre*, grandparents and other anthropomorphic curiosities who collectively contributed to the cacophony.

Outside, the cars had to hoot to make themselves heard. The taxi rank outside the airport doubled as a Lambretta racetrack, with un-helmeted males blinded by their greased forelocks trying not to kill the girls who sat side-saddle on these underpowered collision-bound death traps. The taxi drivers, such as there were, were too busy insulting each other and their fares to pay any attention to me.

All I knew (for then I could speak no Italian) was the phrase *centro città* and that I needed to use it if I were to get to the port, where I had decided to look for rooms and a job. Never underestimate the ambition and imbecility of youth.

My great-aunt, Christine, had warned me against going to Naples, which may have been part of the reason I was there. She was born in 1904. When she was eighteen she had been presented to the King of Italy at a ball in London. One thing led to another, and shortly after that she had received an invitation to a party in Naples, given by a member of the Bourbon family which had ruled there until Garibaldi unseated them. Being keen to see Pompeii and the other treasures of the bay, she had accepted. With a companion she had made her way by train across Europe, taking some practical clothes, naturally. But she had also taken her evening finery and some of her mother's good jewellery. Sadly, her jewel box was taken from her in the tumult at the railway station, and at the ball she had been reduced to wearing what she could borrow from the other young ladies staying at the palace.

And what a palace! The royal castle at Caserta, just north of Naples, is the work of the architect, Vanvitelli. A long association with the Kingdom of the Two Sicilies began when a Count Gaetani made the castle over to Charles III of Savoy, King of Naples. The monarch transformed it into a second Versailles, and it is still magnificent today.

At the party, my great-aunt could not prevent herself from mentioning the loss; it was so distressing her. Her dancing partner, a dashing young Neapolitan prince, said he would look into the matter. Great-aunt Christine thanked him. But how on earth could he make a difference?

It was, therefore, to her great astonishment when the young fellow called on her the following afternoon, and presented her with the jewel case and all its contents intact.

She received it, with adequate grace, but never returned to Naples and warned all her future acquaintances about the perils of the place.

'Imagine a city,' she had said to me, 'where the ruling classes mingle on such terms with the criminals that such a thing could be accomplished.'

She had it all wrong, predictably. He would have spoken to his valet, who would have put the word out. It was more a question of *omertà*[1] than any sordid intimacy with the Camorra, the secret world of Neapolitan organised crime.

I'm afraid the confusion at the airport made me wonder if I had made a wise decision to ignore my great-aunt's advice, but then I saw, as in a dream, a bus. This bus had a sign on the middle of its nose, so to speak, saying, Pompeii, Sorrento, Ravello, Amalfi, Paestum…

---

[1] Respect

Such names! They should have been on its highest brow. I picked up my bags. Ye gods, they were heavy! But I grabbed hold of them and forced my way on board. To hell with Naples, Neapolis, I was off to the bay.

You take the coast road to reach the Bay of Naples, but first you have to get out of town.

We drove through chaotic narrow streets in poor repair, barely missing religious processions, farm vehicles, horse-drawn carts, you name it – it's there. Every driver was leaning on his horn and every pedestrian was shouting at every other. In front of our bus, pairs of youths on motorbikes were playing chicken with our driver. For background music, the sound of Neapolitan song blared from countless cars and cafés. Inside the bus a radio with other views was relaying a raucous football match.

The overcrowded bus arrived at Pompeii just as I could stand it no longer. I got out at the bus station. As good a place as any to start my adventures, I told myself.

If you have never been there, your first sight of Pompeii will not be as you had imagined. True, you'll find the famous ruins of the vast and partially excavated Roman holiday resort, packed to the gills with guided tours. But first you have to deal with the large modernish town that surrounds it.

Very soon I was walking with my baggage along a scruffy high street. I was looking for the word 'Hotel', which I couldn't find. The words 'Language School' would have been equally useful, as I had decided I would teach the natives English. I could speak it well enough, I reckoned. They were going to love me. Goodness, these bags were getting heavy and I was beginning to fantasise.

Every second house had the words *albergo, camere* or *affitasi* in red paint when not in neon. And every third had a sign saying *Qui si insegna inglese*. None of these meant anything to me. I had drawn a blank.

Eventually my right arm fell off, still attached to my suitcase. It was time to take advantage of a brightly lit little place, called 'Bar'. Thank God for the Americans. If not for them it would probably have been called *Qui si beve*.

The Italian for 'beer' is *birra*, so that was easy. As I sat down by the counter, my arm magicked its way back into my shoulder and

I began to rally. The bottle had a great label – a moustachioed old gentleman wearing a hat and smoking a Meerschaum pipe – but the flavour was sweeter and maltier than I was expecting. In fact it tasted like a low-alcohol beer though the Swiss were yet to invent such abominations. I tried a coffee. Ah, that was more like it.

A youngish chap who had been reading a book at a table behind me closed it gently and stood up. He came up to me at the bar.

'Are you English?' he asked.

'So,' said Henry (for that was his name), as I tucked into my second thin beer and a toasted sandwich at his table, 'you have parachuted into Pompeii, having almost no money, no connections, no job and no fixed abode. Would I be right in calling you an optimist?'

I laughed happily. What was he getting at? Wasn't this a perfectly reasonable thing to do?

'Well, then? What do you do here?' I asked. Touché.

'A doctorate. University of Sussex. Archaeology. Managing a couple of digs in the ruined city.' He gestured to his left. 'Have you seen it yet?'

I had to admit I hadn't.

'Let's see what we can do. We'll start with my landlady. She has a number of rooms, some of which are still unlet. We'll have a word with her. And we are just beside a language school called Xanadu. Tell them your name is Kubla Khan, and how could they refuse you?'

His kindness was such that his sense of humour could (just) be tolerated. And it all worked out just as he said. I found myself with a dark room decorated only with a faded calendar showing dreadful religious paintings. There was a single metal bed, the type we had endured at school, which was pushed into a corner of the cell. But I wasn't fussy. I had secured an appointment with the Italian *direttore* of the stately pleasure dome next door.

The pay was dreadful and the hours were long. The school was a cash cow for its frightful management, who were utterly unconcerned either for the beauties of the English language or for the well-being of their staff. The penniless hippies and assorted flotsam who had fetched up there were exploited to the full and seethed with rebellious discontent. It would have been complete hell had it not been for Henry.

He was a great mentor. We spent weekend after weekend among the ruins of the ancient watering hole. He knew everybody and everything; there was nowhere he was not allowed to go. He was also allowed to stay behind when the tourists had been ordered out, and this was our favourite time, when we had the old city to ourselves.

One Saturday he had brought a picnic hamper with him as we set off to see the House of Paquius Proculus. Just inside the door, on the floor, was a mosaic that depicted a chained dog. It was certainly realistic, but whether it was realistic enough to turn the burglars away seemed unlikely. Rather more convincing was the wall painting of the owner, Mr Proculus, with his sweet and demure-looking wife. In the garden was a marble open-air triclinium, on which the lucky young couple would no doubt have eaten al fresco. To this day I am puzzled by the triclinium, whether indoors or out. It simply has to be the most uncomfortable way to eat, leaning on one side and picking off bite-sized morsels from the tray of a passing servant. Thank God and the French for the knife and fork.[2]

Across the road, more or less, was the Thermopolium of Arsellina, and it was there that Henry put down his hamper and announced 'Drinkies!' to a deserted Pompeii.

The word Thermopolium means 'pub' in English. Arsellina's was in a pretty good state of repair, considering that her last paying customer had left almost 2,000 years before. All of the bar fittings were in their original places and it needed no imagination at all to see where the hot or cold drinks would be kept ready for customers. On the floor, exactly where they were left in AD 79, were (and probably still are) urns, amphorae, a funnel and an odd, rather phallic oil-lamp (which will have lit the stairs for some of her customers to quarters where she offered a very different kind of trade).

---

[2] Actually, I have subsequently heard that Caterina de' Medici introduced these culinary refinements to the court of Henri II from the Renaissance confines of Florence.

There is totally legible writing on the walls, probably in Arsellina's own hand, that assures the customers of the wide selection of girls to be found on the floor above. Evidently, they came from all parts of the known world and were of every colour and shape – and probably every age. Lonely foreigners from the whole Roman Empire who chanced to stop for refreshment in this Roman marina would be able to find friendly fellow countrymen and women at Arsellina's. This was a thousand years before the Norman Conquest; London was then Londinium and had been founded just a single generation before. Indeed, there is no evidence of a settlement on the north bank of the Thames before the Claudian invasion of AD 43. What little there was in AD 61 was probably no more than a dozen years old when Boadicea ('Boudicca' to pedants) rebelled, burning the place to the ground. It would be another century before the Romans walled Londinium and began to build in earnest. By then Pompeii had disappeared.

'Not quite the real thing,' said Henry, looking at the bottle of wine he produced from his basket, 'it should correctly be Falernian. The Romans found this Tuscan stuff thin fare.' It was a fine Chianti Classico that he placed on the marble in front of us. Next to emerge from the basket was a loaf of country bread and a shallow dish that he filled with olive oil.

'C'mon, tuck in,' he said.

I wondered if it were just possible that Henry and I were the first Englishmen ever to have been at this bar, idly dipping a crust into the bowl. We would have sat at the counter but its wooden stools had not survived. Instead we propped it up and rested our elbows on the surface, with its great circular holes that should have housed great terracotta urns filled with their flavoured oils. We had another hour of daylight left and God was in His Heaven.

Across the street, and taking up most of the blank wall of a house, were some wonderfully painted advertisements for a forthcoming election, still there and unspoilt from the days before the eruption. Henry gestured towards them. 'So do you believe Caseus Grandis or Shysterius Typicus should represent us at the senate?'

The Romans had a curious 'democracy', if you can call it that. At the time of the eruption, the senate, having enjoyed real power during the Republic, was reduced to rubber-stamping all Imperial edicts. You certainly did not elect Caesar.

Henry explained to me that the Roman senate was supposed to be filled with mature men of noble family, who were genuinely disinterested in power or money, who would rule out of duty and a sense of public service, based on a profound education and long experience of victories and disappointments in love and war. Perhaps our nearest modern equivalent was the House of Lords in the nineteenth century.

'If only we could have that back, instead of the placemen and cronies we have today,' I volunteered.

'You should reread your Plato,' said Henry, agreeing with me (I think). 'He foresaw all the difficulties we now face. Power was doomed to drift inexorably towards the instant gratification always favoured by youth and incarnated by celebrities. The trouble with our modern form of Pericles' flawed invention [democracy, that is] is that the electorate has come to be seen by politicians as "the workforce", or "the tax payer". We have forgotten to remind them that we are their masters.'

I remembered an article in the *Daily Telegraph*. It mentioned a constituent, who, advising his MP on some important issue, had concluded his letter with the elegant phrase, 'I remind you, sir, that you are my humble and obedient servant.'

'That constituent was right,' said Henry. 'In a democracy, these people are there to do my, and your, bidding. Not the other way around. The trouble is in the nature of democracy itself. Too many useless and capricious idiots have the vote. Palmerston had it about right. The more you extend the franchise, the more people you have to bribe with their own money.'

Henry was clearly on a roll, but I wasn't having it. I wanted to stand up for our system.

'At least we can change the way things work,' I replied.

'Well, actually, no. We do have a vote every four or five years, but it has no granularity. Just a stark, binary choice. Keep the liars in, or throw them out and put the other liars in. That strikes you as awe-inspiring? A recipe for constructive change the whole world will want to follow?'

'Well, we are certainly changing the way we educate our children. Look at all these brand new comprehensive schools all over the place. That's progress, at least.'

'Jeremy, you simply have to be joking! Our education has been totally undermined by the idiots who govern us. We had the most modern and successful system in the world, with grammar schools for a few scholarly and academic youngsters and secondary modern schools for the majority. Now we have introduced the American 'comprehensive' system, in the name of calling everyone academic, or equal. We are doomed to return to the levels of illiteracy, innumeracy and general pointlessness that existed before the board schools were introduced in the 1860s.'

'OK, what is the point of politicians?'

'The only thing a state really has to do is to defend its people. But defence is expensive and "dispensable" – except of course in time of war, when it is always woefully inadequate. Our politicians are insufficiently responsible to be trusted with it.'

Henry, for reasons known only to him, thought that dictatorship was the answer. He was a great fan of Mussolini. 'A much maligned man. A fascist, perhaps, but never a Nazi,' he declared.

But dictators aren't the answer, either, I reflected. The word 'tyrant' once meant 'benign dictator', but it cannot mean that any more. Whether the dictator is Stalin, or Mao, or Cromwell, or Caesar, or even 'the proletariat', all power tends to corrupt and absolute power corrupts absolutely. In any case, calling the proletariat the dictator is merely casuistry.

'But England is a democracy, and we're all free, aren't we?' Henry was beginning to sound defeatist and I wanted to cheer him up.

'Don't give me "freedom" and all that American bunkum,' he rejoined. 'Freedom is a fine education. Freedom is being well. Freedom is having no one trying to kill you or lock you up without a trial. Freedom is having a little money. The rest can go hang.'

Henry was getting overexcited. To steer him into calmer waters I gestured towards the election notices painted on the wall behind us, still canvassing for our votes after 2,000 years.

'So, let's get back to these ancient candidates. How should I vote?'

'OK, let's see.' Henry's muse had taken over. 'On my right: Caseus Grandis. He's already a non-exec shareholder and chairman of the Romano-Cornish Tin Mining Consortium. All he wants from the senate are the contacts and levers of power for his expansion into Cisalpine Gaul. His ambitions for the citizens of Rome? That they will help him turn his sizable fortune into a truly vast one. He is in fact a repellent and cruel little toad, a monomaniac sociopathic autodidact. And on the left? Step up, Shysterius Typicus, whose egregious smile tries to disguise the banality of his manifesto; itself a saccharine blend of sentiment, self-importance, half-truths and self-serving pieties designed only to encourage the ill-educated greed of the plebeian rabble.'

I raised my glass to my political mentor. 'You will be pleased to hear that I shall not be taking up either of their kind offers. I shall not be voting at all.'

Pompeii is a life-changing experience. Its miraculous preservation allows one an opportunity to travel in time. The natives have stepped out of the picture for a moment or two and the place is perhaps a little untidy, but the roads are still there.

They still have their pavements. Every so often, a set of stepping-stones allows pedestrians to cross the road while still allowing the carts to pass and the roads to be washed. The depth of the road (relative to the footpaths) allows the street to be flooded while leaving the sidewalk dry.

We saw many ancient urinals let into walls as we walked about. After the Chianti I took advantage of one.

'Aren't we lucky,' said Henry, while I discharged a post-prandial debt, 'that we men have the opportunity to relieve ourselves without scaring the horses? When the Pompeians stopped at these little pieces of pottery they would collect a denarius for having done so. Precisely the opposite of spending a penny. On the other side is a laundry and human urine works wonders on cleaning Roman shirts. The only thing better is camel's pee, for which (if you could get it to do its business when you needed it to) you could earn a whole sestertius.'

As we walked along a distorted little lane near the centre of town, lined with brothels whose mosaics graphically advertised the skills of the ladies who worked there, he asked me why I might imagine they built such a twisted alleyway. 'Everything else in the empire is so dreadfully straight and narrow.'

I had no idea.

'So that their wives couldn't stand at either end and spot their husbands going in and out, of course.'

Henry seemed tireless in his desire to show me the old place and I was his willing student. He paid much attention to the frescoes and their differing styles, from the earliest style which simply 'pretended' to be marble facings for the interiors, to the Second Style, which came into fashion a generation before Julius Caesar invaded Britain. This used *trompe l'oeil* to create false perspectives of columns and extraordinary cornice work, seemingly rebuilding the rendered walls in marble and semi-precious stones. Then came the Third Style, around Our Lord's time, which abandoned the perspectives but introduced some elements of architectural decoration, used to frame small pictures. It is this style that one thinks of as Pompeian, with its use of black, white and London bus red to create a frieze of small pictures around the tops of rooms. But it is the Fourth Style, which effortlessly blends the architectural daydream into great Elysian landscapes, filling them with hunting scenes, seascapes or fantastic villas, which takes your breath away. The images recall Veronese's painted walls of the great villas of the Veneto or the works on canvas of Claude Lorraine. You gasp that they are almost impressionist, or Japanese, as your mind uselessly attempts to find a modern category for them.

It is truly astonishing that we could walk through the ruins at all. After that black river of ash and lapilli had smothered the place in the August of AD 79, Pompeii was left buried under six or seven metres of rock-hard earth.

One of Henry's heroes was an early eighteenth-century architect called Domenico Fontana. He had been engaged in land improvements in the valley of the Sarno, which involved building a tunnel. He had accidentally unearthed some unusual inscriptions that suggested an amphitheatre was not merely intact but the floor of which was thirty feet below where he stood.

In 1748 the excavation was to start in earnest, under the orders of the Holy Roman Emperor Charles, whose selfish purpose was to acquire as many Roman artefacts as he could for his own collection. Then, in 1860, Giuseppe Fiorelli invented the ingenious system of pouring liquid plaster into the spaces left in the ash, and artefacts and even people and animals sprang back 'to life'.

This was Henry's province, and his work continues. It is painstakingly slow. Only two-thirds of the old place has so far been reclaimed.

Pompeii was just 500 metres from the coast at the time of the eruption and had its own little marina. It is now more than two kilometres away from the shore. But the volcano, Mount Vesuvius, is even further. It erupted with such a huge explosion that it beggars imagination. When you look up from Pompeii, Vesuvius is on the horizon. In no way was Pompeii built on the volcano's slopes, as I was taught at school. The ash, the pebbles and the pumice were propelled there through the air.

That May, Henry called on me at the language school. He had had a tiff with his friend, Mario, who ran the bar where we had met. Henry told me he needed some civilised company.

I owed so much to him that I immediately rearranged my classes and we found a café some way from the school where he could tell me his troubles.

Henry had in the past been admitted to Oxford to read Archaeology. This was in the days, according to Henry, when Oxford's entry requirements were focussed on world-class excellence and not on re-engineering British society as part of a neo-socialist fantasy.

All had begun extremely well but, after a term, Henry had let slip that he had paid (deluded idiot) a schoolmate to pretend to be him and sit his Modern French A level on his behalf. He had a mental block (he told me) about this irrational nasal semi-Celtic language whose sound was so frightful that no successful opera would allow itself to be sung in it. I should stress that this was his view, not mine. Had he never listened to Berlioz's *The Trojans*, or Benvenuto Cellini? And what about Delibes? Or Bizet? *Carmen*, to name but one, is arguably the most accessible opera of all time.

News of his barbarous views, plus the revelation that he had matriculated via duplicity, caused his tutor to make enquiries.

The result: he was thrown out on his ear, of course. Happily, Sussex was less pernickety and he had gone on to take a first.

But now it turned out that his old Oxonian tutor had joined the gods at Sussex as his professor and would have the final say in awarding his doctorate. What was he to do? The fellow was about to descend on Pompeii.

How could I help?

'Has he been here before?' I asked.

'Of course he bloody has! He's an archaeologist.'

'I didn't mean Pompeii. Has he done Ravello, Ischia and so on? I mean, this is the Bay of Naples and these are its star attractions. Why don't you offer to be his guide and take him on a tour? And whatever you do, do not miss the cathedral at Amalfi.'

Well, somehow, the deal was done. I, for my sins, was roped in, and Dr Hendricks,[3] Henry and I went on a two-week tour of the Bay of Naples. We took in the endless stairs of Positano and the garden at Lady Walton's villa on Ischia. At Rapallo we watched the butchers' wives tear away the last shreds of pork from the carcass of a pig with a sort of crochet hook. They made sausages in this way, and they were almost certainly the finest sausages I have ever eaten. We saw both blue and green grottoes and ruined Norman castles; and one day we watched a shepherd drive his flock over a cliff into the sea. His sheep fell about ten feet into the Mediterranean and scrambled on to the shore, grateful for their bath and for having had a chance to impress the two huge dogs that had suggested the idea to them.

By the time we got to the cathedral at Amalfi, Henry and the Doctor were like a honeymoon couple. Henry's doctorate was in the bag, I felt. And judging by their devotions to the Romanesque masterpiece so close to the water's edge, their immortal souls were in reasonable shape too.

---

[3] Not his real name.

A Sunday in Borrowed Time
Catedrale de San Andrea, Amalfi

Henry, Dr Hendricks and I must have seemed a little odd as we sat in the piazza overlooking the façade of Amalfi's duomo, the word Italians use for their cathedrals in homage to Filippo Brunelleschi, the first man to build a dome greater than those of antiquity. In my hipsters, Chelsea boots and suede coat, I would have looked fairly typical of my time. Henry was wearing his favourite tweed suit and Dr Hendricks was resplendent in his Panama hat and linen jacket. His was a mellifluous voice. Henry and I let his wonderful words wash us with their wisdom. He was asking us to admire the cathedral's impressive bronze doors. 'They were made by craftsmen from Constantinople, in 1066,' Dr Hendricks told us, with so much pride he might have played a part in their commission.

The church certainly dominated the piazza. Most of what we could actually see dated from the thirteenth and nineteenth centuries. It seemed rather too big for the little town.

I nodded happily as the professor explained and extolled the great building. My beer was slipping down beautifully. It was the perfect foot balm though it had to be taken internally. We had just spent a tiring couple of hours wandering all over the town. Many of its streets double as flights of stairs, but we were now ensconced in a bar in front of an enormous eighteenth-century stone staircase that ascended from the piazza into the cathedral's 'Victorian' façade.

In fact, the oldest bits of the new cathedral of Amalfi date back to the ninth century. Partially built in the moresco style, it has been enlarged and enhanced throughout the centuries. A twelfth-century Romanesque bell tower has been topped with green and yellow glazed tiles to reflect the sun to its returning sailors. It was obviously the town's pride and joy.

I must have been staring at it, as Dr Hendricks read my mind.

'The original frontage collapsed around a century ago,' the professor explained. 'During the restoration that followed, architectural historians discovered in the rubble the original Romanesque façade with its little arches, columns and mosaics. They held a national competition, which was won by a certain Domenico Morelli in 1891. He created a new one, loosely based on the old remains. The venerable firm of Salviati, in Venice, was considered a safe pair of hands, and installed those "Byzantine" mosaics above us, which represent Jesus and the Apostles.'

I looked at it gratefully. This was the best way to do a cathedral. An ice-cold beer in one hand and a brilliant professor on the other. The tympanum was indeed covered with magnificent mosaics.

'The architectonic complex is actually made out of two or three inter-communicating churches, a crypt, a stair, an atrium, a church tower and a significant little cloister called the Chiostro di Paradiso,' continued Dr Hendricks.

'There was almost certainly a cathedral in Amalfi from the sixth century. It will have been a paleo-Christian affair, built in a strategic position in what was then the town's centre, on that little outcrop of volcanic rock. Amalfi's fishermen would have been able to see their church from miles out to sea, then as now.

'Just three arches and some columns survive from that ancient temple, and even those were altered in the seventeenth century for use in the upper crypt of the Crib.

'In the ninth century, the primitive church was rebuilt. When you go in, keep your eyes peeled and you will find marble transennas, banisters and portals from its Byzantine and Lombard phases.'

'Who is it dedicated to?' I asked. I have an interest in early saints.

'Originally, the Virgin, but at some early date it was changed to the Crucifixion. Then, in AD 987, Mansone I, then Duke of Amalfi, persuaded Pope John XV to elevate the see to an archiepiscopate. To force the Pope's hand, Mansone built a new cathedral almost against the old one, and because St Andrew was already the protector of the city, the new temple was also dedicated to him. In 1206, a later duke had the body of the Apostle brought here from Constantinople, at vast expense.'

How can anyone know so much stuff? I wondered. I decided to push my luck. 'When was the Paradise Cloister built?'

'Towards the end of the thirteenth century, at around the same time as the bell tower. It's very unusual. Moresco can be translated as "Christian Arabic". You must both go in; from there you'll get a terrific view of the bell tower.'

Henry and I glanced at each other. It was time to do as instructed. My Michelin guidebook gave the Cloister three stars, which is as good as it gets. Dr Hendricks decided to wait for us in the café. 'I have all it up here,' he said, tapping his own temple. He did too.

Overall, it was just as impressive as the professor had promised. But there was some disappointment in the main cathedral. Apart from a wonderful thirteenth-century wooden crucifix, and a high altar assembled from the parts of a monumental sarcophagus, the columns in the big church were encased in ugly baroque marble that obscured the antiquity of the place. What the cathedral had endured in the eighteenth century was truly horrible. A gold sequin ceiling had been installed in the central aisle, and huge and not very good paintings of St Andrew's passion dominated the place.[1]

But, traipsing around the cathedral, we came upon treasure after treasure. I remember an Angevin mitre made (it seemed) of gemstones and gold, and a pave of 19,000 pearls. A remarkable eighteenth-century sedan chair from Macao caught Henry's eye, and two small chapels, decorated with frescoes of the miracles and effigies of the saints, caught mine. One was of the founder of the Sovereign Order of St John of Malta, the world's smallest nation state, now reduced to a palace in Rome.

That exquisite and romantic cloister, the Chiostro di Paradiso, was easily the most unusual and most extraordinary corner of the complex. It was decorated with delicate and simple interlaced Moorish arches, just as Dr Hendricks had described, and its geometrical purity and beauty made our jaws drop. As with the

---

[1] In 1994 the authorities stripped back of some of the more otiose baroque artefacts, marble and plasterwork, and the ancient form is again visible. Without its original frescoes, however, the effect is rather like a medieval aircraft hangar.

creation of the Holy Church itself, the cloister's creation had been elegant, educated, designed; the work of an architect and not a random builder or felicitous historical accident.

Back in the piazza the professor had ordered another round.

'What about this little city? Why did it merit such a church?' asked Henry.

'Amalfi,' began our professor, 'had been an independent republic from as early as the seventh century. It had rivalled Pisa and Genoa, but in 1075 it fell to the Normans. Sadly, a great deal of it has also been lost to the sea.'

Walking around Amalfi, you somehow know that its early beginnings will be very obscure. It is not even certain when it was founded, or when Christianity first reached it.

'It will have been early, even for Italy, given the trade routes with the East that the south of Italy possessed. Pope Gregory the Great, writing in AD 596, ordered Primenus,[2] whom he addressed as 'bishop of the Civitas Amalfitana', to be 'imprisoned in a monastery as he did not remain in his diocese but preferred to roam about the Campania'. If this Primenus were bishop, then Amalfi must already have had a cathedral,' Hendricks made clear.

'We do know that by AD 1200 there were about 36,000 inhabitants, fifty-four parishes and 279 secular priests.[3] That would make it around ten times larger than it is today.'

Amalfi certainly enjoyed a high position in medieval architecture. Its cathedral, its campanile, its Franciscan monastery; these are breathtaking examples of the artistic movement prevailing at the time of the Normans. The languid Byzantine style blends effortlessly with the forms and sharp lines of northern architecture.

'Medieval scholarship,' Dr Hendricks explained, 'was also well housed in Amalfi, especially with flourishing schools of law and mathematics. Flavio Gioia, famous for the first compasses in Europe, was a native of Amalfi. In honour of King Charles II, a Capetian monarch then ruling Naples, Gioia put a fleur-de-lys instead of an N, to indicate north.'[4]

---

[2] Alternatively spelt 'Pimerius'.

[3] i.e. not monastic priests.

[4] But Gioia was not the inventor of the compass – the Arabs brought them to us from the East.

89

Never again would I have the privilege of such a history lesson in such a location. I began to envy professional historians and archaeologists and felt that I had perhaps selected the wrong subject at Cambridge. Imagine being paid to see these things!

I took my leave of Henry and Doctor Hendricks and caught the train back to my lodgings in Pompeii, with a certain pleasant sadness in my heart.

The year was brisk in any case but now it had donned its roller skates. I decided to stay in Italy. Apart from anything, I was too broke to get home.

Christmas was upon us in a trice and my landlady invited me to dinner with her extended family. Much to her delight, I had second helpings of everything until I could hardly stand. After the enormous and elaborate feast we played board games well into the night.

My job did not allow me to save any money – in fact it was a constant challenge even to buy a coffee on my meagre wages – and I was missing both music and female company – not necessarily in that order.

But by now my Italian really had improved – I was using it every day – and could at last be called fluent. It was time to take the bull by the horns and move to Rome. So I did.

Chapter the Seventh
1972: Penniless in Rome

In which the author arrives in the Eternal City with almost no money and without a job, but confident that something will come up. He has a disastrous attempt to become a male model. He settles for teaching English and for taking tours around Rome – very profitably, as it turns out. He takes to Rome like a duck to water.

Arriving in Rome for the first time, bags in hand and short of a job, gave me a feeling I can only compare with when I walked down King's Parade, Cambridge, on my first day as an undergraduate. I was the most privileged man in the world just for being there.

As a small boy I had seen the old Forum, the Colosseum and some other bits and pieces with my family. I had a distant memory of a hotel, Il Sole, which claimed to be the oldest hotel in Rome. By extension it was probably the oldest in the world. This appealed to me. I remembered it as rather run-down, which was good, as my means were slender in the extreme. I had already learned the most useful word in the Italian language, which is *sconto*. It means 'discount', or better, 'Knock a bit off, governor'. I would have to use this word if I was going to get a halfway decent night's sleep.

I had already acquired the phrase '*centro storico*', or historic centre, but this phrase is rather less useful. The trouble is, the authorities paste it all over the place for motorists who are heading into town, but once more or less in the centre, they see no further use for it. Railways stations are in the centre of towns everywhere in the world. Once there, naturally enough, no further indications for the centre are even considered. I might as well head off in any direction. I weighed up my options, thought about taxis and counted my money. Despite the weight of my suitcases I had decided to hoof it.

I was feeling remarkably cheerful. The weather was fine – a bright, if cool, sunny day in January. My favourite kind, really. And the piazza in front of the Stazione Termini, as the main railway station is romantically called, is a good start for an adventure. Ahead of you is an enormous fountain. To your right is an old church, purportedly designed by Michelangelo. To your immediate left is a bar selling *porchetto*: slices of highly seasoned suckling pig sold in hot crusty buns. Magic.

I must have spent almost an hour in that bar, chatting happily with the railway workers. I was in no hurry, as while I had the name of my hotel, I had no idea how to get there. But my new friends carefully explained to me the route I had to take. About an hour and a half later I arrived in Piazza della Rotonda and at my destination.

It seems incredible, with today's inflated prices being what they are, that Il Sole was in those days a rough and ready sort of place, boasting no refinements of any discernible kind. An ex-policeman who stood for no nonsense ran it, but he was a kind man under his bluff exterior. He found me a room, fairly near a bathroom; at least, it was on the same floor. I tried my word *sconto* on him, explaining that I would be staying at least a month, and he relented, shaving a microscopically small amount from the nominal price. It would have to do. Tomorrow I would have to find a job if I was going to pay it.

The hotel had a sensational location. Opposite its front door was the portico of the ancient Pantheon, a huge temple from Caesar's day. A couple of hundred yards away was Piazza Navona, arguably the finest square in the world. And behind the hotel was a little bistro, da Pepe, where either the owner thought he was a painter, or artists really did pay their accounts with canvas. I have seldom seen a more depressing display of dreadful daubs. Still, if they paid the bill…

But it was to a Chinese restaurant that I went that first night, after I had unpacked and got my act together. I had not eaten Chinese since arriving in Italy almost nine months before, and my goodness how I missed it! I was reduced to a slavering wreck on the pavement outside as I stared at the menu. I took a deep breath, pushed open the door and went in.

I was greeted correctly. A Chinese lady, clad entirely in silk, shuffled over to me and bowed. She indicated a large dining room behind her, entirely empty but for one table, where a girl in her twenties was eating alone. I wondered about the Chinese population of Rome. Maybe they had found a better place to go to, or possibly there were no other Chinese people in Rome. Was there some dark and sinister episode in the Roman past I needed to know about?

I did something that surprised me. It's totally out of character, and I have never done it since.

I walked over to the Italian girl, the one who was dining alone, and said to her, in Italian, 'Do you mind if I join you? I am new to Rome and know no one here.'

She replied in English – understandably, as my Italian was still weak and I had a marked English accent. But it was what she said that mattered.

'Of course, sit down. I have only just ordered myself.'

It seems to me that there is a particular quality to Rome beyond the obvious stuff of its being the world's most romantic city and arguably its most enchanting. Arguably? I'll leave that argument to the Parisians. But Europe does contain a vast number of seriously beautiful cities. Try Bruges, Copenhagen, Prague, St Petersburg, Venice and Salamanca just for starters.

But Rome is always in good spirits. The noise of people in restaurants, or when they talk to each other in trains and buses, the buzz of negotiation in the markets; it is all one contented murmur that bubbles up into cheerfully raised voices from time to time. Even when they are cross with each other, which mainly seems to happen on the roads, their expressions of displeasure are almost comical in their length and complexity. And a really good insult will earn you a round of applause from the spectators who, sure as eggs is eggs, will gather around. For Italian speakers, the best such insult I ever heard went something like this: *Sònate la panza gràvida di quella mignotaccia de tu sorella colle osse de' meio mortacci tua*. I am afraid I dare not translate it.

Rome is probably the last of the great capital cities where strangers will greet each other as they pass early in the morning with a spirited '*Buon giorno!*' If an Italian wears a hat, and many still like to, it will always be raised to a lady, though possibly with a tad too much gallantry.

As I sat down opposite Vittoria, I saw that my first impression of her, that she was sensational, understated the case. She was very tall, possibly too slender for my tastes, but with a perfect figure that her designer clothes did nothing to obscure. She was wearing maybe a shade too much make-up for the dim lighting in the restaurant, but what's this? Complaints, already? Just how good can a first day in a new town get to be?

Well, she asked me what I did, which wasn't much of a conversation, as I did nothing. As yet, that is. I asked her what she did, and she told me the glaringly obvious; she was a model, did the catwalk stuff for Valentino, or one of the other big Roman names.

What was it like? Oh, boring, boring... It is odd how often I was to hear the Romans, in their marvellous city, complain of being bored. Mind you, I was to discover it's even worse in Florence and Venice. Perhaps being bored is a necessary element in the drive to be creative. In Rome, especially, where with every step you take you are surrounded with the works of the finest creative minds of the last two and a half millennia.

We talked cinema. 'You should work in the cinema,' Vittoria told me. 'Rome is big on cinema.' She had plenty of friends who hung about Cinecittà, the Roman studios that are home to the Italian film industry, hoping to get called for work as an extra. She had done it herself when she was young. It paid well, she assured me. You could even live off it so long as you lived at home.

Vittoria had a lovely and infectious laugh. As she described the bullies and primadonnas that were the stuff of her business, and the extraordinary parties they all went to, hoping to resurrect the ghosts of *La Dolce Vita*, I began to laugh alongside her.

What a strange sight we must have been to the inscrutable waiters in that place; a couple who had never met before, talking each other's languages quite appallingly and behaving like long separated friends with years of adventures to catch up on.

Towards the end of that meal, Vittoria asked me if I – yes, me – had ever modelled. If I met her the next day (she passed me an address) she would introduce me to a colleague, and I could give it a go.

'Some men are really sought after and earn enough to buy a Maserati,' she told me, implausibly.

They say there is no fool like an old fool, but then they've never tried a young one. I knew, not suspected, but knew as a matter of fact that I had the posture of a sack of Irish potatoes and the elegance of a taproom drunk trying to explain the ballet. Still, I thought I might have a go.

As I slept in Il Sole that night a tumble of images and scenes played themselves out for me: yachts, white-jacketed crew and a bevy of scantily clad models on the sun deck with signs beside them saying BASTE EVERY TWO HOURS. Below decks, drinking whisky and playing cards were Federico Fellini, Marcello Mastroianni, Anita Ekberg, Anouk Aimée, Yvonne Furneaux, Magali Noël and Valentino with his gorgeous Vittoria. It was a jet set-peopled dreamscape of sails and little seaplanes just off the Costa Smeralda. Heady stuff.

I persuaded the maid to lend me an iron and I attempted to make my suit look as though it had never served as pyjamas.

My goodness, modelling was boring. Vittoria had been right all along. I sat for hours while the girls strutted their stuff, being shouted at, or with dreadful music turned up full volume. The Great Designer looked as if he would explode from apoplexy at any minute. A host of seamstresses descended like a swarm of bees on to the leggy models every few seconds with pins and pegs, adjusting the creations to the girls' reed-like figures – so totally unlike their potential market that the whole thing was close to fraud. There were no men there at all, other than the Great Designer and me.

Finally, after some hours, the girls were sent off for a 'comfort break' and the great man sat next to me. 'Vittoria speaks highly of you, but please don't be offended if I tell you I just can't see it. Why don't you prove me wrong? Walk up and down the stage there, looking natural. No swagger, please. Just look like an English gentleman. Like Steed. OK, I watch you.'

And with that he turned away, in such a manner that he could not possibly watch me. Oh well, I didn't really want to be a model anyway.

Well, I walked up and down the stage. Actually that's not quite true. Halfway along my return journey, the Great Designer shouted, '*Basta!*'[1] I got down, and he clapped once. The single clap was not for me. It was a signal for the girls to return to their labours. As I returned the umbrella to its stand I wondered if could get a job as an extra. Perhaps, in a documentary about the Irish famine, I could play the sack of potatoes.

As I emerged into the street and the ridiculously bright sunshine, I told myself how lucky I was. Imagine the horror of being cooped up all day with a couple of dozen radiant beauties in their early twenties, and I and the gay Great Designer the only men competing for their affections. That was a fate too ghastly to contemplate. I needed a drink.

As I walked past the Temple of Fortuna Virilis, having no particular place to go, I thought it might be time to propitiate the gods. They were clearly taking the mickey. What was needed was a votive offering. But sacrificing a sheep was probably illegal on a number of grounds.

Sitting on the temple steps I lit a cigarette. The smoke rose in the general direction of heaven, where perhaps a tired Roman god noticed it and irritably peered down to earth.

I gloomily studied my copy of *Corriera della Sera*. Oil prices were rising. Stock exchanges were stagnant. Property prices were still unsteady. Recession, stagnation… it didn't seem like the perfect time to give up and head home to a glittering City career.

I turned to the small ads. And buried halfway down the page was one that was possible. It read, in Italian, 'English teacher, mother tongue English, needed for private lessons very early in morning. Please call Rome 1234.'

At 5 a.m. the next morning (I jest not) I was ringing the front doorbell to an apartment in an ultra-modern block of flats. A uniformed maid opened the door and showed me into a largish salon, telling me to wait while she fetched me a coffee. I looked around. The furniture was good; early nineteenth-century Italian. Not a style I admired overmuch, however, when the same period in France, Sweden and England was so much more elegant. On the walls were some paintings of indifferent quality and the bookshelves were occupied by pompously bound classics and about a dozen sporting or media awards.

---

[1] Enough!

Everything had that look of having been bought by an interior designer – except the awards, of course – and I wondered where my host really lived. He certainly hadn't grown up with this lot.

At 5.25 a.m. he came into the salon and I stood up to shake his hand. He was dressed in velvet slippers and a Chinese dressing gown of exquisite silk, below which fluttered the trouser legs of what must have been Jermyn Street's finest pyjamas. He was smoking (a challenge at 5.25 a.m.) a cigarette in a tortoiseshell cigarette holder. He was about five feet tall and his hair was plastered on to his head and parted down the centre. Clean-shaven, he was perhaps fifty years old.

'Do you speak Italian?' he asked in English. I said I did.

'Good. You eat breakfast?' No, I had not.

'Then you come into dining room.'

I followed him cautiously into the dining room. It was another large room, impossibly dreary and filled with heavy furniture. There was a sideboard, and on it a row of silver covered dishes.

'Please help yourself,' he commanded.

I lifted a lid and discovered kedgeree, no less. The next one had devilled kidneys. The third, eggs Benedict. Quite a breakfast, I thought positively. I began to fill a plate with food. He, on the other hand, touched nothing.

'I have been reading P G Wodehouse,' he announced, reverting to Italian. 'From him I have learned what Englishmen eat for breakfast. Personally, I'll just have a coffee.'

He explained himself a little while I ate the best breakfast I had seen for a long, long time.

I did however turn down his offer of a glass of Brunello di Montalcino.

His name was Ettore. He was a director of the Italian broadcasting corporation, RAI. He had to be in his office at 8 a.m. every morning, so I could come at 5 a.m. and we would put in two hours a morning together. Would that be all right?

I looked at the dapper little fellow and wondered. He was clearly a bachelor.

Ettore must have caught my drift. 'I will not receive you like this, of course. You will arrive, and we will jump into my car and go riding, or gliding, or sailing.'

I smiled, the eggy soldier in my mouth making speech impossible.

'We will only speak English. And I will pay you 15,000 lire a session.'

There were one or two reasons why I should say no. And getting up so early in the morning was just one of them. But 15,000 lire? Why, that was, let me see, £75 a week in English money. For two short hours a day!

I agreed. No need to haggle, I thought. Deals didn't get any better than this.

And what's more, it did not even cause me too much pain in the evening, as from that moment on I adopted the habit of taking a long siesta, at first in my hotel and later at Gambrinus, the private beach on the sea close to Rome, on a daybed under the sun.

And it got better. Ettore was as good as his word, speaking execrable English at me while he irritated a horse or piloted a glider frighteningly badly in the Alban Hills at the usual ungodly hour. Sometimes he would show off his personal tutor at the parties he gave for his media mates. If any of them suspected a closer relationship, the girls certainly didn't. I began to meet all manner of people, at first through Ettore and later through each other. My social world was born. I met actors, starlets, polo players and their gamine young arm candy, and Roman aristocrats, of both the Black and Red varieties.

Here, perhaps, I should explain. Romans divide their aristocracy into two types; the Blacks, whose titles had been granted by the Triple Tiara, and the Reds, who had their titles bestowed on them by medieval kings anxious to get them on side. The Reds were generally more fun.

I took drinks with them at the terrace bar of the Eden, or tea with them at Babbington's, or coffee at the Antico Caffé Greco. I even plucked up my courage and asked one of them, a very bright young beauty called Arianna – Italian for Ariadne – to dinner at Alfredo's. In short, I had arrived.

One day, Ettore introduced me to the owner of one of Rome's travel companies. The latter had discovered that I liked to expound on how great Rome was. Would I consider taking guided tours of American tourists around Rome? He would pay reasonably, and he was sure a 'student' could use a little extra.

I really was a student again. I had enrolled on an interpreting course at the *Sapienza*, Rome's ancient university. I was planning a triumphant return to England with a diploma, and, as an added bonus, its student card was getting me into the museums and even the university canteens at a fraction of the normal price. I was devouring museums and galleries by the dozen and this card was proving invaluable.

As instructed I turned up at the Hilton Hotel near Rome and was introduced to my driver, a very charming old boy called Dario. He couldn't speak a word of English, but my Italian was now approaching real fluency. I could even manage a word or two in the local dialect, sometimes called Romanaccio, a coarse blend of Italian and Latin with possibly some Arabic thrown in. It served the Romans as cockney serves Londoners; a badge of authenticity (a Roman born and bred, that is) and a way of excluding interlopers.

I was to take a bus full of American tourists on an orientation tour of Rome. They could get out at the Colosseum – Dario would show me where – for 'comfort' and the chance to buy some souvenirs from a shop belonging to Dario's cousin. I was then to take them to a restaurant on the Via Flaminia for lunch. Another of Dario's cousins was head waiter there. And finally I would return them to the Hilton. It didn't sound too complicated.

So, I took the microphone and pointed out the monuments to either side, giving what I knew of their history and summoning up any anecdotes I had heard on the way. It all seemed to go quite well, and we stopped as planned at Dario's cousin's souvenir shop.

As predicted, everyone got off the bus and took photographs of each other, buying plastic paperweights that were copies of the Colosseum or the Arch of Septimus Severus. As they piled back on board, and just as I was about to tell Dario to drive on, the cousin rapped at my door. I opened it, wondering what he wanted. He handed me a small brown envelope with the word *grazie* scribbled on it.

I resumed my banter until we reached the restaurant, where the deal was that I should eat free, with the driver. I liked Dario, a classic rogue of the old school. He even quite approved of me. He told me some very funny stories. All too soon we were back on the bus and the head waiter had pressed a second brown envelope on me inscribed with the same courteous word.

Finally, we got to the Americans' hotel, and as they all piled out, most of them tipped me in US dollars. Add that to my fee from the tour company, and this was quite interesting employment.

As spring turned to summer I grew into the job. Dario and I became more ambitious and we agreed to extend the trips to Castelgandolfo, the pope's summer palace, and finally an overnight run to Pompeii. Dario had cousins all over the place. Some had restaurants, others sold cameos. One sold lace and crochet work. He even had a cousin who sold genuine Roman antiquities, but whose shop smelled strongly of fresh clay and paint. I decided to avoid that one after a single visit. But the brown envelopes kept coming in.

My commentary was becoming effortless and I frequently went on to autopilot. To avoid boring myself to death I resolved to make my descriptions more interesting. At first I tried statistics. They seemed to go down very well. Take the Colosseum.

'This is the Flavian Amphitheatre, commonly called the Colosseum. A total of 483 Christians were put to death here during the persecutions of the early church,' I would announce. The bus would tilt to the right as everyone climbed over each other to take their photographs. After a while I began to go too far.

'The Colosseum is made up of 4,658,864 blocks of hand-cut stone, and it weighs in at just about the same as the US aircraft carrier *Nimitz*.'

Despite such nonsense, the tips turned out to be more and more generous.

One day, when I was walking my charges around the prison cell that had held St Peter before his crucifixion, one of the ladies stopped me and told me blushingly that she wanted to ask me a very, huh, personal question.

I looked her up and down. Just turned forty, I calculated, which seemed very grown up to a twenty-three-year-old, but still good-looking.

She took my arm and pulled me slightly away from the others. 'It's about love.'

'Shoot,' I said, 'though I may not know the answer.'

'Well,' she continued uncomfortably, looking at her feet, 'did Jesus invent love?'

Well, I enjoy a good bit of theological repartee at any time of day or night, but something told me this was not the right time to dig up some of the old medieval questions on whether Christ ever laughed and so on.

'Yes, ma'am, I believe He did.'

'Well, how did the Romans,' – and here she gestured over the ruins – 'manage to have children before Our Lord was born?'

Americans may not know all the answers, but they sure know some difficult questions.

As for me, one of the truly great summers of my life had begun. I had enough money to manage in some modest comfort. I had a school to attend near the Villa Borghese. And I had all the time in the world to explore what is probably the greatest city on earth.

Chapter the Eighth
1972: A Tour of Athens

In which the author has an opportunity to visit Athens. There is a catch, however: forty beautiful and hyperactive teenage American girls.

Late one morning the director of my tour company rang me up. Could I take three or four days off my other commitments? They had a new contract and it meant a trip to Athens. Could I handle it?

Athens. The life force of our civilisation. The city of the Parthenon, of the School of Athens, of Plato and Socrates. It conjured up a vision of Menelaus, King of Sparta, and that tearaway wife of his who launched a thousand ships. The very name of the Hellenic capital had an ethereal ring to it, a heady cocktail of ancient scholarship and of capricious gods. Of course I'd do it.

My instructions were easy enough. I was to be at Rome's Hilton where a bus would be waiting for me. Dario would be my driver again and would take me and my aspirant fellow travellers to Brindisi whence the ferry would take us to Piraeus. Once in Greece, I would hand over to a Greek travel company, who would have a bus for us plus an English-speaking guide. Accommodation was all sorted. I could join in, or manage my own adventures as I chose. Then the journey would be repeated in reverse, and I would have had the journey a young Roman nobleman in the time of Augustus would have considered a Grand Tour.

Ettore was most accommodating, especially when I explained it was to understand Italy a little better that I sought a few days across the Ionian Sea. Like the putative nobleman whose footsteps I was following, I bought a paperback copy of Pausanias' guide to

Athens,[1] written shortly after Sulla took the place for Rome, and opened it at random, hoping perhaps to discover a Michelin-starred restaurant that Apicius might have dined at.[2]

In the event, the guide was a little out of date. Frustratingly, Pausanias seemed less interested in restaurants than in a great gold and ivory statue of Pallas Athena in the Parthenon, plus a few pictures and portraits. He dwelt at great length on inscriptions recording the laws of Solon. Even before I got there, I had the strong suspicion that Athens would have changed a little since his time.

Dario was all for it. He had a cousin in Brindisi whom he hadn't seen in ages. Three days away? He would wait for us there. Nothing would or could go wrong.

On the due date I arrived bright-eyed and bushy-tailed at the concrete and plate glass portals of the Hilton, which I then thought an excrescence but is probably now listed by Italia Nostra[3] as an exemplar of sixties taste.

The foyer was packed with teenage girls, all slightly under-dressed and all wearing a great deal of make-up. They had bathed in so much perfume that I would not be able to nose a wine for a week. It was an interesting sight, though.

'Here you are then, bang on time,' I heard from behind me, and I turned to meet my travel company's young director. 'Don't panic, but these are your charges. So far, we have taken these delightful young ladies around Rome, Venice and Florence. Their joy was unconfined. Show them Athens, and good luck. And don't do anything I wouldn't do.'

I corralled them as best I could and asked them in a school-

---

[1] His Description of Greece ['Ελλάδος Περιήγησις] is the earliest surviving tourist guidebook and an invaluable text on otherwise indecipherable ancient ruins. It was written in about AD 160.

[2] Marcus Gavius Apicius, who lived in Rome while Our Lord was still alive, was the gourmet who wrote the first known cookery book, *De Re Coquinaria*. Here is an 'everyday' recipe from it. Enjoy!

Patina quotidiana: Cerebella elixata teres cum pipere. Cuminum, laser cum liquamine, caroeno, lacte et ovis. Ad ignem lenem vel ad aquam calidam coques.

[Everyday dish: You crush boiled brains with pepper. Add cumin, asafoetida, salt to taste, young wine already reduced by a third, milk and eggs. Simmer at low heat or cook over boiling water.]

[3] Akin to the British National Trust.

masterish way if they had their passports. They waved them in the air and cheered. I told them where the bus was and the girls whooped, full of the joys of spring. Dario and I loaded their little cases into the hold, all the while wishing we could put our fingers in our ears. Ye gods, it was only 7.30 a.m. in the morning! St Trinian's, I thought, had an American branch.

After around half an hour we were ready for the off. Dario thought we had better take the Appian Way to Brindisi. Most of it was now a motorway but it would still be a marvellous drive.

No Roman can avoid showing the world his capital and Dario was no exception. We drove straight into town, me on the microphone directing the girls to look to their left or right. Suddenly we were driving through the Porta Appia and along the Via Appia Antica, then open to traffic and lined on either side with monuments to senators, generals, admirals and (in particular) to Caecilia Metella, dead these 2,000 years. And then, unexpectedly, we stopped.

I looked at Dario.

'*Un mio cugino*,'[4] he said enigmatically, indicating a huge souvenir shop that seemed to specialise in cameos.

'Ah,' I said.

We disgorged our energetic cargo, which couldn't wait to shop till it dropped.

Half an hour later we were back on the bus and about to pull out. The girls were happily chirping away but Dario seemed to be having some sort of disagreement with his cousin. I got down from the bus, wondering if there was anything I should know or do.

'Your ladies are like jackdaws,' explained the aggrieved shop-keeper. 'They are a plague of locusts. I have been looted. I am ruined! My family is already on the streets.'

Dario shrugged his shoulders, a fatalistic Hebrew gesture that normally works. But his cousin was not so easily satisfied.

'Give me a carrier bag,' I said. 'I'll do what I can.'

I got back on board and took the microphone.

'Young ladies,' I began. There was much laughter, whistling and applause from the audience. 'I am afraid we are stuck here. The owner of the shop has sent for the police and this bus may

---

[4] 'A cousin of mine.'

have to be impounded. We all may be intimately searched by the Italian police. It seems that some of you may have accidentally put a cameo or some other trivial souvenir in your handbags without remembering to pay.

'But I have his agreement that if he gets all his stuff back, he will withdraw any charges and we may safely carry on our journey.'

There was a slow, synchronised sigh. I passed the carrier bag to the first row, where one of the girls dropped something small into it. She then passed it on.

This was a large carrier bag, but by the time it had completed its tour it was brimming with trinkets. I had witnessed an act of mass contrition. Some of the girls remembered items that they had not included at the first pass and wanted a second go. After only a few minutes I had handed it back to the shopkeeper with a fulsome apology.

'Oh, think nothing of it,' he said. 'It happens all the time. But I don't normally get so much of it back. Once or twice I have had to call the police for real.'

He reached into his pocket.

'*Grazie. E buon viaggio.*' He glanced at the girls. '*Mi raccomando.*'[5]

He pressed a fat brown envelope into my hand. I put it discreetly into my breast pocket.

We were on our way again.

It's a long way to Brindisi by road, and despite several pit stops and 'comfort breaks' the girls were sufficiently contrite to ensure that there were no further problems. They had been a little shaken by the thought of the Italian police giving them the once-over and had warmed to me for getting them out of a hole.

They sang a lot on the long journey. I listened to 'The Sloop John B' and similar stuff, sung with enthusiasm, if not ability, for mile upon mile.

Finally we were at the ancient port of Brindisi, in good time for our ferry. My girls were still in a tractable condition and I decided to give them some *Kultur*.

'Brindisi,' I told the girls as we drove towards the ferry terminal, 'is the capital of Puglia. It was a Greek colony until, in 245 BC,

---

[5] 'And be careful.'

the Romans conquered it. Virgil, the great Roman poet who wrote the *Aeneid*, died here in 19 BC.

'Brindisi was conquered by Ostrogoths, reconquered by Byzantines, burned by Saracens and invaded by Normans. From the thirteenth century it was ruled by the Angevins and then by the Aragonese. Then Venice had it for a while, before losing it to Spain. Venice and Spain fought over it but both lost it to Austria in 1707. Thirty years after that the Bourbons got it. Lastly, for six months in 1943, Brindisi was the capital of Italy.

'Look outside. Was it worth the bother?'

There wasn't much to see, of course. Mostly a tedious post-war town. Our friends in the Luftwaffe had done some useful urban clearance, and the USAF had finished the job.

The ancient town's importance was entirely based on its port, with its double inlet, lying at the union of the Adriatic and Ionian Seas. As we drove into the port and its coach park, we could all see the famous Roman columns that must have given solace to so many ancient mariners, but after the glories of Rome itself they left the girls unimpressed.

If we had only had the time to explore; a large area of the Messapian-Roman town is still there, whose houses survive (after a fashion) along a huge and navigable paved road.

But this was Italy. Like everywhere else, Brindisi has any number of monuments of historical and artistic importance, here and there, scattered about. The ancient church of St Giovanni al Sepolcro is reportedly well worth a view, as is the magnificent sixteenth-century Nervegna Palace. And so is the majestic baroque cathedral.

But I was scared to lose any of these sweet young things. Given their obvious lack of enthusiasm for 'old buildings', I chose the better part of valour and aimed straight for the ferry. Dario too thought this a wise choice and in no time we were going on board, Dario behind on the quayside to see us off.

'You won't return alive,' he had promised me cheerfully. 'Check them for drugs. Otherwise the Colonels[6] will have them, and you, for breakfast.'

It was not too long before we had been allocated our cabins and were all at sea for Greece.

---

[6] A military junta then governed Greece.

After I had thrown my case into my little cabin, I set off to find the duty-free shop, the bar and peace in the bottom of a beer glass.

Drugs, I thought to myself. Well, the carrier bag trick worked once. I could always try it again…

An astonishingly good-looking girl came up to the bar and sat next to me.

'Drinking alone, sir? You could use some company. I'll have a peach daiquiri.'

I ordered a vodka and orange from the barman.

'Closest you'll get. Where are you from?'

'Hauppauge. Long Island. Have you been there?

'No. Not yet, I haven't. Should I?'

'No. But there are some real fine places on Long Island. It's just that Hauppauge is a dump. Where do you live in England?'

'In London, mostly.'

'Is that nice?'

'Nice enough, I suppose. It's probably a bit like New York.'

'New York! Wow! Have you been there?'

'Not yet. Should I?'

'Oh yes! I'd show you round. There's the Circle Line – that's the riverboat that goes around Manhattan. And there's the Empire State. And there's Fifth Avenue and the Easter Parade and St Patrick's Day, and the ticker tape for astronauts and presidents and stuff. You'd love it. Tell me you'll come visit? Please? Pretty please?'

I looked at the girl slightly more carefully. She was maybe twenty-one. Or was that an illusion? She had enchanting black shoulder-length hair, an oval face, dark pools of eyes and slightly tanned skin. She was wearing too much lipstick and was sporting a cameo on a chain around her neck. Her V-neck pullover had been sprayed on to a great figure by a car mechanic. She wore a breathtakingly short skirt and a fine pair of legs connected it with her knee length boots.

'Which school do you go to?' I asked, knowing that 'school' can also mean 'university' in the US.

'Hauppauge High. I'm hoping for New York State next semester.'

Well, there was an answer to an unspoken question. She was seventeen.

I heard some giggling from behind me and swivelled around to see the source. A group of about five of my girls was also in the room, watching us at the bar and finding it all most amusing. If they had been thinking what I had been thinking they would have been placing bets.

'What's your name?' I asked my companion, not before time.

'I'm Mimi.' She held out her hand. 'I already know yours. It's Jeremy.'

I shook her hand.

'Look, Mimi, I have a problem which you could help me with.'

'That would be nice,' said Mimi coquettishly. 'Shoot, mister.'

'It's about drugs. Illegal drugs. Do any of the girls have any on them, do you think?'

'Why, Jeremy, you do surprise me! I guess I know where to ask. What would you like?'

'No, it's not for me. It's just that there was a coup d'état a few years ago in Greece and the place is now run by a collective of crypto-fascist Colonels. If they or their dogs find any drugs on the girls they will have to go to prison and it will take ages – possibly years – to get them out again.'

'What's a crypto-fascist?'

'Basically a bloke who likes dressing up in an expensive uniform and hurting people. Or killing them. It doesn't usually matter which.'

'Oh my! What can we do?'

'Well, I thought, if we pass a carrier bag around, like we did on the bus, the girls could put their drugs in it. Then I would put it in left luggage or give it to the Captain to look after until we were back on board in a few days' time. It would mean no drugs in Greece, but your friends could manage for three days, I'm sure. What do you think?'

'If we don't we'll go to jail?'

'I imagine we just might, yes.'

'Have you got a shopping bag, then?'

'Wait here. I'll go and fetch one.'

I went to my cabin where I did indeed have a shopping bag. It currently held a bottle of duty-free gin and a carton of cigarettes. I crammed my booty into my little case and returned to the bar.

But Mimi was nowhere to be seen. I looked around anxiously and spotted her in a corner of the bar with her school friends. I walked over and suddenly one of her party saw me and flicked her head in my direction. The girls all froze and Mimi blushed engagingly. I affected not to notice.

'Here we are – a carrier bag. Are you sure you can manage this, Mimi?'

'Leave it with me, sir. I'll find you in your cabin later.' And all the girls laughed.

Find me she did. It was almost midnight and I had gone to bed. There was a timid knock on my cabin door and I, having drawn a towel around my naked body, opened the door a fraction. Mimi pushed it open and came in. She was in her pyjamas and dressing gown, and was sporting my plastic bag, now almost full of prohibited pharmaceuticals.

'Well done,' I said. Now what was I to do?

Mimi turned the lot on to the bed. There were a dozen lumps of hashish. In even greater supply were 'dolls', pills of every colour that took you up or down. There were a couple of plastic syringes (ye gods!) and two or three stainless steel pillboxes that might have contained anything. The whole caboodle would probably have secured a bungalow in Essex on the open market.

'Have I done well?' asked Mimi. 'Do you want to say thank you?' And she sat on the little bed, apparently not noticing that her dressing gown had fallen open.

I resolved when I started to write this memoir that I would tell the truth, no matter how embarrassing.

So I said, 'Mimi, you're underage. If I did what I would love to do your parents would take a contract out on me.'

'If I let you, they wouldn't. And who's going to tell them?'

I heard a quiet rustle from the door.

'Only all your friends,' I said throwing the door open. Twenty girls, ears pressed against it, fell into my cabin in a parody of the famous scene in the Marx brothers' *A Night at the Opera*.

There was much (fairly) innocent laughter at the way my towel became dislodged but within a minute or two I was alone again, with the 'stash'. But what to do with it?

Early the next morning, as we approached Piraeus harbour just south of Athens, I set out to find a left luggage locker. Of course I failed. I decided to take a steward into my confidence.

A friendly-looking Greek was busy cleaning the deck.

'Do you speak Italian?' I asked, in that language.

'*Neh*,' he said, somewhat confusingly. In Greek, *neh* means 'yes' and a word sounding very similar to 'OK' means 'no'.[7]

'Right,' I said. 'You may be able to help me. I have a parcel here that my party doesn't want to take into Greece. Is there any possibility of storing it on board ship until we return to Brindisi?'

'May I see?' The steward took the carrier bag, opened it and peered inside. His eyebrows went halfway up his forehead.

'You want me to look after this? Personally?'

'Yes,' I said.

'OK,' he said. He then swung the carrier bag by its handle and flung it into the sea.

'I hope that helps,' he said.

I was impressed. But what was I going to say to the girls? Oh well, I would just have to cross that bridge when I came to it.

We were now steaming into the harbour and I could see Piraeus, Athens' port for the last 2,500 years, very well from my maritime vantage point.

Its name, Πειραιεύς, means 'the place over the passage'. At first, Piraeus had been a rocky island that linked to the mainland via a low-lying stretch of land. Seawater flooded it most of the time and its muddy soil must have made it a tricky route, even when 'dry'. But by early classical times the passage was drained and Piraeus began its life as a deep-water harbour.

Pausanias was pretty good on Piraeus, even if his dates were incomprehensible. Thank God for the notes.

Themistocles, I learned, was the first to urge the Athenians to take advantage of Piraeus. He accurately predicted a new attack by the Persians after the Battle of Marathon, and in 492 BC he turned Piraeus into a military harbour. The Athenian shipyards were

---

[7] *Ohi.*

created then, and soon the Athenian fleet was to distinguish itself at the Battle of Salamis.

Shortly after that, a road to Athens was laid and protected with long walls. These were called, appropriately, the Long Walls. Hippodamus of Miletus devised a grid system for the roads of Piraeus. Town planners thenceforward would follow suit, most notably in the USA.

Flicking though the pages, I discovered that during the Peloponnesian Wars, Piraeus boasted three great arsenals that berthed almost 400 ships between them. Not 1,000, Doctor Faustus, please take note. But Athens lost those wars. Under the Spartan occupation her walls were torn down and the triremes in the harbour were seized or burned. The renowned *nausoikoi* ('ships' houses') were pulled down in a special festival, complete with music, singing and dancing. You must admit those vandals had style.

But you can't keep a good wall down, and by 393 BC they had been rebuilt.

But Pausanias runs out of commentary 300 years after that, when Sulla captured Piraeus for Imperial Rome. Greek leadership surrendered to Roman in the ancient world and the Greeks had to wait until the Christian emperor, Constantine the Great, revived it elsewhere.

As it turns out, Pausanias would have been happy to know that under Roman stewardship Piraeus continued happily – until Alaric brought his Goths, of course, and destroyed the port again.[8]

The next thousand years were basically OK, but then Constantinople fell to the Turks. As we docked at the quay, I could see the old customs house and the monastery of St Spyridonas. That was all that remained of pre-Turkish Piraeus.

But with the creation of the modern Hellenic state and the proclamation of Athens as its capital in 1832, the port again gained a raison d'être. It quickly became a great commercial and industrial centre. Magnificent buildings were thrown up, especially the Municipal Theatre, a superb piece of neoclassicism.

Our hotel was the Hotel Lilia. It was in Pasalimani, a pretty natural harbour only a few hundred yards from our ferry.

---

[8] In AD 395.

Our guide, Yannis, was waiting for us as we went confidently through customs, and he had a bus and an agenda ready for me to inspect.

- Day One: an orientation tour of Athens.
- Day Two: the Acropolis and the National Archaeological Museum of Athens.
- Day Three: the Temple of the Oracle at Delphi.

Was I going to join the adventure? You bet I was.

No other city has contributed more to civilisation than Athens.[9] It was the birthplace of Socrates, Plato, Aeschylus, Sophocles, Euripides and so many others. Their offspring, philosophy, logic and ethics, were also born here. So too were humanism and democracy. The light that Athens gave us will never be extinguished.

But I chose to duck the orientation tour. I wanted the noises and smells of a new town, not the view from an air-conditioned bus. I waved off my charges, who seemed delighted with their new and handsome mentor and a few minutes later I caught a clapped out old bus – public transport for me – to the centre of Athens and got down in Syntagma Square. Needing my bearings, I sat down on a shaded bench in the Square, facing the Royal Palace, and opened my little guidebook, where I immediately learned that the word *syntagma* (σύνταγμα) means Constitution.

I put the book down and began to muse on modern Greece, once the world's most famous democracy and now being run by a military junta. How much anguish has Greece suffered from its faith in politicians? Or from the barbarians and their willingness to meddle? When it was finally liberated from the Ottoman Empire, the Great Powers decided that the Greeks needed a king. They chose Prince Otto of Bavaria. They must have put dozens of princely names into a hat. Otto, when he won, was just sixteen.

At the top of Syntagma Square I could easily see the neoclassi-

---

[9] Ὦ ταὶ λιπαραί καὶ 'ιοστέφανοι καὶ 'αοίδιμοι, Ἑλλάδος 'έρεισμα, κλειναί 'Αθῆναι, δαιμόνιον πτολίεθρον! (Oh you, olive shiny and violet crowned glorious Athens, famous in songs, rampart of Greece, divine city!) – Pindar.

cal palace which Otto had built in the 1830s and which his father, Ludwig I of Bavaria, had paid for.[10] The original and mad idea was to site the palace on the Acropolis. Fortunately, this never happened.

Otto came of age in the era of constitutional revolutions. Not even remote old Greece was exempt. Two Greek soldiers, Dimitrios Kallerges and Ioannes Makrioannes, led nationalist troops to the palace and petitioned the King at rifle point to produce a constitution that would make dictatorship impossible for all time. The King obliged.

These Bavarian kings managed the Greek monarchy with an unsteady hand until, in 1923, a plebiscite established the first Hellenic republic of modern times.

An exiled King George II wandered Europe for a dozen years. His luck turned in 1935 when he was invited to take back his throne. But this was the age of dictators and he foolishly granted his prime minister, John Metaxas, too much power. A bad move. By 1941, the Germans (as an occupying power) felt they could safely depose the King – again.

When the Axis went into retreat, the Left now plotted to prevent the monarch's return. Simplistically, or cynically, they associated the King with the Nazis and their collaborators. But Greece's future destiny had already been decided by England and Russia, in a secret meeting chaired by Stalin. Greece would be included in the British sphere of influence in return for Romania, Bulgaria and Hungary coming under friendly Soviet care and attention.

By now, many Greeks wanted the constitutional monarchy to be restored; but as many others wanted a left-leaning republic. It divided the nation and in 1944, as the Nazis went home, came civil war. A demonstration in Syntagma Square turned into a battle. The police fired into the crowd. Many of the demonstrators were armed, no doubt believing that the presence of women would discourage gunfire from the other side. In the event, twenty-three of the agitators were shot dead and several women were among more than a hundred wounded.

The British arrived in 1945 in the role of peacekeepers, to find

---

[10] Now the Parliament Building.

the civil war was at its height, as bitter and ruthless as all civil wars. The British had to isolate the partisans, who were receiving aid and support from Moscow and the GRU. But by siding with former collaborators to create a Greece that would not be communist, Churchill (and later Attlee) ran the risk of aggravating the conflict. The Left was becoming openly Soviet and was trying to provoke a class war of the kind favoured or predicted by Marx. Indeed, we Brits found ourselves defending Syntagma Square and its wealthy Koloniki quarter against the partisan-dominated working-class neighbourhoods that comprised most of the rest of Athens. It was a terrible period. Greece should have been emerging from the Nazi darkness into Allied sunlight, but instead was being led by the Soviets. It provoked widespread despair.

The indisputable resistance and heroism of the Greeks, especially when directed against the Germans, had, in its day, been an inspiration to all the subjugated peoples of Europe. But now, a new world order was on offer, where democracy would hold sway. Prosperity was there for all who would come on board. The partisans and others on the Left refused to recognise this. They continued to intimidate, denounce and assassinate their neighbours – and the occasional British soldier, who manfully tried to keep order unarmed. This was not an economy measure. The surest way of getting killed in 1945 on the streets of Athens was to wear a sidearm.

Both sides, Royalist and Communist, claimed to be acting on behalf of the majority. A referendum was needed to see if the people really wanted to call on their sovereign to return. This time the people voted overwhelmingly in favour of their ruler. Accordingly, early in 1946, the King returned to his old palace in Syntagma Square, the building that was holding my attention, with strong backing from Great Britain, and the civil war began to fizzle out.

Paul succeeded George as king of the Hellenes, and to his great credit he resolved the Cyprus issue, if only temporarily. His son, Constantine II, succeeded him in 1964.

But Constantine too had to leave Greece, after the 1967 military coup. He and his kin fled to England for their personal safety.

King Constantine is still very much alive. He lives in England. His sister Sophia is the wife of the Spanish king, Juan-Carlos. Prince Philip, also a direct descendant of King Otto, is a cousin.

This was the Athens of 1972 where I, with my forty charges, found myself. The Colonels were about to declare their king deposed, which they did the next year.[11]

Syntagma Square is a park with shaded paths, with benches and cafés where groups of Athenians heatedly talk politics. The Greeks are the only people of Europe who read more newspapers than the British, and their papers are strongly (some would say hopelessly) partisan.

It was time to stretch my legs. I decided to have a closer look at the *evzones*, the elite soldiers who guard the palace. They are a curiously attired regiment, obviously chosen for their height and strength. Like the guards at St James's Palace, they were being mercilessly teased by tourists who wanted to make them blink. Every so often they did a little march and dance to break the monotony of standing still all day and they occasionally performed a little kick step in their *tsarouhia* shoes with the large pompoms.

Their pleated skirt, the *fustanella*, was made of many triangular shaped pieces of cloth sewn together diagonally. It had been worn by Greek nationalists in the 1821 revolution. Its 400 pleats symbolised four centuries of Ottoman rule. The remainder of the costume consisted of a white shirt with very wide flowing sleeves, an embroidered woollen vest and a sash worn around the waist. King Otto had himself established the *evzones'* full dress uniform.

To the left of the square, the imposing Hotel Grande Bretagne had been trying to catch my eye. It beckoned me inside.

Here I found the bar and had a cold 'Fix', the local beer. It amused me to ask the waiter for 'a Fix, please'. I was in no hurry.

---

[11] The junta itself was overthrown a year later, but the Greek voters chose not to restore the monarchy. Constantine was stripped of his Greek citizenship in 1994. In 2002 the European Court of Human Rights ruled that Greece had to compensate the former king for property nationalised after the royal family fled the country. Syntagma Square has also seen its shining moments. After the fall of the Military Junta, in 1974, Constantine Karamanlis came back from exile in Paris to lead Greece back to democracy, and it was in Syntagma Square that he first spoke to his newly free constituents.

My girls were probably denuding the trinket shops in Ermou Street, Athens' main shopping district.

I sipped at my beer. The fellow at the bar next to me looked me up and down.

'You're not a tourist, are you?' he said in an American accent.

'Well, I am today. But I am in Greece in order to look after forty of your compatriots.'

'You're a tour guide? That's wonderful! What have you got? A busload of blue rinses from Palm Beach?'

'Not exactly,' I said. 'More like the furies from the *Oresteia*.'

'That might make a story. The name's David Ionides. I'm a stringer for *USA Today* and the *Herald Tribune*. By the way, have you read O'Neill's *Electra*?'

'O'Neill's *Electra*? Have you Americans remade the *Oresteia*? Or perhaps it's a sequel?'

'Ah,' David said with a genial smile. 'I can see your education is incomplete. You have of course been to Athens before?'

'No. This bar seemed a good place to start my personal orientation tour. It's working so far.'

'We journalists tend to meet here for a beer or two. It's an historic place. Lots of history in these four walls.'

'These four walls need a lick of paint, if you ask me.[12] Did the place have a poor war?'

'You've no idea. When the Second World War broke out the Greek military requisitioned it for an HQ. They gave the guests an hour to clear out. Then, during the Nazi occupation, it became the headquarters of the Wehrmacht. Göring, Himmler and Rommel all stayed here. So did Hitler.

'During the civil war it became a base for your British Expeditionary Force. Machine guns and sandbags kept peace in the lobby. A plot to assassinate Churchill was exposed when police uncovered a ton of TNT in the sewers directly beneath the door, a few minutes before the great man's arrival.'

'I'm glad they did. It would have been a pity if his arrival had coincided with his departure.'

'Come on, I've nothing important to do. Let me treat you to that beer and show you a bit of Athens.'

---

[12] The Hotel Grande Bretagne has been completely renovated since 1972.

Never look a gift horse in the mouth, my mother always said.

On emerging from the hotel, we walked along Metropolitan Street, passed a modern cathedral and reached a handsome little square with a wonderfully preserved Byzantine church.

'It's called Hagios Eleftherios,' David said. 'Nearly every stone of this little church was taken from an ancient building or older church. There's a stone from Cana where Jesus changed the water into wine. The church used to be called Panagia Gorgoepikofos – nicknamed 'The Virgin Who Grants Requests Quickly'. Her icon is inside, still ready to perform a hasty miracle.'

The church was utterly beautiful.

Outside, we found a café and David ordered us a *metrio*, or Turkish coffee.[13] I imagined my forty girls looting some souvenir shops.

'Don't worry about it. Athens will actually be richer without a carrier bag or two of toy *evzones*, "ancient Greek" bottle openers...'

'...worry beads, backgammon sets...'

'...cigarette lighters, "Byzantine icons"...'

'...handbags with pictures of the Parthenon...'

'...naughty statues...'

'...and so on.'

I found myself agreeing with him. Even if they were arrested by a very strict and unforgiving regime, the Colonels would soon discover they had bitten off more than they could chew.

Now it was our turn to walk past many tiny shops, all selling cheap souvenirs. 'Fake antiquities are good,' said David. 'If you tried to take the real thing out of the country, the Colonels would have a serious sense of humour failure.'

He showed me the large columns of the old Agora. We found a way in and came face to face with the Thission, the almost completely intact ancient temple to Hephaestus. My hair stood on end, much to David's amusement. 'I said you'd be impressed,' he observed astutely.

Overlooking Monastiraki Square was the crumbling Turkish Mosque.[14] The Mosque is on everyone's map, quite correctly.

'It's named after the Ottoman Voivode[15] of Athens, Tzistarakis,

---

[13] Turkish coffee is called 'Greek coffee' in Greece, of course.

[14] Now restored.

[15] Governor.

who had it built in the eighteenth century. The Athenians liked to believe that each column of the Temple of Olympian Zeus stood on a curse, holding it in the earth. Stealing parts from every surviving ancient building in Athens, Tzistarakis went too far when he removed one of the last remaining columns of the Temple to complete his mosque. The theft of that column coincided with, or unleashed, an outbreak of the plague.'

'I thought the Ottomans were relatively proud of Athens?'

'I think they were, up to a point, but you won't hear a good word said about them today. Certainly, the ancient monuments, according to Ottoman law, were the property of the Sultan, and could not be exploited without his permission. Tzistarakis was blamed for the plague and deposed. They say the temple of Olympian Zeus lamented the loss of its column so loudly at night that nobody could get any sleep. The nightmare finally ended when Tzistarakis was poisoned.'

By an art lover, I suspect.

We now aimed for Plaka, the oldest part of modern Athens.

Plaka is where I would live in central Athens. True, most of its restaurants are typical tourist traps, and the countless shops there are crammed with rubbish. But these are the hallmarks of Bohemia.

We passed a pleasant-looking *cafeneon* where some old boys were playing backgammon. A kiosk[16] was selling everything an American needs abroad; chewing gum, postcards and, to David's satisfaction, *USA Today* and the *International Herald Tribune*. But the tables belonging to the Kostis restaurant[17] that surrounded the kiosk were full of Athenians. There was not a tourist in sight; perhaps because it was a little run-down.

'What have you eaten today?' David asked. 'You can't have any more beer on an empty stomach. Greek food is not too bad. I'll order for you.'

The presence of so many locals inspired confidence and we sat down to a proper lunch, of dolmades and kleftiko, all washed down with retsina. It was a wise move, for it was very good indeed.

---

[16] 'Kiosk' is a Turkish word. It is therefore to be avoided in modern Greece. Use *peritero* instead.

[17] Kostis has been renamed 'The Byzantino' in recent years.

Plaka seemed to fill with Muslim flower girls, shyly pressing roses or gardenias on anyone whose eye they could catch. David waved them away. 'Bloody pests,' he said, with unnecessary aggression.

The streets began to echo to the overtures of street musicians, some of whom had been classically trained.

'Poverty, war or some other terrible circumstance has driven them here. Still, it's better than in Times Square.'

If you listened you could hear real craft. *Dum spiro, spero…*

Some of the large number of people in Plaka who saw fit to importune us while we ate included photographers, people who sold beads and one who claimed to be able to write my name on a grain of rice.

I told David, to his unalloyed amusement, the story of my girls so far.

'What a pity I'll never know how you explain to them why there are so many stoned fish in the Adriatic.'

After lunch we resumed our walkabout. We passed the Ciné Paris.

'This is the finest open-air cinema in the world. You won't see the likes of this in London or Paris, or New York, for that matter. It's on the roof, with an uninterrupted view of the Acropolis. Imagine seeing *Ben Hur* there. It has a bar, and movie-goers can have a brandy and watch an epic with the Parthenon as a backdrop.'

In the street we found a bar, this time part of an ancient distillery, which proffered its precious products by the glass. The ouzo was very mild. Many people claim they don't like ouzo. They have just never had a good one. This was better than being in an insulated bus, listening to girly versions of the Beach Boys' greatest hits.

Now David had resumed his 'professorial' hat, and we put our heads around the door of St Nicholas, in order to add spiritual refreshment to the other kind.

I was in just the right mood to 'discover' a picturesque village of small houses built on the slopes of the Acropolis above the Plaka. It was like being on a Greek island.

'It got its name, Anafiotika, from its original inhabitants, who were stonemasons from the island of Anafi. They built modern

Athens in the mid-nineteenth century,' David explained to his student.

Trying to find our way down, we seemed to get horribly lost (as if I cared) but we did stumble upon the impressive Monument to Lysikrates.

'You see that house next to it? That belonged to the Jesuits. Chateaubriand stayed there, and so did Lord Byron, who wrote some of *Childe Harold* in his room, or cell.'

Plaka was studded with archaeological sites both large and small. The famous Tower of the Winds is a tourist must. For a while it was believed to be the grave of Philip of Macedon, but is now known to have been a first-century weather station, built by the Syrian astronomer, Andronikos Kyrrhestes.

'This was not your common clock,' said David proudly. 'It had a hydraulic movement, no less, fuelled from a reservoir on the south side, and represented the sun, the moon and the five known planets. A few traces of the mechanism remain.'

Its frieze, which represents the winds and their personalities, was both intact and ravishing.

An odd door, without a building attached, caught my eye.

'It's all that remains of the Medrese,' David explained. 'The Medrese was a theological school, founded in the early eighteenth century by the Ottomans. During the War of Independence the Turks used it as a prison, and hanged a lot of Greeks from a giant platanos tree in the courtyard. After the war the Greeks used it for the same dismal purpose. In the minds of gentler Athenians it became a cursèd place. In 1843 the poet Achilles Paraschos predicted that one day the tree would be chopped up and used for firewood. He was right. In 1919 the tree was struck by lightning, was felled and used as the curse had predicted. The entire building itself was then demolished, except for that door.'

It seemed that everywhere I looked in the Plaka there was evidence of some great civilisation – Greek, Roman or Ottoman. Here and there the pavement had been opened to reveal ancient columns, even bits of ancient houses. It was breathtaking, but nothing is beyond criticism. Modern Greek archaeologists might well be accused of zealotry, having sacrificed so many handsome nineteenth-century buildings to expose these ancient remnants.

But compared to, say, Rome, however, there were fewer monuments than I had expected.

'I'll tell you for why. The guy who's to blame was Ali Hadji Haseki, the Ottoman Voivode of the late eighteenth century.'

We sat down at a pavement café and ordered a couple of Fixes.

'Haseki taxed the people of Athens beyond the dreams of avarice,' David continued. 'He bled them dry. Eventually, they had nothing left, and the whole area was reduced to penury. The Athenians were considering a mass emigration, so Haseki decided to build a wall around the city, supposedly to keep the Albanians out but actually to keep the taxpayers in.

'Some of the city's most ancient landmarks and buildings were quarried to build this wall. A great bridge over the Illissos River, a Temple to Demeter and the facade of Hadrian's reservoir on Lykabettos, are lost to us for ever.

'But comeuppance was on its way. His cultural infamy was brought to Sultan Selim III's attention, and Haseki was beheaded on the island of Kos. His head was later exhibited in the Topkapi Palace.'

Plaka seemed to be an island in the heart of the city. I particularly loved the arty if run-down feeling of the place.

I have been back, and it has all been given rather more than a lick of paint. Some people say it has been horribly spoiled. They say the same of Mykonos, of course, or the Upper East Side, or the Latin Quarter, or Chelsea, for that matter. Plaka has certainly changed. My mother, who took a flat in Plaka in 1979 for many years, tells me that the artists who sold their paintings on the street now have their own galleries. The old tavernas have vanished or have been tarted up, and the chap who mixed doner kebabs in his bathtub has been arrested. Plaka may no longer be Bohemia and that is a shame. But, despite the nostalgia, my mother declares it still to be great fun.

My feet were beginning to complain. And it was time to get back to the port.

'I am looking forward to hearing the horror stories of the day,' I said.

'Be sure to let me know how you get on,' said David, passing me his card. 'I still think it will be a great story.'

But when I eventually got there, Yannis claimed that the girls had been as good as gold. It seemed unlikely.

That night we took over a restaurant in Piraeus and broke a lot of plates. The girls were in remarkable form. It was exhilarating but I felt I had drunk and eaten for Britain by the time I hit the sack. I went out like a light.

The Acropolis was on the agenda for our second day, and I elected to join our angelic troupe in the adventure. The place would be packed with tours anyway and I might as well join my own. In any case, our new guide spoke the most idiosyncratic English, which served both to force my concentration and to delight me. He had a certain nationalist passion that I thought terrific.

Mind you, we had to work for it. There were endless steps to climb before we reached the front door, or Propylaea, which Yannis explained had been completed nearly half a millennium before Christ, just before the outbreak of the Peloponnesian Wars.[18]

On the left (said Yannis) was the Pinacotheca, or gallery, and on the right the tiny temple to Nike Athena – Athena of Victory – that commemorates a great victory over the Persians. Not until 1686 did the Turks dismantle it to create a base for their cannon. Its present appearance is due to a painstaking restoration in 1936.

We looked towards Piraeus, where we could see both liners and ferries in the port. And still further away rose the mountains of the Peloponnese. The other way towered the Parthenon.

The main buildings on the Acropolis were built on Pericles's order in the fifth century BC, to celebrate the cultural and political achievements of Athenians.

'Acropolis' means citadel, as opposed to 'polis' (the whole of the city state), and most Greek city-states were built around one. In times of invasion the citizens might gather there. Ancient Greece's most sacred buildings are almost always on an acropolis. A privileged few lived up here too. In fact, there were still houses on the Acropolis until the 1870s.

Yannis reminded us all that Aristophanes had Lysistrata per-

[18] In 432 BC.

suade the women of Athens to barricade themselves up here in protest against the war on Sparta. Depriving their men of sex, cooking and care was a startling and apparently effective strategy. I wondered if telling our girls this story would interest them.

Despite having seen a thousand photographs I was still not prepared for the immensity of the Parthenon. Kallikrates and Iktinos had designed the temple to house a giant statue of Athena, the one that Pausanius had so much recommended. The temple took fifteen years to build before it was completed in 438 BC, and is arguably the most recognisable structure in the world.

Its later evolution took it from pagan temple into church, mosque and finally ordnance magazine for the Turks. Despite this continual change of use, the building was in perfect shape. But that last evolutionary step was a mistake. In 1687, the Venetians bombarded it from the ground. A chance cannon ball hit the gunpowder inside and blew the Parthenon to pieces. *Sic transit gloria mundi*. Its destruction, Elgin's semi-legal pillaging and its subsequent amateurish restoration are all too evident today.

The Erecthion, with its porch of the maidens, or caryatids, sits on the most sacred site of the Acropolis. This is where Poseidon and Athena had a contest over who might be patron of the city. Poseidon's trident, thrust into a rock, brought forth a spring, while Athena merely lowered her spear on to the ground and an olive sapling poked its way through the soil. A panel of divine adjudicators declared Athena the winner and the great city of Athens was born with her name. Poor old Poseidon had to be satisfied with a little village in Syros.

When the Germans occupied Athens, the Nazis ordered the *evzone* who guarded the Greek flag that flew over the Acropolis to remove it. He calmly took it down, wrapped himself in it and jumped to his death. This selfless act of courage and resistance was an inspiration to all subjected peoples.

Long before, below the Acropolis, Herod Atticus, Roman Governor of Attica, built a theatre[19] that is still used today for concerts and ballets. Its quality is impressive. In 1980, while I was wooing my wife, we watched a ballet there.

Less well preserved, but culturally more significant, is the

---

[19] In AD 161.

Theatre of Dionysius. This was (allegedly) the first ever stone theatre. Sophocles, Aeschylus, Euripides and Aristophanes put on their plays here. But high-mindedness does not last for ever. The Romans supplanted the ancient dramatists with gladiators.

Also below the Acropolis is the rock of Areopagos, where Saint Paul spoke to the people of Athens in AD 51. His immortal words are on a tablet, embedded in the stone.

No one, not even Mimi, volunteered to come with me to the National Archaeological Museum of Athens. But they were wrong not to bother. This is one of the truly outstanding museums of the world. If on your journey to Athens you only go to one museum, let it be this one.

The museum itself was built in the 'true style', in the mid-nineteenth century.

The most impressive 'explanation' of why Greek civilisation matters so much is to be found here. In fact, it is to be found just inside the front door. There is no need to go searching for it.

The very second you are inside, you see to either side a pair of Egyptian statues. They are sentinels of some kind. They are not even supposed to be alive. The old gods placed them for you to see so that you would know what would kill you if you committed a sacrilege.

As you walk slowly along the carpet, early gods and demigods are on either side like ushers at a grotesque wedding. But then, one of them puts a leg forward. Not literally, of course, though it might as well be, for the shock you experience. But while the face resembles the Egyptian faces you have just passed, and their stony drapery is similar, this is the first of the Greek statues, and it has sprung to life.

Greek art broke with its predecessors when it strayed from representing the dead and the gods and began to reflect life on earth. This one small step for a man was a giant leap for mankind. I do hope that sentence hasn't been used by anyone else.

Progressing along the corridor, the effect is gradually more pronounced, until you reach the Hellenic period, the work of Praxiteles and the zenith of the ancient world of plastic art, probably never surpassed.

A colossal votive statue of a *kouros*,[20] from Sounion, causes you to stop in your tracks, next to another one, almost wholly intact, with the deceased's name – Aristodikos[21] – still written on the base.

Once you have entered the museum proper, there is a magnificent collection of *steles*,[22] all taking the same form, more or less – a seated person, who has made the journey whence no man returns, accepting the homage of a living one.

A marvellous, fluid composition of a figure riding a horse, and dated to around 380 BC, was found at Epidauros. The uninitiated might be gulled for a moment into thinking that it is a masterwork from our own Renaissance.

Even more glorious is the representation of Aphrodite and Pan, which takes us into the mainstream Hellenic Period, around 100 BC. It was found on Delos, the holy island at the centre of the Cyclades Islands. This statue alone would make the journey to Athens worthwhile.

I had been grateful for the cooling air of the museum and was almost overwhelmed by the heat as I stepped outside. Still, I had seen proof that the Greeks could manage their ancient heritage.

Yannis had decided to take the girls to a place he knew that he thought would suit them and had given me a card. I looked at it carefully and consulted the guidebook. It would need a taxi. I hailed one without any great problem.

For some strange reason, the taximeter was calibrated in lepta, and it took a hundred of them to reach a drachma, which itself wasn't very much. There were nearly 200 drachmas to the pound in those days. I have complained often enough about taxi fares in London, but when I saw the reels revolve so fast I couldn't make out the cost, I relaxed. At least in London you have some idea of what you are going to pay and have some time to worry about it.

I arrived at a sort of hostel, which had a little bar selling Coca-Cola. It was packed with travellers from all over. It had a jukebox and a light show that reflected the music, so to speak. Yannis had

---

[20] Funerary likeness.
[21] Great name, great guy.
[22] Haut-relief funerary plaques.

got it about right. A couple of my girls were playing pool. Others were drinking Coke while fending off the determined advances of any number of Greek boys with consummate ease.

These hostels were the stuff of legend. This one was called the Hotel California. It was run by two Englishmen, Andrew and George, who sailed close to the wind and the law.

You got a bed for 300 drachmas. You could doss down in your own sleeping bag for 200, if you could find a space, and you could sleep on the roof for a hundred. As everyone slept in the nude in the hot Hellenic night, every Athenian pair of binoculars was trained on the roof of this place, from the moment the sun rose until the girls had leisurely put some clothes back on.

The showers were mixed, too, and the locals thought this was too good to be true. Andrew and George found themselves evicting Greeks with purpose-bought brand new rucksacks, posing as seasoned travellers, but whose highest ambition was to share a shower with the Swedish contingent.

'Good as gold, you see? Yannis understands these girls.' He handed me a glass.

'You do, too. You could get a job as a lion tamer.' I meant it.

'Here, put a little of this in your Coke.' Yannis had thought-fully brought a flask with him. It worked wonders.

'OK, tomorrow we see the Delphic Oracle. You coming?'

'Certainly,' I said. I looked at the girls. 'Are they up for it?'

'Oh yes. They have all got cameras and they ask all the boys they see to take their photos. They are having a wonderful time and their parents believe they are being educated.'

'Which they are,' I said. 'Some of what you're telling them will stay with them for ever.'

'OK, maybe you're right.' He didn't sound convinced.

We were back in our hotel in Piraeus a little before midnight. Yannis announced 'bedtime', which elicited a few groans, but Delphi is some way from Athens and Yannis wanted us to leave early. The next evening we would have to take the ferry back to Brindisi, and I was going to have to explain what I had done with their substances.

I got into bed and tried to read a bit about the Oracle, or Pythia. All I really knew was that people had come to Mount

Parnassus from all over Europe to call on the Pythia and have their questions about the future answered. Her answers would determine when farmers should sow their crops or when empires should declare war.

The Pythia strutted her stuff at Delphi for the best part of 2,000 years, until the Goths arrived in AD 381 and sent the circus on its way. Alaric's Goths were devout Christians in rather a stern way, and would not accept that Apollo could or would let his views be known, especially through a woman.

I put my book down. No doubt all would be revealed the next day.

After an early breakfast with about ten ominously silent females – the rest choosing instead to have another half-hour's lie-in – we were back in Yannis' coach. If I hadn't known the girls had been drinking Coca-Cola, I would have sworn they had a collective hangover. A puzzle.

As we set off, Yannis confided in me that he was delegating his duties as a guide to a local chap at Delphi. He had no licence to talk there.

A pity, I told him. He had been brilliantly knowledgeable on the Acropolis.

'Oh, the official guy will be just as good. He'll have done exams on the subject.'

The bus drove along into the hills north of Athens, which soon turned out to be rather steep. Every time we turned a corner, at first a couple of girls would shriek in fake terror. This was an excellent game and soon the bus sounded like a tribe of banshees.

'I want to see their faces when they discover that the Oracle was just hot air passing through a narrow fissure,' said Yannis, with tired glee in his voice.

I opened my book again, though reading wasn't easy. Yannis' theory had been around for a very long time, it seemed. Plutarch, a priest at the Temple of Apollo, was the first to suggest that the Pythia's prophetic powers were due to gases that emerged from a chasm deep underground.

This materialist explanation, however, failed to satisfy the scientists. French geologists surveyed the oracle's shrine in 1927, and found no evidence of either a chasm or of rising gases. They dismissed the story as a myth. If there was no volcanic activity on Mount Parnassus, how could there be any such gases?

Still, the voice on the street stuck with the early theory. Rumour had it that there were not only gases, but they were hallucinogenic. That should amuse the girls.

But maybe a volcano wasn't actually necessary. There are thousands of fault lines in Greece, which lies over the meeting of three tectonic plates. After all, that's what caused Mount Parnassus to exist in the first place.

A major earthquake rattles the faults every century or so and the colossal friction heats the adjacent rocks. Hydrocarbon deposits stored within them are vaporised, the gases mix with ground water and emerge around springs. Who knows what could be produced?

The terrifying mountain drive was finally over and forty hoarse young ladies stepped out of the bus into the fresh air. My ears were still ringing with their sheer exuberance.

The coach park was not far from the rather astonishing circular temple and our new guide stepped up to greet us.

'I am not a teller of fairy stories,' he announced. 'Apollo spoke to no one, here or anywhere else. All that happened here was a succession of crazed young women who liked to fool a lot of gullible men who should have known better anyway.'

I was not immediately convinced he had the right style for my girls, but we would see.

Eventually we were inside, where the Delphic supplicants had stood, hearing strange wheezing noises and having them interpreted by the Pythia. Today the temple was silent, apart from the clicks of forty cameras and a little suppressed giggling. Had I confiscated all their hashish, I wondered?

'Now ladies, gentlemen,' began our guide. 'Before any of you were thought of, before your countries came into existence, before your God and your priests had an Archimandrite or pope to lead them, forgotten kings of long gone Great Powers came here for guidance.

'You see the fractures over there?' He pointed at a number of cracks that could have as easily come through time as from any other cause.

'Strange gases once came through those fractures. Directly below us, the forces of geology – or Vulcan as some would have it – combined to produce mind-bending chemicals that caused the people who came here to trip.'

There was a sharp intake of breath. The guide certainly had their attention now.

'The Oracle had to breathe these fumes all day. She was out of her tiny mind. She was higher than the Rockefeller Center.' He was beginning to enjoy himself.

'One hundred million years ago, when your ancestors were on all fours and slithering about naked in the forest, this great mountain was under water. Its limestone bedrock was steeped in hydrocarbon deposits.

'There are traces in the rocks even today. If you like, go to that fissure there,' and he pointed to a hairline crack, 'and see if you can't smell something sweet and narcotic. The Pythia could.'

The girls needed no second invitation.

In a trice they were climbing over each other to get a whiff of ancient hallucinogen. Mimi glanced at me and came over, ignoring her friends.

'They're so young,' she commented dryly.

'Ethylene inhalation promotes a floating or disembodied euphoria. It is a serious contender for explaining the trance and behaviour of the Pythia,' I heard the guide pronounce.

'That, and social expectations, could easily cause a woman in a confined space to spout off.'

His English was too good. Forty harpies in a bad mood could be a challenge he hadn't expected. Except the girls loved it. They were affecting being stoned, speaking prophetic gibberish. At the expression 'spouting off' they had in unison assumed the posture of a teapot. Or, being Americans, a coffee pot. But the guide was not put off in the least.

'There used to be a small, enclosed chamber in the basement of the temple. If the Pythia went in there just once a month, she could have been exposed to enough narcotic gas to induce a trance.

'Was it Christianity that ended the Oracle? Or was it that the gases dried up? We just don't know.'

But the girls knew. Yannis and I loaded forty semi-comatose hallucinating girls back on our bus, where they predicted the fall of empires all the way back to Piraeus and our ferry.

By eight o'clock that night we were aboard our boat, having said our goodbyes to Yannis, who had certainly earned his fee, and to our driver. We had a lightning supper in the hotel, collected our possessions and souvenirs, and had gone to our allotted cabins for the overnight crossing.

I was fairly dreading what was coming next. Forty pairs of hands outstretched, wondering when what they had entrusted to me was going to be handed back. Despite having had three days to think about it, I still had not a clue as to how I was going to handle it.

Mimi was their spokeswoman, of course. She found me in my usual place.

'That was a good trip,' she said by way of opening gambit.

'Which part of it did you like best?' I asked.

'Definitely the Oracle,' she replied without hesitation. I laughed.

'So did I,' I agreed.

'Sir, Jeremy, the other girls have asked me if you could…' She seemed lost for words. I knew what she was going to say, of course. I intercepted her.

'Mimi, I'm afraid an officer on the ship destroyed the carrier bag I collected from you. He said it was either that or his job. I'm so sorry.'

She looked puzzled for a moment. Then her expression lightened.

'No, actually, it wasn't that. We all knew that would happen. No, we want to play a sort of game, and it needs you. It's not dangerous or illegal or anything. Would you mind? We'd so much appreciate it.'

'Well, what does it involve?'

'It's not easy to explain. The best thing is just to show you.'

'Well, providing it doesn't actually hurt, I suppose I'll do it, whatever it is.'

'Oh, good! You won't regret it. Come on, we're going to one of the bigger cabins.'

I followed Mimi downstairs in a very nervous disposition. I knew she'd be plotting something, but what?

I found myself in a cabin with four beds, bestrewn with clutter. In the middle was a chair, an ordinary dining chair, and around the room, sitting on the beds, were a dozen of my company, looking evil and purposeful.

'Sit there, sir,' I was told, and I obeyed. Mimi went around the back of the chair, and I felt my hands being tied together and to the back of the chair with a dressing gown cord.

'Can you move your hands at all?'

I said I couldn't. It was true. They were very securely tied.

'Good. Now we have to blindfold you.'

So I was blindfolded. I couldn't see a thing.

'Mimi, have you told him the rules yet?' I heard one of the girls ask.

'It's a game we play at home,' Mimi told me. 'We all take it in turns to sit on your knee, say our name out loud, and give you a little kiss. Then we change our order and do it again, but this time we don't say our names. When you don't get our names right on the second round, that girl is eliminated. The game is to see who you end up with.'

Well, what can I say?

The first girl sat on my knee, said 'Suzie', and gave me a peck on the cheek. The second girl said 'Jackie', and gave me a demure kiss on the lips. And the third girl sat on my knee, pressed herself against me and kissed me like a lover. This was Mimi.

And so it went on. One of the girls was very heavy. Another had a brace. But mostly they kissed me with the tenderest and sweetest affection. American high schools must be wonderful places.

After about an hour of this I had 'won' Mimi and I felt I needed a cold shower.

'Will you untie me, please,' I said.

It was only when they took the blindfold off that I saw all the cameras. I am still saving up to buy the negatives.

At breakfast, just outside Brindisi, I told the girls that my poor old mother was an alcoholic and needed her gin. If they would buy a bottle of duty-free liquor before we docked and take it through customs, I would buy it off them on the other side.

None of the girls let me pay, and I ended up with more than thirty bottles of export strength hooch.

After that adventure they would come in very handy.

I gave one to Dario, of course. In a brown envelope, with the single word *grazie* scribbled on it.

Chapter the Ninth
1972: Coffee in Venice

In which the author begins to explore Italy from his base in Rome, travelling first to Venice, the Queen of the Adriatic. This trip is brief, as he is still very short of funds, but it is now revealed to him that the coffee in Italy cannot be beaten and that Palladio was the world's greatest architect, a view he has held ever since.

My first ever visit to *La Serenissima* was by train from Rome. The three days I spent there were an epiphany. I mean it; I haven't been the same since. Incredibly, I got most things right. I would like to take some credit for this but, as everybody knows, it is almost impossible to get anything wrong in Venice.

I arrived at Santa Lucia, Venice's cream neoclassic marble railway terminus (from Mussolini's equally monumental Stazione Termini in Rome) just a few minutes before dawn on a foggy, cold, spring day in March 1972. I was exhausted and in need of a shave, but as happy as a sandboy. I had arrived in a town I knew, or thought I already knew, from the gloom of Thomas Mann, from a few gay moments in *Anna Karenina*, or from a lusty episode in Casanova's memoirs. I looked around the railway station, not just forming my first impressions, but also searching for a chance to freshen up and a matutinal cup of coffee, in that order.

With a few minutes to go before sun-up, I discovered the joys of the Italian 'diurnal' hotel, up till then a wholly alien concept to me. It is what it 'says on the tin': the opposite of its more familiar 'nocturnal' counterpart. For a handful of the small bills that the Italians were using instead of coins (their brand new die-stamping machines had arrived from Frankfurt without an instruction manual) it provided me with a shower and a haircut, a very comfortable place to shave, a newspaper and even a large armchair to sit in and collect my wits after my long journey.

Many say that the 'only' way to see Venice for the first time is from the lagoon, arriving perhaps by liner, past the Punto della Dogana, or by *motoscafo*[1] or *vaporetto*[2] from Marco Polo, its airport. These, I have come to discover, are magnificent too, but if you follow my lead, you will step out of the station on to its steps in the pale dawn light and see – no, hear – the Grand Canal lapping against your shoes. For the station is on no metalled street but opens directly on to the proudest, finest waterway ever conjured up through the arts of man.

But, no time to dawdle. Despite the early light, the mist is still heavy on the Grand Canal and it's time to begin the adventure. Gather your coat around you and breathe a cloud of vapour into the chilly air. Stamp your feet a little, catch the river bus and head off to the Piazza San Marco, the 'drawing room of Europe' in Napoleon's immortal phrase, the single most elegant square in the world.

As I arrived at the quay that serves for a bus stop, the vapour had thinned to an ankle-high swirling wash, lapping the flag-stones in front of the Doge's Palace to my right and the Basilica of St Mark beyond. Across the piazza, the staff at Florian were putting out their tables and irritating the pigeons who clearly believed that their claim to the square had precedence over their larger black and white cousins, the immaculately clad waiters, to whom they bore an uncanny resemblance. As they flapped their wings noisily in the nearly empty L-shaped space, the echoes ricocheted off the Campanile and Sansovino's great library like a great round of applause for a solitary tourist making his way to his breakfast.

I had known of Florian for some time, it goes without saying. Half the writers of Europe seemed to have spent their days there, almost from the moment it opened in 1720.

Drinking coffee is a sociable business. Indeed its only rival is alcohol, and the two are not mutually exclusive, at least in Christendom. But what are the characteristics of a superb bar? If it is to be truly sublime, it will need a chessboard that can be lent out to its more earnest customers, a high ceiling to remove the

---

[1] River taxi.

[2] River bus.

134

more cloying smoke from those fermented *toscano* cheroots and an air of immutability. Add to that basic stock a selection of broadsheets and a *soupçon* of distinguished writers. The latter should not be scribbling away, but should be debating noisily and angrily some recondite issue. My hero, Francis Crick, announced the discovery of the double helix in The Eagle, Cambridge, to a gathering of his disciples. Jean-Paul Sartre and Simone de Beauvoir held the Latin Quarter in thrall as they explored and defined existentialism from their usual table in the Deux Magots during the 1950s and '60s. Florian has all of this, even if the excitable intellectuals have moved on. Its furniture is eighteenth-century (in style, anyway) and the paintings on its walls all date from the time it first opened for business.

Not enough immortality is conceded to interior decorators.

Alone with my thoughts and a *caffè macchiato* ('marked', with a splash of milk), I felt myself in good company. I had declined a newspaper to better enjoy those ghosts of literary Venice who chose to descend on Florian in their Ottoman slippers and silk dressing gowns. True to form, on my left was the shade of Alfred de Musset, the great French playwright, talking excitedly if improbably to Charles Dickens. Proust, preferring solitude on a table a little further away, eavesdropped noiselessly. Next door, the rival Quadri was now opening, and there I could make out the unlikely pairing of the spirits of Byron with Wagner, of Cocteau with Dali.

I picked up my cup and sipped cautiously. It was exactly the right temperature, and with a slightly theatrical gesture, I threw the noble liquor down my throat. Perfect. What is it about coffee? It is not a plausible beverage, at base. To make it taste the way it does takes an enormous amount of effort. The Italians are its master. They will serve it espresso or, if that isn't strong enough, ristretto. They might add a dash of grappa and call it *corretto*. They can dilute it 4:1 with hot water (americano), or lengthen it with hot, frothy milk for a classic cappuccino. Coffee, in Italy at least, is always, but *always,* drunk with sugar. Not to take sugar is to do it a disservice, and if your hosts are truly looking after you they won't let you get away with it.

You are ready for your coffee before it ever touches your lips. In a café such as this, the coffee is almost ground on demand and the air is mixed at molecular level with that most fragrant of aromas. Your nostrils prepared, the coffee explodes on the palate. It has a flavour so familiar yet so easily spoilt that most of us have never enjoyed it as it can be – when produced at Florian, for example. Florian is really just a very grand example of the many Italian cafés that still roast their own beans every day, sometimes twice a day. Their cup is lauded across the civilised world as the very acme of coffee excellence and is, even in Venice, in its most famous café, startlingly cheap. There is no bitterness, no acridity, no hint of that faintly burnt flavour that spoils the coffee the French will serve you. It has a certain creaminess that is best enjoyed in the espresso, for a splash of milk will hide it. Yet a hint of milk is a tribute to the hour, and this was breakfast after all. It was still too early to risk burning my tongue.

It may be that Italian coffee is the best, but the way we drink it we owe, historically at least, to the Viennese. During the Turkish Siege of Vienna, in 1683, a Polish baron called Franz Georg Kolschitzky used his fluent Turkish to slip behind enemy lines. The information he obtained enabled the Turks to be over-thrown, and in their rout they abandoned their cannon, guns and ammunition and 500 sacks of coffee beans. Our young hero liberated the coffee, for 'safe keeping' you understand, while he petitioned the Holy Roman Emperor for permission to go into commerce (a nobleman being otherwise prohibited from trade). On gaining his licence he opened a café called Zur Blauen Flasche.

The Turkish way of making coffee was too bitter for Austrian taste buds, so Kolschitzky filtered it and added honey and whipped cream. The result: the *Einspanner*. So successful was this idea that the entrepreneur engaged small orchestras to play on Sundays and he provided his customers with newspapers. The idea certainly caught on. No less a composer than J S Bach was eventually cajoled into writing music for the coffee houses of Leipzig. But there is more. Kolschitzky's name should be sung out in church with the roster of the saints for his idea of a curiously shaped roll to accompany a coffee, the *Kipfel*, or croissant, in the shape of the crescent moon of the defeated Turks.

In the Austrian colony of Venice (as it was for a long time), a Franciscan monk thought of adding hot milk and refined sugar to the filtered infusion. This variant, which seems to give the coffee a white hood, is the cappuccino, as a White Friar of this order is sometimes called a *Capuchin*. So too is the capuchin monkey, whose white head seems to peer at you from within his monkish robes.

Coffee is the favourite drink of revolutionaries. Perhaps that is why so many governments have tried, unsuccessfully, to ban it. Like alcohol it provokes people to congregate and debate the state of things, the *res publica*, and no earthly government is entirely happy with that, no matter how much they bang on about free speech or the 'free world'.

Coffee had already been banned at least once before it ever reached Europe. In 1511, the Sheriff of Mecca, a certain Kham-Berg, completely lost the plot and had the coffee-swilling faithful evicted from the Great Mosque. All stocks of the stuff were publicly burned, as he claimed that the Koran outlawed all stimulants. Happily for me, and my ghostly companions, the Sultan of Egypt quashed this puritan zeal just eight days later. If he had not been the boss, a coffee connoisseur and a fervent aficionado, coffee might never have reached Europe.

At this time, a fledgling Reformation was making everyone in Europe rather nervous. The Catholic Church was anxious to avoid charges of luxury and self-indulgence at a time when Protestants and Puritans were gaining the hearts of universities and indeed entire kingdoms. A worried Curia in the Vatican ruled that the Muslims had been given coffee by the Devil. This was, according to their theologians, to compensate for their sacrilegious abstinence from wine, which the Bible showed had been enjoyed by Christ and his disciples. They declared the dark 'Islamic potion' to have been sent by the Devil and banned it from Christian tables.

But this early prohibition was not to last. The moment Clement VIII elected to taste it, he decreed that it was far too good to be Satan's handicraft and, moreover, it would be 'inappropriate' to allow the Muslims a continuing monopoly.

But it is the revolutionary aspect of coffee that most worries those who govern us. They really don't like the fact that it keeps young hotheads awake well into the night, free to develop and amplify their repellent political theories. And there is some circumstantial evidence that they are right to be afraid.

In England, Charles II had London's coffee houses suppressed in 1675, but so menacing were the riots that ensued that he was forced to reopen them just sixteen days afterwards. As Jonathan Swift was to remark from the safety of the Enlightenment sixty years later, the key issue of the Reformation was, in his analogy of boiled eggs for breakfast, whether big-enders should kill little-enders or not. But for all his satire, it was a bloody dangerous period.

In Germany and Sweden, at various times during the seventeenth century, several paranoid governments shut down the cafés (though it proved impossible to keep them closed). But the world might have been spared a lot of anguish if Louis XVI had successfully shut the ones in his capital.

At the Café du Foy, in 1787, Camille Desmoulins set off the French Revolution with his speech inciting a baying rabble to take up arms. Seven years later, Desmoulins, and his wife Lucile, would both be guillotined.

Not far away, in the Régence (which had opened much earlier in 1688) the young Napoleon Bonaparte played endless games of chess while waiting for his time to come. 'Strong coffee revives me,' he said, 'it gives me a burning sensation, a gnawing feeling, a pain that is not without pleasure. It is a form of suffering I am happy to endure.'[3]

And though they are odd footsteps to follow in, a century later, Lenin and Karl Marx were to meet at the emperor's old table.

In 1686 a Sicilian gentleman opened a coffee house in Paris. His name, Francesco Procopio dei Coltelli, suggests he was not a man to be trifled with.[4] His *endroit* became widely famed for its agreeable atmosphere, the proximity to the Comédie-Française and its excellent clientèle. It very soon became the meeting place for literati.

---

[3] Quoted by Philippe Boé in *Coffee*, Cassell & Co., 2001.
[4] His nickname implies a stiletto.

For the next 200 years everyone who was anyone (or who hoped to become someone) in the worlds of the arts, letters and politics, frequented the Café Procope. Rousseau, Beaumarchais, Balzac, Verlaine, Hugo, La Fontaine and Anatole France were among the regulars. In the eighteenth century, a new liberal philosophy, that of the Encyclopedists, was expounded and expatiated by Diderot, Voltaire, d'Alembert and Benjamin Franklin, cups of fine espresso coffee in their hands.

The Revolution is closely associated with the Procope. Robespierre, Danton and Marat used to meet there, and a young but promising lieutenant (Napoleon Bonaparte, again) once left his hat here as a pledge.

Voltaire's table is still there, at once a symbol and a testimony of permanence, ready to welcome a writer or journalist, or perhaps a university professor; even a model, businessman or tourist.

In the Café du Chartres (now the Grand Véfour), Murat and Lamartine plotted and agitated. From those deliberations arose the dreadful Committee for Public Safety.

In safe old England there has always been a reluctance to revolt. But in the late eighteenth century, London cafés were political as well. Ozinda's for the Jacobites, the Cocoa-Tree for Tories, and the Whigs found congenial company at the Smyrna and at the St James.

In Vienna, Trotsky played chess at the Central with anyone who dared to sit down opposite him.

As far away as New York, the Burns Coffee House became the HQ of the Liberty Boys, who entertained and fomented the rebel movement of the late 1700s for American independence.

In the end, a fine arabica,[5] perfectly roasted and passed through an espresso machine minutes later, is a bewitching experience, especially when supported with warm new bread and freshly squeezed *sanguinello* orange juice. An espresso is a stimulant, too, especially for businessmen and politicos. 'Coffee which makes the politician wise / And see thro' all things with his half-shut eyes,'[6] certainly works for me first thing in the morning.

---

[5] Such as a mocha or a Bourbon or a Maragogype or a Typica.
[6] Alexander Pope, *The Rape of the Lock*, 1714.

Breakfast, in England at least, can be a proud, magnificent, square meal that prepares a man for his day tilling the fields. But for a lighter alternative the laurels must go to the Italians and the over-modestly named 'continental' breakfast. It is not just that they understand coffee better than anyone else in the world. Breakfast is a court where the other ingredients pay homage to the prince in their midst.

I put my cup down and stood up. By now the doors of the Frari would have opened and it was time to do some culture vulturing. A superb cup. I was restored. No, better than that. I was set up as if I had slept a night in the Danieli.

I spent the rest of this first exposure to Venice following the advice of the guidebooks, which everyone should do. Three days, by yourself, let you ensure that there is a tick in every box – the Accademia, the Ghetto, the Arsenale, the Rialto, the Bridge of Sighs... but no matter how astonishing the lures of the Queen of the Adriatic, it was time for me to head off. At the time I was too poor a student to hire a gondola, or to try a Bellini at Harry's Bar, but I did find myself at one point at an 'undiscovered' restaurant in the Castello quarter, the Trattoria da Remigio, eating a huge bowl of miniature spider crabs with the fishermen. I believe this restaurant is rather better known these days, and their table has if anything became even more exciting. They tell me its nearest rival in putting crabs on tables is in Baltimore.

There was a second 'epiphany' for me in Venice on this short trip. I found myself looking across the Grand Canal at the church of the Redentore. My guidebook told me that the architect Palladio had built it. I felt I knew this style well from England, where he had many disciples over the ensuing centuries.

But as I stood staring over the façade I saw that he had taken the concept of the temple front – columns and pediment – and had combined no less that seven of them to create a renaissance church. One low and broad column was interrupted by another, tall and thin, to create the aisles and the nave. Four representations of the Greek ideal were 'windows' in the front, and the last was the door that let the faithful in.

It was astonishingly successful, and deceptively easy, but I realised that until that point I had never appreciated that these elements could be assembled in this way.

I resolved I would make sure I learned a little more about this architect who single-handedly changed the way Europe looked in the sixteenth century.

When I returned, in 1979, I would come with a suitably loaded wallet and my research rather more complete. But that's another story.

An Orthodox Sunday

San Vitale and Sant' Apollinare Nuovo in Classe, Ravenna

Ravenna isn't far from Venice, but it's on the Italian mainland, and its fifth- to seventh-century mosaics had been highly recommended. 'Possibly the best preserved Dark Age wonder of the world,' I had been told.

Very early in the morning, at least by my unexacting standards, I had walked across the long bridge that connects Venice with Italy and was standing by the main road leading south. I was carrying a large sign on which I had written 'Ravenna', hoping, without much confidence, for a lift.

But I hadn't waited very long when a VW Dormobile stopped and a soberly dressed girl wound down her window. Thank goodness for the ability to pigeonhole people. Her English number plates had already given me the big clue – a light Geordie accent and a pair of bifocals gave me the fine detail. She was in her early or mid twenties, not unattractive, and her heart was large enough to pick up a traveller on the road. She was a young bluestocking, on the road, culture vulturing.

'English? Jump in,' she commanded. 'I'm going to Ravenna too. Octavia,' she said, holding out her hand in a businesslike way.

'Jeremy,' I rejoined. We Brits always like a formal introduction. In two strides I was on board.

'You'll be a student?' she remarked as she pulled away from the kerb. But the audible question mark implied that I was a little old for the job.

'I was,' I said carefully. Having already forgotten that I had just done the same to her, I found it not a little irritating to have other people put me in their little boxes.

'I've never been to Ravenna,' she volunteered. 'Have you?'

'No. All I know is that there is a marvellous church there with some very ancient mosaics. They are of a late Roman Empress called Theodora.' That was in fact the sum total of my knowledge.

'It's a mysterious place,' she declared. 'No one seems to know too much about its origins. No one even knows who founded it. It could have been the Tyrrhenians, or the Thessalians, or even the Umbrians.'

I nodded wisely and said, 'Wasn't it once a bit like Venice?' Her tone had suggested scholarship and I felt the need to add my tuppence worth. 'A few primitive houses on piles in a marshy lagoon. The Romans must have ignored it for a reason.'

'Except they didn't ignore it. The Republic annexed it in 89 BC. Not very much later Julius Caesar gathered his army here, prior to crossing the Rubicon, on his way to Geneva and later to England.' She glanced at me very briefly, perhaps to see if she was boring or overtaxing me.

'In 45 BC,' she went on, 'after his battle against Mark Anthony, the Emperor Augustus asked his famous admiral Agrippa to found a walled naval station at Classis. From that time it never looked back. It was an important port until well into the Middle Ages.'

'Classis?'

'Ravenna's port. Every city has one, you know.'

'Ravenna must have greatly benefited from its federation with Rome,' I said. Easy, that one. Everyone everywhere always did.

'Especially Ravenna. They had to rely on wells before Trajan brought them fresh water. He built them a fifty-mile-long aqueduct at the beginning of the second century,' said Octavia. 'That wouldn't have done the citizens any harm.'

'Founded in 89 BC, did you say? That makes it older than Venice, then. And being stuck in a swamp must have been handy when the Huns began to arrive.' I was uncomfortably aware that I was again making a statement of the blindingly obvious.

'You're spot on.' She glanced at me again. 'When the Visigoths were at their most threatening,' she said, 'the Western Roman Emperor Honorius moved his capital there from Milan. As he saw it, Ravenna would always have easy access to Constantinople and a thriving Eastern Roman Empire. And the swamp helped too. Proof of his sagacity came when Alaric simply bypassed Ravenna and went on to sack Rome, fill his pockets and take Gallia Placidia, Emperor Theodosius I's daughter, hostage.'

'What happened then?' I asked. History, according to Wittgenstein, is just one damned thing after another. From my less elevated perspective I saw it as a compendium of ripping yarns.

'What happened next is somewhat complicated. The upshot, however, was that Gallia Placidia eventually got back to Ravenna with her son, the future Emperor Valentinian III. She had the support of her uncle Theodosius II. With that kind of backing, Ravenna got the peace it needed, Christianity flourished and the city gained its most famous monuments. The secular ones have mostly gone but the Christian ones are all still there.'

She passed me a book, this time without taking her eyes off the road. It was called *Everything You Need to Know about Ravenna but Never Dared Ask*, or something very like that. I let it fall open.

The Western Roman Empire fell in AD 476, I read, sixty-six years after it had abandoned England. The Eastern Roman Empire was to continue for another thousand years. Constantinople didn't actually fall until thirty-nine years before Columbus discovered America. It was curious to realise that some well-informed people would have heard of the fall of the Eastern Empire when young and the discovery of what would be the USA in their early middle age. If these two important dates were exchanged, who knows? Perhaps America would have become an outpost of the Roman Empire. I know some Americans who actually believe it is.

When Italy fell to the Huns, the Eastern Emperor, Zeno, employed an Ostrogoth chieftain as a mercenary to re-take the whole Italian peninsula for 'Rome'. Zeno called the soldier 'Theodoric'.

Ravenna, where he landed, became an incubator for an Ostrogothic kingdom, pledged to the destruction of the Vandals and Visigoths. Theodoric chose to take on the Visigoth, Odoacer, at Verona. Odoacer, running for his life, found his way behind Theodoric's makeshift walls at Ravenna and embedded himself there for three long years. Theodoric tried to starve him out.

Finally, when the Ostrogoth took Rimini, Theodoric was able to sever Odoacer's last supply line and the siege succeeded. The walls breached, Theodoric slew Odoacer in knightly mortal combat.

From then on Theodoric engaged Roman architects to build both secular and religious buildings, including a princely palace near Sant' Apollinare Nuovo, now sadly destroyed. A Palazzo di Teodorico still stands but it is merely an outbuilding of the long-gone mansion.

This was the time of the Arian heresy, but Theodoric, while doctrinally affected, managed to coexist peaceably with the Latins.

'Do you know anything about Arianism?' my new friend Octavia asked me.

'It's about the Trinity, isn't it? Didn't Arians believe that Christ was created by God, and was therefore not quite an equal third of the thing?'

'That's exactly right,' said Octavia, and I was rather pleased. 'Arius was a Christian priest who lived and taught in Alexandria in the early fourth century. He thought that God the Father and the Son were not co-eternal. The pre-incarnate Jesus was divine but nonetheless created by, and therefore inferior to, the Father. Before that the Son did not exist. That made Jesus a "creature", using the word in its original sense of "created being".'

'It sounds pretty logical. Did it catch on much?'

'It certainly did. This attempt to redefine the Trinity was the first serious schism in the ancient Church. The controversy continued for most of the fourth century. It afflicted priests, the faithful and the monks as well as their bishops, emperors and abbots. It infected the imperial house, the nobility and senior clergy for decades, but in the end Trinitarianism prevailed, theologically and politically. That all three persons of the Trinity are equal in One has been an uncontested doctrine in all major branches of the Eastern and Western Church from the fifth century to the present day.'

'Would you mind if I ask you how you know all this?' I asked.

'It's the subject of my dissertation. I'm doing a doctorate on the Primitive Church.'

'That figures… Well, did the early Church fight Arianism with words, or prayers, or with plain old force?'

'All three, really. The Byzantine Emperor, Justinian I, was an orthodox if somewhat fanatical Trinitarian. He invaded Italy in AD 535 and took on the Ostrogoths and their Arian allies. By 540 he had conquered Ravenna, which he made his seat in Italy. The city, and its little empire, was now known as the Exarchate of Ravenna. As such it was an outpost of Byzantium. It no longer even bothered to claim to be a surviving fragment of the old Roman Empire in the West.'

'Your doctorate's in the bag, I can safely predict.'

'I hope you're right. The dons at St Hilda's aren't as easy to please as you.'

She flattered me when she omitted to say 'Oxford'. I kept to myself that I had never even heard of the college's founder or namesake, St Hilda herself. I hoped (for her sake) she was neither a nun nor a nymphomaniac[1] as Hildabeests were reckoned to be. I assumed she was another early martyr.[2]

We had now reached Ravenna, and Octavia was looking for a parking space. What percentage of my life so far has been wasted looking for a parking space? We ultimately found one next to a curious building that I was about to discover was a fifth-century baptistery.

'That's handy,' said Octavia. 'I wanted to start at the beginning. Looks odd, doesn't it?'

'It does, too. It's too squat.'

'That's because the street level has risen almost ten feet since it was built. Asphalt and exhaust fumes have hidden its breathtaking marble columns and darkened the bright mosaics in its arches.'

'Why is it octagonal and not circular?' I asked my cicerone.

'Because it represents the Creation. In the early Byzantine

---

[1] American scientists are still researching a cure for nymphomania.

[2] Actually not. St Hilda was the daughter of Prince Hereric of Deira, a nephew of King Edwin, by his wife, Lady Bregswith. Hilda was probably born at the court of King Raedwald of East Anglia at Rendlesham in Suffolk. In AD 657, Abbess Hilda founded a double monastery of both monks and nuns at Whitby (Streoneshall) and here she finally settled. After a long and painful illness, she died in AD 680 and was buried in her abbey, some way from Dracula's tomb, I suppose. Her miracles were soon reported and she was venerated as a saint. Many pilgrimages were made to her shrine, and an Oxford college eventually named after her, for protofeminist reasons, I think. Her shrine was destroyed and her bones were lost in the Reformation.

Church, God created the world in seven days and rested on the eighth.'

That didn't sound right. 'Did Byzantium have eight-day weeks, then?'

There was silence for a while.

'Come on,' said Octavia, 'Let's go in. Let's see what damage Felix Kibel has done to the place.'

I admit I had no idea what or who she was talking about, but in we went. And it was truly magnificent.

The original floor was yards beneath us but I gathered there used to be some sort of baptismal pool, where penitent pagans could be fully immersed. This realisation is not due to my great genius. It was prompted by the dome. It was lined with mosaics depicting all twelve apostles, gathered around a rather primitive likeness of Christ, up to his waist in the Jordan. The Baptist, standing next to him, is about to pour holy water on to the Holy Head from a dish.

Octavia explained to me that this last detail was added in the ninth century. A Roman artisan, said Kibel, was employed to restore every mosaic in town. He was apparently more interested in showing off his own artistry than in the tedious and faithful replacement of fallen tesserae. In the pristine work, St John the Baptist had held no dish; he had merely extended his hand to place it on our Lord's head to push Him gently into the river.

We were soon on our way again, searching for more of Kibel's restorations to vilify. Octavia considered Kibel little better than the Antichrist.

Our next stop was Ravenna's oldest mosaic cycle. Galla Placidia's mausoleum stands in a ravishing and ancient part of town, accessible only through narrow streets lined with beautifully restored old houses. Everywhere I looked were tall umbrella pines, whose ancestors had been planted by Roman legionaries.

The mausoleum is a small and plain building which you enter through a very small door. It hardly looked worth the trouble, but once inside we both gasped. In fact, people have gasped here since AD 430.

Above our heads was a deep blue barrel-vaulted ceiling, decorated with flowers. Again, over the door was Christ's portrait, set in a gently rustic background. He is in a garden, surrounded by sheep, which contrasts sharply with the next image, in which St Lawrence pauses before stepping on to the flaming gridiron of his martyrdom. Still, even for this doomed Christian, the Holy Ghost is his witness, taking here the form of doves that sip at a fountain behind him. St Lawrence will receive his crown.

Galla Placidia was entombed in the large marble sarcophagus facing the door. Octavia told me that her mummified remains were burned to a crisp when a curious local resident bored a hole in the marble and used a candle to illuminate the interior.

King Theodoric heralded Ravenna's next golden age. We owe him so much; the Arian Baptistry, the Archbishop's Chapel, his own mausoleum, Sant' Apollinare Nuovo and the church of Santo Spirito. And astonishingly all of these are still there.

The Archbishop's Chapel had a floor plan similar to Gallia Placidia's. It similarly had a barrel-vaulted doorway beneath a representation of a youthful, smiling Christ (who this time was dispatching evil, in the form of a lion and a snake). The Evangelists were depicted in the dome, but here they were half-man, half-animal, whereas in the earlier building they had no human elements.

This Arian Baptistry these days appears very stern. When the heresy fell into disrepute, its eight walls were stripped of all decorations and now there is only bare brick. The dome alone survived with its much simpler composition. At least the Baptist is not holding a dish.

'Are you enjoying this?' Octavia asked me, as we headed for a spot of lunch in a pizzeria.

'What do you imagine?' I replied. Not only was I in heaven but I had also fluked a great guide. After lunch we would do San Vitale and Sant' Apollinare in Classe – in Octavia's opinion the two most superb examples of Byzantine art in the world, and both found here. It would have been disrespectful in the circumstances to have mentioned Hagia Sofia, in Istanbul, the cathedral in Monreale or the little royal chapel in Palermo.

But before lunch was over I was able to learn a little more about Octavia.

'I was born and raised in Newcastle,' she told me over that memorable pizza. 'When I was fourteen, my father took me to Durham Cathedral. I suddenly understood a lot of stuff I had just accepted up to then. I really haven't been the same since.'

She had read Theology at her Oxford college. Her game plan required that one day the Church of England would admit women to the priesthood.

'That's a bit unlikely,' I said, discouragingly. 'It would make an eventual communion with Rome impossible. Half the Anglican clergy would desert for Rome at the first whiff of such flagrant pragmatism. And it still wouldn't satisfy the feminists, who before long would want women bishops and even a female Archbishop of Canterbury. How could a pope deal with such a person? The whole church would be excommunicated anew, and just when the original excommunication was wearing off.'

I thought I knew the answers in those days.

'Well, if you're right, and I don't believe you are, then I hit the glass ceiling at curate. But that's good enough. There's still a lot you can do as a curate.'

The thing was, she would obviously make a brilliant priest. She was patient, tolerant, trusting and generous. Her faith was transparent. She was destined to bring consolation to many troubled souls. Paradoxically, I wished her well, while hoping the Church of England – in so many ways the political means by which Britain remained Catholic – would never embark on such a rash adventure.

'Do you have faith – do you believe in God, I mean?' It was such an unusual question to hear from an Englishwoman that I stammered rather when I replied.

'I've thought about this. No, I don't "believe" in God, as if I had a choice. I was baptised a Catholic. My earliest memories include Sunday school in Kensington Square. I don't remember ever debating it, I was simply immersed in it, learning its values innately.' I gestured around me. 'It's as much a part of me as I am British, and a European. I had to study history, but not religion, not really. Even so, my dues are paid. I am a Catholic, even if not a very good one. I don't believe in God, in the sense of having applied my mind to the question. I simply know there is a God in much the same way that I know the world isn't flat but is an oblate spheroid.'

I felt this little speech should do it. We English, after all, were supposed to avoid this subject, together with money and politics.

'And Jesus died to save us? You do accept that?' Octavia was insisting.

'Well, actually I don't know what to say. Whether He jumped or was pushed. The Seven Last Words suggest He was fairly unhappy about the arrangement. But I do believe that the greatest qualities of mankind are now seen to be creativity, a willingness to forgive and an ability to inspire. Isn't that Father, Son and Holy Ghost?'

'But where is the authority for your thoughts? Is it derived from dogma or from scripture? Or are you wallowing in personal opinion, subscribing to no known faith?'

If Octavia was looking for a fight, I was used to this sort of match, having honed my skills (such as they were) for three years in smoke-filled combination rooms.

'Like our other successful religions, Catholicism is a club. It is unnecessary to believe, contrary to the view of Evangelicals and Missionaries. For us, it is enough to be baptised. As soon as that Sacrament is achieved you are on your way. Should you die soon after, God will forgive your deficiencies and admit you to the fields of Elysium. Otherwise, it's limbo. A place where for grown-ups there is tonic water but no gin, and a background din of a billion babies crying.'

'Limbo is Catholic dogma, I believe. There is no mention of it in the scriptures.'

'The authority comes from the Church, whose authority derives from the Apostolic Succession. The Catholic Church has evolved and its dogma has been refined by St Jerome, St Augustine, and the Council of Trent. More time should be given to the Doctors of the Faith, but then' – I suddenly saw a flaw in my argument – 'less time should be paid to the Second Vatican Council. Before that ill-advised council, the faithful could hear in the melodies of the Psalms, in the rhythms of the great prayers, an echo of the original Aramaic, or Greek, or Latin. The congregation was transported back to the time of Christ, and before.'

'Our Archbishop of Canterbury holds his post through Apostolic Succession. And we're fairly big on the Psalms too. It's news to me that you Catholics pay that much heed to them.'

'All right, you win. I suppose I meant the great prayers, the

Sanctus, the Credo, the Confiteor. When I hear the old Latin, *Pater noster, qui es in coelis,* I feel I am hearing the ancient metre that inspired the congregation on the Mount. It takes us back to the original inspiration of it all. The day they tried to suppress Latin was an ill day for Christendom. And now the modernists are trying to expunge the wonderful rhythms and cadences that survived the nationalisation.'

Octavia was unimpressed. 'But don't you believe it should be made relevant, more national, less scholarly and more "inclusive" for those people who didn't actually study Latin? What do ordinary people know, or need to know, about Aramaic liturgy or Gregorian chant? We have to attract the working-class youth in Salford, you know.'

'We're miles apart, Octavia, on this. First, there is nothing national about God. And over the millennia very few churchgoers have actually studied Latin. Latin was already dying by the time of Constantine the Great. The literate had missals instead. The rest heard the same prayers every week, sometimes more often, and they became familiar. They learned them by heart. And seeing and hearing man's attempts to mirror God's infinite beauty, in art and music, is not too good for Salford's working classes. It's too easy to be presumptuous. Maybe a Salford lad has seen a Shakespeare play, or is merely toying with the idea. If you assume his education to be poor too readily you will end by patronising the faithful and infantilising the rite, and making the lad's ambitions pointless, which they are not. You will drive the well-educated and self-educated away. And if they go, who will be left? The Church is too important to be made the plaything of the proletariat.'

'What about my point about a National Church? One fit for Englishmen?'

'But if the Church of England is a National Church, why should it try to convert Nigerians and such? After all, what separates an Anglican from a Catholic is the Anglican's complicity with the Tudor state's confiscations and its readiness to allow the head of the Church six wives. Is that what you want to sell to the Africans?'

'Great. We've come a long way since then. What, I repeat, about the use of a modern, living language?'

'Well, since Vatican II we Catholics are also supposed to celebrate the Mass in English. But what passes for English in our Church is utterly horrible. I so envy you your *Book of Common Prayer*, your King James Bible, and all Thomas Cranmer's prosody. Our wedding service, for example, is either in an incomprehensible and interminable Latin or is a vain catalogue of well-intended anodyne and saccharine rubbish that tries in vain to celebrate what a celibate cannot or shouldn't imagine. But in your *Prayer Book* version, the groom has to swear that with his body "I thee worship". Wow! Now you're talking English.'

'You like all those "thees" and "thous", then? Mostly we're trying to get rid of them.'

'You'll throw the baby out with the bath water if you do. Some words only exist because they are used in church. "Firmament" is an example. Were it not for the Church of England the word would be extinct.'

'I'm not sure we'd be much worse off without it.'

'Ah, you never know how valuable something is until you lose it.'

'You have little sense of the realistic, it seems to me. Most people believe in evolution, I should think. We have to preach to people who have read Darwin. Have you?'

I had read a few pages. My copy of *The Origin of Species* was in Rome. Perhaps it was time I made a serious effort.

'But doesn't it argue that the creation happened, well, accidentally? I thought it was supposed to be an antidote to Christianity. Do you believe in evolution?'

'It doesn't matter whether I do or don't. It's more that if we noisily deny the theory of evolution we lose half our congregation. So we have to work a compromise.'

Our philosophical lunch was over all too soon and we were on the road again. Octavia warned me to expect to be dazzled. We would start with Sant' Apollinare Nuovo, probably the most magnificent survival from Theodoric's realm.

How brilliantly the Byzantines used their mosaics to tell stories! At the far end of the left wall where we started, the Virgin held her baby Jesus. We then stopped at every mosaic in the sequence, 'reading' Our Lord's life as in stills from a film until he finally appeared at the near end of the right wall, a tired and older man in purple, seated on a throne.

The church also boasted a procession in mosaic of martyrs and virgins bearing gifts, led by a Kibel-corrupted trio of Wise Men. It was simply stunning. There was also a tantalising view of Theodoric's long-lost palace.

The heretic king of the Visigoths had had himself depicted, but his portrait had been removed by Justinian, along with the bodies of his Gothic courtiers, whose hands alone are still visible on the columns of the palace.

'This must be as good as it can get,' I said, but Octavia disagreed.

'I don't think so,' she said. And we were off again, this time to San Vitale.

And she was right.

In this enchanting and extraordinary survivor from the Roman twilight, a terrific pair of portraits lives on. Justinian, the Eastern Roman Emperor, and his enchanting wife, Theodora, have been immortalised in mosaic.

'Theodora came from the wrong side of the tracks,' Octavia patiently explained to me, as I stared incredulously at this breathtaking work of art. 'She grew up in a circus, became an actress and prostitute, had an illegitimate child and was subsequently abandoned by her Syrian lover. She was a penniless weaver when the Emperor met her, fell in love and made her his Empress. Theodora had Justinian under her thumb for the rest of her life.'

She had obviously sat for the portraitists of San Vitale. She looks elegant, extravagant and irresistible. Other courtiers are depicted, and similarly their likenesses are individual and not always flattering. Their features clearly correspond to real people. The panel showing Empress Theodora and her court is the most perfect Byzantine mosaic anywhere.

But our adventure in Ravenna was not quite over yet. Ravenna has an eighth wonder.

It was mid-afternoon when Octavia and I drove through some five miles of characterless farmland, passing a couple of ruined churches, in the general direction of the coast. There seemed to be no signposts and we began to believe that we had taken a wrong turning.

We were almost ready to give up and turn back when the horizon was suddenly pierced by a gracious, round campanile, nearly a hundred feet tall. It dates to the beginning of the eleventh century.

Three times in the Second World War it somehow escaped annihilation. First, the Americans missed it during their attempt to liberate Italy by carpet-bombing it. A few months later they actually singled the church out as a target when it became an observation tower for the Germans. Then Providence herself caused the Nazis to flee in such a hurry that they too had to scrap their own plans to demolish it.

Long before, after the great harbour of Classis had silted up, this magnificent basilica was left to the elements. It was pillaged and stripped by any number of profane travellers who happened to wander past. Charlemagne had papal authority to take away from Ravenna anything that he liked. He made three looting expeditions to Ravenna and removed a vast quantity of Roman columns, mosaics, statues and other portable masterpieces to enrich his own Palatine Chapel in Aachen. Almost as notorious was Pandolfo Sigismondo Malatesta of Rimini, who rather later carted off one hundred wagonloads of carved marble.

Getting into the church was a little complicated but we found our way into the nave. Above us weighed a *matroneo* – where women once modestly worshipped. We felt enfolded, closely and yet majestically, by all this architectural and decorative splendour. Few places on earth have such power to stop you dead in your tracks.

The weather was improving and the surviving interior of Sant' Apollinare in Classe was flooded with sunlight. Its nave was divided by rows of splendidly veined marble columns. Octavia and I looked down the apse to where a joyful St Apollinaris stood in a brilliant green garden. This has to be one of the happiest mosaics in existence. Animals gambol gracefully beneath a gold and deep blue sky, where the hand of God emerges from a bank of clouds. Twelve sheep, representing the Apostles, climb another grey-green hill towards Christ, flanked by His Evangelists, who smiles down from the summit. The green, together with a pale turquoise, also appears as a background in the portraits that line the lower part of the apse.

These were the last great mosaics to be completed before Ravenna declined into obscurity, and when the suffocating curtain of the Dark Ages extinguished its gleaming lights.

The light was failing in modern Ravenna, too, when Octavia and I found a little trattoria to grab a last bite before she drove me back to the railway station in Venice. I asked her about the eclipse of Ravenna. How could it have happened?

'The Lombards,' she told me. 'In AD 752, a Lombard king, Aistulf, succeeded in conquering Ravenna, and Byzantine rule in Northern Italy finally ended.'

Charlemagne's father, Pepin, had attacked the Longobards on the orders of Pope Stephen II, who then incorporated Ravenna into the Papal States. Pope Adrian I allowed the Archbishop of Ravenna a measure of autonomy from the body of the Roman Church, following the precedent set by the Byzantine 'exarchy'. It was appropriate enough; the Archbishop of Ravenna was the richest in Italy after the Papacy. But the real 'exarchy' was over and the city was from now on merely a provincial town in northern Italy.

It must have enjoyed a civilised obscurity, however, as one of the most illustrious residents of Ravenna in the twelfth century was the exiled poet Dante.

Octavia gave me her considered conclusion as we drove away, she to visit Venice and me to my train for Rome. Her opinion?

'Ravenna is a museum city. The great city has been set in the aspic of conservation and tourism. Its eight early Christian monuments are less important to the faithful than they are to tourists working their way down Unesco's World Heritage List. After all, we disturbed not a soul in prayer. Both as a vibrant modern town, and as a place of profound spirituality, its vitality has been put on hold.'

And my opinion? Almost the contrary. As a showcase of Byzantine art, Ravenna has no peers.[3] But more than that, I had

---

[3] T S Eliot said of St Apollinaris: '*Et Saint Apollinaire, raide et ascétique / Vieille usine désaffectée de Dieu, teint encore / Dans ses peirres écroulantes la forme précise de Byzance.*' T S Eliot, *Lune de Miel* – Ed.

been transported by the sublime feeling the portraitists, working in what must be the most testing of media, mosaic, had realised especially in San Vitale. Most especially, Theodora's image is still as fresh in my memory as if it were only a week since my visit.

And Octavia? I haven't seen her or heard from her from that day to this, but if the Church of England ever consecrates a female bishop, my money is on her being the first.

Chapter the Tenth
1972: A Guide to Rome

In which the author's sister makes an appearance. Michelangelo's 'Pietà' is smashed to pieces by a madman in the Vatican, and the author shows his sister Bernini's elephant. He reflects on monarchy in general and the Italian monarchy in particular. He gives her a little guided tour and they visit the great piazza of St Peter's on motorbikes, narrowly escaping arrest.

I loved, and still love, the squares of Rome. I love eating in their cafés, peering in their shop windows. If I am in Rome, you will find me examining even their ordinary buildings and trying to guess how old they are. You will find me leaning against some weathered fountain, the Touring Club Italiano's guide in my hand, digesting some scholarly notes about an ancient weather-beaten statue, a frescoed niche in a wall or the site of the burning of a heretic. There is so much here, it is like a favourite book. Rereading is always better than reading for the first time. I go round them again and again.

I tried to explain this to my nineteen-year-old sister, Kate, who had decided to spend a little of her gap year in Rome, learning Italian at a school near the top of the Spanish Steps. I am cheating a little as the name given to this period (between school and university) was not yet called a 'gap year'. In those days most people went straight from school to university. Only Oxbridge applicants had to stay at school for an additional term to take the special papers those universities themselves would set. Theirs was a very different style of exam to the A level, based more on reasoning than on acquired knowledge. After having done these tests, which might lead to exhibitions or even scholarships, the applicants had a 'gap' to fill from January to October. Some students worked, others travelled, but all of them worried themselves sick while they waited for their results.

As for Kate, I had been fortunate in finding her a little flat, complete with terrace, and, as I recall, she was as happy as a sand girl. At first, I had tried to make sure we would spend as much time together as possible; but soon, due to the attentions of a handsome Cuban *chargé d'affaires*, she was busy becoming the doyenne of a rather elevated if ostensibly left-wing circle.

'Going round and round Roman squares? I defy you to make that fun!' she challenged.

It was a challenge I readily rose to. I would start with the square I lived on, the Piazza della Rotonda, home to the Pantheon, the last resting place of the Italian kings, the ancient House of Savoy.

When Kate first arrived in Rome in May we unpacked her small suitcase and together we stocked her shelves with the usual staple of dry spaghetti and tins of tomatoes. Her next-door neighbour had introduced us to her slavering and emaciated German Shepherd. It lived off pasta and fresh vegetables, she explained proudly, as vegetarians who own pets are wont to do. The dog looked at us, weighing up the risks. We were both very skinny in those days, which is probably why we are still alive.

I was still based at Il Sole. The *pensione* was certainly at least 500 years old and must have entertained many an early pilgrim or other intrepid traveller as they battled and swatted their way to the Eternal City through the surrounding malarial swamps. Il Sole, then rather run-down and affordably priced, has had rather more than a lick of paint since those days. My son, who stayed there in 2003, tells me that these days it's well worth a night or two.

Kate was now installed and we agreed she would come to my hotel the next day for breakfast and for a mini tour of Rome.

Sitting alone that evening in da Pepe, buried as usual in my reading – I had determined to elevate my Italian to a level that would not cause my new friends to wince – a very strange thing happened. A Roman burst into the restaurant in a state of abject shock, shouted something hysterical at the clientèle, rushed out and was on his way. The effect of his announcement was to appal the diners. It was all too clear that something of enormous importance had happened, but what could it have been?

I looked about for help, but the others there were in such

trauma that I could not conceive of breaking into their tearful conversations. My nearest neighbour had fallen to his knees and was praying. I could not imagine what had caused this awful scene. Would the assassination of a pope do this? Another world war? Some frightful terrorist outrage? My mind was racing.

Pepe, the restaurateur, was standing close to me, as shocked as anyone. I spoke to him.

'*Cos'é successo*?' I asked. What has happened?

'*Anno ammazato la Pietà*,' he replied, his voice broken with grief.

The diners were now rising awkwardly to their feet and leaving a little money by their unfinished plates.

Pepe went to the door and held it open. He was closing for the night. Never mind that some of us had only just begun to eat.

I rose, too. But what had happened? I thought about his reply.

'They have murdered Pity,' he seemed to have said. It made no sense. It seemed like a line from some depressing Victorian piece of poetry.

Then it dawned on me.

La Pietà was the statue of the Virgin and her dead Son that Michelangelo had carved from a single slab of marble in 1499, when he was just twenty-one years old, and which had instantly raised him to the title of the greatest sculptor the world has ever known, a title he has retained to this day.

In those days it was in St Peter's, in the south aisle, and was difficult to see as so many art lovers, pious and simply curious, wanted to inspect it and touch it. I had admired it a week before, and had noticed that the Virgin's breast was especially shiny.

It is the only work that the exuberant and young artist actually signed, MICHAELA[N]GELUS BONAROTUS FLORENTIN[US] FACIEBAT, on a band across the Virgin's dress.

It transpired that an Australian, Lazlo Toth, whose name ranks high in the annals of infamy and therefore is not to be forgotten, had gone into the basilica with a great hammer concealed under a coat, and in front of a horrified crowd had set about the sculpture, breaking her arms, His feet and so on until he was restrained by a murderous set of Romans and other visitors, who themselves were in turn prevented from killing the man by the Swiss Guards.

When Kate joined me the next day at my breakfast table, just outside Il Sole, she found me in sober mood and with several of the morning papers spread out in front of me.

I shared the excitement of the previous night with her, but she was unimpressed. 'They'll fix it,' she reassured me. 'They knocked bits off the David when they put it up in Florence, and they fixed that, didn't they? I actually feel sorry for Toth. Once inside he'll be beaten to death by the criminally pious. What a way to go!'

Toth was tried and eventually acquitted on grounds of insanity and was sent off to a place for the incurable. But I was with the 'pious'. No punishment would have been too severe.

I sipped at my *spremuta d'arancia* and considered the concept of the 'criminally pious'. Kate was probably right. But it would not be quite as before. It is back and seemingly in one piece, but now it is behind a great wall of laminated glass, said to be able to resist a direct hit from a bazooka. No more young marrieds would rub a breast in the hope of having children themselves.

We stared for a while at the colonnaded façade of the Pantheon in front of us.

Kate was the first to break the reflective silence. 'Let's go in,' she said.

'Yes, OK, but let me take you round the piazza first,' I said.

The Pantheon is a noble building. It is a rotunda, fronted with a fine portico and capped with a stately dome. There is no question that it is the best preserved of all the great classical monuments. Agrippa, the admiral who defeated the fleet of Anthony and Cleopatra, celebrated his victory by building the temple in 27 BC and consecrating it to the seven Roman planetary deities – Apollo, Diana, Mars, Mercury, Jupiter, Venus and Saturn. This was a recipe for disaster. Ours is a jealous God, and with such a dedication it was only a matter of time before it was struck by lightning and burnt to the ground. Some time later the emperor Hadrian rebuilt it, this time with gold- and silver-plated corbels and cornices, which took him nineteen years.[1] These have, naturally, long since disappeared into the fortresses and castles of the robber barons who managed Rome after its fall until

---

[1] Between AD 98 and AD 117.

it regained its feet in the early Dark Ages. The dome of the Pantheon, with its 142-feet span,[2] was the largest of its kind until the fifteenth century when Brunelleschi surpassed it and all of antiquity with his glorious duomo in Florence.

The story goes that Agrippa had asked his architects to build the largest dome in the known world. No one had any idea how this could be done until some bright spark owned up to having a cunning plan.

'I have a cunning plan,' he said. 'We build the curtain walls. We fill the cylinder with earth and shape the soil into a dome. We then lay great marble interlocking coffers on the earthen mound until they click into place and form the roof.'

'OK, I'm listening; sounds good, even, but how do we then get the earth out of the place?' asked one of the more far-sighted members of the company.

'We could announce that there is a gold coin in every cubic cubit. The rabble will do the work for us.'

And that's exactly what happened. The Roman plebs spent months extracting the gold-infused earth from the interior via the great doors until the roof was exposed in all its self-supporting splendour.

As we walked around the outside of the building we could see, behind it, the indecipherable ruins of another ancient building. It was no longer possible to guess what might have been. But I knew, because I had been chatting the previous night with my concierge who, like all such hotel staff, knew everything.

'That,' I said to my impressionable younger sister, 'is all that remains of the oldest skyscraper in the world. It was eleven stories high. Can you imagine a block of flats, eleven stories tall, with no lifts? Well, it utterly exhausted its tenants and, eventually, and for reasons that no one has confessed to, it burnt or fell down. The loss of the first tower block went unmourned, even though the collapse would certainly have killed a few people. The Emperor became very popular when he banned any further buildings in Rome of over seven stories. The study of a little history can be handsomely repaid, and our own dear town planners could have learned a timely lesson here.' In 1972 the town planners in the

---

[2] 43.2 metres.

UK were still building ghettos, or 'council estates', for the poor, based on the tower block concept.

As we continued our walk around the square, we passed the front of Santa Maria della Minerva, the Gothic church whose little forecourt, Piazza della Minerva, had a little gem of a statue of an elephant by Bernini, surmounted by an obelisk.

Forget what I just said about Michelangelo. Bernini is the greatest sculptor of all time. He surpasses Praxiteles, the master of the Hellenic period of classical art of ancient Greece. He outranks Rodin, who was the first of those who followed him who had any chance of overtaking him. He cannot easily be measured against the moderns – the rule book is so different – but I would certainly choose a Bernini over a Moore.

I have never known anyone who does not fall in love with this statue.

Pope Alexander VII placed it there in 1667. The obelisk itself was unearthed two years before at Sais in Egypt and, according to its four lines of hieroglyphics, it had been commissioned by the Pharaoh Apries in the first half of the sixth century BC. The pontiff immediately acquired it for his capital.

But it is as nothing without Bernini's marble elephant beneath it, caparisoned in a great damask battle dress, its tusks turned to defend the church behind it and its tetrahedral howdah from attack.

By now we had circumnavigated the Pantheon. It was time to go inside and take a peek at Raphael's tomb and the last tombs of the House of Savoy, the royal family that had ruled a united Italy from the Risorgimento[3] of the mid-nineteenth century to 1946.

The Pantheon would have faded away, of course, had it not been converted into a church in AD 609. But with the protection of the papacy it flourished. It was used as a last resting place for the great and good, and many of the familiar names of Italian art and letters are there. But it was the space reserved for King Humbert, or Umberto, that caused me to reflect on fate for a moment.

England is a good place to live if you're a deposed monarch. The Royalist Club, under the stewardship of the Marquis of Bristol, used to assemble them every year at a London hotel and

---

[3] The movement that led to the unification of Italy.

throw them a sumptuous banquet. Topping the guest list would be the King of Italy, or the King of Greece, whose sister was to marry the as yet uncrowned Juan-Carlos of Spain. Sultan Ghalib of the Hadramaut,[4] who introduced me to Le Gavroche, was a civilised ornament to this majestic circle. So too was the Emperor of Byzantium, when he could find the time to absent himself from his empire, now sadly reduced to a 'semi' on the Isle of Wight. People were especially kind to him as he was in the habit of conferring great orders of chivalry.

Another habitué was Prince Paul, pretender to the Romanian Crown, who divided his time between London and Paris. On one occasion he spotted a very tight Englishman completely confounded by the traffic on the Champs-Élysées, desperate to cross the road. Doing what we all would do, he took the reveller gently by the arm and led him to safety on the far side. The grateful Englishman looked at his rescuer a little unsteadily and asked 'Sir, so that I may thank you, what is your name?' The Prince duly but simply replied, 'Paul.' There was a silence. And then the Englishman said, 'Tell me, Paul, did you ever get a reply to any of those letters?'

Most of these people, short or tall, thin or fat, conformed to the usual stereotype, except perhaps King Freddie. He was the only ex-Royal to attend these gatherings who was black.

'Now I know you're making this up,' said my sister. 'There has never been a King Freddie. Or has there? Of where, exactly?'

Freddie was Kabaka of Buganda, the richest of Uganda's four ancient kingdoms. Until he was abducted, that is.

On 28 November 1953, the King was just twenty-eight. He was giving an elaborate dinner party in the Ugandan capital, Entebbe, entertaining a distinguished company of chiefs, diplomats and some representatives of 'wider international interests'.[5] The conversation was as ever free-ranging, and the Cambridge-educated king, believing himself to be under Chatham House rules, was incautious in his remarks. He certainly annoyed the British colonial governor, Sir Andrew Cohen.

Towards the end of the evening, the Governor invited the

---

[4] Part of modern Yemen.
[5] Diplomatic speak for 'armaments salesmen'.

king to step outside and take the air. The king graciously agreed. Sir Andrew was Her Britannic Majesty's envoy, after all.

He must have been rather surprised, therefore, when half a dozen commandos appeared from nowhere, tossed a blanket over his head and bundled him into a waiting military car.

Minutes later, the King was unceremoniously dragged on board a transport plane, yelling and screaming all the while. He was always a dapper chap, though full evening dress is not the best costume for international travel – unless you're James Bond, that is.

The King's call for Bugandan independence, and his opposition to a federation of East African countries, was his undoing. Churchill, reading Sir Andrew's reports, called him 'disloyal'.

On landing in the UK, the pilot, Clive Beadon, bowed to Edward William Frederick David Walugembe Mutebi Luwangula Mutesa and apologised for what he had been ordered to do. The King, furious as he was, was able to accept this apology at a personal level. He kept in touch with the pilot for years.

With a pension of £8,000 a year from the British Government – no mean sum in those days – he began to enjoy London society. His first base, at the Savoy, quickly gave way to a house in Eaton Place. Freddie was a bright young chap, and he soon set about renewing the friendships he had made while an undergraduate at Magdalen.

Meanwhile Freddie's removal was proving unpopular among the Bugandans and, just two years later, the Kabaka felt able to return. In 1955 he took his place again on the throne of his native soil.

It was to be a short respite. Seven years later Uganda gained its independence from Britain. Milton Obote became the country's first president, and quickly became a tyrant. In 1966 he used his troops to evict all forces for good, including Ernest Bawtree, the saintly Archdeacon of the western provinces of Uganda and Tanganyika. The civilised Freddie was again exiled to Britain.

This time, the British Prime Minister, Harold Wilson, was only willing to pay him a degradingly meagre stipend. Freddie still visited his friends in Cambridge, where he was something of a star attraction. He was always immaculately dressed, witty, laden with charm, and exuded the exquisite courtesy that befits a king.

On several occasions he was pointed out to me and I remember his elegant form and unhurried stroll across the centre of the sacred lawns.

But despite the brave face he set against his misfortune, he was heart-broken and bereft of the sort of friends that could have been of practical help. In 1969 he died, forty-five years old and quite penniless, in a tiny flat in Bermondsey.

Curiously, I had had the privilege of being presented to King Umberto II of Italy. This had happened in London only a year before, and my sister and I now found ourselves looking at the space set aside for his sepulchre.

King Umberto had been a guest of Peter Thorneycroft, a political industrialist (or an industrious politician) at his flat in Eaton Square. His daughter Victoria had drawn me there – very possibly the most desirable girl I had ever seen. Except for the one I married, naturally. Victoria was a pre-Raphaelite goddess incarnated by the sun from a stained glass window by Burne Jones.

'Tell me about the King.' My sister looked at the place which some royalists hoped Umberto would have for his eternal repose. 'What is he like?'

'He is a sad man,' I told her. 'Tall, wonderfully distinguished, but ultimately pointless. He had been destined to rule – I don't believe he had a plan B. When I met him he contented himself with little bows and curtsies from the Thorneycroft circle. He did not mix or join in the banter or spirit of the gathering. The sadness he radiated prompted me to look up his story.'

Italy, in 1946, was forced by some elaborate political chicanery to convert from a monarchy into a republic. The Americans, loyal to their own tradition, are innately opposed to monarchy in any form. The Italian royals had, in their opinion, earned the castigation of the world for allowing the country to turn into a dictatorship. It never occurred to them that it was their fault; if they had given the League of Nations more support, Mussolini would never have believed he had such a free hand in rebuilding the Roman Empire in Libya and Abyssinia.

At the end of the Great War, King Humbert's father, Victor Emmanuel III, was a young king of Italy. He had been involved with Germany and Austria-Hungary in the Triple Alliance but had always sought cordial relations with France and Great Britain. In 1911, after a brief war against Turkey, he acquired Libya. It's true that during the First World War he had at first tried to keep his country neutral, but in 1915 he finally took his country into battle. On our side, I am pleased to say. He was as yet to claim the titles of Emperor of Ethiopia and King of Albania.

But after the First World War, when every country in Europe was flirting with dictatorship, the king followed the trend and refused to oppose the fascist march on Rome. In 1922 he asked Mussolini to form a government. Not that he had much choice; Benito had just won a general election.

Every country? Yes, even in England. But Mosley never managed to break through. Most level-headed people considered the British Union of Fascists and its various communist equivalents ridiculous. When P G Wodehouse took the mickey out of Spode and his 'Black Shorts' in *The Code of the Woosters*, the cause of British fascism was lost.

Back in Italy, and by way of returning the compliment, the 'modernising' fascist government allowed Victor Emmanuel to remain, but only as a constitutional monarch. Even with his powers curtailed, he was still too powerful to ignore. In 1943, when the Fascist Grand Council voted against continued support of Mussolini, the King dismissed the dictator, placed him under arrest and named Pietro Badoglio, 'the Duke of Addis Abbaba', prime minister. The King, that May, handed all royal prerogatives to his son, Prince Umberto of Savoy, though not yet the crown itself. Umberto was styled 'Lieutenant-Governor of Italy' during this period.

In 1943, Badoglio and his Lieutenant-Governor severed the Axis with Germany. They capitulated to the Allies and offered up the soldiery to the anti-Nazi cause. The Americans refused this handsome gesture, pending the final, unconditional surrender of the Axis. This put Italy in a very difficult position. The Germans now saw the Italians as traitors and frequently attacked their troops on their journey home. The Allies tended to capture the Italians and send them to prisoner-of-war camps, ostensibly to keep them out of harm's way. In the meantime, the Americans landed in Sicily and prepared to drive the Germans out of the country. Their greater concern, however, was to prevent the communists from taking power. Their first action therefore was to release all the Mafiosi that Mussolini had imprisoned and make them mayors, in exchange for a guarantee of the 'gentle' suppression of the communists, many of whom had fought with the resistance.

These were not good times for Italy. The old King, as Rome had not yet been liberated from the German occupation, headed along the Appian Way to the south-east of his country where the Allies had already driven the Germans out. The Americans were demanding his abdication. In the face of such opposition, the King would bow to *realpolitik*.

After the 'armistice' of 8 September 1943, the entire system of government, including the Ministry of Foreign Affairs, fell into deep crisis. The King spent the best part of the next year effectively in internal exile in Brindisi, and the few officials who managed to reach the King's government in the south-east set up a makeshift foreign office and declared the Adriatic port to be the capital of Italy.

An American general was sent to the 'capital' from time to time to ask after the health of the King and Queen. It is said that the only favour the Queen asked of the American was access to a modest supply of fresh eggs. Not until June 1944 was the capital returned to Rome.

In 1943 Crown Princess Maria José, the daughter of Albert I of Belgium, was secretly recruited by the Italian royal house to try to arrange a working peace treaty between Italy and the United States. She persuaded a senior Vatican official, Monsignor Giovanni Battista Montini, to act as intermediary. The envoy was later to be better known as Pope Paul VI. Washington DC, as always, rejected these overtures.

In June 1946 the American-sponsored plebiscite was actually held. The referendum itself was and remains shrouded by questions concerning its legitimacy. The Royal Italian Army was either in prisoner-of-war camps or was sulkily stuck in military camps in territories about to be returned to local management. Millions of ordinary voters, many of them pro-monarchist, were unable to vote because they had not been allowed to return to their own local areas to register. Neither had the issue of Italy's borders, nor the voting rights of those in disputed areas, been satisfactorily clarified. There was an implicit threat from Washington that if the monarchy were not rejected all American aid would be terminated immediately. Allegations have also been made about voter manipulation, while even the issue of how to interpret the votes became controversial, as it appeared that not just a majority of those validly voting but of those votes cast, including spoiled papers, was needed to reach an outcome.

In the event the monarchy lost by a narrow margin. Umberto had by this stage been crowned king, his father having reluctantly and belatedly abdicated the throne a few weeks before.

Well, the Americans won their referendum, and Italy today is a republic. Victor Emmanuel III died in exile in Cairo. His son Umberto, Il Re di Maggio,[6] king for just a month, flew into exile in Portugal from Ciampino in 1946. He died in 1983. He was the last of the Savoyards to have ruled, and his death happened in the 999th year of the royal house. His son, Victor Emmanuel IV, was born in Naples in 1937 and is the pretender. He lives in Monaco. His own son, Emmanuele Filiberto, was born in 1972.

American plans for a US-style democracy backfired some-what, as they always do. Before following his father into exile, Umberto called for the required general election that, with the monarchists unable to vote, promptly returned the only commu-nist government ever to be responsibly elected in Europe. The Americans thought this a worse result than the status ante and cut off their aid anyway. For a time, only Lucky Luciano and his American Mafia came to the rescue – apart, that is, from the thousands of money orders and food parcels sent home from the vast diaspora of waiters, ice cream vendors and factory workers in Germany, France, Britain and even the US.

Happily, Italian communism was not an evil empire, unlike that of Russia and its client states, but a sort of secular debating society, rather keen on long and pompous meetings late into the night. Rather like British trade unions, in fact.

The Christian Democrats took over in the fifties and, more or less, they have remained in power ever since. Despite the frequent

[6] The 'King of May'. He ruled from 9 May to 12 June 1946.

elections – something like ninety since 1946, or an election on average every nine months – this party has effectively governed the country for the last half century, making the country more conservative than any other in Europe except, if you will allow, the old Soviet Union.

'I liked the Bernini elephant,' said Kate, as we came out of the Pantheon into the spring sunlight. 'What else has Bernini done in Rome? Didn't he do the great square in front of St Peter's?'

It was time for lunch and we headed off to da Pepe's. We had a simple meal – *fagiolini al tonno* followed by *costolette d'agnello*, with a carafe of local wine. As I recall we spoke a little about Bernini, but much more about traffic, roads and motorbikes. I had not realised until that time that Kate had a thing about motorbikes.

'I thought I liked Vincents, or maybe Nortons, but these Italian bikes are serious machines. Can we hire one after lunch? Oh, please...'

Well, it would be churlish not to. We found a bike hire shop easily enough and the lies we told about Kate's age did not trouble our consciences over much. The real problem was that neither of us had a driving licence, so we were rather restricted to 50cc mopeds. Still, these were Italian mopeds and looked like Harley Davidsons. They made a creditable racket and very soon we were careering unsteadily through the streets of Rome.

'Let's go to St Peter's and look at the Bernini piazza,' shouted Kate, as we raced along the Pincio. 'I've seen a sign. Follow me!'

So I did, even though it meant riding down a great flight of steps into Piazza del Popolo.

'Come on, hurry up!' shouted Kate. Despite the fact that I was still shuddering like a jelly, I did what I was told. I stepped on the gas.

Suddenly we were at the Via Giulia, and then over the Tiber at the Ponte Sant' Angelo, a pedestrian footbridge.

We could not go wrong. Michelangelo's great dome of St Peter's rose above Rome, drawing us into its hemisphere. Before we knew it we were roaring the wrong way along the Via della Conciliazione, past the 'No Entry' signs and into the Piazza San Pietro itself, where we stopped for a moment.

We knew we were safe from Italian police, now that we were

in the Sacred City of the Vatican. But what about the Swiss Guards? They looked cuddly enough in their Michelangelo uniforms, but they might all be marksmen.

In 1972, the world was reasonably short on terrorists. True, the IRA was blowing things up in England with monotonous frequency. ETA was blowing up policemen and admirals in Madrid. The Red Brigades were kneecapping economics students in Bologna University and were planning to murder their prime minister. The Peruvian 'Shining Path' was deeply worrying. The Holy Land, as ever, was not a comfortable place to make whoopy, and next door the Lebanon was merrily considering the possibility of civil war. 'Weathermen' terrorised the US, and the American government had just finished shooting its students at Kent State University. The Baader Meinhof gang was having fun in Germany and it was only four years since the CRS in Paris had been beating up students and Arabs with impartial enthusiasm. As I said, all quiet on the western front.

No need, therefore, in 1972 at least, for a 'War on Terror', for extended phone tapping, imprisonment without trial, concrete blocks outside the Palace of Westminster, concentration camps at Belmarsh and Guantanamo... but I digress. The Swiss Guards were probably not on an extreme level of readiness.

They are an odd lot, these Swiss Guards. It is the only regiment in the world where the officers are from a lower social stratum than the men. The men, you see, are all volunteers from the greatest, noblest Swiss families. It is an almost hereditary privilege to serve in this regiment, which they do for minimal pay. Meanwhile the officers are merely professional soldiers, drawn from people with talent, rather than coats of arms, and happily receive the generous Swiss military stipend. It must make for the most extraordinary tensions.

As we sat there, we could see three or four of them in the great colonnaded circular piazza in front of us. They seemed to be carrying halberds, or some such ancient instrument of war. Around them milled pilgrims and nuns, busloads of tourists, the holy and the sinful, the usual constituents of God's people.

Kate smiled at me and revved her bike a little.

'Ever scared a nun?' she asked.

'Now, Kate…' I began.

'C'mon, Jeremy, you said how you liked to go round and round the squares of Rome. Now's your chance.'

And with that she set off, passing the sign saying ABSOLUTELY NO CARS OR MOTORBIKES into the immense cobbled forecourt of the largest cathedral ever built,[7] with me just behind her, scattering the faithful like an old-fashioned Protestant at a Spanish procession.

We did two whole turns of the square. We sent convocations of nuns to the four winds. We narrowly escaped collision with a host of pilgrims from the Philippines. Our blood was up as we aimed for a party of English travellers, replete in their tweed skirts and jackets, and we waited almost till impact before we turned away. But before we could execute a *tour d'honneur*, we heard police whistles.

That concentrated our minds rather and we remembered that discretion can be the better option. Before the police actually came to cart us off to Regina Coeli, Rome's infamous high security prison, we were off into Trastevere, to a café in the Piazza Santa Maria where, like tearaways everywhere and always, we felt immensely pleased with ourselves.

---

[7] Or is that title owned by the great church in Seville?

Chapter the Eleventh
1972: Tales from Tivoli

In which the author, with his sister, continues to explore Italy, and now travels to Tivoli, a charming hilltop town half an hour from Rome. They visit the sights and eat a phenomenal meal, for which the restaurateur strangely refuses to accept any money. What on earth is the reason?

History means remembering long-standing debts, and some of them are still outstanding, waiting to be repaid.

I looked at my watch. If we were to get to Tivoli it was time to go now. From Rome's Piazza della Rotonda it's a full ten minutes' walk to the central bus station. I checked my wallet and discovered that there was very little in it. Not because I wasn't earning enough – my little guided tours and the teaching job with my RAI director were both good payers – but I never seemed to have enough cash, as such.

'Look,' I warned my sister, who had just pitched up, 'I am rather short on readies. We can always eat on my credit at da Pepe when we get back' – I had persuaded Pepe to accept my signature – 'but we will have to make do with a bowl of pasta in Tivoli. Will that be all right?'

My sister was at that age when a girl needs three square meals a day, but she bowed to the inevitable.

'Well, I will want the full treatment at da Pepe when we get back. All the courses. Lots of wine. But OK, let's go to Tivoli.'

We had managed an early start and were ready for our adventure. Tivoli is less than an hour from Rome to the north-east. Plenty of time to case the joint before lunch.

Well, I underestimated Tivoli.

According to my guidebook, the Touring Club Italiano's

unsurpassed *Roma e d'Intorni*,[1] it is a picturesque and lively city. I'd say that undersells it. 'Show-stopping' might be a better phrase.

The little city sits high on a plateau in the Ripoli Hills in a sort of geological fold. Its river, the Aniene, is completely baffled by this and has to find its way around the town via a succession of waterfalls and cascades. Kate and I climbed down from our bus in the busy main square and made for the large fountain to get our bearings. The view was enchanting. We could see for miles out over the Roman Campania and in the distance we could even make out the domes and campanili of Rome itself.

Very sadly, American bombers, who mounted twenty-two raids on the town between December 1943 and June 1944, blew almost half the town away. This is doubly sad when you recall that six months before, in May 1943, the King of Italy had surrendered to the Americans and had even offered the Royal Italian Army to the Allies. The Americans seem to have considered this as merely a *beau geste*. The Germans were still there after all. 'If the enemy is hiding in a church,' goes the logic of the new Romans from across the water, 'tough for the church.' Tivoli was of course rebuilt after the war but the new buildings are disappointing. Such are the fortunes of war.

Perhaps the bomber pilots and their masters did not know or care that the delights of this little town had been known since antiquity? Would it have made a difference had they been aware that Catullus had lived there? Or Horace? Or Trajan? Most particularly, the Emperor Hadrian built his 'villa' there – more of a private town, really – as his imperial retreat. A millennium later, Otto the Big established his seat there. But enough, already, I can hear you say. Kate and I were there to see the Villa d'Este.

The Villa d'Este is really a country house, except that it is almost in the middle of town. It had been a Benedictine monastery until the thirteenth century, when a mayor took it over as his town hall. But the real fun began when Cardinal Ippolito II d'Este took over the management of Tivoli in 1550. The Villa, already impressive, became both his home and a marvel.

For generation after generation, the d'Este family adorned the place. Almost every month for hundreds of years they added a

---

[1] *Rome and its Surroundings.*

statue here or an arch there, but it all had to come to an end. In 1914 the lights went out all over Europe and the line could do no more.

After the Great War the Villa passed to the Italian State.

Kate and I loved the house, with its 'modernised' monastic courtyard (modernised in the 1550s with three classical porticos and a fountain representing a sleeping Venus). The old cardinal had built himself a private 'apartment' inside the principal wing: a suite of ten or so rooms with frescoed ceilings. The Roman custodians had furnished them with suitable paintings and furniture. One of the rooms is a throne room, another a private chapel. Too many modern flats fail to include these vital features.

But it is the garden of the Villa d'Este that leaves the firmest imprint on your memory. It is breathtaking, both in conception and location. It is nothing less than the finest garden in Italy surviving to this day.

It's not just the stupendous plants and shrubs, though these would blow the mind of any halfway ambitious gardener. For Kate and me, it was the 500 fountains that grabbed our attention. Everywhere you look, there are fountains, large and small, playing fantastic games with their water, fusing nature and art in an unforgettable way.

The whole thing is made yet more memorable by the noise the whole thing makes; a deep note decorated with a treble descant – loud enough to drown out the sounds of the nearby streets yet producing a haunting aquatic melody. The path called the Avenue of a Hundred Fountains drones almost imperceptibly. A magnificent fountain dedicated to Bacchus seems to chuckle. Another, the Owl and the Birds, has been designed to play a birdsong cantata on some sort of watery organ.

The cardinal had built his own private aqueduct, more than a kilometre long, specifically to divert from the river the water he personally needed. He was a Roman after all. Might as well do these things in style.

It was still early when Kate and I came out of the Villa and into the town to find a café. We found one in the Via Campitelli, where we debated what to see next.

'Let's do the Temple of Vesta,' said Kate.

'OK,' I replied.

That is how debate between men and women is and always has been throughout the ages.

Now, there is a lot to see in Tivoli, and you should go there. These modest recollections are no substitute for a decent guidebook. But though it means breaking my rule, I must tell you about the Temple of Vesta.

This little temple, some will have it, is not Vesta's at all, but rather belongs to the Sibyl. There are others who think it was offered to Hercules. The truth is, no one really knows, and it's not for me to pick a fight with anyone on this subject. Everyone agrees it was built in the last years of the Roman Republic – that is, the time before the generals, or more properly, emperors, took control of ancient Rome.

Whatever the truth may be, it is a small but outstanding circular shrine on a precipitous rock perfectly sited to dominate the deep valley of the Villa Gregoriana below. The Villa Gregoriana, by the way, is not a country house, but a sensational semi-natural park.

The temple had once boasted eighteen slim, elegant columns, finished with Corinthian capitals. Ten of them remain. Above them, a decorated circular stone (or 'trabeation') is carved with period favourites – bulls' skulls, triglyphs, and all the usual designs.

It was converted to Christian worship at some point in the early Middle Ages, which would have saved it from being quarried for its stone. Perhaps its intrinsic beauty held the vandals at bay. In 1828 it was very nearly sold and dismantled; an English 'gentleman' wanted it in his back garden, but mercifully this act of cultural looting was somehow prevented.

Kate and I had a full head of steam by now. We first saw the 'small' waterfall of the Villa Gregoriana below us and walked through the strange arcades that have been carved into the cliffs on either side of it, taking in stupendous grottoes on our way to a sort of parapet, projecting out over the floor of the valley hundreds of feet below, from which we could see the second cascade of angry water.

Halfway up the Grand Cascade we found a belvedere, from which the entirety of the natural spectacle held us dazzled, and where the huge torrent splashed us as it might at the Victoria or Niagara Falls. The landscape bucked and reared like a stallion, the cicadas played their insect symphony and all the while hibiscus and bougainvillea suffused the atmosphere with their overpowering perfumes.

Hadrian's Villa, when we finally arrived there, was no disappointment. After 2,000 years, it remains a semi-preserved imperial villa, a Roman mile in length, or a little less than a kilometre: the Romans had short legs. At one end there is a near perfectly preserved 'Greek' theatre, a riding school and a nympheum; at the other a temple to Apollo, a bathing lake and a *praetorium*, or guardroom, designed to billet a hundred men. Somewhere at its core a huge library presides, with two vast sections for Latin and Greek literature, plus the odd acre of rooms for the personal use of the Emperor.

'If Gulbenkian did this sort of thing with his all money I might feel better disposed towards him,' I told my sister, sniffily. Gulbenkian, 'Mr 5 per cent', was the 1970s equivalent of Bill Gates. He had done a deal with the Middle East oil producers, worth 5 per cent of all their oil revenues. One can jog along on that sort of income.

Hadrian's Villa is the vastest and the richest of the surviving imperial Roman villas. The whole complex of baths, mansions, lyceum, stables and fishponds was built in the second century. The Emperor clearly intended to enjoy himself here, and he 'chose' to die here, aged seventy-three, in AD 138.

After him, successive emperors did the place up a bit, but the barbarians, when they came, undid all the good work and the place began to fall into disrepair. Eventually it suffered the ultimate indignity of being quarried for its stone. Some statues were saved and carted off to various papal collections and, at the time of the Renaissance, some of these were returned to their original locations. But despite the destruction and dilapidations, the sense of scale has not been damaged; nor yet its majesty.

There is only one modern building there, apart from the ticket booth. It is a bar.

The sun was hot and the hour late when Kate and I settled down to rest for a few minutes. Kate, bless her, went for the iced tea. I adsorbed a Nastro Azurro, the best of the mass-produced Italian beers, and only now appearing on the world map.

I checked my wallet again. We had bought so many admission tickets, beers here and teas there, that I was seriously low on funds. I separated from the little sum the cost of our bus tickets home and counted the rest.

'Look, Kate, we have precious little indeed, but we may have just enough for a simple bowl of pasta if we can find somewhere still open at three o'clock. How does the idea grab you?'

'If I don't eat right now you're in real trouble,' replied my easy-going sister.

So we got up and walked back towards Tivoli, hoping to find a *trattoria*, or *osteria*, that might help us out. The food in Rome and its Campagna[2] is always good. It's just that some restaurants are classier than others. A top one will be a *ristorante*, after that a *trattoria* and lastly an *osteria*. That might be restaurant, bistro and café in English.

We got very lost and it was nearly an hour later, in a run-down part of the town, when we came across a bar with a few old boys outside playing dominoes.

'I'm not going in there!' protested Kate. 'They have never seen a woman before except the odd nun. I'm not dressed for it.'

'I'll go and check,' I said, tacitly agreeing with both theses: that it looked fairly unlikely that we would get anywhere, and with Kate's assessment of her very un-nun-like apparel.

There was not a customer inside, but I asked anyway.

The landlord looked at me oddly.

'Where are you from?' he asked directly.

'England. My sister and I are studying here.'

'Come on in. I'll sort you both out.'

But we still had to deal with the difficult bit. The money, or our lack of it. At times like these it's best to take a dilemma by its horns.

'I'm afraid we have very little money. Here it is, all of it. Do you think you can manage two bowls of pasta for this, with maybe a glass of water?'

---

[2] This is a Roman way of saying 'campania romana'. I prefer it to the more orthodox 'Lazio', or Latium.

The landlord looked at me steadily, and across to my sister who was by the door and had pulled the plastic strips slightly to one side. Cheap Italian restaurants often use strips of plastic or metal chains to allow a draught but stop the insects from entering.

'I think I can. Go through that door. You will find a table. Sit down, my wife will rustle up something for you.'

Well, we did as we were told. And it wasn't long before our host reappeared with a couple of plates, a basket of bread and a dish of Parma ham.

We immediately protested.

'We can't do this. We have too little money.'

'I bring you your pasta in a minute,' he said. 'This is my present to the young English couple.'

Well, he left and Kate and I looked at each other. What were we to do? We couldn't refuse it, could we? We were ravenous and he was nuts. But, all things considered, that was OK with us. So we tucked in.

A few seconds later, while we were enthusiastically stuffing our faces, he reappeared, this time with a carafe of wine.

'It's from my cousin's vineyard. It is young, but it is good.'

We spluttered our protests but he paid no attention and was gone. I tasted the wine. He was right. It was seriously good.

'That may have something to do with it,' observed my sister, pointing at one of the gloomy etchings on the wall. I stood up and carried my glass over to take a closer look. It was a large mezzotint of Queen Victoria.

'Unusual to see Her Madge in Italy,' I said, sitting down again.

Kate may have been about to say something but our host interrupted her by now appearing with a great bowl of *vermicelli alla puttanesca*, which he served us at our table. He produced a small cut glass bowl full of Parmesan cheese for us to sprinkle and took the empty carafe away. Kate and I shouted our thanks at the retreating figure.

We tucked into the pasta as if there were no tomorrow. It was obviously freshly made, and the whole thing was proving to be the best meal either of us had ever had. When he returned with the carafe refilled we were no longer amazed and simply mumbled our thanks, our mouths full of Roman excellence.

We had finished everything on the table, including the second carafe, when the door opened again. This time it was our host's wife. She was carrying a great aluminium dish of veal escalopes – *scallopine al limone.*

Again Kate and I protested.

Our hostess said, '*Non caspisco gnente.*' To my skinny sister, she said, '*Va, màgnane un po. Te annerà ben.*' This was like no Italian I had ever heard. But the meaning was clear. We were to tuck in.

A new carafe, this time of a drier wine, appeared, and soon a plumper version of my sister and me were sitting by our empty plates, hardly able to move, wondering what had hit us.

Cheese, cake, coffee, some sort of liqueur, all these things came in their preordained order. We protested each course, but to no avail. These people were determined to feed two tourists who had clearly explained that they had almost no money.

But why?

I thought it best not to ask. Something about gift horses. But Kate had struggled to her feet and was looking at the other engravings on the wall.

'This one's Cavour,' she said. No great surprise there. He was the statesman who almost single-handedly unified Italy under the House of Savoy. He was also the publisher of *Il Risorgimento*, the nineteenth-century underground newspaper that was itself discreetly supported by the British.

'This one's Lord John Russell. And look, here is Palmerston. And Peel. Here's your answer, boyo.'

The pieces of the jigsaw puzzle were beginning to fit into place.

My sister was the family historian, then on her way to Oxford, and the nineteenth century was, and is, her period. I asked her to explain the long and bloody process to me.

'It all began after the dust settled at Waterloo. Pretty well everybody thought that the hundreds of petty European states might be unified under a much smaller number of constitutional governments, broadly defined by the language they spoke. Most commentators and politicians shared the new economic and liberal political ideals that had grown out of the French Revolution of 1789. Italian intellectuals seem to have been the first to pick up the gauntlet.'

'Just in Europe?' I asked her, sipping at my sambuca.

'No, not just in Europe. Washington's government was bea-vering away with its draft constitution. But it was in Italy, Germany, Russia and France where the ideas of the eighteenth-century reformers and *illuminati* really took hold.'

'In Britain, I suppose we sat on the sidelines and complained, as we always do?'

'No, we were anything but insular in those days. From the first, George Canning lent his support to all of these movements. We channelled funds, resources and encouragement into these romantic causes. The Risorgimento might even have failed had it not been for our great Tory statesmen.' She gestured at the engravings on the walls.

'Sir Robert Peel and Lord John Russell?'

'And my Lord Palmerston.' She raised her glass to the etchings.

'What caused all those revolutions of 1848?'

'Well, there had been revolutionary pressure for some time, all over Europe. The Italians simply started the ball rolling. What we now call the Italian Risorgimento began in earnest in Sicily, in January 1848. Just days later, in the northern states of Piedmont-Sardinia, Lombardy and Venetia, the people took to the streets against their Austrian or Italian rulers.'

'Was the *ancien régime* quite defenceless?'

'Of course not. At the first sign of trouble, the Bourbon King of Naples, Ferdinand II, allied himself with Pope Pius IX, and together they condemned the attacks on Austria. As a result, fledgling plans for a common Italian army collapsed. The liberal Charles Albert of Savoy, King of Piedmont-Sardinia, withdrew from the cause after a couple of military defeats at the hands of the Austrian Count Radetzky. That left the revolutionaries, mainly in central Italy and Venice, to fight on by themselves.'

'I'm surprised that the French or the Austrians didn't wander over the Alps for a scrap themselves.'

'You know jolly well the French did exactly that. In the sum-mer of 1849 a French army took the infant Roman Republic by force. May I refer you to *Tosca* for further details?'

'And the Austrians?'

'The Austrians, too. In August 1849 Venice finally fell to Radetzky and the Austro-Hungarian Empire.'

'So the fat lady sang.'

'Eh? Oh I see. But no, it wasn't all over. It's just that everyone now realised that the movement needed more than naive enthusiasm. It needed a dose of pragmatism and diplomacy.'

'Enter Count Cavour, stage left.'

'During the 1850s Cavour led the movement from Turin, having created an intellectual forum in his newspaper, *Il Risorgimento*. This quickly gave the high ground to the constitutionalists. The firebrands (especially Garibaldi) fell from favour, at least outside their semi-fanatical circles.'

'Ah, the press deciding policy again! If only they would just report the news.'

'Well, perhaps, but this time it worked. A fledgling Italian kingdom, united under a royal tricolour and a single government, was delivered to its people in 1861.'

'The Italy we know and love was born?'

'Yes, but the birth was premature and the child still sickly. What sort of union would it be without Venice or the Papal States?'

'You say that we supported the Italians. I suppose we thought of our own United Kingdom as a role model for the Risorgimento?'

'I imagine we did. We English had already rejected a formal constitution, arguing that our body of common law already served as one. But we did force a single language on the Scots, the Irish and the Welsh, emphasising a unified nationhood. We started to revive the word "British" from around this time. But for the Italians, however, the Risorgimento meant freedom from foreign control first, and the introduction of liberalism and constitution-alism second.'

'You keep coming back to constitutionalism. What's so important about a written constitution?'

'Mostly, the function of a constitution is to guarantee personal liberty and rights. The political bits – whether the new country should be a confederation or should be centralised – entailed a lot more debate. In Italy there was also disagreement on whether the newly united country should be a republic or a monarchy.'

'They solved all these issues? Without a civil war?'

'That was down to the genius of Cavour. What he highlighted

in his newspaper was that the radicals distrusted the moderates, centralists disagreed with federalists, and that republicans liked to insult the monarchists. People could see that all this public quarrelling only served to undermine attempts to build a new nation. Italy needed an Italian Legion, or common army, it needed a preliminary constitution applicable to all parts of Italy, and a united front against common enemies, if it were not to fall apart.'

'Their principal enemy, in the most immediate sense, was the brilliant Austrian Marshal Radetzky, I suppose?'

'Hole in one! The very same whose march Johan Strauss has us all twirling for.'

'OK, so tell me about these good fellows on the wall.'

'Right, let's start with Cavour. From about 1852 Count Camillo Benso di Cavour, at that time Prime Minister of Piedmont-Sardinia, began to correspond with Russell, Peel, Palmerston and Disraeli. Cavour was an Olympian, all right; witty, cautious and uncommonly shrewd. He published much of his correspondence in his newspaper.'

'*Il Risorgimento?*'

'Quite. He used the very real menace of further revolutions or civil war to convince his more conservative colleagues that Italy could be united under the House of Savoy, the dynasty of Piedmont-Sardinia.'

'Why Savoy?'

'Easy. Piedmont-Sardinia was then the only Italian state that already had a constitution. It had had an elected parliament since 1849 and this fact alone was persuasive. Most of the other nationalist leaders concurred, with the important exception of Mazzini and his hothead 'democrats', who continued to believe in a popular uprising.'

'And our British role?'

'By 1859 Cavour had successfully negotiated the diplomatic support of the British (and it must be admitted, the French, despite their temporary alliance with the papacy) in order to fight against Austria. He secured the support of the Italian National Society[3] and, frankly, provoked a conflict. This was exactly the

---

[3] A coalition of non-Mazzinian nationalists.

sort of cause that Palmerston and these others adored. They were all for it, in the same way that they had supported the 'British' Don Pacifico in Athens with a battle fleet. The cabinet, especially Peel and Russell, ensured that Britain stayed neutral in the military sense, but not financially. In the end, Austria was forced to cede Lombardy to Piedmont-Sardinia.'

'OK, that's Cavour and the British. What about Garibaldi? You've hardly even mentioned him.'

'Garibaldi was making some headway from the south of the country, supported by his Thousand. They unseated the Bourbons in the south. But he was pre-empted by Cavour, on 12 March 1861, when the Kingdom of Italy was proclaimed in Turin (the capital of Piedmont-Sardinia) by a parliament of representatives from all over Italy.'

'Sorry to interrupt. All of Italy?'

'All of Italy, except Venetia, which remained under Austrian rule until 1866, and the City of Rome, which stayed under papal control until 1870. But once the Papal States, excluding Rome itself, were in the venture, the path was clear to declare Rome the capital of Italy, which finally happened in 1872.'

'Exactly a hundred years ago this year.'

'Precisely. You may have cracked it.'

By 1872 the full Risorgimento of the Italian people had been achieved. And a century later, more or less to the day, Kate and I were looking at these fading engravings in a working-class hostelry in the wrong part of Tivoli, having been treated to a feast befitting an English milord and milady.

We finished the grapes and drained the last drops of grappa from our glasses. As for that pittance we had to pay for the meal, we had no idea what we should do with it. In fact, I still don't.

What we actually did was hide it under the tablecloth.

We composed ourselves and, leaving the private room, went into the body of the *osteria*. We shook hands, rather formally, with the landlord and with his wife. We muttered our infinite thanks. And we were gone.

A very long-standing debt had been repaid, to a chance English couple, who had unwittingly stood in for Lord Palmerston and his queen.

Chapter the Twelfth
1972: Life in Sicily

In which the author continues to explore Italy, now travelling to Sicily, where he lets the journey last a fortnight. He sees the famous sights, or some of them, and discovers the favourite wines of ancient Rome. He meets a poetic taxidermist, explores an underground coliseum, and is joined by a great friend from England.

'Have you ever been to Sicily?'

When Daniele, one of my fellow students at the Scuola degli Interpreti, suggested a week at his people's home in Catania, it was an offer I could not refuse.

At that time I suppose I associated Sicily with the Mafia, perhaps with Nelson's fortified farmhouse at Taormina, and definitely with Garibaldi. I also knew about the dangerous volcano at Mount Etna. I had always wanted to go, having of course heard that the island was enchanting in its special way. I thought to myself that if I was going to go at all, I might as well do the thing properly. I bought the guides and rang around. I even put in a call to beautiful Arianna, a girl who was becoming very special to me, albeit from afar, who had already told me that she had family reasons to go there.

I was determined from the outset to transform a week's house party into an epic two-week adventure.

For some reason I didn't wish to be sociable on the train. I put on a suit (wearing a suit is always the best way to carry it) and had my copy of *The Origin of Species* to hide behind. My progress with this book had been slow. Maybe on the long journey I would discover why I was a fool to consider the spiritual and intellectual far more important to selection than the carnal and venal. Darwin's animals seemed to have been made for all the wrong reasons.

I stood on the platform in Rome waiting for the Reggio train to pull in. It would pull out again twenty minutes later, but I had been advised to get there early if I didn't want to stand all the way.

The train came sedately alongside the platform, gradually slowing to walking pace. But this was not the 7.13 a.m. into Waterloo. At five miles per hour, all its doors sprang open. The very second it was safe to jump, the train discharged its human cargo, like a dog shaking off the rain. The passengers launched themselves straight at us and I was foolish enough to stand back for an instant. Half a dozen nuns instantly took my place on the platform's edge. Within moments the stampede was out and away. Empty of its human cargo, the train still juddering to a final halt, the outward bound started to board the train.

Boarding this train was, perhaps still is, one of the black arts. It takes at least two people to secure a seat: one to leap on the train, pushing anyone else who is trying to do the same out of the way. The other must hurl the luggage – suitcases, rucksacks, baskets of live chickens – through the open windows. The one who is already inside picks up the luggage and spreads it over the seats that he and his extended family intend to occupy.

I was now in acute pain, one of the nuns having elbowed me out of her way rather too sharply, but I persevered and forced my way on. The nearest compartment to the door had a Sicilian family already ensconced and they were proprietarily opening their hamper and organising lunch. I was forced into their company by the throng behind me, and retreat was not physically possible. I pointed to the seat by the window, apparently not taken.

'*Posso?*'

'*Ma va! Come no? Si siede, pure.*'[1]

So I sat down. Surprisingly, I had a window seat. The train had stood in the station for under half a minute and was already full. The corridors were filled to bursting with cheerful lads (mainly) who knew they would stand the whole six-hour journey. Perhaps they would work some kind of roster with their friends. I wouldn't put it past them.

I shook hands with my fellow travellers, who exuded a collec-

---

[1] 'May I?' – 'Of course, please take a seat.'

tive rustic dignity. The oldest shawl-enwrapped female was in charge of the food, and her elderly weather-beaten husband was in charge of the wine. A demure young daughter had the mineral water and her husband had bought tins of pop for the three grandchildren. A rap on the window from a sandwich vendor on a bicycle gave us the chance to buy anything we might have forgotten. I declined his offer, for no good reason. Did I really believe I could get through the crowds to a hypothetical restaurant car? I must have been mad.

Despite my suit and my book, the Sicilians were not going to leave me alone.

The smallest of the children began my interrogation.

'Is that how you speak Italian in England?' she asked. 'And have you met the Queen?'

In this the Italians have much in common with the Americans.

The paterfamilias now bent forward in a confidential way.

'This man on the moon,' he began, 'It's not true, is it? The Americans have made it all up?'

The journey, which would begin in another quarter of an hour, was shaping up well.

It was difficult to form a detached opinion of these generous people as I tucked into their food and drank their wine on the long journey south. Again and again it crossed my mind that I had met similar people in the west of Ireland, or in Scotland.

Their willingness to share their food with me, together with a concomitant insistence that in exchange I join in with their family wholeheartedly, was touching and instructive.

They pressed me on some issues of our way of life in England. The Queen, I learned, paid all our medical expenses. If only their old king had done something similar they would not have had to become Italians. We had a sense of society, the way politics had advocated in their old Greek days. A sort of civic pride that they could learn from. No one ever dropped litter in England.

I would have hated to disillusion them.

What I felt at first to be a delightful informality was, however, nothing of the kind; their inclusion of this unfortunate single man, with no kin to look after him, was not more nor less than their formal duty. If any of them were travelling in England, alone and a long way from home, wouldn't my people take them in, do the Christian thing?

This idea of generosity spoke volumes about the hardships they must have suffered, not just over a few short years but over the long centuries.

The Sicilians are an island race too, and that came through very clearly. They had a loyalty to each other that surpassed any division of class or wealth that might apply on the more ambitious and successful mainland. While these were 'ordinary' people, they had cousins who were 'professors' and who knew people in the local government. As this word (professor) covers the whole gamut of academe from primary school teacher to emeritus professor of astrophysics, it is linguistically uninformative.

They were never ill. And the grandmother could paint. They were grand people, albeit living simply, due to the way God allocated His favours.

The wine came from a friend's, or cousin's, vineyard near Palermo. What did I think of it? Was it not as fine as Chianti or Barolo? Why could it not get its DOC, its appellation?

I tasted it more carefully. I learned that, like most Sicilian reds, it was made from the nero d'avola grape. It had balance and good length. It had been well aged in oak, for perhaps a year, but it was still a young wine. We were probably drinking it decanted straight from the vat. Yet it was fit for the gods. I knew the ancient Romans had appreciated Sicilian wines, though I had not knowingly drunk one myself before that time. I readily fell in with the old man. It was indeed tragic this wine was not more widely known.

'Better than your English wines, I'll bet,' he said proudly.

'No contest,' I happily agreed.

How short the journey seemed! Within what seemed like minutes we were at Reggio di Calabria, where most of us were bound for the ferry to Messina in Sicily.

Sadly, I lost my new friends on the boat, for they were surrounded by literally dozens of friends and neighbours, all with stories to tell. Instead I found a little bar on board and had a coffee. I felt oddly isolated in a way I seldom did. Was the strange sadness I suddenly felt the result of my mind having been broadened?

I had an hour or two to kill before my onward train to Catania, so I took in the Messina museum. Sadly I had not the time to do that exquisite little place and its Caravaggios justice, and soon I was back on board, pulling out of the rather quaint little station and on my way south. The track ran alongside the coast almost all the way, passing names steeped in history – Taormina, Acireale to my left, the great mass of Mount Etna to my right.

And at Catania railway station my student friend, Daniele Catanagni, met me, with his father and sister. After the usual concerns that I had not eaten enough or might be in need of coffee or water or even a beer, I was swept off to their fortified farmhouse on the slopes of the volcano overlooking the sprawling city of Catania itself, capital of eastern Sicily.

We sipped our iced tea that afternoon on the 'lawn' in front of their ancient house. It wasn't really a lawn. Only the extremely rich have lawns in the English sense in Sicily. The water is far too scarce. But the Sicilians have found some green ground cover that is very nearly as good. Wear shoes, though.

It occurred to me to ask about this brooding hill behind them. It is still active. In winter people ski on it; in summer they stare anxiously or resignedly over the crater's edge into the sulphurous smoke below. In modern times there had not been too many eruptions, I was reassured, but the volcano had a fickle temperament. Lava flows and earthquakes had got as far as Catania on several occasions. In 1169 Catania had been almost completely destroyed by a particularly violent earthquake. Exactly 500 years later a particularly destructive volcanic eruption took place that had practically taken out Catania. And adding insult to injury, before the town had been completely rebuilt, it was followed in 1693 by yet another devastating earthquake. The most recent eruption had been thirty years before my visit, which must have let the pressure off the thing for a little while.

'Time for another?' I asked.

'Another iced tea?' These Sicilians have a sangfroid to impress the stiffest upper lip.

'We have a real treat for you tomorrow,' said my friend Daniele. 'We have managed to get permission to visit the "secret" amphitheatre. Almost impossible to get. You are going to find this unforgettable.'

Catania, it seemed, has three ancient theatres. There is a small one, built on an earlier Greek theatre, which is open to the public. In its day it could accommodate as many as 6,000 spectators.

The Odeum, not far away, is an even smaller theatre, which could hold about 1,300.

But the largest amphitheatre was probably able to seat some 14,000 spectators, and was right in the centre of town. It was a completely Roman structure, built in the second century AD. Only a small part of is actually visible today; lava and the passage of time have meant that most of it is now below ground. Buried it may be, but it is still vast and, exploring its underground network of passages and rhythmically repeated alcoves, it reminded me forcibly of the Roman Colosseum.

We surfaced after an hour or so and spent the rest of the day strolling around this neoclassical city, only stopping from time to time to refuel.

I was shown the impressive imperial Ursino Castle, built as a coastal fortress on the orders of Emperor Frederick II von Hohenstaufen in the first half of the thirteenth century. The castle is still there; it is the coast that moved.

Then there is the duomo. The cathedral was begun in 1092, though what you see is mainly baroque or eighteenth century. It is dedicated to a certain St Agatha, who was so virtuous a virgin that when, in the early Middle Ages, the volcano began to spew lava in the direction of the city, she was sent to stand in the path of the flow. It was unthinkable that God would not save her, and to accomplish that, He would have to halt the eruption. Well, the citizens were half right. The eruption stopped at St Agatha's feet, but the poor saintly girl was vaporised by the heat and ascended to heaven in a cloud of smoke. An unusual martyrdom.

Most of Catania's wide streets and fine palaces were built during the eighteenth century, coinciding with the Bourbon redevelopment of Naples. Architecturally, the similarity between the two cities is striking.

During the eighteenth century, noble families from all across eastern Sicily began to build their palaces in Catania. The social and economic rivalry with Palermo, which still continues, is plain to see. If Catania is somewhat more industrial, and Palermo the administrative centre, Catania is much less chaotic than its rival, and its streets and squares are a good bit cleaner. Organised crime, which certainly exists, is slightly less pervasive here than in Palermo. And most Sicilians, even Palermitans, would agree that it's generally easier to do business in Catania than in Palermo.

Dinner involved a casseroled pheasant and an introduction to a particularly brilliant local red wine. To this day I retain a special place in my palate for the great Sicilian reds, especially the Duca Enrico I had that night.

The following day we were off to the coast, to the lovely fishing village of Acitrezza, where a long line of rocks, something like the Needles off the Isle of Wight, stretch out to sea – recording where Hercules had thrown them during his labours.

Daniele had arranged that we would be welcome on one of the brilliantly painted boats. We spent the day at sea, trying not to get too much in the way. We helped the fishermen pull in their nets and were rewarded with red mullet and octopus to take home for our supper. But before we were permitted to drive home, the fishermen wagered I could not manage a wine glass of the local liqueur, Fuoco di Etna. Let it never be said I duck a challenge. Firewater perhaps, but it was delicious. For more than thirty years I have been looking for another bottle.

Driving in rural Sicily, while looking for the remote house of one of Daniele's friends who had turned into a kind of recluse, we passed by dozens of mandarin groves. In every field, half asleep, half alert, was an old boy on a stool, leather hat tilted forward over his face, sawn-off shotgun on his lap. They call this weapon a *lupara*, and the word has long stuck in my memory. The joys of scrumping must be unknown to Sicilian youth.

Eventually we found the extraordinary log and brick cabin that Ricardo, Daniele's old school friend, had built for himself, right in the centre of nowhere. At first it seemed it was half shed and half man-made cave, but as we approached I could see that it was deceptively spacious.

I was informed that its owner, Ricardo, had gone back to nature, in despair of human society. Happily, with Daniele and me, he seemed disposed to make an exception. Ricardo had let his reddish-brown hair – facial and tonsorial – grow as nature intended. It almost completely obscured his face, fell six inches below his collar and it emerged again from his jerkin over the back of his hands.

When I say Ricardo had returned to nature, I mean that he had turned feral. He lived for nature. Every morning he would wake in time to be at his chosen location in the wild as dawn rose. There, armed with nets or camera or shotgun or fishing rod, he would commune with the animal kingdom from the perspective of one who is at the top of the food chain. In the Bible it is writ 'and Man shall have dominion over the rest', and Ricardo took this as a papal injunction.

Most of his victims would never have expected they were about to meet their Maker. Their nemesis came camouflaged. Ricardo dressed mainly in odd leather clothes, so used and worn as to have disguised their human manufacture. When he was in the open air, he was something like a large and intelligent super-dog, with a slightly greater ability to converse with humans than the average mutt. I suspected that his sense of smell had similarly evolved.

But he was generosity itself towards Daniele and me. I noted that Daniele glanced at me from time to time, as if to measure my reaction, but I am afraid I was only wondering about the use Ricardo made of his standard lamp. As for his victims, they had had the ultimate honour bestowed upon them, for Ricardo was a brilliant taxidermist. His cabin was filled with every animal you can imagine, and one or two you cannot.

On near invisible fishing twine, suspended from the ceiling, a flock of geese flew through his living room. Eyeing them impotently from a corner, a fox was locked in a state of eternal cunning, his mask an essay in mute speculation. Arranged in tableaux around the room were groups of field mice, several large rats and an otter. A mother duck and her dozen ducklings were off on their adventures into the kitchen. There were snakes and lizards, and a goat with a great beard faced the back door with its head down, ready to deter any burglar. On one of the curtains a wise old owl stared fixedly at us while we sipped some kind of rose hip infusion.

Ricardo asked me rather gruffly if I had read any Italian literature. It seemed a bizarre question in this strange and frozen still life, but I nodded.

I had started on the books that Italians are forced to read while they are at school, in an effort on my part to pick up the references they routinely sling into their conversations. This was not as hard as it might sound. Kate had instructed me to read *The Leopard* in order to understand the Risorgimento, and I now reread it (as *Il Gattopardo*) in Italian. That was difficult; Lampedusa's vocabulary is so vast he had me burrowing in my dictionary every two minutes, but I was hypnotised by the sad beauty of the piece. It is written in a language entirely appropriate for a prince who is marking both the heights and the end of the Bourbon dream for Sicily, which the House of Savoy will eclipse.

Having read and, in some instances, learned by heart, some of Michelangelo's sonnets, I had tried my hand at Dante. I had embarked on a tough diet of Castiglioni and Machiavelli, of Ariosto's *Orlando Furioso*, of Benvenuto Cellini and Vasari. My copy of *The Origin of Species* had been recently neglected. I would put that right, I resolved yet again. It's just that it was so, well, mechanical.

I also went through the libretti of every opera I managed to see, in Rome, in Verona, at San Carlo, in Tuscany and Spoleto, in Umbria. It was an ambitious programme, but by now my Italian was really coming up to speed. A month could easily drift by without my speaking English at all, except with Ettore and on my guided tours, and I was glad of it. If nothing else, fluency in this euphonic language would be the finest treasure I could hope to have with me the rest of my life.

How very different an approach to Ricardo's. He, by contrast, had started to learn great chunks of Shakespeare, in English. This was truly astonishing, as he did not actually speak English. He would read the Shakespeare in a contemporary Italian translation, and then, very carefully, learn the English version phonetically. Predictably, he made mistakes aplenty, though I had not the heart to correct him. But there, in his cabin, and under a suspended pair of fruit bats, he quoted the great pessimist soliloquy from Hamlet, in English, understanding every tortured word and introducing a magical Italian rhythm into a work of art that should have been well beyond his reach.

All too soon it was time for us to leave. Ricardo thanked us formally and graciously for our visit, offering Daniele a bottle of his tangerine liqueur and me a stuffed shrew, holding an acorn, in a miniature glass dome.

Not everybody has the same ambitions. I wished I might have had Ricardo's great and particular fortune: to find his singular way in the dark wood when the true path is so badly obscured.[2]

The week had flown by in Daniele's magical company. The next phase of my Sicilian adventure was heralded by the proud arrival of my old friend, Johnnie FitzHerbert. He had received my instructions and had arrived from Catania Airport with ambitions to see the hilltop village of Corleone, preferably with a pair of local beauties.

Johnnie could drive a car, unlike myself, and he had hired a decrepit but open-top old banger – an Alvis, I believe – somewhere in Catania, and he had arrived at the house in it like a firebrand crazed by an excess of d'Annunzio. The car, which today would be painstakingly restored, was then a great big noisy thing with running boards, just about held together with rust.

'C'mon, hands on socks,' he greeted me. 'Fish to fry!'

Johnnie had adopted a very strange way of talking that owed something to Wodehouse or, more likely, Dornford Yates. But at least he was a civilised fellow and had bought into my plans with enthusiasm.

We lunched one last time with Daniele and his kin, exchanged gifts, and set off on the road – first stop: Piazza Armerina.

'Can't we go straight to Corleone?' Johnnie asked rather petulantly.

'No,' I replied firmly.

Johnnie was obsessed with the Mafia. The film *The Godfather* had recently been released, and everywhere people were humming its catchy tune; except, that is, in Sicily, where the Church had recommended giving it a miss. I had seen it in Rome and had immediately fallen in love with Simonetta Stefanelli, the Italian

---

[2] '*Mi ritrovai per una selva oscura / Chè la diritta via era smarita.*' Dante, *L'Inferno*, 1314.

actress who played Apollonia, the ill-fated first wife of Don Michael Corleone. I had first seen her in *Homo Eroticus*, a highbrow film the plot of which escapes me, and in *In the Name of the Italian People*. With *The Godfather* she had become an international star.

Johnnie had fallen for her, too, but then the Pavlovian Johnnie fell for every woman. He had also been stirred by the rugged vision of Sicily in the film. It was all I could do to stop him from going directly to Corleone to pay homage at the shrine. There is a shrine to Mario Puzo, surely?

But Corleone would have to wait. Our first stop was Piazza Armerina, with its very large Roman villa, and its magnificent floor mosaics. Nothing really prepares the visitor for its huge scale, and Johnnie was gratifyingly impressed.

'You've some rum ideas of what constitutes fun, old boy, but you're spot on about this place, by God,' he confided to me, though I could tell that until we hit Corleone he would never be truly satisfied.

The villa is one of the largest Roman patrician dwellings of its kind to have survived from antiquity (as opposed to imperial palaces like that of Diocletian in Split, or Hadrian's in Tivoli).

Thousands of square metres of mosaics cover the villa's floors.[3] A rugger pitch's worth of them. They depict scenes from everyday life in the fourth century, such as hunting, and drinking cocktails beside the swimming pool. They are utterly transporting. One of them shows women in two-piece swimsuits, bikinis no less, working out with barbells. It could have been Beverly Hills. Our guide, on the other hand, thought that the style of the mosaics had been influenced by the North African motifs of the Romans. Well, I'm not going to disagree with her.

I was struck by how very different the architecture was from the remains at Pompeii. Johnnie got quite involved and called me to come and inspect some water pipes visible near the entrance. For some reason he had not expected the Romans to have running water in lead pipes going to so many of the rooms.

Back in the jalopy, we headed for Syracuse where I had booked us rooms for a couple of nights.

---

[3] 3,500 square metres, to be exact.

After an early breakfast our first stop was the cathedral. It turned out to be a near-perfect Greek temple, wrapped in an elaborate baroque casing. The fifth century BC Athenaion, together with the Temple of Minerva, forms a large part of the building. It is one of the few surviving examples in the whole of Magna Graecia of a temple being turned into a church.

Everywhere you turn in Syracuse you see this unbroken continuity with its ancient Greek past. To discover that the Corinthians founded the city in 734 BC comes as no surprise.

Even somewhere as ancient as Syracuse has an 'old' quarter – in this case an island called Ortegia. As any fule kno', *ortygia* is the ancient Greek for 'quail', which were presumably plentiful here a few thousand years ago.

Ortegia can boast the freshwater Spring of Arethusa. When poor Arethusa was desperate to escape the clutches of the river god Alpheus, she called on Artemis for help. The hunter goddess, who never much cared for men, transformed the maiden into a spring, whose extra virgin water remains as eternally pure as Arethusa herself. Johnnie and I felt distinctly wicked as we sipped at her fountain.

Syracuse was the city of Aeschylus, Archimedes and Pindar; it was easily the most important city in Magna Graecia and for a long time it challenged Athens, Carthage and Rome for predominance in the ancient world.

The old town has a Greek amphitheatre that is carved out of the rock. The nearby Roman one is also in good shape. The Greek theatre is semicircular and open, the Roman one oval and enclosed, which in point of fact is how most of us can tell the difference.

But Johnnie was keen to see the Ear of Dionysius. Dionysius was the original 'tyrant of Syracuse', the classic example of a good guy who turns cruel when given too much power. The 'Ear' was formerly a limestone quarry. Dionysius used to set his prisoners to work here, cutting great stone blocks for his palaces and his public projects. One day, his superintendent came to him to report a great discovery. The prisoners had discovered a cave that had exposed a flue that led to the surface some 300 metres above. A trick of the shape of the quarry had created an acoustic phenomenon. The quietest of whispers in the cave, muttered from one conspirator to another, could be heard as if it were a whisper in your own ear, at ground level discreetly and well out of sight. The tyrant quickly exploited this. All work in the cave was halted and a set of fine chairs and a table were placed in the cave. The prison guards were instructed that the place was to be reserved as a shelter for the senior enemy officers who had been captured and put to work in the quarry. On the top, where the sounds of conversation emerged, Dionysius built a small temple, where he, or his agents, would listen to his enemies talking secretly about their own kings' ambitions to overthrow the tyrant. All very gratifying.

It still works. Johnnie whispered things to me – he at the bottom, me at the top – along the lines of 'I'm ready for a spot of lunch, old chum,' and 'Where do the girls hang out?' I heard him as plain as a pikestaff.

We took in the extraordinary necropolis and the archaeological museum before the light began to fail. The museum holds a little Greek statue, the Venus of Syracuse, which may even be by Praxiteles. It is the loveliest study of the female form, and I am afraid that set Johnnie off again. For my money, the museum is unmissable; a trove of rare loveliness.

I had discovered one of Caravaggio's Sicilian paintings in Rome, in the marvellous gallery in the Villa Borghese. It is the sublime and strange painting of an androgynous, bacchic and beautiful boy, St John the Baptist, who seems to stretch languidly between the sacred and the profane. The staff of the Baptist forms no cross (contrary to usual practice) and in the background, such as it is, a ram is eating grapes.

In Messina there are two Caravaggios. 'The Raising of Lazarus', painted in 1608, was commissioned by a man called Lazzari for the high altar of a church owned by the Padri Crociferi, a healing order. All very appropriate.

The other is the 'Adoration of the Shepherds', painted in 1609 for the Franciscans at Santa Maria la Concezione, near Messina.

But there is a better one still in Syracuse. Caravaggio's 'Burial of Saint Lucy' hangs in the local public gallery. That alone deserves a detour.

St Lucy was a local saint of Syracuse, who was denounced as a Christian by her former suitor and died under torture in AD 304. It is likely that the artist worked at speed to deliver the picture before her feast day. The painting shows the unfortunate saint dead, and on her back, in the middle ground of the painting. Her face is that of the classic Italian beauty, olive-skinned and oval-eyed. She forcibly reminded me, with a shiver of recognition and excitement, of Arianna.

Two massive workmen are busy with their spades, digging her grave. To the back of the painting a group of spectators is struck with awe or conscience that such a tragedy has unfolded. Behind them all is a Roman arch, simplicity itself, setting the period without ado. The viewer is forced back to the time of the Church of the catacombs.

Apparently, Lucy's head was severed from her body. This idea seems to have depressed Caravaggio, who decided a small slit in the front of her neck would be quite enough, thank you.

Muscular gravediggers emerge from murky shadows. The mourners are so much smaller that they seem some distance away. An officer directs the operations from beside a bishop. All the onlookers are obscured by shadow, excepting a young man above the saint who stands out poignantly in his red cloak. Characteristic of Caravaggio, the lamplight imitates the action of the sun by falling from the right. The artist has distanced the viewer from his subject in a way that seems to suggest it all happened so very long ago.

Johnnie was impressed with St Lucy. 'Why don't we see if we can't find ourselves a girl like that?'

Maybe, just maybe, I already have, I thought to myself.

But out loud, I felt the need to dampen my old friend's ardour.

'It'd be us with our throats cut if we did. The local lads all carry knives.' I wasn't sure if this was true, but there was a sense of honour and vendetta in the Sicilian air.

'There is nothing to surpass Syracuse,' Johnnie declared, 'so why don't we now go straight to Corleone?'

But I had it differently planned.

Chapter the Thirteenth
1972: Love in Sicily

In which the author continues to explore Sicily, now travelling to Corleone, the hilltop town so associated with The Godfather. *He discovers one of the wonders of the world, the Palatine Chapel in Palermo, and has a rendezvous with a very lovely Roman girl in a grand hotel.*

Johnnie FitzHerbert and I arrived at Agrigento the next afternoon, having taken on board an early lunch on the way.

Unesco has now listed Agrigento as a world heritage site. Today, in 2007, there are almost 800 such sites in the world. In 1972, however, its importance had not been recognised – except, of course, by everyone who actually cared.

Agrigento was founded as a Greek colony in the sixth century BC and quickly became one of the leading cities in the Mediterranean. From the sea, its magnificent Doric temples dominate the Grecian city and dramatically underline the old port's supremacy. Much of the ancient town must still lie almost unspoilt under the groves and orchards that the temples stand in.

The present town is over a kilometre from the temples, and is yet another Norman foundation. With the departure of the Byzantine and Saracen administrations, Agrigento's importance declined, but it was restored to a great extent under Norman rule when its fine churches were constructed in or close to the town. Nearer the coast we could see a number of archaeological digs, presumably to uncover the earlier Hellenistic and Roman towns. And right on the water's edge was Akragas.

Akragas was Agrigento's original name. It was the name of its source, or spring.

Its story is impossibly ancient. After a first blossoming under a certain Phalaris,[1] about six centuries before Christ, it developed further under the great general, Theron,[2] who sent his troops to join in the Battle of Himera in 480 BC, where they succeeded in routing the Carthaginians.

During the later Punic Wars, Agrigento was destroyed several times. The Romans heavily besieged it in 261 BC. But it was often rebuilt, and every time bigger and better.

No less a giant than the ancient poet Pindar[3] described his birthplace as 'the most beautiful city of the mortals'.

But Akragas' most famous inhabitant was the philosopher and scientist Empedocles, who lived there between 490 and 430 BC and outranked even Pindar in the catalogue of human genius.

This impressed me, but Johnnie was less moved by this astonishing fact.

As far as the Norman town was concerned, he was in no mood to visit its stunning churches at all. Partly I blame the weather. It was a little sultry and the midges or mosquitoes had taken a fancy to him. Happily, these little so-and-sos have always left me alone. He consented to visit the Valley of the Temples, but only after we had bought a couple of bottles of local white wine and had borrowed a couple of glasses from a restaurant.

And why not? Is there anything so very wrong with sacrificing an afternoon to a glass of wine or two?

In case you believe it somehow sacrilegious or self-indulgent to imbibe in such a spiritual place, I should tell you that drinking wine is an activity much recommended in the Bible. It is an essential activity if you are to prepare for Heaven, as God also enjoys a glass from time to time ('Should I leave my wine, which cheereth God and man…?' Judges 9:13).

Jesus ratified this at the last supper, when he announced that while he had drunk his last wine on earth, he would 'drink it anew in the kingdom of God' (Mark 14:25).

Johnnie's and my mood happily migrated from the academic into the sheer bliss of communion with history – eternity, perhaps – on the Doric ridge of a town that was old almost before

---

[1] 570–554 BC.
[2] He ruled from 488–471 BC.
[3] 518–438 BC.

the New Testament was a twinkle in the eye of the prophets.

There is a lot to see there for the serious student, not just the ruins of numerous temples but also necropoleis, houses, streets and everything else one would expect to find in an ancient city. There is a small amphitheatre, several auditoria and a fine archaeological museum.

The three great temples are a little damaged, naturally, after the best part of 3,000 years. Around them, great slabs of stone are strewn about, often carved with triglyphs of ancient design, which conspire to make the scene resemble a work by Piranesi. The Temple of Juno is in good condition, even though it was built in 450 BC. It is similar in style to the temples at Paestum, just south of Salerno on the Amalfi coast, which I had seen soon after my arrival in Italy. The Temple of Concord was built around 440 BC and is in even better condition. The original dedication is not known; this name was given to it quite recently. A number of its *telamones*, or large segmented stone columns in the form of human figures, have escaped being 'preserved' elsewhere.

Johnnie and I sat in the shade of an olive tree and sipped our wine. It was a working day and we had the place pretty much to ourselves. And as we talked the nonsense that wine and youth makes it necessary to talk, Johnnie banging on about *The Godfather*, and me repeating my anxieties over ever getting a real job, a goatherd appeared from beyond the necropolis to our east and drove his herd just past us, his goats looking us over and shaking their heads and bells as if to reproach us for our unnecessary vanity and sophistication. Why did we not just embrace their simple rustic truth?

And later, as the sun set, lights set discreetly into the hill came on and the illuminated temple became a sight to behold. It was sensational, but we were calm about it. At this time in our lives the gods were granting us such marvels nearly every day.

The first miracle the next day was that the jalopy ever made it up the hills and round the hairpin bends that lead to Corleone.

The steering was terrible and I feared for my life while Johnnie muttered incomprehensible things about overhead cams and double-declutching. We drove past fields filled with purple blossom, with drystone walls like those in Yorkshire.

But make it we did and in due course we reached the market town that played such a starring role in Francis Ford Coppola's celebrated movie. But it's not as small a town as one might imagine. It's actually quite large.

I regret to say we got rather lost. Eventually we found a bar that looked sufficiently like the one where Don Michael met Signor Vitelli for the first time. It might have been the same place. Johnnie always thought it was.[4] We sat outside, as in the film, and Johnnie, who up to now had declined to speak Italian, proudly asked for a carafe of the local red wine with surprising eloquence.

'*Una carafa di vino rosso, per favour,*' he had said.

'*Subito,*' the waiter had replied, and had retreated indoors to find one.

Johnnie was ridiculously pleased with himself after this simple sentence, and I understood him only too well. This was the first time he had ever spoken to another man in another language, and to find himself perfectly understood was a thrilling experience. It had been exactly like that for me some years before when, on a school trip, I had first remonstrated with a particularly truculent French waiter. Languages make the world – or more exactly, that bit of the world you are permitted to explore – so much larger. Johnnie's universe had just doubled in size.

We ended by eating in 'Signor Vitelli's'. Three or four curious townsmen drew up a chair and accepted our offer of a glass or two. They were happy to share their experiences with us. Coppola's film crew had spent three weeks in the town something over a year before. They hadn't filmed that much, mostly the square by the church, a procession and some general views. It had been difficult to deal with their special food requirements and crowd control proved a problem, as everyone wanted to be in the film. Hundred of extras were expensively recruited, mainly to keep them corralled and quiet.

But just three months ago, after much pleading with the local priest and the mayor, a viewing had finally been negotiated and the town had turned out in force to watch the film in their

---

[4] It wasn't. The restaurant in the film was filmed at Savoca, near Taormina. It proved impossible to shoot the scene in the narrow streets of Corleone.

ancient cinema. To a man, and especially to a woman, they were disappointed, even angry. They had been led to believe that the whole film took place in Corleone, or at least in Sicily, not just one or two little scenes. More importantly, the film glamorised the Mafia. The female natives of Corleone, often widows, had particular reason to loathe the Mafia, despite the fact that the protracted war between the 'godfathers' of Palermo and Corleone had made the town the Mafia capital. It was a dangerous, corrupting organisation that brought everything it touched into disrepute, and it was on their doorstep. It weighed on them, and their husbands' businesses, like lead. Who in their right minds would want to invest in Sicily?

Even non-commercial posts, like the director of a local hospital, were open only to Mafia appointees, as also were some of the top positions in tourism. What sane doctor would want to work in such a place? He would have a better career on the mainland.

The film was hardly an advert for Sicily, said one. Al Pacino was not 'Italian enough', said another, though I must say that did seem a little unfair. The lack of hotels of international standard had been an irritant to everyone. The natives of Corleone had felt a little slighted by the American attitude to their best rooms. But to treat the Mafia, this social cancer, as glamorous? That was outrageous. All in all it was not a happy experience.

I had been wondering about the Mafia too. If it hadn't been for Johnnie, I doubt I would have asked.

'Surely the Mafia is slowly dying out?'

There was an intake of breath.

'True,' we were told, 'the Mafia is invisible to the tourist; there is very little obvious crime in Sicily. Even street crime is rare. The Mafia doesn't allow it, of course. But the Mafia 'folklore' of film and television has led the public into some unfortunate delusions about life in the west of Sicily.'

We learned that the Mafia does exist – it remains one of Sicily's most serious social problems. Mafiosi kill people. *The Godfather* was set in 1947. Up to 1944 the Mafia had been suppressed (though not completely destroyed) by Mussolini. But when the Americans landed, they released all Mussolini's prisoners and had them elected to office. This was done to oppose

Communism, of course. The Mafia would guarantee the safe election of a Christian Democrat majority. As a strategy it was reasonably effective. In the election that followed the war, the Christian Democrats won every seat in Sicily, while the rest of the country voted the other way. But they were then free to rebuild their organisation, and since that time they had gone from strength to strength.

'They have never been the charming fellows depicted in American movies,' our new friends explained. 'In every village there is a Mafioso who is searching for *picciotti*,[5] to enlist. They offer a career that will take them from petty crime to murder. Many turn into contract killers, often employed by rival Mafiosi as they squabble over the meagre takings in this poor island. They are ruthless drug dealers. We have a terrible problem with our children. And the fee for a corpse is said to be pitiably small. But why stop there? They run prostitutes and protection rackets. They intimidate magistrates, to the point of murdering one every so often, *per incorrigiare gli altri*.[6] There are three murders a week in Palermo alone. Almost every day there is some account of a dreadful villainy in our newspapers.'

It seemed that the Mafia was almost as powerful in 1972 as it had been in the days before Mussolini dealt with it with a dictator's fiat. Murder levels in Palermo were the highest in Europe, as they had been for a century, except for the short time when the little town of Favara overtook it. There was a ten-year period, in the 1930s, when only one man in Favara died of natural causes.

The conditions that foster such crime are rooted in traditional aspects of Sicilian life. Patronage is key; there are long-standing norms, such as the need to be 'introduced' or 'recommended' to somebody before business may be done with them. These practices conspire to promote the kind of introspective and secretive environment where organised crime can thrive. The Sicilians call this mindset *Mafiosità*, in which elegant shrug is insinuated that the line between being the criminal and his

---

[5] Petty criminals.
[6] '*Pour encourager les autres*.' Voltaire's damning indictment of the British for the shooting of Admiral Byng seems to ring in all European ears.

accomplice is a fine one. Many Sicilians, though not by choice, end up dealing indirectly with organised crime or political corruption.

It is also difficult to avoid when the Mafia controls entire sectors of the Sicilian economy. The Mafia has murdered many courageous magistrates and judges since the war. The two most famous belong to a time after this narrative. Giovanni Falcone and his closest friend, Paolo Borsellino, were killed in two separate and ruthless explosions in 1992. Ironically, perhaps, both these courageous men came from poor parts of Palermo.

Falcone was one of the main organisers of the 'Maxi-trials' that saw hundreds of Mafiosi prosecuted in cages in a specially built courtroom in the mid-1980s. Many were convicted of crimes including murder, kidnap and extortion. These trials have broken Mafia power, for a while. It was Falcone's persuasion of a *capomafioso*, Tommaso Buscetta, to inform on his brethren that was his historic achievement.

Afterwards, the Mafia sent a warning to anyone else seeking to damage their organisation. Falcone was killed with his wife (also a judge) and with his three bodyguards, on the motorway between Palermo Airport and the city of Palermo. A bomb had been buried under the asphalt of the airport road and was remotely detonated directly under his car.

After Falcone and Borsellino's deaths, their murderer, Salvatore Riina, was arrested. He is still in prison (in 2006). Palermo Airport is now known as Falcone-Borsellino Airport in honour of these two brave men. A memorial to them by a local sculptor has been erected there.

Organised crime, with political corruption, exists everywhere. It's not confined to Sicily. It's just that it happens to be more violent in that handsome island and more a part of their way of life. Catania boasts that it is afflicted to a lesser extent by this deadly virus, but the rivalry between the two largest Sicilian cities has been a fact of life for generations.

But Johnnie was the sandboy of the proverbs. He was in paradise. Our trip to Corleone was the very apotheosis of a travelling man's fate. He could die now, secure that he would go to Heaven.

It had been a fine lunch for us both, in a little square by an old church, near the open air market, at a rickety table outside the restaurant, involving a generous plate of *spaghetti alla carbonara*, and pleasant conversation with our recently acquired local friends, who were surprisingly forthcoming with their unexpected views.

Johnnie now wanted to return to Catania and thence to London, his business in Sicily done, but I managed to persuade him to give me a lift to Monreale. I could manage from there.

A Saracen Sunday
Santa Maria, Monreale

I am happy to report that Johnnie came with me to see the cathedral in Monreale with its exquisite cloister, before setting off alone to wherever he had hired the car and onwards back to England.

The dazzling mosaics in the interior of Monreale Cathedral have rightly made this church world-famous. Their ravishing beauty creates an atmosphere of solemnity, tranquillity and awe. They cover most of the cathedral's walls, except where the walls are finished in white marble bordered with inlaid polychrome and Cosmatesque patterns. The mosaics are the world's largest display of this art, no longer surpassed in scale (as once they were) by Istanbul's Basilica of Hagia Sofia, or even in beauty, as one can argue for the older San Vitale Nuovo in Ravenna. But the Turks destroyed many of the enchanting mosaics of Istanbul when they took ancient Constantinople for the Prophet in 1453. And Monreale's challenge to Ravenna is spiritual.

Just by itself, the exquisite cloister of the old Benedictine abbey would make Monreale world-famous. Hundreds of columns, some with mosaic inlay, each with its meticulous stone-carved capital, enclose the cloister gardens. Their capitals each tell a story; there are Bible scenes, lives of the saints, Norman knights in action, and gargoyles. The knights in particular remind you forcibly of the Norman knights in the Bayeux Tapestry. They make an Englishman think of home.

The crowning glory of the cloister is its 'Arabian' fountain, almost a mini-cloister within the cloister, surrounded by its own four-sided colonnade.

When Johnnie and I returned to the cathedral, we were taken aback to discover a mosaic icon in the cathedral's main apse near the altar, representing Thomas à Becket. A long way from home, it was extraordinary to light upon the first work of art anywhere honouring our greatest English saint.

When you start to look for them there are English connections aplenty. Work began on the cathedral in 1174. The English martyr is probably represented there because in 1177, at the age of twenty-four, the Norman King William II of Sicily, nicknamed 'the Good', married Joan, the daughter of King Henry II of England. William's father-in-law had just commissioned the murder of the turbulent Archbishop of Canterbury in 1170. Just three years later Becket was canonised. Three years? The Vatican could move fast in those days.

William II built this dazzling cathedral to establish the Roman Catholic Church, then known as the 'Latin Church', as the official Church of Sicily. There were still vast numbers of Orthodox Christians (the 'Greek Church') and Saracens (as Muslims were then called) in twelfth-century Sicily. Although Orthodoxy was permitted and Islam tolerated, their king embraced the authority of the Bishop of Rome.

But despite William the Good's earnest efforts to make his kingdom a Catholic one, his habits were unusual, to say the least, for a Christian monarch in the Middle Ages. Muslim ministers, including astrologers and doctors, dominated his court. He was also keen on local customs; not only could he speak and write in Arabic, he went the whole hog. Most notably he maintained a harem.

Most of the major work at Monreale was completed before the King's early death, when he was just thirty-six, in 1189. The cathedral's two huge main doors are a masterpiece in bronze, signed and dated by their maker, Bonanno of Pisa, in 1186. They are made up of various scenes from the Old and New Testaments, and are opened for weddings and other festive or ceremonial occasions held in the cathedral. The side portal was also built that year.[1] Its door frame is in the 'Arabic' style, with a dazzling geometric mosaic, as is the Saracen roof of the cathedral, which is superbly carved and painted.

The light was fading as we looked out over the panorama from the belvedere, a hundred yards or so from the cathedral. You get

---

[1] 1186, by Barisano da Trani.

to it (here is the secret) through a courtyard near the cloister. Pass through an archway at the south-west corner of the piazza, go about twenty paces through this courtyard to another archway, and you'll be there directly. It is well worth it. The views over Palermo and the valley between Monreale and Palermo – the Conca d'Oro[2] – are simply spectacular.

I felt transported, believing that I would never again enjoy such magic.

But there I was wrong, as I was about to discover.

I waved Johnnie goodbye as he set off for home. He was going to tell the world about his lunch at Vitelli's place in Corleone. I was bound for Palermo, and to get there meant climbing on to a rickety old bus. When I eventually arrived at the central bus station I hired a taxi to my hotel, the Villa Igiea, and was in good time for dinner.

I had a couple of things to do now that I was in Palermo, the last place on my first tour of Sicily. I felt I had taken a reasonably good first bite at the island, but there was so much I hadn't done. I hadn't seen Taormina, for example. Or Cefalù. Well, these places would have to wait.

On my working list for Sicily only two items remained. The first was planned for the following morning. It was the Capella Palatina of the Norman Royal Palace in Palermo, an awesome jewel so heart-stoppingly sublime that it counts as one of the wonders of the world.

The second, designed to follow hard on the heels of the first, was lunch at my hotel. I know, it sounds a disappointingly small ambition after all the *richesses* of the trip, but that girl that I had met and nervously dined in Rome had agreed to meet me there. Bright, beautiful Arianna was the kind of girl you would take to the finest place on earth, and my research had suggested it might be this grand hotel, overlooking the bay.

I ate simply and had an early night. I slept very well. I woke early and went on to the balcony of my room, overlooking the town and the Mediterranean. A knock at my door told me that my clothes, almost two weeks' worth of laundry, were washed and ironed. Room service now arrived with a cappuccino and a glass

---

[2] Golden conch, or sea-horn.

of orange juice. I had another twenty-four hours in Sicily and I was going to make the best of it.

I regarded myself in the mirror. Just turned twenty-three, and comfortably able to pay for a couple of nights in a grand hotel. Not bad, eh? I debated whether to wear the seersucker jacket and Panama. Why not? Suitably clad, I read the notes in my guide and set off for town with a spring in my step. The most phenomenal building in the world awaited me. It would be followed shortly by the company of the most feminine girl in the world; so intelligent but so modest, so adventurous yet so restrained, so classical yet so modern, with the charisma, the presence of a film star, and yet so private, so discreet.

Well, you set these things up in order to fail, but I cleared the first hurdle with no problems. The Capella Palatina was everything it was cracked up to be. The exquisite craftsmanship of the mosaics of the palatine chapel in Palermo's Norman Palace is today the only real competitor that Monreale now has left. It is not grandiose, like Monreale; the place is so small that the mosaics have a haunting immediacy that's wholly enveloping. It's almost as though the whole wealth of Monreale is concentrated into a private house.

The Capella is a single elaborate work of art. Not only are the mosaics every bit as good as the unsurpassable ones at Monreale, but the roof is domed and constructed as in a Moorish palace and lined with yet more priceless images. You feel like a diamond in a mirrored jewellery case. This art is self-sufficient; it is a universe of the sheerest epoch-defining artistry. Nor can it ever be bettered.

And yet, somehow it does not overwhelm. It manages to reach out to you at a human level; its stories are all familiar, all its characters are sad and noble, or proud and haughty. How many places are there that can distil such genius into so small a space? Genius here, as in a sonnet, is concentrated and confined.

To say that a visit to the Palatine Chapel is a life-changing experience may understate the case. It is thirty-three years since I was first there and I have never seen anything before or since that comes even close. In fact I have checked, returning with my wife and son in 2003. It hit me anew with the same impact and vigour as it had the first time. Anyone who goes to Sicily without seeing the place is an ass.

Chapter the Thirteenth

Conclusion

After a long while I looked at my watch. It was time to head back to the hotel.

The Villa Igiea may well be the best-known hotel in Sicily. It's either this one or the San Domenico Palace Hotel in Taormina. Like the other, the Villa Igiea is set in superb terraced gardens, filled with jasmine. Ernesto Basile built it high over the bay of Palermo at the turn of the nineteenth century in the art nouveau style. He was also responsible for its extraordinary furniture and fittings.

The concierge told me my companion had arrived and was already in the single room I had booked for her. I made my way to the bar. I ordered a glass of prosecco and waited as coolly as I could manage for her entrance.

When Arianna arrived she looked simply magnificent. Dressed in uncreased linen (how is that possible?) and some very simple jewellery, she seemed unspoiled and fetchingly demure. But I was already old enough to realise that in such women appearances deceive.

Beneath her super-cool exterior she was a coiled spring. Lightly tanned, her exquisite complexion appeared all the more striking. She radiated health and self-confidence. I offered her my arm, and as we went to our table every eye, male and female, was on her.

Over a terrific lunch she brought me up to speed on our Roman circle of friends. For my part, I tried to tell her that she had something of the face of Saint Lucy in her, as I had just observed in Caravaggio's breathtaking painting in Syracuse. I decided to omit the detail that St Lucy had just had her throat cut.

We ordered *pasta con le sarde*. It is the simplest dish, made with wild fennel, fresh sardines, anchovies, saffron, sultanas and pine nuts, and it's quite scrumptious. I know I had a veal steak for my main course, perhaps a little unimaginatively, but I was very hungry and it had been a long while since I had been in such a restaurant. And then we finished our lunch with a cassata, which is complicated to make but mouth-watering to eat. It's a pastry dish, whose main ingredients are ricotta cheese, candied fruit and almonds. Nor was the wine a problem; between the two of us we did splendidly with a bottle of Duca Enrico. I may have had the lion's share. It was the second time I had tried this outstanding ambassador for Sicily. It goes very well with gossip and even better with a little flirtation.

These were still early days of my international seduction skills, but the mere fact that she had accepted my invitation gave me confidence.

Arianna's family lived near Palermo. Her father was a property developer, I vaguely remember. She confided in me that she had told her parents that she would be arriving a day later than the truth. Tomorrow she would ring them up from the airport, asking them to pick her up. But today she was here, at my lunch table, with twenty-four hours conjured up out of nowhere. But she had agreed to my invitation subject to an important condition: that she would have her own bedroom.

She had looked rather circumspectly around the dining room as we sat down, and I surmised she was making sure that no one she knew, or her parents knew, was there. And then she relaxed, so I concluded that the coast was clear.

It was hot outside our air-conditioned hotel, and many of the wiser Sicilians would take to their rooms after lunch for a brief siesta and renew their strength to take them into the Sicilian small hours.

We ordered a coffee, and I a grappa, to finish the meal. She was leaning over the table towards me when I lit a match for her and she pressed my hand very sexily as she guided the light towards her cigarette.

The only Italian I knew that might plausibly work for me came from Don Giovanni, but Da Ponte knew a thing or two about seduction and I thought I would borrow his best shot.

I sat back in my chair and looked at her appraisingly in the soft light.

'*Che labretti sì belli, quelle dituccie candide, che occhi bricconcelli…*'
She smiled both thoughtfully and decisively.
'*Me lì luzinghi,*' she replied.[1]

'Before we take our siesta,' I said, 'you must see the view from my room. It is unforgettable.'

'I should love to,' she smiled again.

My train left Palermo for Messina and Rome the next morning. I only just caught it. Words cannot explain how tempted I was to forget that train and stay in Sicily for ever.

---

[1] 'What lovely lips, what slender fingers, what roguish eyes…' And she replied, 'You dazzle them [i.e. you are enticing me].'

Chapter the Fourteenth
1972: Vicenza's Mansions

In which the author travels to Vicenza in search of Palladio, the most famous architect of the Renaissance. He is delighted by an innkeeper's daughter and manages to wangle a private tour of the Villa Rotonda. All in all he thinks that a reasonable percentage of his Christmases have come in one job lot.

There is a Renaissance architect who has changed the way that all of us, from Shanghai to Cirencester to San Francisco, see the built environment around us.

His world standing is as widely recognised as is Shakespeare's or Mozart's in their different fields and, despite the great claims that could be made for Lutyens or Vetruvius or Gaudí or even Imhotep, it is Palladio whose signature is seen on almost every building that can remotely be called classical.

His pivotal invention is what we would today call a country house.

Palladio's career began in earnest when the pathfinding rich and nobles of Venice, who had been experimenting with building their retreats on the Venetian hinterland, lured him to Vicenza. While Venetian society of the 1500s was still intensely feudal, it had one very attractive feature. If you bought an estate in the swamps to the west of the sea-girt capital, and undertook the challenge of draining it, the Doge was prepared to grant you a title – a noble title. True, it wouldn't be the coveted 'nh' or 'nd' of the lagoon, but nonetheless a proper title from the Holy Roman Empire. No titles were permitted in the Republic of Venice, other than 'Doge', which is a dialect form of 'duke'. Instead, the most serene grandees had to content themselves with those letters before their name, standing for *nobil homo* or *nobile donna*. But if you took the reclamation option, you could even turn into a prince. Being a prince was very desirable. A prince could use the royal 'we', for example, though don't try this at home. When the Duke of Wellington, who had been given this honour by the Prince of Orange, ruler of the United Netherlands, began to use this privilege in England, he was booed to the rafters, as was Margaret Thatcher.[1] Even our own dear queen prefers to begin her Christmas broadcast, 'My husband and I...'

The rich and ambitious of Venice, and sometimes from far beyond, produced ducats and dinars, drachmas and thalers by the cartload for the Doge's ambitious project in the Veneto, buying almost barren land at prices to rival fertile Tuscany. And Andrea Palladio was there for them. He built them scores of magnificent villas within easy range of the little garrison town of Vicenza, and in the centre of the city he erected a theatre for his newly ennobled patrons. As a man, his beneficiaries rose to the task and came to town as often as their carriages would bear them, keen to show off their nobility, erudition and, well, their fine clothes.

I had arranged to team up with my old Cambridge friend, Alexander, at a bed and breakfast that I had discovered in the Touring Club Italiano's brilliant little guide.

Local trains were very unpredictable, even in those days, and I arrived rather late. Alex had got there long before me and his room was strewn with his stuff. Of the great man himself there was no trace.

It was time to gather my thoughts in the sitting room – the *salotto* – where the landlady was happy to make a fuss over me. I glanced into their little dining room, where a pretty girl was practising at her piano.

'My daughter,' explained our landlady.

But I was here to see the villas. Pretty girls can be found everywhere, I told myself. I needed particularly to see the Villa Rotonda, on which so much of English eighteenth-century architecture was based. Indeed, Lord Burlington's Chiswick House was almost a replica. The villa was not half an hour from Vicenza by open landau. It was still privately owned – and not open to the general public – but I would be happy just to see it from the outside.

In Joseph Losey's film, *Don Giovanni*, the Don's *casinetto* (in

---

[1] 'We are a grandmother!'

which he seduces Zerlina) is played by this villa. For the Don himself, Losey had local hero, Casanova, in mind, but Ruggiero Raimondi had to suffice. A very good job he made of it, too. Since then I've seen this film five times on the big screen. More times than any other single film, in fact. Nevertheless I agree with Bernard Shaw in his view that there cannot be a perfect version of this opera (as it will always be impossible to gather together a perfect cast) but Losey comes about as close as you can get. Losey's Don is such a grand figure, whose courage is infinite, whose manners are charming and whose ruthlessness is his damnation.

On the other hand, by way of wholesome contrast, I am sure Andrea Palladio's original patron, Paolo Almerico, was wholly respectable. He must have been. After all, he was an Apostolic Referendary, or Principal Private Secretary, to two popes, Pius IV and Pius V. Almerico had lived in Rome, probably near the Pantheon, which may have been part of the reason why he thought his new house should have a dome. His was in fact the very first private house since antiquity to have one. He had Palladio build him a villa on top of a hill, with no less than four Ionic porticos each with five classical life-size statues, facing the four compass points. These *pronaoi* are attached to what seems to be a two-storey cube, itself crowned with a shallow hemisphere clad in terracotta pantiles. Simple lawns fall away from the house, except on one side where a sloping and walled ramp or road has been carved into the hill to allow carriages to drive up to the steps. The drive has walls on top of which stand classical figures every ten metres or so, holding torches or books to illuminate the visitor literally and figuratively.

Goethe was deeply impressed.

Today I have seen a splendid villa called La Rotonda, half an hour from the city, on a beautiful hill... Maybe art has never before reached such a level of magnificence... Thus the villa can be admired from every part of the region, and also the view which can be admired from the inside is one of the most delightful. One can see the Bacchiglione flowing, bringing the boats down from Verona to the Brenta...[2]

---

[2] J W Goethe, *Italienische Reise*, 1816–1817.

Art is evolutionary, not revolutionary. The passing of time makes this obvious. Throughout art's history, critics have maintained that their own epoch is unique in taking a revolutionary new direction, but a hundred years later we discern that such supposed mould-breakers were in truth just part of a trend, standing on the shoulders of giants. Artists used to delight in their scholarly pedigree, even revel in it, but latterly their game has been to make you mistake these piggybacked pygmies for the colossi themselves. Their stacks of bricks, pickled sheep or unmade beds, desperately trying to shock a non-existent bourgeois complacency; are merely *objets trouvés*, dredged up by *enfants terribles*, jejune and immodest successors of Marcel Duchamp, who pre-empted and outclassed them all with his urinal of 1924.

So Palladio did not arrive in Vicenza like an architectural Big Bang, creating everything out of nothing, as some architectural historians will have it. For nearly a century, successive Doges had promoted the Veneto's draining and cultivation. It had been a great plain about as hilly as Suffolk, peppered with the occasional castle or tower. The merchants of Venice were not initially happy to inhabit such an inhospitable place, where feudal armies and *condottieri* roamed at will in search of a scrap.

But in the half-century before Palladio's arrival, Vicenza began to develop a home-grown strain of seriously rich merchants who wanted their homes to outshine anything built before. This was a comparatively easy challenge, as the local heritage amounted to no more than a clutch of fortified farmhouses and some militaristic barracks.

The *arrivistes* began to realise their showy ambitions in the *quattrocentro*. The fifteenth century in almost all of Europe was a period of awesome prosperity, and when the Catholic Church was at its richest and most powerful. When the great merchants were amassing their vast fortunes from spices, silks and silver, the Reformation was still about a century away. Luther had yet to pin his theses to the church door at Wittenberg (in 1499), and Henry VIII would wait until 1535 to dissolve the English monasteries. The incomers brought with them a flood tide of money, together with a small army of tutors (Frenchmen, Greeks from Constantinople, both before and especially after it fell to the Turks in 1453, and perhaps one young and extraordinarily talented Englishman). Vicenza's streets thronged with Latin scholars, professors of oratory and rhetoric, and masters of dancing, fencing and riding, all keen to build schools for those who could pay the fees. The young Englishman? Shakespeare wrote *Othello*, *The Merchant of Venice*, *Two Gentlemen of Verona* and *Romeo and Juliet*, and centred them all on the Veneto and its capital, Venice. Could this be a simple coincidence? The Vicenza or the Verona of his day would have been an ideal place for an educated young man to spend a gap year. So would it be, today.

The first Renaissance architects to build in Vicenza were Cornaro, Sanmicheli and Sansovino. While these talented men had discovered how fertile their building plot truly was, it was only after Palladio was sent for, to teach at the Accademia Olimpica in the 1550s, that the Veneto and the world would change forever.

Vicenza's greatest school – its Cambridge, perhaps – was the Olympic Academy, as it modestly called itself. It met at Sansovino's Odeon, until Palladio built them their theatre. It was from the old Odeon that the master's *Four Books of Architecture* were taken for publication to the printing presses of Venice in 1570, and it was this collection that has been bought by every architect in every country in the world ever since. These books have changed the way every city and town looks today.

Some years later I asked Jon Harris, the Cambridge artist, to explain to me the particular magic of a Palladian window. It lies in the purity of the geometry, he told me, and that remains true even when stripped of its carved or stucco detail. In fact, without the decoration you could be forgiven for believing you were looking at an ultra-modern building, so pure and geometrical are the lines.

As there was still no sign of Alexander, I decided to go and find this famous theatre – the Teatro Olimpico – and tackle the genius of the place head on.

From the street, the Teatro Olimpico looked smaller than I had imagined. The façade was that of a severe Georgian building from the 1750s, slightly resembling Trinity College in Dublin in a softer, whiter stone. No, hang on, that can't be right. Actually, it's 200 years older than that. It is actually older than either Shakespeare's

Globe or Marlowe's Curtain Theatre. It was built when Queen Elizabeth I was newly on her throne and had only just erected the long-demolished earliest buildings of Trinity College, which the Palladian ones were to replace two centuries later, with the notable exception of the Rubrics.

On entering, I realised at once that it was not only a place of entertainment, designed to deliver Pindar or Aristophanes to an educated and appreciative audience, but also a lecture hall, where scholars would analyse the Renaissance as it unfolded. This was the apogee of our European civilisation, but it was for an elite, of course. There were simply too few cattle drovers or private soldiers who could improvise in iambic pentameter or toss into their casual prose a judicious alexandrine or two.

The Teatro Olimpico is an amphitheatre in the Greek style. The semicircular tiers of seats are carved in stone and are ranged around an orchestra pit. Immediately in front of this is the vast proscenium, so wide as barely to provide for wings. If you turn yourself around and look behind the rows of seated scholars there is a blind screen, pierced only to admit the studious via a grand staircase. The screen is set with life-size stone portrayals of the illuminati of the School of Athens, half-emerging from their shallow niches. Above the screen is a gallery, difficult to see behind the phalanx of some thirty classical figures who defend the sanctum from the sophisters beyond.

Looking straight up, I was surprised to discover the theatre was roofed over. A flat ceiling covers the entire amphitheatre, painted to resemble an oddly northern sky of cumulus in a pale azure. How it's supported defies the imagination. But the best was yet to come.

The shallow stage has a monumental architectural backdrop, as befits a Greek theatre, in Palladio's favourite soft and white stone. Seven bays and three tiers of Corinthian pilasters reconstruct full-scale the monumental backdrops we have all seen in the ruined theatres of Thrace, Catania, and Pompeii.

And behind even this tremendous sight, slightly obscured by this stone curtain in front, is an entire Renaissance city of streets and palaces stretching endlessly away in every direction, carved in a pale wood. Palladio has been able to achieve the impossible by distorting the perspective – a fully three-dimensional trompe l'oeil, if you will – so that the 'houses' at the end of this startling prospect are scarcely a metre tall. But the effect is not merely stunning; it is magisterial, for it amounts to a magnificent lecture in stone and wood, delivering the rules of a new architecture and architectonic with such force that its authority would hold sway for the next three or even four hundred years.

It was all rather overwhelming. I emerged into the street wholly dazzled by what I had seen. I stopped at a *trattoria* for a simple plate of *pasta al burro* and a glass or two of white Pino Grigio wine from the Tyrolean Alto Adige. What on earth was Alexander up to? He should have come with me. Unlike most of the marvels of the world that claim to be unique, this theatre is the real William McCoy.

I got back to our digs at about ten o'clock that night and found our landlady there, plying Alex with a local wine. She had taken rather a shine to him. Her pretty teenage daughter sat shyly in the background, glancing our way every now and then. Or was she glancing my way?

Alex was delighted to see me, and I him, and he told me of his evening. He had accompanied his Vicentine *amore* to an evening of local talent, Vivaldi, Monteverdi, Scarlatti and Gabrieli, at a concert at the Casa del Capitano in the main square. And in the interval, she had secured him, no, *us*, an introduction to the Capra family, owners of the Villa Rotonda nearby, supposedly the most striking of them all. And they had volunteered to open the place up for us the following morning.

I was tired when I went upstairs and closed my door on the outside world. There was no lock, but who needed one in a place like this? I turned on my bedside light, cleaned my teeth, put on my pyjamas and climbed into bed. I picked up my book, that essay in materialism that is *The Origin of Species*, and began to ingest its wisdom.

I heard some footsteps come very quietly along the corridor outside and stop at my door. The quietest of knocks – designed not to be answered if I had fallen asleep – made me speculate. Had Alex forgotten something?

'Come in,' I said in English. The door opened. And in came

the young pianist, still dressed in her little skirt and pullover. She was holding a magazine behind her back. She looked nervous.

'*Accòmmodati*,' I said. She looked around, and sat on the far end of my bed.

'You are very nice,' she said in English, after a moment or two.

'Thank you,' I said. My mind was racing.

Silence prevailed for another few seconds. She then crossed her arms in front of herself, took the hem of her pullover in her hands and took it up and off over her head. She was wearing nothing underneath.

After a while she spoke. 'Do you like me?' she asked.

Words failed me. But then I half-collected my thoughts.

'*Sei bellissima*. You are gorgeous,' I said. This had the added advantage of being true.

'You don't think I am too young?' she persisted, growing in confidence and turning her matchless torso this way and that.

'No,' I said. 'You are very grown-up.'

She moved about six inches nearer me.

'Would you like me to stay?'

This was not the sort of question that has baffled philosophers and scientists down the ages.

'Do you dare?' I asked.

'No,' she said. 'I have brought you this.' She passed me the magazine. It was a copy of Playboy.

'The girls in this are even more beautiful than me,' she said.

'I don't think that can be true,' I said, realising sadly that I had lost a game the rules of which were almost wholly unknown to me.

She put her jumper back on.

'Maybe we can go for a walk tomorrow morning? The countryside is very pretty here,' she said.

But I had my trip to the Villa Rotonda all brilliantly planned. What on earth could I say? Perhaps I could stay another night…

'Would you really show me around tomorrow? After lunch? I would love to see all your favourite places.'

'After lunch? Well,' she said, 'I might. If I'm here.'

And with that she was gone.

I woke the next morning to a very curious noise, which

seemed to come from just outside my bedroom door. It was a human noise, somewhere between a hiss and a gasp and a sneeze. As it didn't stop, and as I had to get up anyway to grab a light breakfast and organise a taxi to La Rotonda, I threw on my dressing gown and opened the door.

What I saw was difficult to believe.

It was our landlady, on her knees, outside the single bathroom that served our floor, with her eye to the keyhole and having difficulty suppressing a full-scale attack of hysterical laughter.

I closed the door behind me gently but she heard and leapt guiltily to her feet.

'I don't like to pry,' I asked diplomatically, 'but what on earth are you up to?'

Her face was so red with excitement and her eyes so swollen with hilarity, it was extraordinary that she could speak at all.

'It is your friend, Alessandro. He does not sit on the lavatory like a gentleman, but perches on it like a huge egg-laying bird!'

The grotesqueness of this observation caused me to laugh out loud and I heard a sudden movement from inside the bathroom followed by the unmistakable sound of the chain being pulled. Our *signora* rushed downstairs 'to make the coffee', giggling like her fourteen-year-old former self being asked to sit next to Marcello Mastroianni.

I, too, thought discretion the better part of valour and re-treated until Alexander had emerged, checked the coast was clear and made for his own room to get dressed and ready for breakfast.

Our hostess served us and, every time she caught sight of Alexander, she looked as if she was going to get another fit of the giggles. Alex leant forward and addressed me conspiratorially. 'What the devil is the matter with her?' he demanded justifiably, looking at me as if I might have had something to do with it.

I described the scene as I had seen it. Alex blushed, the deepest crimson I have ever seen on a man.

It turned out he was a bit of a hygiene freak and, in order to protect himself from any unnecessary exposure to infection, he had long espoused the Arabic posture when using the loo. In Europe, where these matters are usually conducted on a porcelain pedestal replete with wooden lid, it meant climbing on to the thing and delivering, so to speak, from a great height. Presumably our innkeeper had fancied him (he was very good-looking) and was hoping for a sight of her Adonis in the altogether. What she saw was way beyond her wildest expectations.

In a way I regret that I had lacked the necessary scientific or medical curiosity to take a peek myself. But it wouldn't have had the same magic for me as it had for her. I also guiltily regret that he became known as the 'stool pigeon' for many years to come.

La Rotonda, in the clear spring morning light, was as magnificent as it could be. Not only was it grander than I had imagined, but the interiors, frescoed down to the last square inch, dazzled the two of us. Our guide, Alex's noble friend, seemed quite astonished that we could be so moved. But then, she lived with this sort of thing every day. Sometimes it is better to be a visitor than a resident.

We had an exceptional tour of the state rooms and after some time we went upstairs for a glass or two of prosecco, the Italian equivalent of champagne. Don't be snobbish about this wine; at its best it is nearly a match for its famous Gallic rival.

The house is an essay in geometry, a cube built around a cylinder surmounted with a hemisphere. The state rooms – the piano nobile – are above a suite of commodious storage rooms and cellars that allow the villa to pretend to be a farmhouse by informing the guests of the historical links with the fields that sweep down from the house. The chief room is at the centre and rises the whole height of the building into its dome. The walls are entirely frescoed, perhaps not as enchantingly as the walls of the Villa Barbaro at Maser,[3] but superbly all the same. All the rooms on this floor have fine stucco work and false architectural detail made of plaster, which merge into the trompe l'oeil wall painting of colonnades and architraves. The whole thing is a riot of colour, with not much in the way of furniture – it would hide the walls – and reminded us that guests in their elaborate dress (huge bustles for the girls, rapiers for the men) would have found it easier to mingle standing up.

Upstairs, which you reach via a narrow staircase set into the fabric of the walls, the house is laid out around the dome, which

---

[3] There, the frescoes are by Veronese and mark the perihelion of house painting.

is a little impractical. But in 1972, the family was blissfully relaxed, and pictures of children on horses offered a homely contrast to the stateliness below.

As we made our way back into town, Alex confided in me how extraordinary he thought it that since the 1950s these houses were in a near-terminal state of disrepair.

Alex had concluded that the only reason why villas of the Veneto had survived was because of an odd conspiracy of landowners, historians and local government, the last with a greedy eye to tourist revenue. At least they understood their extraordinary patrimony had value.

Whatever the cause, seen together they are truly one of the unsung wonders of the world. For Alex their survival was the stuff of optimism.

I agreed that there might be something in the air. But overall the forces of darkness were prevailing. There were whole streets of Georgian architecture still being pulled down by (elected) vandals and philistines in Dublin. The English upper class was continuing to demolish its grander country houses. The Americans, who had so little heritage in any case, were busy destroying Penn Central Station in New York. The Russians were filling their country houses with lunatics, and the East Germans had just blown up the Kaiserhof.

I felt myself that we would have to wait until the twenty-first century before the long process of reinventing civilisation might begin in earnest.

I recalled my many conversations with Henry in Pompeii. His assessment of the twentieth century – 'a catalogue of death, depression and philistinism, visited upon us like plagues' – rang in my ears. Over the seventy-one years that had passed since Death had opened the batting for the Boers in 1901, all four horsemen of the Apocalypse had returned every twenty years or less. The Boer War, the 'Great' War, the Russian Revolution, the Spanish Civil War, the Second World War, the nuclear bombing of Japan, the Korean War, Suez, the Malayan 'insurgency' and the Vietnam War: it was a sorry roll-call indeed. In 1972 another world war was not too implausible a prospect. Journalists were writing of 'mutually assured destruction', which they gaily abbreviated to 'MAD'.

Henry would have had us believe that a love affair with politics was the reason why we had seen professors of music being made to work in salt mines or having their throats cut in Russia, in China, in Cambodia...

'The "enlightened" imposition of *égalité* and the removal of "superstition" was not only the cause of the Cultural Revolution; it was the reason for the original "genocide",' he had told me. 'The Committee for Public Safety had coined the word for the eradication of priests and monks during the French Revolution. It was too new a coinage for it to be used to describe the systematic extermination of the North American Indians, but it fell back into currency in our "modern" twentieth century, in Asia, Europe and Africa, where it is guaranteed to continue.'

'Your friend Henry needs to cheer up,' said Alex. 'Education, especially history, is the way out of all that stuff. Truly educated people don't make the same mistakes twice. That's what education is for.'

'I wouldn't rely on History O levels for a social immunisation,' I said. 'Our greatest ever entrepreneur described history as "bunk",[4] and he may be right. What passes for history in schools is a sordid narrative of the lives of slaves or servants. Past glories and great men are more and more left unsung. And as for the Arts, our parents and grandparents thought the only viable art form was at first futurism, and since around 1925, modernism. Try to build a Gothic building today and see what the critics would have to say.'

'I meant education in general. Overall. The mind-stretching stuff that you and I had. Or claim to have had.'

'Well, as you're shifting ground, even education, as opposed to child minding, is itself highly suspect.' Henry's views had infected me. ' "Progressive" governments have more or less abolished it, in the state sector at least. After all, if we were to teach our children what we know, we might indeed be able to vaccinate them against

---

[4] I didn't know it then, of course, but Bill Gates has recently followed Henry Ford's famous dictum with an offering of his own, calling history 'an obsession with the rear-view mirror'. Gervas Douglas has suggested a way of breaking a driver out of such a fruitless reverie. 'Get Microsoft to design the car, of course. It will spend so much of its time breaking down that you won't have time to look back.'

the cult of modernism. The prevailing view, however, is that for the long-term benefit of the race, it's best that our children flounder in ignorance. That way, so goes the thinking, not only can they not repeat our mistakes, but it's cheaper.'

'Well, how do you imagine we have got to this impasse?' asked Alex, smiling slightly.

'I think it's guilt,' I replied. 'Even today, it is obvious that the twentieth century is a vile century. Its denizens, when not killing each other, leave behind a consuming worm of guilt. The fault lies with our parents and grandparents who, having survived their generation's turmoil, decided to reject wholesale all the self-confidence, knowledge and bourgeois certainties of the nine-teenth century. Our grandparents, especially, banished the link between application and excellence. They are iffy about excellence itself. You can forget taste. The near-continual horrors of the twentieth century convinced them that the Truth must lie in the future; that there was never a Golden Age. Don't turn around. Don't speak to your parents. Your grandparents were fools. "Forward, not back!" That's the depressing catchphrase.' I was on a roll.

'But,' said Alex, 'there are always contrarians. People like us. There are lots of us who believe that education is the means by which one generation talks to the next. It's to us, a privileged minority perhaps, that society must turn to fund and spawn a steady restoration and recovery of our heritage. We must trust ourselves to overthrow the relentless, destructive process called "the future". Let's appeal to their pockets. Economically speaking, it's more expensive to destroy than to restore.'

'Well, I hope you're right,' I said. 'But in the meantime, let's see as many of these villas as we can before they fall down or are sold for scrap.'

It may be that the Villa Rotonda is the loveliest of all the villas, but it has many competitors. Alex and I had planned to see as great a number of these palaces as humanly possible, starting with the Villa Valmarana ai Nani, famous for the inspiring frescoes by the Tiepolo father and son team. We also decided to see the Villas Manin, Loschi Zileri, Foscarini and Selvatico, this last with its remarkable staircase that descends from the house, through the park and straight through a collection of tenants' houses. Some, like the Villa Serego, are so stunning they make your heart ache. There are more than a hundred villas worth a visit in the Veneto alone. As the *Guide Michelin* would have it, *ça vaut le détour*.

But all that could wait until the next day. Which left me a spare afternoon. I asked myself an important question. Had I given the picturesque city of Vicenza, and its surrounding woods and copses, enough attention?

I had an idea…

Chapter the Fifteenth

1972: Roman Holidays (Part I) – *La Dolce Vita*

In which the author finds his feet, socially speaking, and begins a programme of theatre and opera going which is to last him all his life. He learns about the origins of Rome Airport – which are more interesting than you might suspect – and how to torment a taxman. He hears of a dinner so grand it is still talked of 400 years later and he meets a Sardinian girl…

My self-appointed task in Rome had been to master the language and it was nearly completed. I was beginning to reflect on coming home to a sensible job in England. But there were still some adventures to be had in the Eternal City (including sitting my diploma), and in the summer of 1972 I decided to share a flat with a Florentine friend of mine, Sandro Ridomi. He was the son of a famous publisher, but was fed up with Florence.

'My people have been in the same palace on the Lung' Arno for 400 years. The man on the street corner who sells me a coffee, his people have been doing that for 400 years. The beggar outside the church – his people have been doing that for 400 years. It's a bore.'

So he had bought a little place in Rome, in the Via del Coliseo. He had a spare room, which he was looking to rent out, and I jumped at the chance.

When I finally said goodbye to Roberto, the bad-tempered landlord of Il Sole, where I had put myself up for so many months, he told me that I was welcome to take up residence again, any time I liked. That discount that I had mentioned so many times? Next time I would get it. No, he really meant it.

Now began the high period of my stay in Rome. I had, and leapt at, a chance to see *Tosca* at the Rome Opera which, given the subject matter, was a sine qua non. Rather more cheerful entertainments were the operas at the Terme di Caracalla, and an outstanding *Aida* will always remain with me. Since that performance I have always felt that too many operas lack live elephants. I also started to go to the theatre. One curious evening I saw Pinter's *Homecoming* in the majestic theatre in the Largo del Torre Argentina. At the time I was surprised and delighted that the leading actress took her clothes off on stage – the first time it had been done in Rome and, therefore, the beginning of a new era. But 'homecoming' was in my mind and began to prey on it.

In Rome I had met a strikingly good-looking young Romano-Venetian, Violante, who lived with her parents in a superb apartment occupying the top three floors of a palace literally on the left-hand side of the Spanish Steps. She asked me outright if I were thinking of packing my bags and memories and taking them to another place.

'Because,' she said most generously, 'if you are, then I will give you a farewell party.'

The idea of a party, at the end of September, perhaps, began to grow on me. I had an awful lot of friends I wanted to thank with declarations of eternal friendship.

One of these was Lanfranco. Lanfranco's father was a Count from Lombardy who lived in a fine apartment in his family's old palace in the so-called Piazza delle Tartarughe, right in the heart of Rome. There is a breathtaking fountain in the square. It was said that one of Lanfranco's forebears had it built overnight in order to impress and seduce a young beauty.

Before the last war, the Count had mixed in the wrong circles in a vain effort to reinvigorate his house's ancient position in society, and he had fallen in with a fast and dishonest set of Mussolini's placemen.

They had introduced the Count to a club where poker was played for high stakes and had let him win for a while. But then they had ceased to smile and had taken off their jackets. Now reduced to a single floor of his old palace, his castle in Lombardy still in unrestored ruins, the Count had taken to playing chess, at first as an amateur and later professionally. He had achieved Grand Master as early as 1934 and had never lost a tournament until he retired twenty-seven years later.

But he had not lost the taste for a gamble. I would pitch up, once a week, and we would sit down with the chessboard. He would fetch a bottle of Lombardic rosé, and we would play ten games. If I won just one of the ten, he would pay me 10,000 lire. If he won them all, then I would pay him.

He never paid me. Not even once. But I considered 10,000 lire a small fee for being coached by a player of this standing and I paid up cheerfully week after week.

Mind you, Lombardic rosé is not the greatest wine in Italy. A better place to go for a glass of something actually drinkable was a little wine shop on the Via Mario de' Fiori (a turning off the fashionable Via Condotti).

You would not know from the outside that you could buy wine by the glass in this Enoteca.[1] Cheap plastic strips admit you into a plain little room stacked with wine cases, some made of wood, most of cardboard. The wines come from all over Italy, and Nicoló's prices are very reasonable. But go in a little further, go right into the shop, and you will find a minuscule counter which doubles as a bar. On a shelf behind the landlord are a number of silver cups, some rather large, that have been won at the races by a long line of horses from the mighty Torlonia stable. There are photos, too, of racehorses bearing Prince Torlonia's colours. And at the makeshift bar there are two or three, and very occasionally four, gentlemen representatives of Rome's most ancient noble families talking racing and arguing the odds.

One of the most distinguished of the habitués was Alessandro Lante, or Don Alessandro Lante Montefeltro della Rovere, to quote the name on his cards under his ducal coronet. Alex is a direct descendant (whoops! Sorry, I mean collateral descendant) of Pope Sextus IV. All you need to stay in business as an aristocrat in Rome, I had been told several times, is to have a pope in the family every 300 years. This meant that Alex really needed to encourage one of his cousins to seek holy orders. His family's most recent Pontiff was the aforesaid Sextus, from whom the word 'Sistine' derives, and who was the pope who commissioned Michelangelo to do some interior decoration in the old Curia in the early *cinquecento*. He had come close, however, when another Don Alessandro Lante had received a pink hat in 1813.

---

[1] Oenoteque, or wine store.

Another regular was Prince Civitella-Cessi, familiarly but confusingly known as Don Alessandro Torlonia. He was there most days. The bar doubled as a remote office branch of his stables. It was certainly handy for the old boy, who was then in his sixties. His palace – one of the grandest in Rome – was a stone's throw from this little den.

Torlonia was the fifth prince of that name. His mother, Mary Elsie Moore, was the heiress daughter of the American businessman Charles Arthur Moore, a hugely successful shipping broker and hardware manufacturer in Connecticut. On that distaff side, his grandmother was Kate Moore Campbell, herself the subject of many stories in Europe. When she died, her obituary declared that 'she left the world as she might have left the Ritz, with little tips for everyone'.

Torlonia's personal fortune, whose origins were old even by Roman standards, grew considerably with his great-great-grandfather. This was the banker-prince who had managed the papal finances through most of the eighteenth century. In 1794, out of heartfelt gratitude, the Pope created him Duke of Bracciano and Count of Pisciarelli. Obviously this was not nearly enough, so in 1803 the Duke persuaded the Pope to allow some of his other great estates to be acknowledged in the same way. The 'Servant of Servants' agreed, and he added the marquisates of Romavecchia and Turrita, and the principality of Civitella-Cesi, to his aristocratic titles. By now he was on a roll. From 1809 he was styled 'Roman Patrician'[2] and from 1820 he could call himself Duke of Poli and Guadagnolo. This, needless to say, is a very much abridged list of his titles. He was the duke of that very Poli whose waters flow to the Trevi Fountain in the centre of Rome, and there he built himself an occasional residence, one wall of which is the fountain itself. The banker, naturally enough, was also the builder of the famous Villa Torlonia near Rome.

I asked him, when I felt sufficiently confident, why he had seen fit to rent his villa to Mussolini as an official residence.

'Well, I was much younger then, of course. The villa had fallen into disrepair, and being on the scale it is, I had no idea of how to finance its restoration.'

---

[2] *Patrizio Romano* (or *Patricius Romanus*).

'So the Fascists offered you a huge amount of money? The sort of thing no one can refuse?'

'On the contrary, they offered me one lira a year as a rent. But it was still a good deal.'

'I don't understand, Excellency. How does one lira a year work out as a good deal?'

'Well, you've been there, I imagine. The villa was begun in 1806 for my ancestor, Giovanni, the banker. His architect was Valadier, the neo-classicist, who also built the Pincio and laid out the Villa Borghese. It took him an age to finish it. The first member of my line to live there was Giovanni's son, Alessandro.'

'I haven't ever been in,' I admitted, 'but I've been around the park. I visited a marvellous "Moorish" kiosk, and all sorts of other exotic garden pavilions.'

'Ah yes. Did you like our "English" garden? It's said to be one of the best of its kind.'

'I adored it.'

'Excellent. We are talking to the government about opening it to the public. And our collection of statues, too.'

'From what I saw from the outside, the villa looks to be in pretty good shape.'

'Exactly. That was the point of the deal. It would have cost us millions to restore it. The deal meant we could let the Fascists do it, and we would take the villa back just as soon as the regime fell.'

'But that might have been hundreds of years?'

'So what? Torlonias have been around long enough. We could wait. And we were right. Mussolini spent almost a million dollars on the restoration; he fell, we're still here, and we have it back.'

'But you must have had some regrets about dealing with those gangsters?'

'Yes, indeed. The Duce forced me to allow him to turn the third- and fourth-century Jewish catacombs underneath the landscaped park into a bomb shelter. That was indeed philistine, but I could see no way around it. The government says that even that can be put right in time. We shall see.'

The Prince, popularly thought to be the richest man in Rome, had recently been in the newspapers. Like all such people he was deeply put out by the way the press treated him.

There is a gossipy side to the Romans' largely generous character which allows them to embroider a good story until it becomes palpably implausible. It is obviously untrue that the Prince would seek to pay any less tax than he was required to do. Nevertheless, the Roman papers had delighted in recounting the story (as they insisted had happened) about the most recent princely engagement with the taxman.

It was well known in Rome that before the war the Fascists had wanted to quarry the family for funds to finance Mussolini's mad visions of a new Roman Empire. But the Torlonias are of banking stock – their origins are at least as much from the purple of commerce as from the ranks of the aristocracy – and there was a deal to be made with them. It concerned a farm owned by the family, almost on the coast to the west of the capital. The name of this farm was Fiumicino.

Most of the flat, swampy lands that separate Rome from the sea had been uninhabited, except by brigands, masochists and depressives for many centuries. The problem was malaria. The only remedy was the wholesale use of DDT, a disturbingly powerful insecticide powder that was dropped in great clouds from biplanes. It was effective enough. Its only downside was that it caused the farm workers to wheeze a lot and then die.

But Italian scientists had for once come up with a truly ingenious solution: the water buffalo.

These stately creatures like nothing better than to pad about in swamps, devouring the river grass, and while they potter about they crush the larval mosquitoes underfoot, since the fledgling beasties metamorphose from cocoons on the underside of the water's surface. What's more, the farmers now have an extra source of income, for buffalo milk makes the finest mozzarella money can buy.[3]

So Fiumicino had a reprieve of sorts, and embraced the new technology with renewed fervour. Of course, the presence of a few water buffalo did not actually add much to the value of the land. The land was always fundamentally poor, compared with (say) the farms of Tuscany or the Po valley.

---

[3] Want an odd job? Try milking a buffalo.

So when the Fascists decided they needed a brand new all-singing-and-dancing runway, near Rome, it just happened that Prince Torlonia owned a site flat enough and large enough to support an airport fit for a European capital; no, correction – the capital of the Roman Empire.

The negotiation will have been long and hard, but Mussolini owed the Prince a favour, now that he was living in the Villa Torlonia. Torlonia stuck to his guns and eventually disposed of an estate of swamp, mosquitoes and buffalo at a fabulous price to the Fascist government. This enormous deal, and some of the fee was actually honoured, restored the young prince to his place at the top of the pile in Rome.

This influx of funds proved especially useful while he sought credibility with the Spanish court. He had met and was pressing his suit on the Infanta of Spain, the title always given to the eldest daughter of the King of Spain, and who was very probably the most eligible spinster in all the parishes of Catholic Europe. Their fantastic wedding, on 14 January 1935, was easily the most lavish in Madrid in the twentieth century, and Torlonia took home his blushing Beatriz de Borbón-Battenberg, daughter of King Alfonso XIII of Spain[4] and of Queen Victoria-Eugenia, herself born a princess of Battenberg, with a stupendous dowry.

Don Alessandro Torlonia had a slight American accent when he spoke English. This was probably due to his Hollywood connections. His youngest sister, the princess Donna Marina Torlonia di Civitella-Cessi, was grandmother of the American actress Brooke Shields. And also he was first cousin of Dr William T Close Moore, the father of actress Glenn Close.

Well, perhaps not unnaturally, the Italian tax authorities had little patience for Don Alessandro's plea of poverty. So he invited the chief tax collector to come over to Palazzo Torlonia in person.

When the inspector arrived, he was more than a little surprised to be admitted to the house by the Prince himself. At no time were any flunkeys to be seen. With elaborate courtesy, the Prince ushered the taxman into the great salon, known to all Italians from the countless lavishly illustrated books on the Renaissance. In pole position were two chairs. One was a gilded fauteuil from

---

[4] Fr Alfonso de Zulueta's godfather.

the early seventeenth century, the other the sort of rickety item you see in a farmhouse kitchen.

Sitting the taxman on the antique museum piece, the prince gestured helplessly at the walls, where dark oblong spaces showed clearly where paintings had once hung.

'The horses, my dear sir,' explained the Prince with an economical gesture. 'They ran off with all my money.'

As the prince expounded on the terrible reversal of fortune his kin had endured, the tears began to well in the taxman's eye; he had a heart.

And his cheeks were still damp as he walked back to his car, parked some way from the palace, past the rows and rows of stationary furniture vans, waiting patiently in the Via Torlonia for the 'all-clear'…

The Romans are famous for these theatrical gestures.

The Florentine banker, Prince Chigi, during the Renaissance, had invited Pope Alexander VII to dine in his 'little' villa perched on a cliff overhanging the Tiber. His palace in Rome was still being built.

The Pope arrived in due course with a small retinue of around forty secretaries, *camerlunghi*,[5] cardinals, his confessor and other dignitaries of pivotal importance to the Holy See. The Chigis, princes and dukes from Tuscany and Lombardy, received them all with lavish hospitality. When at last the papal party was shown into the great dining room, the table was groaning with crystal, gilded silverware and solid gold ornaments that had been made in Florence expressly for the occasion. On the centre of the table was a scale model of the newly rebuilt Basilica of St Peter, spun out of sugar filaments, whose windows were paned with slices of almond and whose dome and surrounding cupolas were made from a glacé melon and caramelised white peaches.

Following the Pope's intoned grace, which combined a blessing on the Chigi household with a benediction, a formidable feast was served to His Holiness and his party. The footmen, behind every guest, poured the finest wines the Frescobaldi estates could provide. And finally the meal came to a very satisfactory conclusion.

The Pope rose to address his host. 'Your Excellency,' he began,

---

[5] Chamberlains.

'will you allow us to express our thanks for this sensational and magnificent dinner you had advertised to us as a simple repast?'

The Prince now rose to reply to his sovereign.

'No, Your Holiness; it is the House of Chigi that is honoured for all time by Your Holiness' acceptance of our unworthy supper. As such an event has never and cannot ever be equalled in our history, please permit me to make one final little gesture of how unrepeatable is the honour you have done us.'

And with that he clicked his fingers. The footmen threw open the great windows over the river a hundred feet below, and the glass, the silver, the ornaments – everything that was on the table, the output that every artisan along the Arno had slaved over for ten long years of patient craftsmanship, was carried in the priceless damask tablecloth and hurled out into the air and into the raging torrent of the young Tiber beneath.

The Pope was said to have been impressed. He said as much as he and his party returned to their carriages for the hour's drive back to the Quirinale.

It was only when Pope Alexander was safely out of sight on the road to Rome, along a road that the prince had lit with torches all the way, that the banker's men hauled on the nets they had carefully set in the Tiber below and retrieved their master's priceless artefacts.

The Chigi's town house, Palazzo Chigi, today serves as a base for the prime minister, as his official residence.

It is just around the corner from Piazza Navona, arguably the most incredible square in Europe. Despite the fact that it is a tourist trap, its magic is undimmed. The sheer scale of Piazza Navona makes it able to handle even the ghastly influx of high summer; though someone should tell the world's backpackers that Rome is at its most uncomfortable in August.

Of course, some of the tourists do not come from so very far away, and they are not all there just to rubberneck at Bernini's fountains or at the Palazzo Massimo alle Colonne just out of sight behind Palazzo Aldobrandini at the end of the 'square'. Though perhaps they should, for the architecture of Palazzo Massimo is particularly elegant and it is one of the most successful examples of early Roman mannerism.

My usual spot in the piazza was Sabatini's, a perfect little café for me to take a coffee in the open air and peruse the paper. In 1972, nothing much was happening to entice me back to the Anglo-Saxon world. OPEC had raised the price of oil to record levels. Sheikh Yamani had informed a panicking market that in real terms the hike was not really so very life threatening. The Shah of Persia had been on television, casually telling us that a high price was in our interest, as it would spur us on to find alternative fuels. The government in Rome had decided to allow cars on to the streets only on alternative days, depending whether their number plate ended in an odd or even number. Most prosperous families had immediately bought another car.

I put down the newspaper in disgust. And as I did so, I noticed that there, at my table, doing her nails no less, was a strikingly pretty, almost gypsy-like girl. What cheek!

'I'm sorry,' she said. 'Was this chair taken?'

I looked at her more carefully. 'No, help yourself,' I said. She studied me in a provocative way.

We both asked each other simultaneously, 'Where are you from?'

'England,' said I. 'Sardinia,' said she. At the same time. And, at the same time, we both laughed.

We talked happily for perhaps half an hour. She told me how enchanting Sardinia was, how sometimes they would visit the Costa Smeralda, though the shopkeepers were only interested in the rich and did not make them welcome. She told me that her kind was sometimes called *banditti* by the newspapers, who understood nothing, because it was a tradition to do these things, not the terrible crime they said it was. And she demonstrated to me how she could smoke a cigarette the wrong way round – the lit end inside her mouth. This was to avoid attracting the attention of the police when they were about their business at night.

By now she was sitting square on to me, her ankles turned around the chair legs, her dark and wilfully unkempt hair setting off those pools of dark light that were her eyes. She was the kind of girl you could imagine playing Carmen and meaning every word.

I was very flattered by her smouldering attentions.

'Are you in Rome with your family?' I asked, in a Prince Charlesy sort of way.

'Not really. With my fiancé.[6] He has business here.'

'Is he about?'

'He will be. In about half an hour. Do you have a cigarette?'

She held my hand with both of hers while she lit up. My pulse began to race.

But I had another appointment. She seemed genuinely surprised when I put my papers together and stood up.

It was the first Wednesday in the first month of the summer with an 'r' in it, and the Palazzo Massimo alle Colonne was open on that day to the public, for two short hours. It would be my only chance to see inside.

Am I a complete idiot? I silently asked myself, as I prepared to part company with the siren. I'm little better than a trainspotter…

'Come and see me tomorrow,' she commanded. 'I will be here. Same time. At Sabatini's.'

---

[6] '*Affidanzato*', or '*fidanzato*'. Perhaps 'boyfriend known to parents' is a better translation. Many Italian girls have several *affidanzati* before they marry. For practice, I suppose.

Chapter the Sixteenth

1972: Roman Holidays (Part II) – *E Pericoloso Sporgersi*

In which the author learns of Rome's oldest family, of Napoleon's son the 'King of Rome', and reflects on the arts over coffee and profiteroles with an ex-convict in the elegant Caffè Greco. He drinks champagne at the Spanish Embassy to the Holy See, and prepares to say goodbye to Rome with an immense party overlooking the Spanish Steps.

The Massimo family had ordered their palace to be built after their old one had been destroyed during the sack of Rome of 1527. Unusually, the monumental façade, with its six ground-level Doric columns, is convex, in order to allow it to follow the old Via Papale, now renamed the Via Vittorio Emmanuele, and to take advantage of the foundations of an old Roman theatre.[1] A smooth rustication covers the adjoining walls and the upper storeys, which are perforated with rectangular windows on the piano nobile. There are two further storeys with smaller, square and rectangular windows above. The stone frames are simply detailed, with a ribbon motif on the higher storeys. The overall effect is severe.

But even from the outside you can see the architect[2] faced a difficult architectural problem. On the inside, the ingenious ground plan approaches the contorted site as a challenge and sets rectangular rooms around rectangular courtyards, linking them axially to the palace entrances. This palace is a masterwork.

In contrast to its forbidding exterior, the interior halls, court-yards and rooms are elaborately ornamented with decorated walls and both coffered and vaulted ceilings. The first courtyard is a

---

[1] The Odeon of Domitian.
[2] Balthazar Peruzzi.

cluttered treasure trove of statues, bas-reliefs and other bits of classical ruin. The first floor above opens on to the courtyard in a fine loggia, with gilded and polychrome vaulting. In the second courtyard there is a nympheum. If socialism were really a force for good, everyone should have one of these. That would be equalising upwards indeed.

It may be a great status symbol to have had a pope in the family, but the Massimos go one better. In the seventeenth century one of the Massimos was canonised. There is a little chapel where the saintly remains are interred. On the anniversary of the canonisation the palace is opened to the public. Hardly anyone seems to know this and I had the place to myself. True, one of the Prince's retainers followed me at a safe distance, eyeing me up and down suspiciously. But despite the temptation, I left everything where I found it. Most of the stuff worth nicking was too big and heavy to pocket, anyway.

At one point I caught sight of the Prince himself. Only the owner of such a house will walk backwards into a room while talking to a secretary who (judging by the distant clatter of her stilettos on the marble floor) was over a hundred yards away.

Somehow it reminded me of a story I had heard about one of his ancestors.

Napoleon had sent word to the Roman nobility that the Pope, at the time under house arrest in Fontainebleau, was to bless – and by implication crown – the infant King of Rome, the future Napoleon II.

This sad boy lived just twenty-one years, between 1811 and 1832. The Emperor insisted that he be called King of Rome for his first three years, but after that Napoleon changed his mind and insisted that the boy be known as the Prince of Parma. In 1818 he changed tack again, and from exile declared his son to be the Duke of Reichstadt. Well, what's in a name?

As Napoleon's abdication in 1815 was in favour of his son, Bonapartists referred to him from that moment as Napoleon II, but he never did rule in France. In fact, after 1815 the boy was kept 'prisoner' in Austria, under a very comfortable 'house' arrest, free to travel within Austrian boundaries. The 'prison' was a suitable palace. He died there, barely out of his teens, of tuberculosis.

In 1940 Adolf Hitler transferred the boy's remains to France, as a gift. They are now in the great mausoleum at Les Invalides in Paris, lying beside his father's. The pitiful life of the 'Eaglet' is the subject of Edmond Rostand's sad and magnificent drama *L'Aiglon*.

But let me retrace my steps. When the Emperor arrived at Fontainebleau in 1811 with his infant son, he gave an audience to all the Roman nobility, including the supreme pontiff in his role of King of the Papal States, and who was effectively Napoleon's prisoner. Blue-blooded Romans were 'permitted' to make the long and dangerous overland journey to pay homage to their new sovereign.

As they knelt one by one before the Emperor and his baby boy, an aide would brief the Emperor as to whom they all were. From time to time Napoleon would exchange a few imperial bons mots with a grateful subject.

The Roman aristocracy could not be blamed for considering this Napoleon Buonaparte a Corsican peasant, though modern historians believe he came from *gentilhomme* stock.

But when Prince Massimo tried to rise, the Emperor leaned forward and spoke to him so that all could hear.

'They tell me, Prince, that you are descended from Fabius Maximus. Is there truth in this?'

The Prince looked up at his new overlord, a man whose recent and modest origins had already been obscured and reworked. He smiled.

'I really cannot say with any certainty, sire. It is merely a rumour that has circulated in my family for the last 1,800 years.'

The palace next door to the Massimos belongs to the Aldobrandinis, who own that vast villa that dominates Frascati. The better wine from there bears their label. I had been their guest many months before. Below us, in Piazza Navona, strange, pagan festivities had unfolded to mark the end of the twelve days of Saturnalia that follow Christmas.

They were hospitality itself, but the stately splendour of a private party could not compare with the noisy and cheerful celebrations in the public square below. Bad children are given coal (made of extruded sugar) and good children are given money (made of chocolate wrapped in gold foil). All of Rome congregates in Piazza Navona to catch a glimpse of the *befana*, the witch who is allowed on this day to give the Romans a hint of the religion that Christianity replaced.

Overall, the Romans have masses of style which shows in most things they do. Take coffee, for example. When in need of coffee in Rome, take my tip and have one from time to time in the Antico Caffé Greco.

This is simply the loveliest little place in Europe to partake of an espresso. For some marvellous reason, no moderniser has wrought his evil improvements on it since 1770, except to install a discreet but very decent espresso machine.

True, it can fill up with Japanese tourists, who take a lot of photographs of each other. But this is a small price to pay for the marvellous paintings all over the walls and the impeccable service. It's a little eighteenth-century jewel, on the Via Condotti, just below the Spanish Steps. And the best paintings there may be the ones by Angelica Kauffmann.

Kauffmann was born in Switzerland in 1741 where her father, Johann Joseph, trained her in painting from a very early age. As soon as she grew up she developed her skills in most of the major European cities, including Milan, Florence, Rome, Venice and London.

It was in England where she was most admired, particularly for her talent as a portraitist. In 1768 she was nominated as one of the thirty-six original members of the newly founded Royal Academy. She returned the compliment by settling in London, where she died in 1807, sixty-five years old.

Angelica Kauffmann is one of the few female old masters to feature in the history of European art.

But why should there be so few feminine old masters, so to speak?

Yes, I can understand why there has been such a small number of scientists or engineers of the fair sex. Indisputably, the education system used to be biased against them. Madame Curie is the proverbial exception.

But why is it left to Clara Schumann to be the only great female composer?

Why was Angelica Kauffmann's example followed by so few other women?

Great writers too, despite that curious season when the genius of Austen, the Brontës and George Eliot arose, are predominantly men.

Even female romantic poets, like Elizabeth Barret Browning, have rarity value.

What accounts for this? British lady watercolourists were all over Italy in the eighteenth century and, thanks in part to Byron, all over Greece in the nineteenth. Where are their works? In which galleries?

Every house of even modest gentility had a Broadwood Grand, or at least a spinet or clavichord. Where are the concert pieces penned by the female hand? Jenni Murray's explanation (that all women are utterly blameless and unfairly put upon, whereas all men are rapists or child molesters) did not ring true for me.

These were my thoughts in the Caffé Greco as I patiently awaited the arrival of an English lad whom Sandro had wanted me to meet. He had told me that Peter was an interesting example of the merits of a modern British education.

'Nice chap,' Sandro had said cryptically, 'but always talk to him in English. His Italian is truly horrible.'

Peter was indeed a nice chap. As I ordered my usual cappuccino and profiteroles (he had tea and a Welsh rarebit) I tried to get him to tell me a bit of his story. I was keen to learn why his Italian was so frightful that even Italians, notoriously bad at languages as they are, preferred to address him in English.

It seemed he had been raised in Chingford, or Dagenham, but had been dissatisfied with the narrow horizons of both his school and his parents. He had decided to go abroad, just like that. No plans of any kind. I warmed to him.

'I had to find some way of supporting myself, but I don't have an accent like yours that people want to learn. So I thought I'd sell a little grass. It's easy to grow here and I had seen people selling it on the Spanish Steps.'

Whenever I walked down the Spanish Steps from the Hotel Hassler, where I had recently taken to breakfasting on the terrace – with a view to die for – I was routinely accosted by drug pushers. It was no big deal. I was only surprised that anyone dared

Piazza San Marco, Venice, March 1972

Doge's Palace, Venice, 1972

View from hotel window, Venice, March 1972

Fancy dress party, Rome, 1972.
I am dressed as an early archbishop of Canterbury.

With two young friends in the Roman Forum, 1972

In a bar in Sicily, 1972

My sister, Kate, and my brother, Giles, in Paris, 1973

– the Roman police had countless closed-circuit cameras focused on the steps and regularly took these idiots away by the cartload.

'Anyway,' he persevered, 'I was making a reasonable living when I was taken by either arm and thrown into the back of a police van. They took me to Regina Coeli, the fearful lock-up, and took away everything I had on me, including my belt. Without so much as a "by your leave", they banged me up.'

'So you demanded to see the British Consul?'

'Well, I would have done if I could have done, but the fact is I couldn't speak a word of Italian and no one could or would speak a word of English. So they just left me to flounder. I tried shouting and sign language, but they wouldn't have any of it. I knew my parents would be going frantic with no idea where I was, and if they had known I was sharing a cell with seven other guys who made cannibals look like Texas Rangers it would have been even worse for them.'

I digested this simile for a moment.

'So how did you get out?'

'Well, after a while, you begin to pick up the lingo. After six months, you are fluent, I can tell you. One of the rapists was really helpful with the grammar, and the child molester was really patient with me, forcing me to do my homework and my revision.'

Just like the ones who taught me at school, I thought.

'Eventually, I was able to make myself understood to a relatively friendly warden. A couple of days later a British official appeared and he got me out. No trial, nothing. Just banged up and then thrown out. Not even given the chance to say goodbye to my new friends. What sort of a country is this, anyway?'

Just behind him was a Kauffmann portrait of a romantic poet, dressed as a Greek freedom fighter, about to banish the Ottomans from the Hellenes. I was beginning to doubt that the neckerchief was the only thing they had in common.

'At least you learned Italian,' I said.

'Well, it's more Roman than Italian,' he admitted. 'It is possible that it is a little rough and ready.'

And with that, he clicked his fingers for the waiter and said in perfect Romanaccio, the Roman dialect, 'Oi, dungface, go and fetch my sodding bill before I slit your horrible little throat.'

The service is certainly prompt in the Caffè Greco.

Having waved goodbye to Peter, I passed the bottom of the Spanish Steps and that heart-stopping little fountain, la Barcaccia, carved by the great Bernini's father in 1627. Next door there is the seventeenth-century Spanish Embassy to the Holy See, where I was expected for a glass of champagne.

How I got to know the ambassador is hard to remember, but it may have had something to do with his comely daughter, Ana.

The Spanish take the Vatican very seriously, and their embassy to the Holy See is far grander than their other one in Rome, to the Quirinale.

The building is a little stern on the outside, but don't let that fool you. Inside is a fine atrium with columns and then a little courtyard with its own fountain.

The interiors, or at least the ambassador's apartments, are decorated in the Pompeian Third Style. The only other house I have seen that is so strictly antique is Ickworth in Suffolk. But at Ickworth this decoration is confined to a single room. In the Palazzo di Spagna, as you step off the busy street, you enter into the ancient world. Highly recommended at the end of a long day.

I always drank champagne there. Champagne, expensive any-where, was doubly so in Italy, so it seemed a real extravagance.

'Let me share a little secret with you,' his Excellency confided in me. 'I buy the stuff at the Vatican supermarket, duty-free.'

It had never occurred to me that there was a Vatican super-market. How very practical these priests are.

Half of Rome seems to know about the supermarket. You can fill up your car there. You can buy a Ferrari there. It's like a duty-free Harrods with H R Owen and filling station attached, and it's all there for the convenience of those who have abjured wealth and material possessions the better to follow in the footsteps of Our Lord.

The letters SCV in Vatican number plates stand for Sacred City of the Vatican (*Sacra Città Vaticana*). But the Romans say they mean *Se Cristo Vedessi*: 'If Christ could but see'.

An early night, another day. Back from teaching English to my eccentric RAI student, attempting to learn white water rafting, I found my way to Sabatini's in Piazza Navona. I took my usual table. Almost instantly I saw the Sardinian girl again. This time she was not in the mood to sit down but was standing near the café, smoking and chatting with a group of mates.

I put my newspaper down and went up to her.

'Do you remember me? We met yesterday. You're from Sardinia.'

'Of course I do, English.' She stuck her cheek forward and I kissed it.

Some of her friends had now spotted me and had stopped talking. One of them, clearly their leader, was a streetwise ruffian with designer stubble. There was something missing in his manner. Any concession to humanity, perhaps. His eyes, of cornflower blue, had no kindness in them of any sort.

He pulled the girl up sharply by her elbow and said something to her in urgent tones that I could not decipher. She replied equally volubly, adding only a famous Italian gesture. He then came over to me with a tight smile on his face.

'OK, English, there is no problem. This time I leave you alone and you will be able to walk away. But let me teach you some Sardinian manners. You say "Good morning" to the *fidanzato* first, not to his girl. Better for you that you know this.'

And then they were off, with purpose in their gait. And so was I, somewhat shaken, in the opposite direction. What sort of an innocent fool was I? It was not as if the newspapers did not report the kidnappings of tourists in Rome and Florence with dreary frequency. Sardinians were in the news. In Tuscany especially they were proving to be the most ruthless sort of atavistic barbarians. Sometimes the bandits had tied their victims up in thin wire while ransom negotiations took place, dragging on for weeks, and the poor wretches had to be fed by hand the occasional sandwich. And yet, there I was, entranced like a rabbit in a huntsman's torch, being baited into their lair. Had the girl's sensational appearance undone my instinct for self-preservation or my sense of danger? How many people have been charmed by complete strangers into going along to some dark place or cave, in civilised Italy or in the hills of Afghanistan? There is no easier victim than your willing star-struck idiot.

I had to get my act together if I was going to enjoy my lunch at the Polo Club. *Tutta Roma* seems to be a member of this place, and in summer you eat around the pool. The moment I got there I bumped into Caroline Swan, an English friend, who was in deep chinwag with Violante – that same Violante who had promised me a party.

'I'm off too,' announced Caroline. 'I've been in Rome long enough. I'm going to take a place in Paris. Some friends of mine have been accepted at INSEAD, and I'm going to share a flat with them in Neuilly. You should think Paris, too.'

'I've heard of INSEAD,' I said. 'It's Europe's leading business school, in Fontainebleau. Its students have to be trilingual and have three years post-university experience. They tell me that job openings and plane tickets from around the world are pinned to the notice board at graduation time. Your mates must be very bright.'

'So you are still set on leaving us?' asked Violante. 'Have you decided on a date for our "do"?'

'Not really, but I suppose it had better be soon. Can we make it late September? I must get back to London at the same time as the new batch of graduates are doing their rounds.'

'Of course we can. Let's say the thirtieth. Do you want to use my invitation cards?'

In the end I did take a few from her, but mainly I just rang around. It was a two-day telethon, but I invited almost a hundred people. I had been putting down roots and that had never been the plan. It could never be the plan. I might be able to earn a penny or two odd-jobbing, but if I were not to scrounge for the rest of my days I needed my own money, and to me that meant the City of London. But I frankly confess my heart was only just in it.

There was time for one quick outing for a week to Porto Ercole, staying with friends who sailed from there, before I was back in Rome. I was probably the saddest man on earth. Rome had metamorphosed into a lover, and I was letting her go because I could not afford her. I was being practical, which is a girly trait and is best avoided by real men.

The day assigned for my farewell party seemed to rush up on me. Violante made all the preparations herself. It was to be a memorable affair at her breathtaking apartment.

When the day came, her palatial flat filled rapidly with the astonishingly glamorous gilded youth of Rome. From the outset everyone seemed to be having a jolly time. Mainly they all knew each other, anyway. Violante had spared no expense, and fine wines flowed like the Trevi fountain.

For me, however, it was rather different. Through most of that party I was close to tears. I had fallen in love, with Rome, with my friends, with Arianna, and to all of these I had to say goodbye.

When the sun went down, the Roman roofs turned pink and the city's terracotta rendering began to glow like an Irish peat fire. Floodlights lit the great dome of St Peter's, which dominated the roofscape to the south-west, and behind us the great church of St Trinità del Monte came to life, reflecting a yellow light down the famous *scalinata*. Leaning over a railing I watched the crowds in Piazza di Spagna milling about far below, buying roast chestnuts from the Abruzzese street vendors, elegantly greeting each other on their *passeggio*, and carrying huge bags from the fashion shops in Via Condotti, each containing little more than a handkerchief with a label.

I turned back to my – Violante's – party. I forced a smile or two and kissed cheeks and shook hands with the most remarkable bunch of people I had somehow collected from almost my first moments in the Italian capital. Ettore, for example. He was always more than a pupil. He was my friend and was there with at least a dozen of the talented people he had introduced me to. Also there was the couple who ran the guided tours I so much enjoyed giving. All the people I had met via Sandro, or Violante, or Lanfranco, or any of them – they all showed up to see me off. Only Vittoria, my first Roman friend, had not made it. She was probably on a yacht off the Costa Smeralda.

Sandro, my flatmate, came over to me and put an arm around my shoulders. 'I thought Englishmen had stiff upper lips,' he said. 'It's not for ever. You'll be back. Everyone comes back to Rome. Anyway, you promised you would come with me to the Mille Miglia, or the Twenty-four Hours at Le Mans. Count on me, I'll make sure it happens.'

Sandro was mad on motor racing and never let the chance of talking about it pass him by.

A very decent jazz combo struck up at 10 p.m. and continued until well after midnight. Waiters rushed everywhere with trays of food, successfully depriving anyone of the need to make excuses and go on for dinner elsewhere.

I danced with Violante several times. I danced with everyone a few times. But my last dance was with Arianna, the sweet Romano-Sicilian to whom I had grown so close.

And that was that. My homecoming had begun.

Rus in Urbe

The Sistine Chapel

There is only one way to see the Sistine Chapel in all its glory, and that is to run like hell.

I had a personal need to be alone in there. I was planning to kneel at an altar at which countless popes had knelt, and pray for my return to Rome. Given the location, the odds suggested that God would listen.

The Vatican is a delightful, if miniature, city state, filled with palaces, parks and gardens. It's set like a jewel in the heart of the Italian capital. Deservedly, it gets the lion's share of Rome's tourist trade, but to see its treasures you must get up before the sparrows clear their throats. Be at the appropriate doors at 7 a.m. and wait patiently for the museum to open at 9 a.m. Once inside, your tickets in hand, run through the Vatican museum, the 'secret archives', the statuary and the antiquities, pass the great art gallery, paying its contents no heed whatsoever. Follow the signs to the Sistine Chapel, and after the best part of half a mile up and down stairs you will find yourself almost alone in this most sublime of chambers, searching uselessly for somewhere to lie down and catch your breath.

If you follow this advice, you will have the place to yourself (if I am not there with you) for almost twenty minutes before the others get there.

It is possible, as you will know, to pay a considerable fee and book tickets that avoid (some of) the queuing, but you will still need to run when you get through the doors. Half an hour after the museum opens, the Sistine Chapel is like the Piccadilly Line in the rush hour.

In 1972, the ceiling was cracked, smoke-stained and faded, lit by electric light, and most convincingly looked all of its 500 years. Modern restoration has successfully revived the place and made a dispassionate appraisal of this astonishing tour de force much easier. The 'ice cream' colours are today very vivid, which they need to be now that the ceiling lights have been removed.

The Creation, above you, and the Last Judgement, in front of you, represent two considerably different styles of painting, even though the same artist painted them both. The Last Judgement is Mannerist. The much earlier Creation is Late Renaissance.

While both are astonishing works of art, there is no work of art that is beyond criticism. If you share my tastes, you may feel that the maestro's reputation rests on his sculpture, particularly his Pietà and his David, and that the enormous momentum generated by these two pieces carried the great man for the rest of his life beyond the first division (where he deserves to be) into a category of his own (where he does not). If only his work on Pope Julius II's tomb had been completed as first conceived! What a work that would have been.

This is not to neglect his architectural legacy. In Rome, just to raise your head is to be reminded of the enormous dome of St Peter's which was merely the most conspicuous part of his contribution to the 'new' basilica.

The Sistine Chapel is roughly fifty years older than the Bramante/della Porta/Michelangelo cathedral. It was built between 1475 and 1483, under Pope Sixtus IV. Its main use today is as the Curia. Grand official ceremonies, such as conclaves and papal coronations, are held in it. Even when it was merely a palatine chapel inside the old Vatican fortress, it loved its ceremonial.

The chapel is rectangular. The Old Testament was painstakingly researched by the scholars of the age to determine the dimensions of the Temple of Solomon. It is not a simple rectangular block – it has a flattened barrel vault with small side vaults over six centred windows. But the floor tries to be as ancient as the Old Book itself: its fifteenth-century pavement is in *opus Alexandrinum*.

The chapel is divided in two by a *transenna*. The larger part, which includes the altar, is reserved for religious and clerical events. The smaller one is for the faithful.

When television cameras are present, Raphael's tapestries cover the walls, which gloriously depict scenes from the Gospels and the Acts of the Apostles.

The chapel was dedicated to the Virgin Mary on her feast day, the Assumption, on 9 August 1483. This date happily marks the very zenith of the *quattrocentro*.

From the outset, the papacy commissioned great painters to embellish it and the list of artists they have employed reads like a *Who's Who* of the Renaissance. The walls are painted by Perugino, Botticelli, Ghirlandaio, Roselli, Signorelli and their respective workshops, in which painters such as Pinturicchio, Piero di Cosimo and Bartolomeo della Gatta became almost as famous as their masters.

The pictures appear to follow historical and religious themes, selected and divided according to the medieval notion that partitioned world history into three epochs: before the Ten Commandments were given to Moses, between Moses and Christ's birth, and the Christian era thereafter. But they have a special purpose, a political one. They are there to underline the continuity between the Old and the New Covenant and the transition from Mosaic Law to Catholic Rule.

The political dimension is especially obvious in the positioning of the Moses and Christ cycles. Sixtus IV wanted everything to bolster his papal authority, whose mandate ran from Moses to Christ, and whose ultimate authority was conferred by Christ to Peter, upon which rock He built His Church.

Both in Perugino's 'Christ Gives the Keys to Peter' and Botticelli's 'The Punishment of Korah', in the background rises the triumphal Arch of Constantine. This is the emperor who baptised the known world as Christendom, and gave the Pope his title of *Pontifex Maximus*. But a coin needs an obverse and a reverse. By so pointedly displaying the arch, Sixtus IV was less reinforcing his papacy and more declaring himself a Roman Emperor.

The great Botticelli was prolific in the Sistine Chapel. Michelangelo was to paint over many of his frescoes, but three of his scenes remain: 'Scenes from the Life of Moses', 'The Temptation of Christ' and 'The Punishment of Korah'. But how 'good' are they?

If I may presume for a moment to the lofty heights of an art critic, these are certainly not the best Botticellis I have ever seen.

Those would be in the Uffizi. In fact, in all these Sistine works his painting appears a little weak.

Perhaps it's because the Sistine Botticellis have as much to do with politics as with art. In the centre of the triumphal arch, the artist has written, 'Let no man take the honour to himself except he that is called by God, as Aaron was.' This is to warn heretics and Protestants that dire punishment will be inflicted on them. Aaron's divine authority, in the fresco, is illustrated appropriately – he is actually wearing the Triple Crown.

And not far away Perugino continues in the same vein. His Christ is giving Peter the keys to the Kingdom of Heaven.

In 1508 the greatest ever makeover in history began. Pope Julius II commissioned Michelangelo Buonarroti to repaint the ceiling, which until then had depicted nothing more profound than golden stars in a blue sky. It took him until 1512 to complete, the best part of five years.

Bramante, that genius and fellow architect of St Peter's, imagined a special scaffold, suspended with rope in the air. But Michelangelo suspected that this would leave holes in the ceiling once the work was over, so he designed a scaffold of his own. He built a flat wooden platform on brackets, cantilevered out from holes in the wall, high up near the top of the windows. Famously, he stood or lay on this scaffolding while he painted.

The stories of the difficulties associated with such a colossal work are the stuff of legend. The first layer of plaster began to grow mould because it was too wet. Michelangelo stripped it down and began again, but this time with a new mixture, *intonaco*. This new rendering, which resisted mould, entered the Italian building tradition and is still in use today.

When Michelangelo started work, he chose the brightest colours so that they should be easily visible from the floor. On the lowest part of the ceiling he painted the ancestors of Christ. Above this he alternated male and female prophets, with Jonah over the altar. On the highest section he narrated nine stories from the Book of Genesis.

Michelangelo's commission only required him to paint a dozen figures, the Apostles in fact, but when the work was unveiled, more than 300 were revealed to an awestruck pope. His figures showed the Creation, Adam and Eve in the Garden of Eden and the Great Flood.

His sketches show that he used male models, even for the females. Perhaps female models were rarer and costlier than male ones, or maybe he just liked them less. In my view it is one of the weaknesses of this Olympian work that his females almost always appear too masculine.

The story of the later Last Judgement[1] began in 1533, when the Medici pope, Clement VII, suggested to Michelangelo that he should paint the altar wall of the Sistine Chapel. Michelangelo lived at that time in Florence, where in 1516 he had been sent by Pope Leo X to work on some of his family commissions.

Florence was still stretching her muscles. In 1527 she had taken advantage of the sack of Rome (under the direction of the Holy Roman Emperor) and with the confinement of the Medici pope to Castel St Angelo, she had established herself as a republic, free at last from Medici clutches. Michelangelo was released from his labours in the Medici chapel in San Lorenzo, and was redirected to building Florence's new military fortifications.

They were to be of little immediate use. The Florentine Republic was soon defeated, and the Medicis reassumed their control of what was again their Duchy. Michelangelo found himself in a difficult position, as he both feared and hated the young Duke Alessandro de' Medici.

The artist had also been committed to finishing Pope Julius II's enormous and elaborate tomb, for which he had already been partly paid. Michelangelo was being torn in two.

Rome found a way through the minefield. Clement VII pardoned Michelangelo, sent him back to San Lorenzo, reduced the scale of the old pope's tomb and ordered Michelangelo to commute between his ducal patrons in Florence and his papal ones in Rome.

In 1534, when Pope Clement died, Michelangelo must have imagined that his duties in the Sistine Chapel would be awarded elsewhere and that he would be allowed to complete Pope Julius's tomb. But that was not his fortune.

---

[1] For some historical details about the Last Judgement, I have referred to Marcia B Hall's informative *Michelangelo: The Frescoes of the Sistine Chapel*.

Paul III, the new pope, treated Michelangelo's excuses with contempt.

'For thirty years we have had the wish that Michelangelo serve us. Now that we are pope, can we not gratify it? Where is his contract? We want to tear it up.'

So, Michelangelo was redirected to the altarpiece, the Last Judgement. It took an age to prepare the wall for fresco work. Sebastiano del Piombo had helpfully prepared the wall for an oil mural, using his own (successful) technique. But Michelangelo, ever the primadonna, watched and criticised for nine whole months before declaring the surface unsuitable.

Perhaps he did this because he was aware that in 1535 his contract for the Julian tomb would expire. But the sands ran out and the artist was compelled to start work.

As soon as figures began to appear in the *intonaco*, a furious argument between Cardinal Carafa and Michelangelo broke out. Carafa ranted interminably about immorality and intolerable obscenity, and that Michelangelo had allowed innumerable naked figures to show their genitals. A censorship campaign, known as the 'Fig-leaf Campaign' was organised by Carafa and Monsignor Sernini, Mantua's ambassador to the Holy See.

When the Pope's own Master of Ceremonies, Biagio da Cesena, said that it was mostly disgraceful that in so sacred a place there should have been depicted all those nude figures, exposing themselves so shamefully, and that it was no work for a papal chapel but rather for the public baths and taverns,'[2] Michelangelo planned his revenge. He worked da Cesena's likeness into the fresco as Minos, ruler of the Underworld. It is said that when da Cesena complained to the Pope, the pontiff replied that his jurisdiction did not extend to hell, so the portrait would have to remain.

But the fresco was to be bowdlerised. The artist Daniele da Volterra, the 'breeches-painter', performed the cover-up.

Of course I cannot better Giorgio Vasari's description of Michelangelo's frescoes. In *Lives of the Artists* he wrote:

---

[2] Public baths and taverns must have had some interesting décor schemes in those days.

This work has been and truly is a beacon of our art, and it has brought such benefit and enlightenment to the art of painting that it was sufficient to illuminate a world which for so many hundreds of years had remained in the state of darkness. And, to tell the truth, anyone who is a painter no longer needs to concern himself about seeing innovations and inventions, new ways of painting poses, clothing on figures, and various awe-inspiring details, for Michelangelo gave to this work all the perfection that can be given to such details.

And Goethe, too, in his *Italienisch Reise*, delivered a succinct accolade: 'Without having seen the Sistine Chapel one can form no appreciable idea of what one man is capable of achieving.'

Werner Herzog, the German film-maker, was also motivated to write:

Many years ago I went to the Vatican and looked at Michelangelo's frescoes in the Sistine Chapel. I was overwhelmed with the feeling that before Michelangelo no one had ever articulated and depicted human pathos as he did in those paintings. Since then all of us have understood ourselves just that little bit deeper, and for this reason I truly feel his achievements are as great as the invention of agriculture.

Yet, some limited dissent is surely allowable. The sheer, unimaginable scale of the frescoes so dwarfs your perception that it is all too easy to be dazzled. I have already mentioned that the female characters in the great frescoes look like athletic young men with female bits glued to their upper torsos.

In my opinion, too, the trompe l'oeil, necessary to place figures in the vaulting to either side, fails in places to convince. Michelangelo has overdone the foreshortening in a leg here or an arm there, and a number of the figures appear distorted.

And is it just overfamiliarity that makes me believe that the spark between a white-bearded God and a handsome, Olympian and slightly limp-wristed Adam is just a bit, well, corny?

The previous tradition of representing God was in a blaze of white light, sometimes emanating from an *arc-en-ciel*, through which the dove of the Holy Ghost could be seen. Michelangelo's God is too patrician, too Parnassian, and too human for comfort.

To me, at least, it suggests that we have made Him in our image.

But at least my prayers – that I would return to Rome – were heard. I have been back many times.

Chapter the Seventeenth
1972: Spending in Sardinia

In which the author makes his way from Rome to Paris by land and sea via Sardinia, where he sees flamingos and walled cities. He finds the world's most perfect hotel and spends his every last penny. Arriving in the south of France, he is befriended by prostitutes, invited to join the Foreign Legion, learns how to pronounce 'Marseilles' and attempts to avoid buying a train ticket to Paris. He is shocked by Parisian early-morning drinking and discovers the Latin Quarter.

The easiest way to London from Rome is by plane. It is also the dullest.

The trouble with flying is that no travelling is involved. All that happens is that you turn up at an airport, get shouted at by dematerialised people, mainly reminding you that a moron like you has probably got a suitcase with you and that you should remember to take it when you go. You get pushed and corralled through ropes like so much cattle. Countless humourless apparatchiks ask you endless silly questions.

The Duke of Marlborough was once asked at check-in whether he had packed his own bags.

'Of course I bloody didn't,' he replied, before he could stop himself.

When you finally get on board there is a conspiracy to play the world's most irritating music to you. This is apparently intended to calm you down. You squeeze into the narrow little seats and wonder what to do with your legs. A man begins to give you his views on immigration, which he will do until you land. You are offered a cooked meal, no matter what time of day it is. Nobody in their right minds wants another lunch at 4 p.m. Afternoon teas, on the other hand, replete with scones and clotted cream, would be another matter. I've tried to tell them. I have.

You are then disgorged at an identical airport, where you do the whole thing again in reverse, except that you have to wait for your baggage to appear for inexplicable ages in some vast airless, bar-less, seat-less room in front of a stationary carousel. You have arrived at your destination with no hint of the huge distance you have travelled. You haven't felt the climate change. You have no clue that there are whole mountain ranges and a great sea on the flight path between Rome and London. You have experienced nothing of the differences in culture of the peoples you have passed over.

No, I was not going to fly. I was going to do it the hard way.

I took the train from Rome to Civitavecchia. For half the journey the train ran along the coast and I stared out to sea. A vast blue nothing. It seemed a metaphor for where I was in my life. Where exactly was I going?

At the port I found my way to the ferry to Sardinia. Of course, in the narrow geographical and literal sense, I knew exactly where I was going. My first stop would be Cagliari, the capital of the island and its most southerly town. My sister had sent me a postcard from there, saying how much she had enjoyed flirting with the *banditti*, but getting shot at by the police appealed less to me than it had to her.

The walk-on tickets (for passengers without cars) were absurdly cheap. Soon, with a great bass hoot, we were pulling out of port.

Everyone on board had a friend or relation on the quayside to whom they were waving goodbye, and even though I knew not a soul down there in that throng, I too waved goodbye.

But the big philosophical question would not go away. Where exactly was I going? Was it really my lot to be confined to a desk in a vast and silent office, one of a hundred similar prisoners, with an office manager pacing up and down and putting endless files in my in-tray? I would probably never see Rome again. True, there might come a time in my dotage when I would tell my children about it.

'Gather round, kiddies,' I would tell them. 'Go to Rome. It's the only town in the world that says goodnight to you. Have a glass of champagne on the terrace of the Hotel Eden. When the sun begins to dip in the west, directly behind the Basilica of St Peter, listen to the angelus bell toll from every direction. Watch the whole great city glow with satisfaction and bow to you and to its great floodlit churches with ancient courtesy. Or be at the Forum and watch the cats, those slim and feral Roman hunters, emerge from their afternoon sleep and bring the ruins to life.'

Thinking like this was not going to help. I went in search of the bar.

A few hours later Sardinia appeared off the starboard bow.

A couple of beers had steadied my nerves. I began to be more positive. I had been greatly cheered by the dolphins, or porpoises, or whatever they were, chasing our ship out of their territory.

And now I was standing in the noisy bustle of a Sardinian harbour, watching the natives rope their countless suitcases on to the tops of their little cars.

The Costa Smeralda is about as far from Cagliari as you can get and still be on the same island. It is at least a hundred miles to the north. Getting there was my next challenge. Sardinia suddenly seemed rather large.

I had already booked a hotel at my destination, the Cala di Volpe hotel in Porto Cervo. I had allowed myself two nights on the road in order to get there, giving myself time to drink in the Sardinian countryside and see a couple of churches. I figured that I would be able to find somewhere to doss down en route, given that we were just out of high season. If necessary I would rough it a bit.

My map showed only one road out of Cagliari that was going anywhere at all and I walked to the bus station with my blasted suitcases. The two I had taken to Italy all those months ago had long been replaced with the largest ones I could find. And I imagine you know how much books weigh...

Any bus going out of town would do. I would get on the first one and get off again when I was bored. Let's see how far we can get.

It was almost two hours before the bus got to Oristano, half-way up Sardinia on its west coast. The clocks were striking six o'clock as I got off the bus, wondering if this pretty little town would have anywhere I could put my head down. I strode purposefully into the first hotel I saw, the Mistral. Fully booked. No restaurant. Not a good omen.

But the owner had a cousin who had another hotel, much nicer than this one, called Mistral 2, hardly any distance. Could he see if they had a room? Just a quick call should do it.

I agreed, naturally, especially when he directed the porter to drive me over there and carry my suitcases in his car.

The little 'sister' hotel just down the road was, inevitably, on the other side of town. It was also a palace of a place compared with the Mistral. Oh well, it was just for a night. But it too had no restaurant. The owner reached for his telephone. Before I knew it I was booked into a restaurant called Il Faro, almost on the shore itself. I would love it, he told me. 'Simple fare, typically Sardo,' he said. 'It's surrounded by dunes and little lakes, all filled with flamingos. And the food is unbeatable.' I didn't need any further persuasion.

There was a moment or two for me to explore the town and I walked around a bit. The walls were rather spectacular, but I supposed they needed to be, given Sardinia's history of plagues, Moroccan invasions, Saracen raids, a Spanish conquest and its eternal home-grown dreams of independence. From the top of the walls I could easily see the flamingos. I had thought they lived in East Africa. I had never known that they came to Europe.

Inside the walls, the town is medieval. The centre of town has a fine cathedral with a great octagonal bell tower, and the 'modern' buildings include a number of seventeenth- and eighteenth-century palaces of real distinction.

But my time to explore was short. I was off to the 'simple' restaurant that, I had no doubt, belonged to a cousin of my hotelier.

This was the first time in my life I had eaten elvers, or baby eels. I had a huge plate of them and tucked into them with gusto. Elvers are the tops. The main course was *pecora con patate* or roast mutton with sautéed potatoes cooked in oil and rosemary. It was, I was told, the house speciality. I had a fine carafe of wine, probably the local Capichera, and I finished with a blancmange. I had hated the stuff at school, but the Sardinian version was something else. Not even close, in fact – it was utterly sensational.

Eventually a taxi came for me and took me back to town. Me and my *The Origin of Species* – the book I was still struggling with – had had an unforgettable evening. The food had maybe been a little more poetic than the words.

My bus for Olbia left at 11 a.m. the next morning, and being determined to see the Basilica of Santa Giusta, a couple of miles south of the town, I was up very early. After faffing about with the taxi driver and getting slightly lost, I barely had time for the briefest of glimpses, but I do recall how charming it was from the outside. It is on my list to be revisited.

And now, on board a bus for Olbia. I ought to be able to get there in time for a late lunch.

Maps are misleading things. On mine, the distance checked out at around seventy miles. Just how long could that take?

But a map never really tells you how mountainous your road will be. Sardinia is severely hill-infested. Bang in between Oristano and Olbia, the Gennargentu range rises almost 2,000 metres, almost twice as high as Snowdon or Ben Nevis. To make matters worse, the road was tremendously narrow and the bus often had to stop to let school buses get by. My stomach was rumbling, the bus was uncomfortable in the extreme, and my suitcases were almost certainly going to fall on my head from the narrowest possible rack above me. That fellow over there, effortlessly strap-hanging, had occasionally glanced my way. He was smoking a cigarette the wrong way round. I was beginning to have uncharitable thoughts about Sardinian drivers, bandits and schoolchildren.

Sometimes the enormous mountains rose as cliffs on our right and fell into the abyss on our left. Sheep wandered into our oncoming path with ovine disregard. At least the driver was determined and we accelerated into every piece of straight road. Unfortunately, as soon as the road bent again he piled on the brakes. It was the sort of trip people pay money for at Alton Towers, but it was not designed to get us from A to B in any great hurry.

We reached Olbia bus station at 9 p.m. that night, where I managed to check into the Centrale without a hitch. The hotel was worthy but dull, but I was so exhausted and keen to move on it didn't matter at all.

Dawn came and I woke early. I looked out of the window. A bonus: the weather was absolutely perfect. I told myself, hang the expense. I would take a taxi the few short kilometres left to Porto Cervo. I was looking forward to the treat I had promised myself, a week of self-indulgence at the Cala di Volpe hotel.

The Hotel Cala di Volpe overlooks the eponymous bay that defines the exquisite emerald coast of north-eastern Sardinia. It's less a hotel and more a serenely sculptured piece of Arcady. The whole complex is a subtle blend of understatement and elegant glamour. Behind it the hills rise, stern and sunburned, rustling with lizards and bandits. Towards the sea are unspoiled beaches of white sand and the luminous Mediterranean Sea.

The place looks like an ancient harbour with a recent coat of paint, but the Aga Khan's architect, Jacques Couelle, created the place from scratch. His object was to build the absolute opposite of an American hotel, and he made the place resemble a charming fishing village. He constructed 'ancient' bell towers, stone terraces, irregular pantiled roofs and vaguely classical porticoes, and they all blended effortlessly into the shorescape and its private marina. It made you wonder why there had not been a fishing village there before. Some of the guests may not even realise that the whole thing sprang into life in the late 1960s.

I liked my room. It was spacious, well furnished and had great views over the sea. No seaplanes, I noticed, as I stood on my terrace, a glass of prosecco in my hand. Only enormous yachts. I unpacked and wondered what to do first.

Wandering around the 'village', I remember the atmosphere being pretty relaxed and informal, and I half expected to bump into people I knew only from the cinema.

It certainly felt expensive. They say that in a new Rolls-Royce the only two sounds you can hear are its clock and the sound of the petrol tank emptying. I could hear the latter sound from my wallet. I will admit I was a little scared by the prices. The *à la carte* menu for dinner would cost me two days' work alone. Well, I was closing a chapter of my life, not trying to economise.

I told myself that if I had wanted to go home the hard way, I was getting something pleasantly wrong. It really hadn't been that hard so far.

It was a fairly international clientele. There were many English voices, and not a few American ones. Italians were there, but not many. Despite myself, I kept staring at people's faces. I was hoping to recognise a star of the silver screen.

During the next couple of days I went snorkelling, riding, scrabbling over the rocks and filling my face with lobster from the magnificent buffet lunch table. I had a protracted but unsuccessful attempt at learning to waterski. Some of the time was with my new friends, a pair of girls from Virginia in the US who were travelling. They were not to be mistaken for tourists, they told me pointedly. I also met a man from Milwaukee who was carrying photos of his two adorable children back home. Happily he was into golf and I lost him to the links. Topless beauties filled the beach to my constant distraction, and I was a small boy in a sweet shop, except that I was inexplicably lonely and puzzled by my own decision to leave all my new friends behind me.

At least I had no need of ready money. Everything was charged to my room, even in the few shops and bars that had nothing to do with the hotel.

I had been there for just two nights when the manager caught my attention after lunch as I came back in to change for the beach.

I assumed it had been decided that I was beginning to bring the hotel into disrepute by my constant failure on waterskis. But I was wrong. I was about to have a lovely surprise.

The manager looked up from his books as I approached and looked behind me into the foyer. A little smile played for a moment across his face.

I turned around to see what he was getting at and saw, on one of the wicker chairs, Arianna, in a hat and making a million dollars look like small change.

'You told me where you were going,' she said as I sat down next to her. 'So I decided I needed a day or two by the sea. I hope you don't mind.'

I had been feeling that Rome was lost forever to me, but I had overlooked the simple fact that Romans also like to travel. And here was the sweetest Roman of them all.

I prattled on happily about the joy of seeing her, and how she should move her stuff into my room immediately, while she waited for my seam of enthusiasm to exhaust itself.

'I came to give you a leaving present.' She fished around in her bag and brought out a little box. 'It's a souvenir of Sicily.'

'May I open it?' I asked.

'Of course you may. I hope you like it. I imagine you will.'

I undid the wrapping carefully and opened a cardboard box, to reveal a small *krater*, an antique Grecian drinking cup. It was black, with two unbroken handles, and had traces of a hunting scene painted on to the outside. As far as I could see it was utterly unscarred in its 2,500-year voyage through time.

I looked up at Arianna who had been watching me carefully.

'You're a little unused to affection, aren't you?' she said.

I blurted out my thanks a little clumsily.

'Never mind that. I'm glad you like it. Treat it carefully. Now, I'm going to my room to get changed. I'll join you on the beach in half an hour. What's the waterskiing like here?'

Very correctly, she never gave up her room during the days that followed, though she would spend all of the day and the better half of the night with me. But by breakfast she was designedly by herself in her remote bedroom, in some other part of the complex. An ambitious bellboy, who always found her alone, delivered her cappuccino and newspaper to her. Her reputation was absolutely safe.

And then, quite suddenly, Arianna checked out. My time was up too, my bags were packed, my *krater* carefully wrapped in a pullover, and I was at reception about to settle my account.

I had felt quite prosperous, even rich, when I had set foot in Sardinia. Arianna, while scrupulously paying for her own room, had allowed me the pleasant gallantry of spoiling her to the best of my ability in the bars and restaurants. Even so, the room rate was the killer. As I put my cases into the hotel car, which was to take me to Porto Torres on the north-west corner of the island, I had the fortune of the church mouse of legend.

This was the era before credit cards. All money was cash, personal cheques or 'travelers checks' [sic]. I counted and recounted what remained of my funds very carefully. I could barely make it home. I would need to tread very carefully.

A little later that day I was by the ferry terminal in Porto Torres, having let my driver go without tipping him. I kept looking around for him, expecting him to come for me with his *lupara* – his sawn-off shotgun – and with cigarette smoke coming out of his ears.

So far so good, I thought, as I went aboard. The ferry was bound for Toulon, in the south of France on the western edge of the Côte d'Azur. The game was still on. Only its Italian phase had finally drawn to an end.

Or had it? Arianna's last words to me were that she would see me in Paris. I had naturally agreed, but I was planning for London.

'It's not so far. I'll let you know when, and you can drop everything. Will you do that?'

Paris is closer to London than is Manchester and Arianna had guessed shrewdly. I would indeed drop everything for her.

My boat crossed the remaining chunk of the Mediterranean at a stately pace and I enjoyed the cruise.

I considered what I would do once I was in the south of France. I had good schoolboy French – I had a decent O level and it had been my second language at my school in Rome – so I would have to see how the wind blew. I looked at a map. On arrival I could turn left and go to Marseilles or right and head towards St Tropez, Cannes and Nice.

There was just one vicious blood-sucking fly in the ointment. After the Cala de Volpe treatment my wallet was close to redefining the elusive concept of a perfect vacuum.

Marseilles, second city of France. I thought of my friend Johnnie, who had always wanted to come here. Something to do with *The French Connection*, his second favourite film after *The Godfather*, and when we had paid our homage to Corleone his face had been a joy to behold. It would have been fun to see his big red enthusiastic mug again, wondering where the action was.

Actually, William Friedkin's *The French Connection* really is a brilliant film. It had just come out and I had seen the *policier* in Rome. Apparently the plot was loosely based upon an actual investigation that led to what was then the biggest heroin seizure in US history. Marseilles was mentioned, if briefly, but the film was really about New York. Its views on law enforcement were a little cynical, but Gene Hackman's Popeye Doyle was an Oscar-winning portrait of a brutal, pushy, alcoholic bigot in New York's anti-narcotics police. It also had a show-stopping car chase – even today it remains one of the best of its kind. And it had Fernando Rey, the brilliant Spanish actor that Buñuel had made an international star, as the bad guy. He portrayed the most Machiavellian and charming drug runner on any cinema screen at any time. Some people can hold the screen to the exclusion of the rest of the cast, and Rey was one of that privileged band.

But there was another reason why it was to Marseilles I turned and not to St Tropez. I had remembered that I had a little money untouched in my British bank account and I had rediscovered my battered chequebook. Marseilles was big enough to have a British consul, and I thought he would be bound by the bonds of nationhood to cash me a cheque. With Herculean strength I picked up my bags and headed for Toulon railway station and the short journey along the coast to Marseilles. What muscle tone I would have, I thought to myself, masochistically.

Once in Marseilles I took my two huge suitcases and my poor self down towards the port to find a cheap hotel. I changed what was left of my money into French francs at a kiosk that gave me an abysmal rate and charged commission on top. Not often you have to tip someone for ripping you off.

Eventually I found a run-down bar with a flickering sign saying '*Chambres*', and I thought that would have to do. I struggled inside.

Everyone looked at me curiously. I could tell what they were thinking. Why does a young man like that wander about at night with a pair of suitcases filled with barbells? Seems a no-brainer to me. It was my way of keeping fit.

The lady by the cash register and the cigarettes looked me up and down.

'You want a room? You are alone?'

Odd question. I was rather obviously alone.

'How long do you want the room for?'

'Just one night,' I replied, slightly baffled.

'The whole night?' And one of the eavesdropping customers, a gnarled and rebarbative sailor, let out a long low whistle.

'The whole night,' I confirmed.

The *patronne* made me pay in advance – rather a lot for a flea-bitten dive like this, but frankly, until I could cash that cheque, beggars couldn't be choosers.

Having carried my bags upstairs and locked them in the odd little room – filled mostly by an oversized bed with pink nylon sheets – I went back down to see if either the bar or somewhere close by might be capable of giving me supper.

This time I looked around more carefully. Most of the customers were Berber Arabs, or looked it. The men were wearing working clothes. My first impression was that they worked on the ships in harbour, and that seemed to fit. They were speaking French, but not a version of the language that I could understand. In fact, I wondered if it actually was French. The girls, of which there were a surprising number, were something else again.

In very different ways they were mostly wearing a combination of black and red clothes. Fishnet stockings, sometimes in good condition, continued the nautical theme. They swapped banter with the seamen by jiggling their bosoms at them, and the sailors brushed them away like flies, preferring their Ricards or Pernods. My God, what sort of a place was this?

I must have said this out loud, because a salt-encrusted tar answered me with overblown courtesy.

'*M'sieur, vous vous trouvez chez Mme Renard, au bord de l'eau,*'[1] and he laughed. And so did I.

As it turned out, I had a great evening. The sailors tried to teach me a little French, or Arabic, and the girls made a great deal of innocent fuss of me. I had a great bowl of bouillabaisse and I went to bed a happy, well-nourished and drunk young man.

I walked through Marseilles the next day, my bags safe in the hotel where I had spent the night, as happy as Larry.[2] Despite a hangover, I was not carrying my barbells and this alone was grounds for cheer. I arrived at the offices of Her Britannic Majesty's Consul General at about 10 a.m. and addressed myself to the receptionist.

---

[1] 'You are at Mme Renard's, on the waterfront.' '*Au bord de l'eau*' is pronounced '*au bordello*'.

[2] A cousin of the sandboy.

'I would like to see the Consul General.'

'Have you an appointment?'

'No.'

'Then it is impossible. He is very busy.'

'It's very important. Please tell him there's an Englishman in reception who needs to see him urgently.' That should do it.

'I am sorry, m'sieur. He has several appointments already. He cannot see you.'

'Well, please tell him that I'll wait till he has finished and I will see him then.' I was not going to be thrown out by this jobs-worth of a secretary.

The girl glanced across the vestibule at a uniformed man whom I had not previously noticed. Perhaps I was wrong. Perhaps she really was going to throw me out.

I tried to put on my most ingratiating smile. 'Please,' I said, 'it really is urgent.'

'Is it about the Foreign Legion?' she asked.

'The Foreign Legion?' I gasped. 'No, it isn't! It's a personal matter.'

'Oh, very well. Let me have your passport. Go in there and wait until you are called.' And she pointed to a reception room, wallpapered in orange hessian and filled with classroom chairs. Very up-to-date, I thought, very modern. None of these aristocratic chintz-loving Foreign Office types need apply for this posting.

In the reception room were a number of down-and-out peo-ple who eyed me suspiciously. It may have had something to do with the Valentino tie I had chosen to wear that morning. Well, the girls at the hotel had liked it, I wanted to tell them.

A well-dressed young lady came into the room and looked around at us. 'Smith, John,' she said in a bored voice. 'Repatriation.'

And a sorry-looking fellow got up and wandered into the Presence.

If they didn't cash my cheque, that would be me, I thought to myself.

The fellow sitting next to me had closely cropped hair and a blue spot on his left cheek. Tattoos were breaking out from under his shirt. He was busy struggling with a form on a clipboard on his knee. He turned in his seat and spoke to me.

' 'Ere, what's this?' he said. 'They've given me a new name.'

'Really?' I said.

'Yeah,' he continued. 'I used to be called John Trevor, but here on the form it says Trevor John. I like that.'

'Yes. Trips easily off the tongue.'

'What's that? Oh, I see. Yeah, does sound OK, doesn't it.'

We were already firm friends.

'What are you here for?' I asked.

'The Legion. I tried to join the British Army, but they wouldn't have it. They said I'd be better off in the Legion. So here I am.'

The British Army (in 1972) had not done a lot of fighting since the end of the Second World War. I know, there was indeed Korea. Yes, the Suez Crisis, too. And the Mau Mau uprising. And then there was Ulster. There is always Ulster. But Britain then was nothing like as belligerent as it is now. And this fellow looked a bit too useful for simple peacekeeping activities.

'Can you help me with this form, mate? Only I'm not that good at words and that...'

I helped him fill in the waiver that let the Queen off the hook if the poor chump got shot at by those pesky Arabs. I witnessed it and told him to sign on the dotted line. To my surprise, he actually marked the spot with a cross. I had never seen that before, except at the cinema. I was visibly surprised.

'Well, thanks, mate,' Trevor John said to me. 'You going for it too?'

No, I'm here to be repatriated, I thought. But to my surprise, the girl remerged and called my name.

'Macdonogh, Jeremy. The Consul General will see you now.'

I am pleased to relate that the Consul had a rather more comfortable private office than his waiting room.

He passed my passport across the desk to me.

'Well? What can I do for you?'

'Er, the fact is, I've run out of cash and I need desperately to cash a cheque.'

'To cash a cheque? You force my secretary to make an unscheduled appointment for you, claiming it's "urgent"? I thought you might have caught terminal clap. Or murdered a chorus girl.

I'm not here to cash your effing cheque. There are half a bloody dozen British banks here in Marseilles. Take your chequebook to any one of them. And don't waste my time again. Next!'

So I slunk off with my tail between my legs. But I had learned something, I thought, as I cashed a cheque at the branch of Barclays across the road from the consulate. It was that her Britannic Majesty's Consul General had pronounced the word 'Marseilles' as '*Marsails*'. I have tried to affect this pronunciation ever since.

Now for Paris. My batteries (or wallet) recharged, I retrieved my suitcases and waved a cheerful *au revoir* to the ladies of the night. I took my copy of *The Origin of Species* out of a case and slipped it into my pocket. Maybe I would read some more of it on the train.

I carried my bags to the St Charles railway station and checked them in as left luggage. It was a ten-hour trip by rail to Paris and I might as well save the cost of a hotel and do it overnight.

So I had time to explore the town a bit.

The building that dominates the town is the Basilica of Notre Dame de la Garde. It took a while to get up there, but it's very impressive when you arrive. From the terraces I could easily see the fortified island of the Chateau d'If, where Edmond Dantès was incarcerated so long and so unfairly. If you need further details, read *The Count of Monte Cristo*, by Alexandre Dumas.

The town is a bit dilapidated, it is true, and maybe a bit 'ethnic' here and there, but there is still a certain faded nineteenth-century splendour to it. The stock exchange, for example, is particularly imposing.

I felt a spot of lunch coming on and headed towards the busy narrow streets of the old Panier quarter. The houses here are all built on the slopes of the great hill, and as I wandered around looking for a cheapish bistro I kept getting glimpses of the Mediterranean beneath me.

In the end my imagination ran short and I treated myself to a second bowl of bouillabaisse over lunch at a bistro just by the noble neoclassical town hall.

After lunch I strolled around some more. A fine old bell tower caught my imagination. There is also a superb and unbelievably ancient abbey, close to the port, the crypt of which was the first church in Provence to see Christianity, at a time when the town was still called Massilia.

I had indeed cashed a cheque but I would still need to be careful. To save money I had a great scheme. I would get on the train without a ticket. The train would stop many times over the 500 miles to Paris and whenever the ticket collector came, I would admit to having boarded at the previous station only. That way my ticket would decrease in cost in direct proportion to the laziness of the conductor. I was doing SNCF a service, I told myself. And I would have a little more to spend in Paris.

My feet were killing me after all that rubbernecking when at last I pitched up at the station for my train to Paris. I headed for the middle of the train where I found a second-class compartment. I was in good time and secured a window seat and a place on the rack for my two huge suitcases. I tried to make them as secure as I could. If one of them fell on a passenger during the night I would have a manslaughter charge on my hands.

And now the train began to fill. The first person to come into my compartment was a young man, about my age, struggling with his own pair of giant cases.

'Ça serait libre, cette place là?' he asked, pointing at the seat opposite me. I nodded.

'Good, good,' he said to himself in English, and filled the rack opposite mine with his own cases. If anyone else had any luggage they would have to leave it in the corridor.

'You're English, too?' I asked.

'Yes, yes. Been staying with friends along the coast. Time to get home and back to the varsity.'

It seemed a long time since I had heard that word.

'Cambridge?' I asked.

'The very same.'

The carriage filled and somehow there was room for everyone and their belongings. And the train pulled majestically out of Marseilles' great railway station and aimed for the capital of France.

The Englishman and I chatted about this and that, trying to find if we had friends in common. I don't recall that we did. And two stations had passed without a collector. I had saved at least fifteen francs.

Then the man appeared, in his grey uniform and quasi-military cap.

'*Vos billets, s'il vous plaît, m'ssieurs-dames.*'

I suddenly realised that I hadn't the nerve to go through with my scam. The other passengers would denounce me. I would be taken before the Committee for Public Safety, where I would be condemned by a People's Tribune and then whisked off in a tumbrel to be guillotined. Was it worth it for fifteen francs?

I explained that I had got on the train at Marseilles.

'*Sans billet, alors?*'

I agreed. I had no ticket. I was running late and thought I could buy one on the train. I was terribly sorry.

The ticket collector did not seem in the least put out. He wrote me a voucher, and charged me the fare for it. I would present this voucher in Paris to the police there, and they would probably allow me to exchange it for a ticket. That way I could leave the station. If not I would be taken before the Committee for Public Safety…

He did not have to say the rest. I was rather ashamed of myself, too. He checked the others and then left. Silence settled on the compartment for a while.

'I had a mate,' began my new friend, 'who once thought he could get away without paying in France. He boarded the train at Lyons, bound for Paris, and climbed on to the luggage rack, covering himself with his coat and a pullover.'

'What happened,' I asked. 'Did he get away with it?'

'Well, the conductor came into the compartment, which was otherwise empty, and said, "*Votre billet, s'il vous plaît, monsieur.*" My friend knew he had been rumbled, so he pulled the coat from his face and said as politely as possible, "*Excusez-moi, monsieur le conducteur, mais je ne suis pas une personne, je suis un bagage.*" And the conductor simply looked at him and replied, "*Alors, monsieur le bagage, votre ticket, s'il vous plaît.*" '

The excitement over, the elderly train made its stately way to Paris. Night fell and the train rattled on. There was a self-service restaurant on board and at one point I went there and grabbed a roll or two and a minuscule bottle of wine. Not a patch on the Italian equivalent, I thought loyally.

And then I slept until early the next morning when the train juddered into the Gare de Lyon, right in the heart of Paris. My dreams were a troubling helter-skelter of images of Italy and friends from Rome, dominated by the adorable Arianna. I felt as if I were the sole survivor of some terrible war, and all these people and places now survived only in my memories.

I brought my suitcases down from the rack, with a little help from my fellow countryman, and I found a porter to help me get them to the barrier. But when I was ready to face the fury of the French railway police and exchange my voucher for a ticket, I saw that there was no barrier and that I could walk freely into Paris. So I told the porter to take me to left luggage and I booked my bags in. Those wretched cases. All the books I had bought in Italy were in them. So was half a case of Sardinian wine and a bottle of grappa. Were it not for an ancient *krater*, the temptation to throw them into the Seine might have been irresistible. That and the fact that they were far too heavy to fling anywhere.

I looked at my watch. It was almost 5.30 a.m. Let me tell you something: at 5.30 a.m. there is little in Paris going on in the way of excitement.

I found the gents and managed a shave of sorts. In Italy there would have been a diurnal hotel, I thought to myself, like the ones in Venice and Rome. These Frenchies have a lot to learn.

The next step in the long recovery period, having slept so fitfully in a second-class railway carriage for what had seemed an eternity, had to be an espresso.

I had no particular place to go but I had resolved to see a little of Paris before I made my way to the Gare du Nord and back to Blighty. But first things first. I walked out of the station and found a bar across the road that was opening up.

I took my seat by the bar, entirely made of wrought zinc, and ordered an espresso and an *orange presseé*. A rushed Parisian sat next to me and ordered '*un p'tit coup de rosé*' with his coffee. I had never before seen anyone drink wine that early in the morning, unless it were before going to bed.

Now the earliest phase of the rush hour was beginning and the little café began to fill. I had my guide to Paris in my hand and was sleepily trying to work out an agenda for myself. After all, this was almost the first time I had ever been in Paris (as an adult, at least) and if I were to work in that City office for the rest of my days, I should at least be able to say I had been there.

I looked around as I reached for one of the boiled eggs in a little rack in front of me and peeled it absently. Almost everyone seemed to have a stiff drink. Over there was a man drinking half a pint of lager. It was a quarter past six in the morning, for goodness sake! That chap there had ordered a glass of Calvados, no less. My neighbour had taken a second, admittedly small, glass of wine. Were they all alcoholics?

I paid up and wandered down to the river, which wasn't far, and crossed on to the Left Bank. I strode on past the Jardin des Plantes and into the Latin Quarter, so called because scholars used to come from all over Europe to study there, and where until the Revolution they were taught and spoke to each other in Latin. They called this Latin in France their 'lingua franca'.

Paris is a more complex city than Rome. Unlike Rome, which evolved (admittedly painfully), Paris was built in a succession of destructive waves, and only the smallest traces of the Roman, Merovingian, Carolingian, Medieval, Renaissance and Neoclassical remain. Today it is largely an Edwardian or belle époque city, and it encapsulates the flowering of Europe just before the wheels came off in 1914. It also seems to me more secretive than Rome; more like London, perhaps, in that its many districts differ so markedly from each other. The V^e *arrondissement*, where I now was, was far too grand to be a student district, and yet it had dozens of cheap little hotels and economical restaurants. I checked a price here and there. Yes, they really were affordable.

There was a pervasive sense of scholarship. Paris was still selling books in cardboard covers from stalls on the street, waiting for the proud owner to put them into his own binding – half calf, full morocco, just so long as it fits into the library, *mon cher*. There were dozens of little shops selling paints and artists' materials – so many that there had to be a thousand artists within the square mile surrounding the Sorbonne, all painting away furiously.

As I walked, I passed schools that have vanished forever. A police station proclaimed its maiden name to have been the Collège des Bernardins. From the street I could make out a bit of a fourteenth-century cellar and a refectory. I walked by the ancient rue des Écoles and stopped to admire a bravura doorcase that, according to a small brass plate, led into the seventeenth-century Collège des Lombards. Inside the Collège des Trente-trois had also left behind a few scanty remains. Who were these Lombards, or these Thirty-three?

I found an atmospheric student bar, Les Pipos, and ordered a nice cold beer. I looked around for the debate. When I had been at school, Jean-Paul Sartre and Simone de Beauvoir were still meeting at the Deux Magots, and Juliette Gréco and Boris Vian held a rival court at the Café Flore. My parents' generation had seen Apollinaire, Breton, Hemingway, Picasso and Modigliani at the Dôme and the Coupole in Montparnasse. Some artists paid in kind – the wall paintings at the Coupole are now protected by the French government. There would have to come a time, I resolved, when I would get to know Paris as well as I had come to know Rome.

What I didn't know then, was that that time was almost come.

But now, it was time to finish my first walk through the Quartier Latin and survey Paris from the steps of their Pantheon, before retracing my steps and collecting my luggage.

I think I remember seeing the station bar, or restaurant, called Le Train Bleu. But I was too young and too skint to realise its importance. I, and my cases, descended into the Métro and headed across Paris to the Gare du Nord, to what was left of my journey back to London.

Was I evolving, like one of Darwin's weird creatures in the Galapagos? If so, I had been living in the most fertile environment for it. Or was I actually getting sillier? The irritating, insistent strains of '*Arrivederci, Roma*' that kept coming into my head seemed to give me the clue.

Chapter the Eighteenth
1972: Coming Home (Part I)

In which the author returns to a London on the eve of economic collapse. He determines to enjoy himself. He 'walks' Diana Dors and he meets Lady Diana Cooper. At a very grand party he is presented to Princess Margaret. At Simpson's in the Strand he drinks a very fine wine, which is to have a long-lasting effect. He gets a temporary job at Harrods, from which he is quickly fired. But an opportunity arises, as they always do, and he heads off, this time for Paris.

My train back from the Continent let me out at Victoria Station, where an English summer shower sent me scuttling for cover. I found a concrete umbrella in the shape of The Shakespeare which, despite its hallowed name, was one of the grottiest pubs in London. I made a few telephone calls. I was now on home territory and confident of my future. If I had managed to survive in Rome, then London (where I thought I knew all the angles) should be a doddle.

Two years had passed since Cambridge and I felt I had been vastly improved by my experiences. From being rather insular and singularly useless, I was now a true cosmopolitan. I could speak Italian like a native. I could even manage a passable Roman dialect. I figured I was now commercially desirable. My time had surely come.

Only it hadn't, predictably.

I ended up in my mother's Kensington flat, which didn't seem to please my doting parent. 'So you're home again,' she stated pleasantly. 'I expect you'll want feeding. Well, you know where the kitchen is.'

For a few days I spoke to agencies that dealt with graduate employment, but I drew a blank.

'Don't you read the newspapers? The City is in free fall. The

SE30 Index has fallen from 500 to 200 in the last month. Oil prices have doubled. The secondary banks have collapsed. Edward du Cann is under arrest. Property isn't worth a penny. Get back to Europe.'

So I tried the agencies that dealt with temporary staff.

After a dispiriting few days, I found one that could use me. The job was with Harrods, as a shop assistant. My job was not over-arduous. It consisted mainly of being as unctuous as humanly possible. Perhaps even more so.

So I joined the staff of the boutique on the top floor, wittily called 'Way In'. Despite the fact that the Beatles had officially broken up over a year before, the shop believed itself to be the epitome of the swinging sixties. As I recollect, the wallpaper was by Brigit Riley. Every time, every morning, I saw that wallpaper and remembered Oscar Wilde's much-quoted last words: 'Either that wallpaper goes or I do.'

But at least I was earning enough money to get by, and my old friend Sian Rhys let me rent a room in her new flat in Notting Hill, which got me out of my mother's hair.

Sian used to cook up great bowls of spaghetti with a ragout she called '*Bolognese*', seriously inaccurately. I loved her bohemian 'just drop in, darling' dinner parties, where cheap wine flowed all night and when her slightly effete circle dazzled each other with their poetry, or in the case of Piers de la Force, with tales from Glyndebourne, where he had somehow contrived to be a member. True, the place was a little untidy – it had been months since anyone had seen the floor – but we can all get a little obsessive about hygiene. Mind you, if anyone from the HSE had seen it, the power hoses and decontamination squads would have been in there in two shakes of an eviction notice.

A couple of months passed easily by in this desirable residence. I remember a smooth and uncomplicated sex life, punctuated by countless supper parties and an infinite amount of cheap red wine. The two wines we seemed to favour were called, from memory, Vieux Septic and Guttrotti. At one of these impromptu soirées, her brilliant friend David Levy seemed delighted to see me. David was a genius of the Right when that wing of intellectual debate was almost unrepresented. Indeed, he championed the ultimate lost cause, the *Action Française*. Alas, the professor is now dead. Aids took him in 2003.

'I didn't realise you were back, Jeremy,' he said. 'Look, there is a favour you can do for me. I had volunteered but it really isn't my thing. Can you take a girl to a dance for me? Thursday night. It'll be great fun. And you won't need any money.'

Well, it is self-evidently true that I was very much more positive, in every possible way, about women than David was, and I could even understand why the idea of a dance would depress him. And the offer was for the competed-for Thursday night.

The grandest events in London are always on Thursday nights. Friday night is impossible, as everyone is off to the country, and Saturday night is lager night and not a pretty sight. London at weekends is like a desert island, with the penguins or turtles swapped for grinning grockles chewing their gum or candyfloss and feeding the pigeons. Ugh.

I decided to accept David's kind invitation. He scribbled down the details. I had to be at such-and-such an address in Eaton Square at 7 p.m., neither early nor late, in my dinner jacket. The unknown lady would be introduced to me then and I would 'walk her' to a big charity dance at The Dorchester. Nothing further would be expected of me, except that I could turn her around the floor if she thought that an edifying prospect.

I put the details in my pocket.

My 'spag bol' was interrupted by a call from my mother. While I had been an undergraduate, I had been asked to show a French student called Charles-Henri around the university. He was a charming fellow and I had thoroughly enjoyed introducing him to our little student circle. Now it seemed he wanted to meet me in London.

I rang him the next day from Way In at Harrods during a quiet moment, trying to avoid getting caught by the floor manager. Charles-Henri was staying at the Savoy. For a twenty-three-year-old he had style, I can tell you.

'Jeremy,' he said when I got through to him, 'do you remember telling me that it was possible to eat well in London? Well, I am here again and I have found absolutely nowhere. Let me take you to dinner but you choose the restaurant.'

In those days the top French restaurants in London were the Caprice, Mme Prunier's, the Mirabelle and the Écu de France. The Italians I favoured were La Famiglia and La Paesana, where I had opened accounts. You see? I had learned something from my time in Italy. In fact, I managed to organise a dinner party for my sister Kate's twenty-first at La Paesana. All on credit, naturally.

There were some superb Indian restaurants, notably the Star of India in the Old Brompton Road and Khan's and the Standard in Westbourne Grove. But Charles-Henri could not be taken to an Indian restaurant. So where was it to be?

In the end I tossed a coin between Rules and Simpson's in the Strand, and Simpson's won. I was going to show him English cooking at its best and watch him eating his sceptical Francocentric words. I booked a table a few days ahead.

But first on Thursday was the little matter of 'walking' this unknown girl, and there I was in Eaton Square, ringing the doorbell, feeling somewhat doubtful.

A Filipino girl, dressed as a maid may have done fifty years before, opened the door to me. But I had come to expect this sort of thing in Eaton Square. The rich watched *Upstairs, Downstairs* on television just as avidly as the rest of us. This TV soap about masters and servants had grabbed the nation's attention and nobody dared miss an episode. Everyone will have had their different reasons, but for the nouveaux riches it was a useful handbook on how to live properly. By 1972, even the slowest-witted of us had finally realised that Britain had not always been the austere post-war ruin-infested prison camp that we had been brought up in, and that before the (great) war there had been a better way.

I was led into a drawing room, where a number of very well dressed people were chatting away. They all used cologne, which made for a heady atmosphere, and one of the men was wearing white gloves. I could have sworn that another was wearing make-up. There was a marked deficiency in the lady department, I thought, looking around.

I could tell immediately that no one knew anyone else there well. A little too much courtesy and interest, and no small talk about little Veronica's riding lessons.

My host was shaking my hand, very warmly. He discreetly indicated my fellow revellers. 'Sorry about this lot,' he said to me. 'Bit complicated to explain. David tells me you are a high-flyer – know how to behave – and my wife felt that none of these could deal with someone like Diana. She has real class, or likes it, anyway. And she'll be here in a second.'

As it turned out, we didn't have to wait even that long, as the maid opened the door to Diana Dors.

Diana Dors had been one of the icons of the English film industry of the 1950s. Sometimes styled the Englishman's Brigitte Bardot, she had been a rather better actress than her screen goddess typecasting had ever let her prove.

But this was 1972 and her figure, framed in the doorframe as if she were waiting for the final flashbulb to fade, had grown slightly fuller than it had been in her nubile days. In fact, she resembled Mae West, heavily corseted into a body-tight sequinned tube that flared beneath the knee, Spanish gypsy-style.

I was immediately presented to her.

'Miss Dors,' I breathed, as she held out her hand for me to kiss, 'What joy! I must have done something very good in a previous life.'

'And so must I,' she cooed.

This sort of mush may have seemed appropriate, but the lady was in fact more Epping Forest than Beverley Hills. It was strange hearing her talk in a sort of halfway house between LA and Dagenham, but that was how she sounded. She actually lived in Buckinghamshire at the time, with her much younger and quite ungovernable lover, Alan Lake.

That she was a gorgeous blonde actress cannot be gainsaid. Even so, the 'English Marilyn Monroe' (another of her labels) was an inadequate moniker. She began her career long before Norma Jean and had proved herself to be a fine actress, even if she were so often cast as a 'gold-digging' blonde. Her career in films had actually begun as early as the 1940s.

She kicked off her career at just thirteen as a pin-up girl. Then, barely fifteen years old, she signed with J Arthur Rank. Her break was with *The Shop at Sly Corner*, and as soon as she was allowed off her 'sexy siren' hook, she was off.

She even starred in cameo roles. And when, many years later, I last heard of her in action she was playing, to countless ovations, opposite Adam Ant's Prince Charming, as his Fairy Godmother.

She had not always been Diana Dors. She had been born on 23 October 1931 in Swindon. Her name was given on her birth certificate as Mavis Fluck, but she and a wholly concurring agent had decided to go for a new Christian name, coupled with her mother's maiden name.

'Fluck' would have certainly been problematic. In fact, only five years before, the Foreign Minister George Brown had got himself into serious trouble with a Mrs Fluck.

A tabloid had called Mr Brown 'the very a-b-c of a foreign secretary: alcoholic, bibulous and crapulent'. Or was it 'abrasive, bullying and cantankerous'? Difficult to say which did him the most justice. As Sir Humphrey might have put it, 'Not precisely the right temperament for the Foreign Office.' Even he realised this in 1968, and resigned. But this was just the last and most successful of his attempts to resign. They had happened so often that there was a joke in circulation while I was at school. A Downing Street aide rushes into Harold Wilson's office clutching a piece of paper and tells him, 'We've just received a resignation letter from the Deputy Prime Minister.' Wilson wearily replies, 'Just put it on the spike with all the others.'

On one evening Brown phoned Prime Minister Wilson at 11 p.m. to say he had just had a row with his wife and would have to resign. Ten minutes later his wife rang. She told the Premier to take no notice.

Later that same year, Brown and Wilson were in a meeting, disagreeing about the role of Number Ten staff in foreign policy. Brown, who perhaps had had a sherry, suddenly demanded a shorthand writer so that he could dictate a resignation letter. When this was refused, he tried to phone his office to dictate his resignation in the form of a press release. The Downing Street switchboard disconnected the call.

A little later he returned. Wilson then remarked that 'now that the eighteenth resignation was out of the way, we can discuss the matter further' – when Brown stormed out again. His nineteenth 'nervous breakdown' still ahead of him, in the morning he was back at his desk.

In 1970 Brown published his memoirs, which he named *In My Way*. On hearing the title, Wilson commented that it was very appropriate, because that was just where he had always found George Brown over the years.[1]

But it was as a diplomat that he became the stuff of legend. Never mind the stories of his wanting to dance with Mrs Golda Meir, or those concerning his unnatural attraction to the Cardinal Archbishop of Lima.

The story I loved most was when he had to give a speech to the Women's Institute. The President at that time was a Mrs Fluck. I am not sure that she was any relation of Diana Dors. But either way, the not-yet retired Foreign Secretary duly appeared to give the ladies the benefit of his wisdom. He was assisted by a loyal junior.

'Foreign Secretary,' began this hapless civil servant, 'you must remember her name. It is Fluck. Please do not get this wrong.'

'How could I get it wrong? It is the easiest surname in the world to remember. Count on me, I'll be fine.'

And with this the eminent British politician took the stage and made his opening remarks.

'It is with great pleasure,' he began, 'that I am able to intro-duce to you delightful ladies your hard-working and effective president, Mrs... Mrs... ah... excuse me a moment, if you don't mind.' He pretended to cough into his handkerchief.

It was obvious to everyone that he had forgotten the presi-dent's name. From this moment the Amazon Nation saw him as an ambassador of the enemy.

'It brings me great pleasure,' he resumed as if there had never been a problem, 'to introduce to you the brilliant and attractive president of your association, Mrs Clunt.'

I decided to take no such chances with Miss Dors, née Fluck.

'Now tell me about yourself,' she said, focusing her eyes and pointing her ample figure at me.

'Not much to tell, really. I speak Italian.' It was the single accomplishment I felt I had.

'Really? I love Italians,' said the 'hurricane in mink'. 'Tell me, how do you say "shall we dance" in Italian?'

---

[1] Some of the detail is from a memoir by Brian Walden for the BBC.

I loved her. She was a complete charmer and danced exquisitely. I enjoyed myself enormously. I was seriously struck by the sheer brilliance of my companion. She was the only person worth speaking to in our strange party, and she seemed to repay the compliment. When the time came I returned her to Eaton Square, where she gave me a chaste kiss before I wandered home. Maybe I had been hoping for more.

Diana died in Windsor on 4 May 1984, of cancer. The loss to me, and to millions of British film-goers, was that of losing a friend.

There was a surreal quality to London then. Blackouts came all the time and made life unpredictable. Hospitals found it especially challenging. A pal, Bob Norfolk, had made enough money to buy a Bentley, having cornered the market in candles and selling them on to restaurants and friends alike. What a strange business life is.

Quite by chance I bumped into Artemis Cooper, an old acquaintance, who was by now at Oxford with my little sister. I was keen to renew my slight acquaintance with her father, the historian John Julius Norwich, as I felt that I might be able to earn some money on the lecture circuit. I was duly invited to drinks in Little Venice where, by implication, my eligibility as a speaker would be judged.

The house was everything I love: 'grand Bohemian' you might call it. Most of the walls were given over to library shelves, except where there was a need to hang a painting. The furniture was an essay in eighteenth-century restraint.

As I arrived, in the best European tradition, I was immediately offered a glass of champagne.

There were a dozen or so friends of the family there and I was in no hurry. Artemis knew I needed to speak to her father and would point me in the right direction at the appropriate time. Meanwhile I mingled with the guests.

This sort of society is for me much easier than the very grand stuff where you are defined by your connections. Here was a coruscating world where your conversational skills mattered even more than the innate good breeding I suspected to be more or less common ground for the guests.

It is inappropriate at this sort of party to sit if just one lady is standing, but across the room on a Chippendale sofa was sitting a very beautiful older woman with her dog – Doggie III, if I remember its name correctly – and a small gathering of devotees had brought in their chairs and had sat around her, the better to hear her every word. I looked at her carefully. It was Lady Diana Cooper.

In itself this was not so very odd; after all, as she was Lord Norwich's mother and Artemis's grandmother.

I joined the little circle and was immediately made to feel like an old friend.

'It's Jeremy, didn't you say?' she said. 'What are you up to? Are you still "doing the season"?'

'No, not really, Lady Diana. I've got a little old for it. I have been to one or two parties in the last few weeks but they have all seemed a little juvenile. Are there any grown-ups left in London?'

Lady Diana Cooper, née Manners, was born in the great ante-bellum age and grew into the most fascinating girl in London. The 1930s were her heyday. She was then the most talked about celebrity aristocrat in London. Evelyn Waugh had immortalised her as 'Mrs Stitch'. Arnold Bennett did the same for her in his character 'Queenie Paulle'. For D H Lawrence she was his 'Artemis Hooper'.

She had witnessed from the inside the great long summer's afternoon of the Edwardian age. That evening, I saw her immutable beauty as clearly as Asquith had. Indeed, that prime minister had forgotten himself (and Margot) for her. In fact, all her lovers were privileged men. By all accounts she had conquered Chaliapin, the greatest opera singer of his time, Lord Beaverbrook, who was arguably the most powerful, and Lord Wimborne, supposedly the richest.

When, after the Great War, the fledgling British film industry started to make films in Technicolor, it turned to Lady Diana. To the gossip columns she was the unmarried daughter of the Duke of Rutland and she was the heroine of every article. She was also far too bright ever to have been an 'it' girl.

Duff Cooper was the fortunate man she married, and he was a diplomat, writer, statesman and philanderer. She accepted with consummate grace her husband's frightful behaviour in Singapore, in Algiers and in Paris, where they were posted.

She was not only the reigning beauty of her generation; she was its most celebrated wit. Hers was an adventurous and sometimes bawdy sense of fun, and she brought to society a sense of theatre. She was famed for her entrances and, when she departed for the next party on her busy social round, for the emptiness she left behind.

'Well,' she said to me, 'I have been invited to a party that won't be too young for you.' Her tone ticked me off a little for my pomposity but simultaneously encouraged me to believe there were some parties still worth attending.

'Paul Channon is giving some sort of thrash at his place in Essex. I'll see you are invited.'

We talked a little about Rome. And then Artemis signalled that I might grab a little of her father's attention and so I made my excuses, kissing her cheek but somehow wanting to kiss her hand.

Lord Norwich felt I was still too young and perhaps under-qualified for the role I had in mind. Oh well, it had been worth a shot. But Lady Diana was every bit as good as her word. A suitably thick envelope fell on to my doormat a few days later. It had to be thick, because the envelope contained an engraved pasteboard invitation to a dance in Essex, courtesy of Mrs Paul Channon, together with a second invitation to a dinner party before the dance, to be given in London, and a number of maps that explained to the motoring classes exactly where they had to be and when. Mrs Channon's husband was then a junior Conservative minister, if I recall correctly. Paul Channon's father, Chips, had also held the same Southend seat, and in Cambridge days we had joked that the seat was hereditary. Paul was later to serve in the government as President of the Board of Trade and Secretary of State for Transport. His career was finally to unravel in the Guinness scandal, in the late 1980s.

I was to be in Upper Phillimore Gardens, in Kensington, at 7 p.m. 'for 7.15'. I knew from experience that these very tight arrival times meant that the *quart d'heure de politesse* was not an option. My hostess in London was to be Mrs Blackwell.

I suppose these parties must continue today as they always

have. But it is difficult to believe that they are as grand today as they were in the early 1970s.

At the appointed hour, my taxi deposited me, in my old and seasoned dinner jacket, at the front door of a large villa in Kensington. A busy catering person let me in and pointed me downstairs.

'Dinner is in the cinema,' I was told. I forged ahead, to discover that the huge basement to this Victorian house had been transformed into a single room, now filled with small tables that would each seat six or eight people.

About half the guests for this dinner party had already arrived and were swirling around the black-walled room looking for their name cards in the candle-lit darkness. I found my name and was amazed to find I was in the same mini-party as Winston Churchill. Not the prime minister and wartime leader, naturally, but his grandson; the great man, Sir Winston, had died in 1965, reputedly after declining a dukedom from a grateful monarch.

A waiter refilled my champagne glass and the screen at the end of the room flickered into life. Mrs Blackwell had selected *The Gold Rush* for us – arguably the greatest of Charlie Chaplin's silent films. It would play havoc with the duller conversations, I thought. But there I was wrong. There were no dull conversations.

Nearly a hundred of us sat down to an exquisite dinner, while Chaplin's 1929 tramp sought his fortune and love with Georgina Hale in Alaska. As I spoke to the enchanting girl on my left, Charlie was in that cabin, teetering on the cliff edge or eating his boots.

And just when a terrific dinner was ended, our hostess tapped a glass and told us the cars had arrived. Mrs Blackwell certainly had a sense of style. She had hired a great fleet of black and stately limousines. They were outside, ready to drive us to Ongar in Essex. Ongar was on the tube in those days, the Central Line to be precise, less than twelve miles from the future Stansted Airport. Instead of extending the line to the new airport, the government chose to close the station and disconnect the airport. Just on whose side is the Minister of Transport?

Henry Paul Guinness Channon was, at the time I am writing of, a young man at the peak of his fortune and destined for high places. All his connections were superb.

Our cars drove up to Kelvedon Hall, a neat Elizabethan country mansion in red brick, in its own park (and long since converted into offices and a call centre). We formed a majestic if sombre motorcade, but the contents (i.e. ourselves) were in high spirits. The cars came to a halt and we were ejected from our hermetically sealed comfort on to a red carpet.

'Ah,' one of my travelling companions observed, 'royalty. Straighten your ties, gentlemen.'

We found our way inside. To either side of the entrance were staterooms but we went through into the courtyard, which had been laid with a wooden floor for the dance. A marquee roof had been erected over the dance floor, which would otherwise been open to the elements. Some of the party were already there, and the other dinner parties, in London and Essex, were already relocating to the new venue.

I heard my name announced and shook hands with my hosts, who smiled vaguely and let me pass on without further comment. Within seconds yet another glass of champagne was in my hand and I looked around for a familiar face.

This was not a society dance in its most limited sense. I had been to many of those, where all the guests are usually childhood friends. This one was much more elaborate. There were TV presenters and actors, there were industrialists and the holders of real power, and there was indeed senior royalty, wonderfully incarnated in the person of Princess Margaret.

I danced with an old girlfriend for a moment or two and found myself on the floor being accosted by a fairly belligerent Reginald Bosanquet, who was at that time the leading news presenter on British TV.

'I know you,' he growled in that superb voice he had. 'Your mother is a member of the Chelsea Arts Club. I know her very well.' He seemed genuinely astonished that he knew someone as young as me.

It was true that my mother was a member in that famous club in Old Church Street in Chelsea. But it was not really true that I knew Bosanquet. I had spoken to him a few times but I had formed a terrible view on political journalists in general – one I have never revised.

All classes of people have their toadies, and power is especially attractive to sycophants. Some important people like to revel in adulation, and political journalists oblige. Lobby correspondents, newsreaders, even editors all have opinions for hire to the highest bidder.

People like Bosanquet probably begin their careers in a level-headed way, but gradually they come to believe in the politicians on whom their careers depend. After a while they persuade themselves that their heroes are neither liars nor cheats. To identify such weaknesses would render the commentators themselves ridiculous. The inevitable result is that they will support the dishonest antics of the governing class through thick and thin. And famously confusing the very different words 'cynical' and 'sceptical', they adjudge all of us who would actually prefer our country to be run by Olympians whose word was good, as being either apathetic or alienated.

Interestingly, I mused, the word 'sycophant' derives from the Greek for 'fig'. I must find out why one of these days.[2]

Bosanquet was a giant in the toad pond. I mean by this that you actually wanted to hear his opinion. As a consequence he was courted by power. His attraction lay partly in his voice, which lay somewhere between James Mason and Richard Burton. He also had a certain matinée idol quality.

'Jeremy,' said the great man, displaying a flawless memory for names, 'be a good chap and fetch me a large whisky and water from the bar. I'll be out here on the floor.'

There was no reason not to be helpful and my friend and I moved away. I fetched a whisky as ordered for the great journalist.

By this time, Bosanquet's companion had re-emerged from wherever she had gone and was back on his arm. It was Princess Margaret.

Reggie accepted the drink, one arm around the princess, without any particular ceremony. I felt my services could be dispensed with when to my great surprise, and incidentally raising my opinion of him greatly, he paused for an instant.

---

[2] Συκοφάντης means a 'fig-shower' i.e. someone who shakes the tree to show the figs, or someone who informed against persons exporting figs from Attica (a fig-informer); hence an informer or slanderer; a frivolous liar – Ed.

'Ma'am,' he said, 'may I present an old friend of mine, Jeremy Macdonogh?'

She smiled at me. Not a simple courtly acknowledgement but a full beam laser-powered smile that illuminated the entire dance floor.

Not many people, perhaps, remember just how beautiful Princess Margaret was. Even fewer remember just how talented she was. But what I recall was her dazzling courtesy.

As I nodded a little bow and muttered, 'Your Royal Highness,' she rounded on me.

'Can you sing? Take photos? Speak French? Play the piano? Do impressions?'

'Not yet,' I improvised. 'You see, no one before you has been kind enough to give me a shopping list.'

And then she laughed. What a delightful laugh she had.

Bosanquet smiled the most impossibly welcome smile at me and said, 'Come with us,' and I followed him and the Princess off the floor into the body of the house. If I am not imagining it a hundred eyes were on me.

I found myself in a 'small' drawing room somewhere inside. Smoking cigarettes and drinking coffee, or in Reggie's case, whisky, were a number of older people who clearly had no interest in turning a number on the dance floor.

'Jeremy,' said Princess Margaret, who will not have forgotten my surname but flattered me to the rooftops by ignoring it, 'can I introduce you to Arnold Goodman, the chairman of the Arts Council? And this is Harold Lever. He makes soap.'

'How do you do,' I said. To myself I wondered, How am I ever going to be able to tell this story? No one will ever believe it.

At this time these two lords were constantly in the newspapers.

Arnold Goodman was, from 1963 to the mid-1970s, probably the most powerful non-elected figure in Britain. His trick was to know everybody who mattered. This skill was then called 'access'. His power was based on it.

He first made an impact when he defended an infamous libel case. The *Spectator* had accused Nye Bevan, Richard Crossman and Morgan Philips of being drunk at a socialist conference in Venice. Goodman won the case with consummate ease.

Impressed, Harold Wilson chose him as his lawyer after the 1964 election, and for the next six years Goodman had the Prime Minister's ear.

By the early 1970s Goodman was the most dominant legal figure in England. He was feared by a generation of journalists. His skill at extracting the most fulsome apologies in libel cases had become legendary. His mere existence seemed to stop unwelcome stories before they even appeared. Robert Boothby and Jeremy Thorpe were just two of his clients. He was 'a taxi for hire' in his own words, and was probably one of the most extraordinary figures Britain produced in the last half of the twentieth century.

I also knew of Harold Lever's reputation. Lord Leverhulme (for this was his noble name) was that strange conundrum, a British millionaire and a Labour Party politician. For some time he had been Wilson's economic adviser.

Leverhulme had started out as a soap wholesaler who expanded his father's business (Lever Bros) into a multinational monster (Unilever). His father had founded Port Sunlight, but despite his career as a brilliant capitalist, his son had always espoused the socialist cause at the expense of the philanthropic one of his father.

A Labour Party politico, Hugh Gaitskell, who for a moment had forgotten that socialism is about power and not about ideals, asked him, 'What kind of a socialist are you? You married your wife because she's worth four million!'

'I married my wife because she has four million?' spluttered His Lordship. 'I would have married my wife even if she only had two!'

Midnight had come and gone and Mrs Blackwell, heiress to most of the Crosse & Blackwell fortune, had allowed her cars to retreat to London. When this dawned on me I realised that I was stranded in Essex.

'I don't suppose I can scrounge a lift home,' I said like a penniless student to Princess Margaret and Lords Leverhulme and Goodman.

'Take my car,' said Lord Leverhulme. 'Goodman here will take care of me, won't you, Arnold?'

Which is what happened. Having had rather too much to drink, I fell into the back of Harold Lever's enormous Phantom VI and was driven back to the sixty miles or so to Sian Rhys's flat in Westbourne Grove, where I tipped the driver much less than he deserved and carelessly, even chirpily, woke up my flatmates as I made my way to bed.

The next day I was back at my temporary job at Harrods. The morning started predictably enough, in that I arrived late, and with a heroic headache.

Way In did a reasonable trade and on most days the time passed quickly enough, so I thought I could manage. All too often, however, the customers were a little scarce and when no one came to disturb our peace the hours would sprout extra minutes. On days like those, we floorwalkers began to devise little practical jokes to help the time go by.

There were no cheque guarantee cards in 1972, and it was left to the discretion of the shop assistant to ask for identification. I hated being bored, and on the day I was due to meet Charles-Henri it was rather a relief to see a customer come in. I had sent my colleague over to the repository in Barnes to collect a dozen 'Grecian bends' – a very ancient sort of bustier that the warehouseman was guaranteed never to have heard of – and I was eagerly waiting to hear the result. The customer, a rather attractive young lady in her late twenties, found me alone in the shop. From behind his desk the manager glanced at me and nodded.

'Are you the shop assistant?' she asked me, looking around the shop to see if there were anyone more suitable.

'I am.'

'Then follow me.'

We walked around the shop, the customer choosing a pullover here and a pair of jeans there, then changing her mind and repeating the exercise for a scarf and a belt. After almost an hour of indecision she finally decided that the only thing in the shop worth having was a pair of reflective sunglasses. They were outrageously expensive, in my opinion, but I did not share it (my opinion, that is) with her. I had been over-forcibly reminded of my low station and was getting resentful.

At the till she asked me if she might write a cheque. I decided to insist on identification, which I was always supposed to do but hardly ever did – most people simply didn't carry any and it could end up being a bit embarrassing.

But the customer had her passport on her.

'Lady Sarah Coke?' I said. And then I made a terrible mistake. I smiled and added, 'Any relation of Old King Cole?'

Well, my attempt at levity, which is what I thought it was, went down badly. The manager appeared to see what was causing the kafuffle and the upshot was that I got fired on the spot for being impertinent to a member of the English aristocracy. My real crime was in not knowing that her surname was pronounced 'Cook'.

So I was in an odd mood when I met up with Charles-Henri that evening at Simpson's in the Strand. I took him to the men-only dining room, 'the Divan', on the ground floor, the very idea of which was enough to send him into paroxysms of amazement at the English and our peculiar ways. How I wish we had still some peculiar ways left. But a modernist-feminist conspiracy has legislated them all into oblivion.

My job was to order the food, his to order the wine. So I plumped for potted shrimps to start with and then I ordered the roast beef and Yorkshire pudding from the trolley for us both.

Meanwhile, Charles-Henri had been conducting a quiet conversation with a highly impressed wine waiter and had then concluded, 'A bottle of number eighty-three, then, and would you decant it, please?'

My memory of the food has faded – I am sure it was delicious. It always was at Simpson's. But my memory of the wine is as fresh now as it was thirty-five years ago.

Charles-Henri had ordered a burgundy. To be exact, he had ordered a Clos de Vougeot, Grand Cru, 1955, from the Dijon end of the Côtes de Nuits.

This was the first time I had experienced a wine of this stratospheric quality. To tell the truth, I had always suspected that the great fame of some of these wines was a little exaggerated. What a fool I was.

They say that the northernmost Burgundy reds are aromatic. That was an understatement. The bouquet was an adventure, a doorway to an Aladdin's cave of aromas. The wine was perfectly balanced – not neutral at all, but with the acid pulling in a dynamic equilibrium with the fruit, the tannins, and the lightest vanilla from the oak. The texture was between velvet and silk. But there were so many distinct flavours, all of which were separately discernible. This wine had so much character. It was almost operatic, and compared to the single instrument of a cheap red wine, this was a Mozartian sextet. It was utterly memorable and the experience lives with me still. I was hooked. From that day fine wine has proved to be a consuming if expensive hobby.

'What do you think of it?' Charles-Henri had realised that we had lapsed into silence.

'Rather good, actually,' I said.

'You know,' said Charles-Henri, 'that this was Napoleon's favourite wine. Whenever his troops marched along the Route Napoleon, which connects France and Italy, they would pass by the gates to the *clos* where Vougeot grows. They were ordered to salute the vines, and they still do, to this day.'

'Hmm,' I said. 'You French are so very different to us. I can't see the Brigade of Guards saluting a brewery. But I'll agree it's difficult to believe this wine could ever be bettered.'

Despite a difficult day, the good company, wonderful wine and a very decent dinner had combined to raise my morale. I was able to describe my circumstances to my French friend with reasonable good humour.

'Did you know,' said Charles-Henri, 'we have a *chambre de bonne* – a maid's room – above our flat in Paris? You could think about staying there, quite free, if you want. It's not terribly comfortable, but it's clean and private and you could come and go as you liked. It seems to me that you would make your way easily in Paris, better even than in London, just at present. Why don't you give it a go? For funds, you'll teach English, or do tours, just as you did in Rome. Give it some thought.'

I peered out of the window into the Strand. It had begun to rain. I thought about Paris. Yes, I would give it a go. What had I to lose?

The newspapers were reporting a suicide in the City. Some poor fellow had thrown himself out of a window. In the event it proved not to be a stockbroker, but a window cleaner who had missed his footing, but this was not known at the time. The papers were calling it the 'Crash of '29 Revisited'. Would the government fall? Would Britain need a loan from the IMF? The share index had fallen to a third of its previous high and there was no reason why it should pick up. Winter would be tough. There wasn't much for me in England.

I could already get by in French, after a fashion, but it would be a fine thing if I were able to speak it the way I could now speak Italian. Then I would be able to join a company that traded with the Common Market. All the more so if the UK could bring itself to join in the European Project with a little more enthusiasm.

Chapter the Nineteenth
1972: Arriving in Paris

In which the author returns to Paris to take up residence in the attic of a smart block of flats. He finds work as an English tutor to a film star, discovers a superb Bloody Mary at 5 rue Danou, buys some shoes and a dinner jacket and assumes the genial role of boulevardier. He learns about the St Bartholomew's Day Massacre and that the choucroute *season begins in October.*

It took me less than a week to put my London affairs in order, say goodbye to a few friends, and cadge a lift to Heathrow. The logic was incontrovertible. I had neither job nor prospects in the UK. I had passed a couple of magical years in Italy. Ergo, Paris was the place to be. It would be like the sequel to a great film, and the sequel stood a chance of being even better than the original.

I arrived at Charles-Henri's apartment building just off the avenue Mozart, my small case in hand, all ready for a short stay in his *chambre de bonne*. I would soon hit a seam, I told myself, and then I would move into my own flat.

The avenue Mozart is in the XVIe *arrondissement* of Paris; its Belgravia, perhaps. The whole quarter is slightly stern, eschewing the hints of Bohemia that are associated with the rest of the French capital. There are a few bars, frequented in the most part by the Portuguese servants of the *haute bourgeoisie* that favours this part of Paris, but none of them (the bars, that is, not the servants) looked especially inviting. Local restaurants are mostly of the *brasserie* type, suggesting a clientèle of bachelors or husbands whose families were away at their *petites terres* or country places.

I rang the *sonnerie* at the slightly Germanic front door of Charles-Henri's building and it clicked open automatically. I stepped inside and looked about.

The building was typical of the territory. The whole edifice had been conceived towards the end of the nineteenth century to resemble a Renaissance palace around a small courtyard, but one with lifts. A corkscrew stair, rather like the one in the cloister of Tours Cathedral, was tucked, unused, into a corner. The concierge directed me to the lift that I took to the second floor, where I met a beaming Charles-Henri.

'Excellent timing, my dear fellow. I'll tell cook we are one more for dinner. For the time being, let me take you straight away to your room, where you can change into something suitable, and then come and join us for an early evening drink.' Charles-Henri really does talk the best kind of top-drawer English.

Charles-Henri and I took the lift to the top of the building, wandered down a dim and narrow corridor to find a small door that opened on to a fragile wooden set of steps up to a further storey. This was the floor for the maids; a sort of female aerial colony. If any of the gentry below had male servants, it would not do to have females in the same apartment. That would be considered a poor show, even if the servants were married. So the males got a bed in the big flat and the females were consigned to these simple rooms far above. How they had children I've no idea.

I looked around the little room I had been so very kindly allocated.

Charles-Henri read my mind. 'It's not much, is it? But it is the best of the three allocated to us.'

I looked around at the little steel bed and the modest arrangements. The Baby Belling, a portable oven characteristic of bedsits at the time, would make some sort of cooking possible.

'What about bath times?' I asked Charles-Henri, who was still studying my reaction. 'My rubber ducks need exercise.'

'Let me show you.' He led me along the narrow corridor with its sloping ceiling (it was built into the mansard) until we reached a door marked with an enamelled oval, '*salle de bain*'. It revealed a clinical-looking room, smelling strongly of disinfectant and as clean as it is possible to be, with an ancient and spartan bath and an antediluvian shower.

'That will do nicely,' I said, hoping the shower would not prove diluvian. What did I expect? The George V?

Charles-Henri headed off home and I returned to my palatial apartment and fell on to the bed. The mattress felt surprisingly good. There was an hour or so to go before drinks time, at least in England. Or was England an hour ahead?

I took *The Origin of Species* out of my jacket pocket and put it on the bedside table. I promised myself I would make a real, final effort to finish it this year. But not this very minute. I unclipped a duty-free bottle of whisky. It was time to give Greenwich Mean Time the benefit of the doubt. I lay on my back and lit up a cigarette.

These days, smoking is an almost forgotten pleasure. At the time of writing it has been twenty years since I last smoked. It has become inconvenient, unfashionable and expensive.

But then, it was another thing. The great conductor Otto von Klemperer smoked a pipe. Given half a chance he liked to conduct his orchestra with it. The Berlin Philharmonic found it a poor substitute for a baton and, when from time to time he replaced it between his teeth, it threw them into cacophonic confusion. Eventually they persuaded their First Violin to remove the thing from the Great Man before the rehearsals even began.

A worse case even than Klemperer's was the Prussian general, Gebhard von Blücher, whose troops famously helped Wellington defeat Napoleon at Waterloo. The General would indicate where his men were to go by waving his boxwood pipe around in the air.

In the manner of great men of style, Blücher employed a 'pipe keeper' who rode beside him at all times, no matter how danger-ous the battle. His job was to keep his general's pipe alight. During the battle of Waterloo, the pipe keeper may have smoked more than a hundred pipes on his master's behalf.

As I lay on my bed, it occurred to me that this sort of selfless service could inspire fantasy. A cocktail barman, perhaps, always ready with a perfect Manhattan? A Playboy Bunny? Or a sober philosopher, armed with useful thoughts from Montaigne or Marcus Aurelius? Or all three? This thing has potential.

The French expression *'casser la pipe'*, usually translated as 'to kick the bucket', comes from those gallant days. Wounded soldiers, when on the operating table, were asked to bite on their pipes during the amputation or whatever. If he died, the soldier would let his pipe fall to the ground and the surgeon would know to move on to the next case.

My cigarette had run its course. I was much refreshed. I had to 'put on something more suitable', so I put on a tie and headed downstairs.

Charles-Henri's family was most welcoming, if a little old-fashioned. It was obvious that I would have to be on my very best behaviour.

After a glass of champagne, a servant in a white jacket came in to tell Charles-Henri's mother that dinner was ready. He said, as I recall, *'Madame la comtesse est servie.'* In France they say, 'Madam is served', whereas in England we are told that 'Dinner is served'. Odd that there should be a difference, really.

Dinner that evening was quite charming. Their dining room was a large oval, decorated entirely in hand-made, early nine-teenth-century Chinese wallpaper. A few pieces of chinoiserie provided the necessary furnishings. There were two large doors cut into the walls, decorated in the style of the building – a severe and marvellously restrained art nouveau – which worked rather well with the room. The door to the kitchen was neither framed nor decorated but was wallpapered, so that when closed it became invisible.

The food was simple and elegant, a *salade d'endives* followed by roasted quails with sautéed potatoes. We drank Beaujolais throughout. A perfect light supper, in fact.

It was almost midnight when I bade everyone goodnight and headed upstairs to my spartan quarters.

At the British Council, the next day, I inspected the notice board. Companies and individuals wanting English tutors would sometimes advertise there, I had been told, and I wanted to check it out.

There was just one vacancy there that morning. A French actress, Bulle Ogier by name, wanted someone to bring her English up to speed. There was something vaguely familiar about the name. 'Irregular hours but decent pay', said the ad, and I decided to apply.

Mlle Ogier had suggested we meet at a café in the Beaubourg,

in a *zinc* in the rue de Montorgueil. '*Zinc*'? The older bars in Paris
– at least the better ones – have their counters made entirely of
zinc. I have absolutely no idea why.

It was not too far to walk – about an hour through the loveliest
parts of Paris – and as I did so I racked my brains for where I had
heard her name before. And then it came to me. I had seen her in
Buñuel's Oscar-winning *Le Charme Discret de la Bourgeoisie* only a
week or so before.

I found the little bar easily enough and there, already seated in
a corner, was a blonde in beret and sunglasses, perhaps in her
early thirties – every inch the film star trying hopelessly to look
anonymous.

'Tell me about yourself,' she commanded in lightly accented
English. I obliged. Like most twenty-three-year-olds, I felt the
precious little I had to relate was rather a lot. I was learning
French. No, I didn't know how long it would take. I had rattled
on for too many minutes before I thought that this nonsense
must have been boring her. I changed tack and asked her to tell
me about herself.

She had begun her career in the little theatres you find all over
Paris. She worked those bijou stages for more than five years, and
in the process she had met half the people you need to meet in
France. Jacques Rivette had taken a shine to her and had cast her
in *L'Amour Fou*, in 1967. Since then she hadn't looked back.
When Buñuel had given her a starring role in *Le Charme Discret* in
1972, her sixteenth film, she began to attract international
attention. That meant Hollywood, perhaps. Whatever it meant, it
also meant English.

I agreed that I could go to her apartment in the Marais and
teach her for two hours a session. But her hours were erratic. She
would call me in the morning when she knew she would be free
in the early evening. Could I start that same evening? Yes, I could.

Charles-Henri was amazed when I told him.

'Not only do you find a job on your first day in Paris, but
you're teaching one of the most ravishing women in France. How
do you manage?'

I won't deny I was rather pleased with myself as well.

I picked up some other work, teaching a class organised by the town hall for young working people (*jeunes ouvriers*, as the French like to call them). They were charming and hard-working but it was my occasional lessons with Bulle that I particularly looked forward to. We had managed four sessions a week to begin with, but it had eroded to one as Christmas drew closer. Paris was an expensive place and making ends meet was also becoming a challenge, especially now that I was beginning to live a slightly turbocharged life.

Charles-Henri had decided to introduce me here and there to people he knew who, it seemed, could all speak near-faultless English. They must have all had Scottish nannies. Mostly they were curious to meet Bulle's private tutor. She was very much more famous than I had realised, and I found myself with a growing number of invitations on the shelf above my metal bed. My address was excellent, even illustrious. If my new friends could only know how very un-palatial my particular circumstances really were.

One day I shared with Bulle the secrets of my social success and she claimed to be delighted to learn that I was being presented as her mentor.

'We must cover the other end of your story. Come and meet some of my friends on Thursday night. I'm giving a little dinner party.'

Bulle had arranged to take over the oddest little restaurant I have ever been to. It was called, appropriately enough, Le Curieux, as it served as an antique shop during the day. At night, a space was cleared for about a dozen covers and it became a seriously chic restaurant. I know the Gasworks restaurant in Fulham, London, had something similar. The downside to the Gasworks was that its food was frightful.

It was difficult to know what to wear and I rang Charles-Henri. He suggested a conference at Harry's Bar. Its address (5, rue Danou) is engraved indelibly on my memory.

This was Hemingway's bar. I don't know if you are a great fan of his. I am, and not just for literary reasons. Solely on the grounds that he invented the Bloody Mary, it is reasonable to petition the angels on the old man's behalf for his safe place in paradise.

Harry's Bar is close to the Opera House – the Garnier one, that is – and is decorated with the armorial bearings of most of the Oxbridge colleges, plus a number of colleges in the United States. Charles-Henri was already there when I found the bar. He was rather pleased with himself as he had found my old college's coat of arms and had secured a pair of seats under it.

'You'll need a decent pair of shoes,' said Charles-Henri, who seemed to have a thing about footwear, 'so I'll take you to Weston's. They are the best shoemakers in Paris but you know that already. They used to have a branch in Jermyn Street.'

I smiled ambiguously. I had never even heard of them.

'You need a new dinner jacket. I'll take you to my chap. He'll run you up a stylish one for not too much. You need to cut a dash.'

Charles-Henri's English constantly amazed me. How could anyone speak it so well? His accent was so good you knew he could not possibly be from England. Only the Indians speak English that well. He didn't look Indian, though.

The dinner was not black tie, I told him. I needed to look more Bond Street than Savile Row.

'Say no more,' said Charles-Henri. We set off along the Rue du Faubourg St Honoré and peered in a few shop windows. The clothes were marvellous, but their prices were surreal.

'Just choose a few things,' said Charles-Henri. 'You can pay me back when Bulle Ogier pays you next.'

Thanks to Charles-Henri's generosity, I arrived at Le Curieux looking a million dollars. It was almost literally the case.

In the candlelit gloom I could just make out a long thin refectory table, awash with crystal and ebony-handled cutlery. Napkins were folded into bizarre animals or birds. How do they do that stuff with napery?

Torches also lit the room, and I mean the genuine flaming kind, hanging away from the walls. Strange pieces of dark lacquered furniture surrounded us like natives around a missionary's clearing, and three or more suits of armour were set around the table like medieval footmen. Huge candles lit the table, which would allow us to see the faces of the people nearest to us. In the general darkness little pools of light were visible where the picture lights threw the odd eighteenth-century courtesan into sharp relief. And some of them were *very* odd.

Bulle pressed a glass of champagne into my hand the very second I found the party, after I had first collided with a Louis XV escritoire in the gloom. She was all over me, making me feel as if I had some merit in some way, which I didn't. But she was such a star, and if she wanted to make a fuss then that was more than OK by me.

And as we took our places, I saw in the dim light that across the table from me sat Fernando Rey, the veteran actor, who had been my hero ever since I had seen him in *The French Connection* a couple of years before. Rey had made over 200 films, starting way back in 1935. With hindsight, I would especially recommend *Illustrious Corpses* (1976) and *That Obscure Object of Desire* (1977). Until his death in 1994, if I heard that Rey was in a film, I would drop everything and see it that same day. Pathetic, isn't it?

It was Rey's remarkable work with Luis Buñuel during the 1960s and 1970s that made him internationally famous. He became, in all probability, the first Spanish actor to be a household name around the world.

Rey astonished me when he told me his favourite British actor was Oliver Reed. His favourite American? Gene Hackman, it went without saying. We traded a bit. I put up Diana Dors. Yes, charming, under-exploited, perhaps. What about Richard Burton? Good at priests, he said. And we both laughed. Fernando Rey had made priests a speciality, and I had seen him in communion with the infinite in *The Last Days of Pompeii* and *The Return of the Magnificent Seven*.

If only I could remember all the showbiz anecdotes that flew about that evening, but my French was still weak and many of them went clean over my head.

But as I drifted off to sleep that night I wondered if many twenty-three-year-olds could arrive unannounced in Paris one month and be at such a dinner party the next. I must be getting something right.

I was beginning to meet a lot of people. A cousin of Charles-Henri's, Olivier de Caumont la Force, decided to further my cause and introduced me into his circle.

I mentioned my English friend, Piers de la Force, and admitted to having known him since my teens. I wondered if he might be a relation of Olivier's?

'It is not possible! In fact, your man is a fraud. There are no "de la Forces" outside France.'

Olivier was clearly proud of his ancient name, but he was wrong. There is a powerful Portuguese line of that name who produce a marvellous port. And I was confident that Piers's family was the real thing, too. Why, Piers's elder brother is called Tarquin, and what could be more plausible than that?

'The reason why I am so sure,' explained Count Olivier, 'is because all my ancestors were murdered on St Bartholomew's day, 1572. All, that is, apart from one fourteen-year-old boy, the heir to the dukedom, who survived by the most extraordinary of miracles. And as we all descend from that one little boy, we all know one another.'

Olivier knew that I had heard of the notorious massacre, but he felt I should have a better understanding of what had actually happened. He had met Englishmen who liked to dismiss it as merely an act of wanton Catholic savagery, and the couple of sharp questions he put to me quickly demonstrated that I was in no position to defend the Faith or the French for their terrible crime of 400 years before.

He determined, like a good historian, to set the scene fairly before me.

'Without knowing about this massacre, you cannot possibly hope to get beneath the skin of modern France,' he began. 'These shameful things – whether at Drogheda, Glencoe, Nagasaki, My Lai or Belsen – they leave their mark on a nation's soul.'

Olivier leant back and spoke with a sadness of biblical proportion.

'These terrible acts echo down the ages, cursing their perpetrators' children and grandchildren for untold generations.'

France, he explained, was not a comfortable place to live in the second half of the sixteenth century, any more than was England under Elizabeth I. A lot of effort was put in by the Queen Mother Catherine de Médicis, or Caterina de' Medici if you prefer, to create some form of neutrality between the Catholic and Protestant leaders. She invited the Huguenots' chief, Admiral de Coligny, to join the King's Council. She tried to arrange a marriage between the Catholic Margot de Valois and the Protestant Henri de Navarre, and she despatched a younger brother of the king to court the Anglican Queen Elizabeth I.

It was none of it any use. The tension continued to mount in towns and in the countryside.

'It beats me how Protestants could despise the Catholics with such vehemence,' I volunteered. 'It's rather like the branch of a tree insulting its trunk.'

'Ah. I'm afraid you have it the wrong way round. Our house was Protestant then. Our hero was Calvin. At first our great preacher was rational, and was all for peaceful coexistence, but after a while he began to contradict his earlier teachings. One day he declared that a prince who persecuted the Protestant Church had forfeited his right to be obeyed. One of his acolytes, François Hotman, went so far as to recommend a "Frankish" constitution. If it had been implemented a king of France would have had to be elected by the people and could had governed only through their consent.'

I could see the problem with this sort of arrangement. It might have led to all sorts of trouble. If a king were elected from the people by the people, who would be there to protect the people from their own greed, their need for instant gratification and their general venality?

'Most French people could see through it too. This sort of doctrine was far too revolutionary. The people of France began to associate the Protestant faith with treason.

'The Protestants, in order to survive the long years of persecution, had created a cell-like structure of congregations, consistories and synods where people in the group stuck together and helped each other, both in matters of religion and everyday business. As with the Jews, their "secret" organisation was met with suspicion. The task the Huguenot leaders faced was to ensure that it did not mutate into outright hostility.'

'Give me the economic background, Olivier. We are always told that economics explains everything.' Though privately, I have never accepted this Marxist approach to history.

'All right, here I go. The Huguenots worked harder than Catholics, mainly because they were able to work through the hundred or so Catholic feast days. This made them very attractive to capitalists and merchants, but not to Catholics. They dominated the new technology, typesetting, publishing and even bookbinding. They were mostly literate, as well. Huguenot schools emphasised literacy, mainly to understand the Scriptures better. However, these skills became translated into countless newspapers and tracts.'

'Didn't the Catholics write them off as boring Puritans?'

'Again, you seem to have it upside down. From the Catholic perspective, the Protestants actually seemed to be sex-mad. Women participated in Protestant rites. Men and women sang and studied the Bible together. This came close to a sexual fantasy for Catholics, who took great care to segregate the unmarried. The Huguenot doctrine of a "priesthood of all believers" led to a wicked rumour that Protestant worship must involve some kind of orgiastic ritual.'

'But the Catholics must also have benefited from the improving economy, surely?'

'The improving economy? Who said the economy was improving? On the contrary, the ground was fertile for a revolution. The costs of food, fuel and shelter all rose sharply throughout the 1560s. The difficulty of making ends meet, the rising homelessness, the increasing urban poverty, coupled with an unfocused anxiety about the future, created a fearful society that was looking for scapegoats.'

'So, all hell broke loose?'

'In a word. The Catholic reaction was fierce in the extreme. The population suddenly realised that the Huguenots were heretical. When Catholics saw cobblers and washerwomen and other such riffraff debating the message of the Bible, they were appalled. It seemed like a disease in the Body of Christ, and Catholic firebrands were now openly advocating the purging of this infection, in the name of God.'

All of this unease, unrest and intolerance must be taken into account when you consider what actually happened on 23 August 1572, said Olivier. A worried Paris had just seen the wedding of the nineteen-year-old and Huguenot Prince Henri de Navarre and his appealing Catholic Margot. The festivities were still going on, almost a week later. Almost every Huguenot in France had turned up in Paris for the event. Henri himself brought 800 mounted noblemen from Navarre in his train.

'The trouble – the real trouble, that is – broke out on 22 August.'

An assassin shot at Admiral de Coligny. He wasn't killed outright, but he was severely wounded and his arm was shattered.

Coligny was a loyal subject and believed that he enjoyed royal protection, so when fellow Protestants and sane Catholics advised him to flee the city he simply refused. He could easily have made it to the safety of one of the many Protestant strongholds, but he stubbornly chose to sit the crisis out.

But he was wrong about the King. During the night of 23 August, the vacillating monarch met his mother Catherine de Médicis and his brother Henri d'Anjou in the Palace of the Louvre, where they decided to murder Coligny. And not just the Admiral. All the other Huguenot leaders were also on their hit list. Charles IX reportedly said, '*Mieux qu'on les tue tous afin que personne ne puisse jamais rapprocher ce geste à nous.*'[1]

Some of the household soldiery were sent to deal with Coligny. The killers burst through the door of his lodgings and their officer, Besme, sword in hand, addressed his startled victim.

'Are you Coligny?'

Coligny replied, with great sangfroid, 'Yes, I am he. But you, young man, should respect these white hairs. What have you in mind? You cannot shorten by many days this life of mine.'

But even as he spoke these sad words, Besme thrust his sword into the admiral, pulled it out again and thrust it deep into the poor man's mouth. Now the soldiers had their turn and plunged their own swords into what we can only hope was the lifeless figure at their feet.

Coligny's body was thrown through the window into the courtyard below. The king's men who had remained below wiped away the blood that obliterated his face. It took them a moment or two, but they confirmed that it had indeed been Coligny. Besme,

---

[1] 'Well then, kill them all so that no one is left to reproach us.'

returning from the scene of the crime, gave the corpse a kick for good measure.

The Chevalier d'Angoulême, another Catholic firebrand, wheeled his horse around and shouted, 'Come on, friends! Let's finish what we've started!'

Soon the cry of '*Aux armes!*' came from all around. Some of the rabble emerged and ran to Coligny's house, where they shamefully mutilated the body. Eventually they cut off its head, in order to package it up and send it to Rome, of all places.

The crowd, not satisfied in the least, retrieved what was left of the unfortunate admiral and dragged the corpse through the streets to the Seine.

There, some children threw the body into the river, but a new crowd showed up and dragged it out again. They hanged Coligny's remains by the feet in iron chains on the gibbet at Montfaucon. Then they lit a fire underneath, which charred and disguised the unrecognisable lump even more. Coligny, as Voltaire dryly observed some years later, was tortured with all the elements, 'since he was killed on the earth, thrown in the water, placed on the fire, and finally hung out to dry in the air'.

Friends, later that night, took him down from the gibbet. What was left of him was taken to Chantilly and interred in the Duc d'Orléans' chapel there.

As dawn broke that St Bartholomew's Day, all hell was breaking loose. Somehow both the militia and the general population went on the same rampage, believing themselves to be sanctioned by both king and Church. Many Catholics painted white crosses on their hats and went around gaily butchering their soberly clad neighbours. The killing spree went on for three whole days. Nobody could bring the thing under control until more than 10,000 people had died.

The Huguenot prince, Henri de Navarre, consummated his marriage to his beautiful Catholic queen in their bridal suite. Outside their locked door, presumably while Henri's mind was on higher matters, his entire entourage of forty Protestant gentlemen was put to the sword. When he emerged the next day, the Prince, together with his cousin the Prince de Condé, was dragged before Charles IX. They were both threatened with death if they did not convert to Catholicism, and they did as they were told. Navarre became a ward of the Court for the next four years, defended but living in constant fear of his life. This is when the future King Henri IV of France and Navarre memorably declared that '*Paris vaut une messe*' – sometimes translated as 'Paris is worth the candle'.

Over the next few weeks the massacres spread to the provinces. It wasn't clear at the time but this was the beginning of the eclipse of the Protestant church in France.

'It's unbelievable that Europeans could have behaved this badly,' I pronounced. 'Were you de la Forces in Paris that day?'

'No, heaven be praised. We were in our old donjon, or castle, at La Force, in the Aude. We were among the most powerful Huguenot nobles in France, but we had been warned not to attend the royal wedding.

'But we were anything but safe where we were. Within two weeks of St Bartholomew's day, crazed common soldiers, homicidal militiamen and murderous peasants baying for blood surrounded our castle.

'They laid siege to the stronghold, but my forebears had been taken by surprise. Our provisions could not last long, so we decided to saddle our best horses and make a break for it, through the baying hordes, to safety. Our retinue would give us cover with a rain of arrows to either side of our path.'

'Did it work?' I asked, transfixed on the edge of my seat.

'It might have worked, had it not been for the local militia, who were helmeted and armed with firearms.

'We flung the doors open and came out at speed, the duchess in her carriage at full tilt, closely followed by her duke and their son. Father and son shared the fastest horse in their stable. Behind these came the rest of the family, tutors, chaplains, dancing teachers, masters of rhetoric and all the other human paraphernalia of a grand sixteenth-century household.

'Our terrified soldiers, firing their arrows from the battlements as fast as they could manage, had almost no effect. The rabble, which charged the procession, fired their pistols and crossbows at us.

'Our carriage was easily overturned, and my ancestor the duchess was pulled out and away to an ignoble death.'

'Were the men all right?' I asked.

'No. A round from a handgun pierced the duke's armour and threw him and his fourteen-year-old son, Jacques-Nompar, from his horse, which itself was felled by an arrow.

'What became of François de Caumont, Duc de la Force, is lost to history. But his heir, little Jacques-Nompar, fell into a hollow in the ground and curled up into a defensive ball, just as his father's horse fell on top of him.

'The young man was trapped under the dead horse, while everyone he had ever known – his parents, his siblings, his tutors and servants – were put to death around him.

'Their bloodlust satisfied, the mob returned to its hovels, except for the looters, naturally, who plundered the castle and tore the rings and jewellery off the bodies beneath the walls. Then even they went home.

'There is no question that Jacques-Nompar would have been murdered or died of exposure if he had done anything other than what he actually did, and stayed out of sight under a dead but warm horse. The mayor of La Force sent teams to bury the dead, and eventually the boy was revealed, desperately weak and hungry, but otherwise undamaged, his little sword at his hip and his signet ring still on his finger for all to see.'

'So the Protestant princeling survived?'

'Jacques-Nompar de Caumont la Force grew up a Catholic. He grew to be governor of Béarn and, later, of Navarre itself, after Henri de Navarre had relocated to Paris. Henri became the Catholic King of France, after having been merely the Huguenot Prince Henri de Navarre. After some dangerous political intrigues, Jacques-Nompar submitted to Henri IV's successor, Louis XIII. He was a great soldier. He campaigned in Piedmont, taking Saluces in 1630 and defeating the Spanish at Cariñena that same year. He took Philippsburg, captured the great general Colloredo, and was made a Marshal of France.

'By the time he died,[2] his castle was rebuilt, and his fortunes were restored. It was not, however, a permanent victory over destiny. The castle was again attacked in the French Revolution. That time it did not survive.'

---

[2] 10 May 1652.

'And the Huguenots?'

'The St Bartholomew's Day Massacre destroyed the Huguenot leadership. An unrepentant Prince of Condé escaped to Germany. Coligny's younger brother, Andelot, was sent to Switzerland, where no doubt he prospered.'

'Oh!' I said, 'I am looking forward to telling Piers he is an impostor.'

'No, don't do that,' said Olivier, who was never that strong on jokes. 'Let me do it. It is only right.'

Both France and Paris were built in a succession of destructive waves, probably the key feature of the national character. France has been overrun by Ancient Greeks,[3] Celts or Gauls, Romans, Huns, Vandals, Goths, Franks, Merovingians, Carolingians, Normans, English, Crusaders, Burgundians and, predictably, the Germans, who have played away three or four times so far. It is a huge country, and is vaguely defined by a common language. At least it is written the same in Metz as it is in Gaillac, even if the natives have to concentrate a lot when they meet.

Because the country has been reinvented so many times, the French are inured to disaster. What would be unthinkable in England – their Revolution is a good example – was possible in France precisely because it had happened so many times before. That is why they are on their Fifth Republic, and have experimented with Bourbon and Bonapartist monarchies, sometimes alternating between the two. There was even a Louis-Napoleon, who presumably offered the best of both worlds.

The revolutions of 1848 in Europe were as nothing compared to the great dislocations the French have suffered. But in the process, they created the proudest middle class on Earth. The French bourgeoisie defines France – not its peasants or its aristocrats. The aristocrats are mildly disliked and they keep to their own circles. The peasants and *la classe ouvrière* are permanently furious, largely unmanageable and scarcely represented in the Assemblée Generale in Paris.

France today is a sort of bourgeois conspiracy. The two main political parties, one of the Centre-Left and the other of the

---

[3] Marseilles and Nice were both Greek colonies.

Centre-Right, fight each other in public but tacitly conspire together to keep the working classes and the peasants out of power.

By way of example, before the Revolution, no one could hunt except the nobility. Only the heir to the throne was called 'Monsieur'. Since the Revolution, everyone can hunt, and every Frenchman is called milord or milady (which is what monsieur and madame actually mean).

The English seem incapable of understanding this. When we recently banned foxhunting, some people thought the French might be sympathetic. The French are simply baffled. For we have introduced a ban that prevents ordinary people from hunting and allows the rich, who can easily travel to Ireland or France or Germany, to continue their sport. In France, everyone has the right to hunt. A British Labour Party, notionally socialist, has introduced a law the most recidivist, atavistic and aristocratic Frenchman could only pray for.

Similarly, when an Englishman, with his schoolboy French, goes into a shop and asks for a French loaf, he may say cheerfully, '*Bonjour! Je voudrais une baguette, s'il vous plaît*,'[4] and be baffled by the froideur of the shopkeeper he has apparently offended. 'Ah, the French,' he sighs, not understanding anything.

But the French Revolution, through a curtain of pain, levelled upwards; not downwards, as socialism tends to do in the Anglo-Saxon world. Whole social classes, previously without education, now found schooling forced upon them at rows of wooden desks in depressing schoolrooms. All the French became lords and ladies – and how they insisted on it! The Englishman in the boulangerie, had he remembered to tack the word 'madame' on to his short sentence, would have been rewarded with a great smile.

The sadness of France's destructive history is also written into the national character. So many French people have died in too many wars. Napoleon alone killed more than half the men in France aged between sixteen and forty. He abandoned two of his three *grandes armées* to a lingering and fatal exile, one in Egypt and the other in Russia. A substantial percentage of the natives of the Baltic States, especially Lithuania, descend from these homesick

---

[4] 'Good morning! I should like a baguette, if you please.'

soldiers. In the savage 'pacification' of the Vendée, revolutionaries hunted royalists like vermin, and in other parts of the country they concentrated their priests into warehouses and burnt them alive, or chained them in barges and sank them with cannon fire.

It is the French who gave us the word 'genocide' all that time ago, in the closing frames of the eighteenth century. We wrongly credit the Germans with this neologism.

But they also gave us the word 'civilisation'. And which nation has explored the meaning of courtly love more that the French? Read the *Roman de la Rose* or Beaudelaire's *Les Fleurs du Mal*, and ask if such works could have been written by, say, an Italian. They could not. From Montesquieu to Verlaine, from Molière to Beaumarchais, from Proust to Camus, these ideas are endlessly rehearsed. And even today, in our materialistic world, when a French boy asks a French girl out on a date, the whole process will be courtly in a way that has hardly been seen in England these hundred years.

Saying that, he will probably take her to dinner and on to a nightclub, the same way we all do. And despite its reputation, and its famous nightclubs, Paris is not really a late night city. Sure, if you want to dance, Paris has a sample of the finest nightclubs in the world. There is also some late night cabaret, of usually a satirical or an erotic nature, and sometimes both.

But don't try to find a mere restaurant open for business at 2 a.m. You will walk your shoes off.

One of the exceptions is Le Buffet, a *brasserie alsacienne*, which really comes into its own in October, once the *choucroute* is declared *en saison*.

This is one of Paris's great historical restaurants. For many years it was called Le Buffet Germanique, but after the Franco-Prussian War[5] it was thought prudent to shorten its name to Le Buffet.

It is the tiniest of restaurants, which you won't stumble across by accident. Probably for this reason it was and still is the rendezvous for writers and artists, musicians and celebrities, none of whom ever seems to eat before midnight.

You can't even see the walls of the place. There are so many paintings hanging that sometimes they overlap. Not all the artists

[5] 1870–1871.

are unknown, either, and there are works by Emile Breton, Eugène Perrin and many others. If you're interested in art, get there early, because by 2 a.m. the place is packed and there will be no way you can treat the place as a gallery. There are also poems and graffiti on the walls in illustrious manuscript; there are bits and pieces by Emile Zola, by Paul Arène, by Georges Nardin, some in vile prose and others in sublime poetry. Caution is advised – some of the philosophical diatribes would make an entire Turkish regiment blush a deep crimson.

Madame Clarisse, the *patronne*, seemed to know everyone personally from their second visit onwards. For some reason she took a shine to me and I never had trouble getting a table. It did pay to telephone, though, even if she would always ask me why I bothered.

Many, even most, British people have lost the habit of eating seasonally, but on the continent there are people who will tell you with pride that they do not own a freezer. Buy what you need for a day or two, and then buy again. The first tomatoes, or asparagus, or potatoes, are all treated as events worthy of celebration, especially as the French have tired of the food of the previous season. In October, their great event is the first *choucroute*, or 'sauerkraut', as it is better known in England.

Cabbage is fermented, lightly pickled and flavoured with cloves and other spices. The resulting improbable confection is then brought to your table in a great steaming mound, with pieces of bacon and a frankfurter or two sticking out at a rude angle. It is washed down with beer (traditionally Kronenbourg) or with a thin red wine like an Alsatian Pinot Noir.

And my goodness, it is succulent! For about a month, nobody eats anything else. And then, by November, Paris has tired of it again.

How these restaurants keep going out of season beats me.

On the wall at Le Buffet is a little drawing by a competent cartoonist of the late nineteenth century. It has a drawing of two Prussian officers, one very tall, one very short, staring at the Mona Lisa in the Louvre. Both are covered in medals and carry huge swords, and both are wearing hats brimming with ostrich feathers. And both are staring grimly at the painting, sweat bursting from their brows. There is a caption below.

'Two Prussian officers practising a smile,' says the caption in an elegant French hand, 'for it is rumoured that the natives of Alsace-Lorraine have a sense of humour.'

I was beginning to enjoy Paris a lot.

A Revival Sunday
1973: Notre Dame de Paris

In which the author begins a vain attempt to visit every cathedral in France. He begins to realise the debt France owes to Viollet le Duc and to the Gothic revival.

My great-grandfather, in 1899, made an intelligent New Year's resolution: never to dine in a house where he could not stay the night. My rather more modest New Year's resolution for 1973 was to visit every cathedral in France. I suspect that my ancestor also knew from the outset that he would be defeated, just as I was. I had just no idea how badly.

I needed help, and I put in a call to my old friend, Gavin Stamp, a brilliant architectural historian with whom I had been at Cambridge. I was thrilled when he said he could manage a weekend in Paris.

Paris has two cathedrals, St Denis and Notre Dame, but the former was really an abbey, or had been, so Notre Dame won the toss. Gavin and I set off for the Île de la Cité, he with a battered *Baedeker*, and I with my paperback edition of Darwin's *The Origin of Species*. This latter, as Piers de la Force had warned me, would serve as an antidote against any too fervent meandering into the lush meadows of Catholicism.

Notre Dame is a glorious church, but you know that already. Everybody with the smallest strain of wanderlust in the whole wide world has been there at some time in their lives. This was to be my first time (at least as an adult) and being in my own right a tiny sample of the whole world, I was similarly knocked out by it.

'So when do you think it was built?' Gavin and I were in front of its west façade.

'Very early Gothic,' I replied, unhesitatingly, as we stood outside admiring the deceptively self-confident frontage. I felt I was finally becoming rather good at guessing the dates of buildings.

'*Nul points*,' said Gavin. 'What you can see is an illusion. Most of it actually dates from the first half of the nineteenth century. Not only are you wrong, but by 800 years, either way.'

'Either way?'

'The bald fact,' said Gavin, 'is that Notre Dame cathedral started its long life about 1,800 years ago. Its first incarnation was as a Gallo-Roman temple, dedicated to Jupiter. Future transmogrifications turned it from a paleo-Christian basilica into a Romanesque church.'

'But this version we are looking at. That will be twelfth-century, won't it?'

'Up to a point. True, it was begun in 1163, during the reign of King Louis VII. His pope, Alexander III, together with the customary papal entourage, had made the long journey from Rome to Paris along the old Roman road to lay the foundation stone. For the next 200 years no one could see the new cathedral, draped as it was in linen sheets and wooden scaffolding. At long last, in 1345, the building was topped out and its modest clothes removed. An archbishop arrived with a pair of scissors to cut its ribbon and it was immediately, stylistically speaking, 200 years out of date. The building is of course characteristic of the time it was begun, not the year it was unveiled.'

'So what I can see is early Gothic. I was right.'

'As I said, only up to a point. It's true, that for a while the great church had an easy time of it. Despite the wholesale destruction of its medieval tombs on the orders of the proto-modernist Sun King, the body of the church survived in pristine splendour until the end of the eighteenth century. But then came the French Revolution.'

We went into the glorious nave. It was all too easy to picture the swarms of sans-culottes coming on to the island from its Left and Right banks, jeering and baying, armed with spades and muskets. Their banners read '*Liberté ou la mort*' – an insane excuse for the destruction of their past and everything fine that lay in their path. How many shocking sins have been committed under that label of 'Liberty', or 'Freedom'? This apparently noble war cry must have been the cause of more pain, destruction and despoliation than any other. The theory goes, no matter what atrocity you commit, if it's in the name of Freedom, it's OK.

Everything of beauty in France was systematically pillaged and plundered by the populace during this ghastly experiment with social engineering. Everything not nailed down was stolen. Even the great bells only narrowly missed being melted down.[1]

'You commented on the finely sculpted kings and queens that decorate the great portico,' continued Gavin in professorial mode. 'They are all new. The rabble set upon the crowned figures from David's royal lineage. They deliberately smashed them, in the deluded belief they represented the kings of France. Inside the locked doors, the priests and curacy prayed that the hordes would not find a way in. But their prayers were not answered; they were seized and sent to prison where they thought they would await "re-education". This was not their fate. They were eventually concentrated in warehouses and judiciously burnt alive. The French coined the word "genocide" to describe this heroic purification of their race in the name of Liberty.'

We walked along the aisle towards the choir, where the mob had smelted the plate and turned it into ingots to sell in the bullion markets.

'They were doubly feeble-minded,' said Gavin, 'as the price of bullion crashed after the sudden release of so much of it into an open market. The wooden statues, some of which dated from Gallo-Roman times, were used as firewood for their makeshift foundry. For months a delinquent populace had free rein, until at long last their adventure playground was prised from their destructive hands by the Committee for Public Safety. The venerable institution – Notre Dame, that is – was now dedicated to the incomprehensible Cult of Reason, and later to the Cult of the Supreme Being. And this wonderful nave was used as a warehouse for the no doubt "rational" storage of food and forage.'

The noble church, insulted and brought into disrepute, was then systematically starved of public funds.

---

[1] Not just in France. Two hundred and fifty tons of lead were stripped off the roof of Salisbury Cathedral by Oliver Cromwell and converted into musket balls, leaving the cathedral open to the elements. Happily the rafters, 28,000 tons of English oak, survived their enforced nudity, while they waited for the Restoration.

'In a fit of profound Gallic depression, it decided to fall down,' Gavin pronounced.

'But it is still here,' I replied, 'and it looks to my casual eye to be in pretty good shape.'

'Yes it is. The miracle is down to Viollet le Duc. By the mid-nineteenth century, France was slowly sobering up. A global Gothic revival was underway and the government asked two architects, the short-lived Lassus and the great Viollet le Duc, to undertake the cathedral's restoration. Their work began in 1845 and took twenty-three years. Nor did it stop at restoration. Viollet le Duc decided on a few improvements and he included within his project the spire and a sacristy that, oddly enough, the cathedral had never previously possessed.'

'So, at least in 1868 it looked the way it does now?'

'Yes, but a semi-grateful Paris was able to enjoy it for just three short and happy years. After that the Parisians experienced another of those destructive paroxysms that so regularly convulse French history.'

'The Commune?'

'The communards, practising their primitive brand of communism, torched the place in 1871. They piled the ancient and elaborately carved pews, some recently placed there from neighbouring churches, into a bonfire right here, in the centre of the nave. Everything wooden was fed to the flames, including those few extraordinarily ancient statues that had miraculously survived the previous assault. But the stone, much of it newly carved by Viollet le Duc, survived more or less unscathed.

'You say it looks "pretty good". But it is sobering to imagine what this church has lost. Not just its plate, its spoons and chalices; it was denuded of its medieval carvings, and its famous frescoes were lost to the fire. St Louis, that great and pious king of France, had placed the Crown of Thorns here in 1239. This unutterably holy relic was carelessly tossed to one side and later lost in the Revolution. I only hope some Catholic family somewhere has it in its attic.'

For an Englishman, the great cathedral has particular importance. Huge parts of what is now France were once under English rule. Indeed, Henry VI, King of England, held his coronation in Notre Dame in 1430.

The Scots, too, have their own ghosts here. Mary Stuart, whom we usually think of as Queen of Scots, was crowned Queen of France here, early in her unfairly truncated and tragic life. When a mere slip of a girl, she had married François II.

'The most dazzling coronation the cathedral has ever witnessed,' continued Gavin, as we emerged from the sacristy, 'was on 2 December 1804. After being anointed by Pius VII, Napoleon famously dispensed with his pope and crowned himself – and then, for good measure, his wife Josephine. The Emperor rather resented this old church. He later built a huge Arc de Triomphe at the top end of the Champs-Élysées. His first specification was that his arch should be physically larger than the entire façade of Notre Dame.'

'I suppose that at some point another wave of violence will overtake France.'

'It's a racing certainty,' agreed Gavin, peering at what looked like a bullet hole in the stone. 'As recently as the solemn *Te Deum* Mass, given on 26 August 1944 to celebrate the arrival of the Allies and Liberation of Paris, Nazi sympathisers occupied the galleries and frightened the congregation by firing both inside at the faithful and outside at the crowd surrounding the cathedral. Mercifully no one was killed.'

It seemed to me that there are grounds for optimism and celebration. It's not just that the church has somehow survived its ordeals. The fact remains that France, when she needs to, can throw up an architectural genius on the scale of Viollet le Duc. Walking around the huge church Gavin pointed out to me which bits were original and which bits were by this talented 'Victorian'.

Gavin Stamp, a proselytiser for the Gothic revival, had founded the Cambridge University Victorian Society soon after he had been admitted to Caius as an undergraduate. Viollet le Duc, while French, was exactly his territory.

Gavin's hero, Sir John Summerson, writing in 1948, had concluded that 'there have been only two supremely eminent theorists in the history of European architecture – Leon Battista Alberti and Eugène Viollet le Duc'. The latter was born in Paris in 1814 and died in Lausanne sixty-five years later. Le Duc's Gothic revival was vehemently opposed by 'rationalists' – whom we would now call 'modernists' – and Viollet le Duc's eloquence was crucial in the eternal debate on 'honesty' in architecture. The engineer's victory on behalf of the romantics was merely temporary, as 'honesty' was eventually to win and eclipse all revival styles. By the mid-twentieth century, architects were effectively prohibited from borrowing from the past; modernism became essentially negative. But, at the beginning of the nineteenth century, style and art still dominated European taste, and informed and imaginative reconstruction was duly rewarded.

The French Gothic Revival, as Gavin pointed out, began in the early 1830s. In England it had begun considerably earlier, probably with Horace Walpole's eighteenth-century Strawberry Hill, his castellated Gothic home in Twickenham. As early as 1747, Walpole made his intentions clear: 'I am going to build a little Gothic castle at Strawberry Hill,' he wrote, and he asked his friends for any fragments of old painted glass, armour, or anything 'gothick'. They all obliged. He spent the rest of his life dedicated to this pursuit.

'His little piece of crenellated paradise was bulldozed in the 1980s, almost under the eyes of an indifferent and negligent local council,' the author of the Piloti column in *Private Eye* was later to comment.

In France, the parallel movement was forced on the nation by the need to restore so many medieval buildings – mostly damaged in the Revolution.

Prosper Mérimée, Gavin patiently explained to me, is the insufficiently sung hero of the restoration of the ruins of France. Born in Paris, the son of a painter, he studied law before becoming a hugely successful French author. His meteoric career began in 1825 with six short pieces – *Le Théâtre de Clara Gazul* – that he attributed to an imaginary Spanish actress, the eponymous Clara Gazul, and it made him his first million. Another marvellous hoax was to follow. He published a collection of supposedly Illyrian folk songs, purportedly penned by a mysterious 'La Guzla'.

But it was not as an author that Mérimée was able to command the services of Viollet le Duc. Mérimée, on graduating from his *grand école*, had entered public service. Under his own name he became the Inspector General of Historic Monuments. In due course Napoleon III awarded him an impressive budget that greatly augmented his immense private fortune, which he had already put at the disposal of France.

Gavin felt that Mérimée's foresight in sending Viollet le Duc to Vézelay, Carcassonne, Notre Dame and St Denis was one of Europe's greatest strokes of luck.

'So what,' asked Gavin, 'if the modern taste for "authenticity", or "honesty", finds Viollet le Duc's restorations too free, too personal, even too interpretive? Wherever you stand in this controversy you must know that many of the monuments he restored would otherwise have been lost.'

So, when you are next in Notre Dame, think about this praiseworthy revivalist and light a candle for him. And buy one of Gavin's books.

Chapter the Twentieth
1972: Christmas in Munich

In which the author is invited to spend Christmas in Munich and to fly there in a two-seater aeroplane. This also gives him the chance to visit Heidelberg on his way home, where he experiences his first fast food.

It was startling to realise that December was already upon us. Parisian hours must be shorter than British ones.

Charles-Henri, whom I had not seen for a while, abruptly summoned me to dinner in his parents' flat. Charles-Henri's father, Comte Charles de Bartillat, was a diplomat, at that time looking after French interests as their consul general in Munich. His son had a proposition to make to me.

'Have you ever heard *Stille Nacht* sung by Germans?' Charles-Henri asked, à propos very little.

For a moment I couldn't think what he meant.

'*Stille Nacht*?' I replied, vacuously.

'Yes, Jeremy, sharpen up. I mean *Stille Nacht, Heilige Nacht*. It's the world's most famous Christmas hymn. Come on.'

'Oh right, Silent Night. Er, no I haven't.'

'You do in fact realise that it is a German hymn, don't you?' I nodded furiously. 'I didn't think you did! You English are famously ungenerous when it comes to the Germans. It's their big Christmas number. They give it the whole wellington. Huge male voice choirs. Not a dry cheek in the house.'

I nodded happily and helped myself to another sliver of perfectly pink *gigot d'agneau* from the servant.

'Well, I want to press on with your education. I have just bought a Piper Archer.' I was obviously still looking baffled. 'It's a little plane. Why don't you come and do Munich with us over Christmas? Only the Germans truly understand Christmas. You will learn how the thing is done properly.'

I had to consider this invitation carefully. I had been planning to go to London and catch up with my family. They looked up to me. They worried about me. They needed me…

'I'd love to come. How superb. You really can fly?'

'Certainly can. My licence arrived yesterday, full spec. I can fly at night, in icy weather, whatever it takes. I've bought two pairs of goggles. Europe's already a doddle, even if the United States may take a little longer.'

Preparations for the big adventure now began.

Charles-Henri had discovered an ancient military greatcoat, full length in fawn leather, in a long neglected wardrobe in his country house. He gave it to me proudly. 'Not much in the way of heating in the air. This will keep you warm.'

I was grudgingly allowed to take the bare minimum – my new shoes, a toothbrush, my new dinner jacket – and the two of us set out by car for Le Bourget, the old airport just north of Paris.

Charles-Henri seemed a classically 'privileged' young man. But despite his ancient name, his family – together with most of France – had lost most of its fortune during the long years of recession that led up to and followed the Revolution. Following those dark days they had adapted, and evolved from aristocrats to country gentlemen. No doubt, they would have continued in that pleasant but simple mould until one of their number, in the very early twentieth century, fell in love with a smart American heiress, Anna Gould.

Miss Gould was connected to the Morgan dynasty, whose name lives on in such companies as Morgan Stanley, Morgan Grenfell, J P Morgan, and Morgan Guaranty. In the manner of those days she set out to find herself a titled husband. Money was not an issue, she had enough of that. She had $19 million, which was quite a lot, even in 1906. But what she felt she lacked was a pedigree.

She came to Paris and everyone with a suitable number of quarterings on their escutcheon was presented to her. The competition for her hand was intense, but in the end she plumped for Charles-Henri's grandfather, the handsome Count de Bartillat.

Writing him an enormous cheque, she immediately arranged the nuptials, and the lucky Count set about restoring his ancient seat at Bartillat and commissioning a suitable house for his young bride in Paris. He built her a palace, in the Champs-Élysées, to a peerless specification. Anna's favourite colour was pink, so the house was too, which was particularly striking as almost every other house in Paris is white or in stone.

For a time, their life together was the stuff of fairy tales; an orgy of shopping and socialising. What parties they gave! The Empress Eugenie would sit across their table from Sarah Bernhardt, and a cantankerous Guy de Maupassant would entertain them all.

The Count, however, wanted to restore all the practices of his class, and this was his undoing. When Anna discovered that her husband had installed a delightful soubrette in the Île St Louis, whom he visited every day between five and seven o'clock, she sued for divorce. Americans consider infidelity (or 'cheating' as they coyly call it) a far more serious affair than murder.

With scarcely a dent in her colossal fortune, she let the Count keep his hubris, horses and houses, plus a little money, a million dollars or so, and promptly married the Duke of Talleyrand-Perigord, who did not (as far as anyone knew) keep a mistress. He probably didn't; he was rather older and very much more earnest.

A chastened Count de Bartillat sold the Paris house. It is now the French Travellers' Club. It is very grand indeed. I can vouch for that.

As far as Charles-Henri's aeroplane was concerned, I blamed the freezing cabin on the relative penury of the de Bartillats. Charles-Henri's aeroplane had no heating, so far as I could tell. I wasn't even sure it had a compass. Nevertheless, the two of us taxied to a runway, got clearance for take-off and we were away, I in my leather greatcoat and Charles-Henri covered with maps, or charts, or whatever they're called.

'We'll fly low and follow the road. Absolute cinch. We'll be in Munich in no time.'

About half an hour from Paris we hit cloud.

'Not a problem,' said the pilot. 'I'll just take her down a little lower.'

I have to say that flying at around fifty feet was exhilarating, to put it mildly. Most of the time I felt I was within handshaking reach of my Maker. We were so low I could easily read the signposts on the road beneath us. Every so often, Charles-Henri would pull the plane up. 'Just avoiding that pylon,' he would happily explain.

Then the rain set in.

'We are going in the right direction. I'll just hold this course. We'll be fine, don't you worry. Maybe I should give us a little height.'

So we carried on merrily, without (as far as I could tell) any idea at all as to where we were.

'Let's see,' said Charles-Henri after a long while. 'We must be getting close by now.'

All we could see was cloud, above, below, all around. Were it not for the noise and the cold we might have been wrapped up in a duvet.

Charles-Henri now busied himself in his maps. The plane flew itself. 'George,' explained Charles-Henri. 'He's a better pilot even than me. If I'm right, we should be there any second now.'

And suddenly the clouds cleared. Bang ahead of us was a great wall of enormous mountains. And we seemed to be on a collision course.

'That'll be Germany, all right. What do you think of it so far?'

'Most impressive,' I said. At least we could see where we were going.

We touched down at Munich airport as promised and, impossibly, on schedule. It was late December, icy and wet. But a car was there to meet us and we were home and dry.

Charles-Henri's father had taken a place in Schwabing, a slightly louche area of Munich. Needless to say their apartment was the epitome of elegance. But I was travelling, and my job was to see the town. And after a warm supper and good night's sleep, that's exactly what I did.

May I make one little point about the pronunciation of the name of the capital of Bavaria? Munich is our word for München, which is their name. So stop pronouncing Munich as if it were something from an opera by Wagner. 'Munick', if you don't mind. If you want to sound German, use their name for the place. All right, I've got it off my chest now.

Marienplatz is at the heart of Munich. It is here, on the *Alte*

Rathaus (town hall), that you find the incredible clock tower. The nearby and associated giant glockenspiel plays its tunes three times a day. It's a marvel.

There is also the Viktualienmarkt, which is the kind of foodie market you simply need to see to believe. It's not just German food – the Austrians, French and Italians are especially well catered to. Charles-Henri and I had a hot dog, a bratwurst, complete with Munich mustard, from a stall. It was quite delicious.

Munich was founded sometime in the eighth century. Its first building was a monastery, called by local people '*Bei den Munichen*', or 'At the Monks' ', and around it grew a small settlement. Its later growth was the result of a stratagem of Duke Henry the Lion, who destroyed a bridge near Föhring that used to carry the salt trade, and built a new one in 'Munichen'. The Duke then charged a toll. A council was called in 1158 at Augsburg, and Frederick Barbarossa gave his seal of approval. The Duke's fortune was made.

The Munich we saw that December chimed sadly with us. Earlier that year the city had hosted the Olympic Games. It was an occasion that was completely overshadowed by the terrible assassination of the Israeli Olympic team at the hands of terrorists. Charles-Henri and I conferred. We thought we would give the Olympic Park a miss.

'Let's go to the pictures,' said Charles-Henri. At first I thought he meant the cinema, but he meant the *Alte Pinakothek*. There are some real goodies there. Dürer's 'Self-Portrait' and 'Four Apostles', for example. Rubens' 'Self-Portrait with his Wife' is a star performer. Botticelli's 'Pietà' is not exactly trivial. And Altdorfer's 'Battle of Alexander at Issus' is rather classy, to say the least.

The *Neue Pinakothek* has the new stuff: Goya, marvellous German Romantics like Caspar David Friedrich and French Impressionists, including Manet, Renoir and Cézanne.

Before long we were exhausted and needed a beer. Why else should we be in Munich? In or very near the Odeonplatz we found a vast *Bierhalle*, which Charles-Henri thought would do the trick. The sun was well over the yardarm and all those pictures

326

had provoked a major thirst. A quick litre or two of Löwenbrau would do nicely.

'We should get a chance to sing their anthem,' said Charles-Henri. '*In München steht ein Hofbräuhaus – oans, zwoa, g'suffa!*'[1]

We wandered into the taproom and looked around for a table. It all looked perfect and suitably ancient, but it had been destroyed, like so much, in the war. Valentin Emmert, its first tenant after the war, had taken the Hofbräuhaus ruins in hand as early as 1945. He patched up the place as best he could and kept the restaurant going. The Reception Room had to wait until 1958 to reopen, in time for Munich's 800th anniversary celebrations.

'Hitler himself came here,' said Charles-Henri, cheerfully. 'In November 1921, in fact. He made a speech to a hall filled with his opposition. A fight broke out, when 400 Marxists in the audience tried to disrupt the Führer, attacking Hitler's fifty-strong SA team with the beer mugs they had hidden under the tables as ammunition. Hess played a leading part in the brawl and suffered a skull injury for his pains. Hitler made a great thing out of it in *Mein Kampf*, calling it a 'baptism of fire' for the SA, who won the day.'

The place was packed out and a long queue was forming of thirsty revellers-in-waiting. Charles-Henri would have none of that. Right in the centre was an empty table, and we sat down at it.

It took about half a second before a great mass of angry Germans, wondering why we were sitting there, surrounded us. Could we not read? A great sign, in Gothic script, hung over our heads. RESERVED FOR VETERANS OF THE ELEVENTH PANZER DIVISION, it said (in German, obviously). So now I knew what you had to do to get a drink round there. We left the *Bierhalle* somewhat sheepishly, followed by a rumble of concentrated Germanic disapprobation. Not a comfortable feeling. Back in Odeonplatz we actually managed to get a pint. It tasted very good, but once again the war had intruded into our lives.

In England, there is no pub (at least, where I have ever been, and I've been to quite a few) where a table might be permanently reserved for military veterans, not even the Coldstream Guards. And we Brits are mostly very proud of our army. The Germans

---

[1] 'In Munich there's a Hofbräuhaus – one, two and down the hatch!' It was written by Wiga Gabriel to words by his friend Klaus Siegfried Richter, in Berlin.

would seem to be even more enthusiastic supporters of their military, suggesting that the regular Wehrmacht has earned little opprobrium from its willingness to obey Nazi orders during the war. Perhaps the German people are more capable than the British of separating military orders from their over-arching politics.

Scarcely a regular member of the *Marine*, the Luftwaffe or the Wehrmacht was charged with war crimes or faced the long drawn out trials at Nuremberg and elsewhere after the war. By unwritten convention, neither Hollywood nor the British film industry treats regular German soldiery as bad guys. In this vein, only top Nazis, the SS and the Gestapo were convicted of crimes against humanity. On the whole I believe this to be fair.

But if the forces of the Wehrmacht were not the bad guys, then with whom exactly were we at war?

Today, Germany is a strong and proud democratic nation, so vehemently anti-Nazi that it borders on paranoid. Germans today mostly realise that the defeat of the Nazis was a victory for ordinary German people, and combined with the massive help they had just after the war (from the Americans under the Marshall Plan) they have put their country back to where it should have been.

The irony is, with the benefit of hindsight, it is clear that we British did not defeat Germany. At the time, the USA and the Soviet Union won that war. Germany is at long last back to where it started. And contrary to the official verdict, as seen from 1973, Britain it was that lost.

The enemy? Churchill's decision was to attack the German people. We used phosphorus and primitive napalm in Hamburg, when we first changed our minds about not bombing civilians. We went on to use incendiary bombing, saturation bombing, carpet-bombing, night and day, raid after raid, on Frankfurt, Düsseldorf, Dresden, Berlin...

Despite the evident fact that there is no longer a Nazi Party in Germany, and this vile political theory is disproved for all time, we never specifically attacked National Socialism.

True, the question of targeted assassinations sometimes came up. But such ideas were vetoed immediately. Beyond doubt, we had men that could have taken out Hitler and his fellow gangsters, even before war had been declared.

But we are a Christian country, so we're told, and St Aquinas's rules of a 'just war' specifically exclude such keyhole surgery. The Jewish tradition is more accommodating. Israeli soldiers regularly terminate 'enemy ringleaders',[2] usually with a sniper's bullet, or a shell from a tank. This way they also lose a fair number of innocent bystanders, plus an occasional journalist, but they don't seem to worry overmuch.

There were many plots to assassinate the Führer and his henchmen during the war itself, sometimes led by brave Germans themselves – not the British, nor the Americans, and certainly not the Jews. In the main it fell to French, Polish and Italian partisans to focus their attacks on the *fons et origo* of this disgraceful cancer – the political officers and the war machine. Heydrich, for example, got his comeuppance at the hands of two brave Slovakians. But Britain pointedly refused to assist such 'good Germans' as von Trott zu Solz and von Stauffenberg.

No, at the time our politicians spared their politicians, out of professional courtesy, and convinced the British people that we were at war with all Germans. Hence the saturation bombing. Germany was a democracy, after all, and in a democracy the people are to blame for the idiocies of their masters.

We British would wait until the war was over before we attacked the Nazis themselves, and then we did so in specially created 'courts of law', based around newly invented, retrospective 'international laws' that knew the sentences they wanted before they began the trials. Even so, the results still baffled many onlookers. Most notable was the case of Albert Speer, Nazi minister for munitions, who was allowed to survive. Speer had been the chief deployer of slave labour under Nazism. If anyone deserved the sentence of death, it was he.

When Munich was ready to metamorphose from monastic chrysalis to urban butterfly, the monks engaged Italian planners to lay out the city. More recently, it has metamorphosed a second time. The centre of Munich has been rebuilt since the Second World War. It has been a painstaking labour, a reconstruction

---

[2] The name traditionally given by military governments to the opposition.

from memories and old photographs of the town before the Nazi madness. The more important buildings defy belief – it is as though they had escaped the terrible bombing altogether. The less important ones show a few short cuts – trompe l'oeil here and there – but the whole effect is very pleasing.

Why didn't we, in England, rebuild our cities to their pre-war pristine beauty? I had the odd experience of visiting Coventry when I was at school. It was a hymn to the urban motorway. Aside from the cathedral precinct it was impossible to see that this had been our finest medieval city, with endless streets of half-timbered buildings. No, we had to be 'modern', and Sir Basil Spence's frightful 'cathedral', which sits pretentiously on part of the site of the ruined one, already looks dated and tired. Nothing ages quite as fast as a modernist building.

And now that the Germans have finished their patient re-building, we face the extraordinary fact that the Second World War has left more of a permanent scar on the English urban landscape than it has on Germany's.

Those Munich days went famously. They actually got better. Charles-Henri's little sister, Caroline, joined us and we went as a party to see the Nymphenburg Palace.

The Wittelsbach summer residence is in the western part of Munich. It is delightfully baroque. Its grand park contains the enchanting Amalienburg hunting lodge, a moving rococo masterpiece by the architect Cuvilliés. It would make a perfect stage set for *Rosenkavalier*.

The old ruling house's principal seat is on Max Joseph Platz. It is an extraordinary confection, having been frequently embellished with courtyards and fountains over its 500 years. The staterooms are magnificent, and the Treasury is truly impressive with its incomparable display of royal paraphernalia.

I was so delighted to be forcibly reminded of the splendour and genius of Germany in these wonderful places that I resolved to put the Nazi issue to one side. Germany is, after all, the country of Beethoven, the greatest artist of all time and not merely the greatest composer. On 23 December we all attended a formal concert in the *Alte Pinakothek*.

Our party wore evening dress. So did about half the Bavarians.

The other half wore their national dress. The girls each wore a dirndl, a close-fitting bodice, a pleated skirt of oblong panels and the whole thing made up of vaguely rustic fabrics and trim. The ancestry of both the word and the shape may lie in young country girls' non-formal, working day dress. *Dirndl* is also the Bavarian word for 'girl'. Whatever, they looked utterly charming.

Their men, in their loden coats and formal lederhosen, to my eyes at least, looked rather odd, but it was plain to see they were proud to be Bavarian.

The concert was a joy. The music was stirring and moving. As Richard Strauss's *Metamorphosen* came to its resolution, I glanced around the auditorium. Tears were flowing freely down male and female cheek alike.

Germany's music has helped persuade me that the Nazi period was a vile but temporary aberration in the history of this noble and breathtakingly talented people. From Heinrich Schütz through J S Bach to Richard Strauss and even Anton Webern, high nobility shines through.

If we're talking music, of course, the experimental or modern stuff is mainly meretricious rubbish in Germany, just as it is everywhere else. German modernists especially have convinced themselves that all musical form is somehow fascist, to be avoided like the plague. This can make late Schönberg or Stockhausen an acquired taste.

But Anton Webern could do it, probably because he wrote before the Nazis spoilt the fun for everyone. His 'Three Little Pieces' (1914) for cello and piano is a masterpiece. So are the 'Six Bagatelles' for strings and the 'Six Pieces for Large Orchestra'. His 'Opus 29' comes highly recommended.

This very modern music is also wonderfully brief, which helps too.

The greatest new works by any German, and which will endure until the last syllable of recorded time, are all by Richard Strauss. The 'Four Last Songs' were written in 1948, just a few short months before I was born. Most people seem to find that Elizabeth Schwarzkopf recorded the loveliest version, but listen anyway to the voice of Gundula Janowitz, clear as a boy soprano, and dare to tell me she does not steal the diva's thunder.

Christmas 1972 was as a German Christmas is supposed to be.

The snow lay thick on the ground and the great Christmas tree in Marienplatz towered over the surrounding buildings, hung with coloured lights and countless ornaments, and underneath the citizens placed little presents to be given to orphans and any hapless children that were in hospital.

After a marvellous feast, eaten on Christmas Eve in the French tradition, Charles-Henri's father ordered the car to stop a few streets from the cathedral and we walked on snow-clad and moonlit pavements the last few hundred yards. It was cold – and why not? It was almost eleven o'clock at night. The stars hung over us like Christmas lights, and every so many yards there was a brazier, glowing with red-hot coals, for us to warm our hands. Everywhere there were stalls selling chocolate and chestnuts, bratwurst and beer, or *Einspanners mit Kipfel*. Children were everywhere, hurling their snowballs at each other, and the sound of childish laughter and their squeals of surprise made the streets of Munich an untrammelled delight.

As St Mary's bells began to sound for the faithful to begin their vigil, we filed into the great church to the sound of Telemann. And as we looked for our places in the hymnbooks, the choir sang '*Stille Nacht, Heilige Nacht*', just as Charles-Henri had promised.

It was a profoundly solemn and magical moment; a bit schmaltzy, I admit, but then the Germans are given to sentiment. But you would have to be ascetic in the extreme not to have been enthralled.

Charles-Henri's house party was off to Innsbruck for the New Year and I had lessons to give. I decided to make my own way back to Paris. I was in no great hurry. I explored the railway timetables to see if I could break my journey somewhere interesting. I could. Early on 30 December I got down from my train in Heidelberg.

Heidelberg is justifiably famous for its huge but ruined castle, which sits on a high ridge overhanging the most picturesque little town, complete with winding alleys.

It is also the seat of Germany's greatest university, founded in 1385, which I was particularly keen to see. I knew, beyond any question, that my old alma mater was the greatest university in the world. But periodically, suggestions that there might be a rival somewhere came to the surface. I considered it my duty to quash such impostors in person.

I had already consigned the Sorbonne to the 'also-ran' category. The *Sapienza* was charming but a factory. Trinity Dublin was fine, but it was just one college, after all. Salamanca and Cordoba, Coimbra, the University of the Flowers in Cairo and at a push even Oxford; these were also on my list, and one day I would get round to them too. The very old university at Louvain looked rather promising, but since the Flemish and the Walloons were still at daggers drawn there it would be a bit like studying in Belfast. In the event, Louvain, which had educated Erasmus, was about to break under the strain. The French-speaking students created their own purpose-built university at Louvain-la-Neuve, just over the Flanders border into Brabant. The 1970s saw the ancient library divvied up on a 'one book each' basis. *Sic transit gloria mundi.*

I will readily admit that one's first impressions of Heidelberg's 'Old University' are encouraging. Before you even get to the front door, in front of the building itself, you come face to face with a magnificent fountain, crowned by a lion. You are left in no doubt as to the Palatinate's military power and intellectual ambition.

The current university buildings, dating from 1712, are in a stern neoclassical style. The Old Assembly Hall, its finest room, was tastefully added on in 1885.

Once inside I craned my neck and took in the vast ceiling paintings, depicting the university's four great faculties: Philosophy, Medicine, Law and Theology. On the front wall a huge painting[3] showed the arrival in Heidelberg of Pallas Athene, goddess of wisdom. Bronze figures to the left and right symbolised the genius of science. Everything to remind the boys why they were there.

But what made the university so uniquely German was the tiny Students' Prison, behind the university in the Augustinergasse. From 1778 until 1914, students were imprisoned here for *Kavaliersdelikte* – the mainly minor transgressions which were fashionable among the university's undergraduates, most of whom were members of fraternities.

---

[3] By Ferdinand Keller.

I found the curator at my elbow.

'Do you know why we locked up our students?' he asked.

I hadn't the faintest idea.

'Typically, the students were sent here for disturbing the peace, especially after their ritualistic heavy drinking sessions. They also liked to insult the authorities or play jokes on them. And then there was illegal duelling. Depending on the offence, imprisonment would last from three days to four weeks. They were allowed, however, to attend lectures. After class, the juvenile delinquents had to return to their prison. Many of the prisoners 'decorated' the walls with graffiti and paintings. This is their 'artwork'.

I find the duelling tradition a telling one. I had already given it considerable thought, as an ancestor of mine, Felix Macdonogh,[4] had defended Richard Brinsley Sheridan on a charge of duelling.

Traditions linger on, and courage can be reinforced with the appropriate martial skills. German students see their duelling scars as badges of honour. Even though duelling was officially banned, there were illegal duels all over Heidelberg as recently as the Great War. Even today I suspect the practice is not extinct. Walking the dog at dawn in 1900 must have been positively dangerous.

Duelling was not practised by the ancient Greeks or Romans, but it certainly existed among the Gauls and Germans from those days, according to the ancient historians,[5] and was so firmly rooted in the heathen customs of the Gauls and Germans that it survived their conversion (largely by Irish missionaries) to Christianity.

The Burgundian King Gundobald actually declared duelling lawful.[6] His reasoning rested (he thought) on a moral premise; that God could not allow the innocent to be defeated in a duel, nor would a guilty party pretend to the judgement of God as proof of his innocence and then pick a fight while known to his Maker as a perjurer.

---

[4] Felix Macdonogh was the lawyer and father of the journalist of the same name, better known as 'The Hermit', who wrote for the *Spectator* during the French Revolution and the later Napoleonic wars.

[5] Diodorus Siculus, Velleius Paterculus and others.

[6] d. AD 516.

The Church disagreed. St Avitus, Gundobald's contemporary, protested angrily. He pointed out the innate contradiction between Gundobald's cruel law and the clemency of the Gospel; God might very easily permit the defeat of the innocent.

In the event his argument prevailed, and the papacy came out against duelling. Nicolas I (858–67), in a letter to Charles the Bald, described the duel (*monomachia*) as a presumptuous teasing of God.

In tournaments and in personal disputes the old pagan instincts of the Germanic and Gallic peoples came more and more to the fore. Seven hundred years later, duelling over questions of honour had increased so greatly and so widely that the college of cardinals that gathered for the Council of Trent felt obliged to act. They decreed that:

> ...the detestable custom of duelling which the Devil hath originated, in order to bring about at the same time the ruin of the soul and the violent death of the body, shall be entirely uprooted from Christian soil.

They declared terrible ecclesiastical penalties against those princes who allowed duelling. All participants were automatically excommunicated. If any were killed in a duel they were to be deprived of Christian burial. Seconds who advised or assisted were also to be refused the sacraments.

These penalties were constantly escalated. Benedict XIV decreed that duellists should also be denied burial by the Church, even if they had not been killed in the duel and had received absolution before their death. Pius IX extended this rule to include kings and emperors, if complicit.

Governments, too, took steps against the evil of duelling. In 1608, Henri IV of France issued an edict against the practice. If anyone killed his opponent in a duel, he was to be executed. Penalties were also enacted against both issuing a challenge and accepting one.

Under Louis XIII, in 1626, the laws against duelling were still further reinforced. But the effect was perverse. Duelling increased alarmingly in France. The number of French noblemen who fell in duels in the middle of the seventeenth century was estimated by Theophile Raynaud to have been enough to man an entire army.

An association of French noblemen then signed a 'declaration'.

> The undersigned publicly and solemnly make known by this declaration that they will refuse every form of challenge, will for no cause whatever enter upon a duel, and will in every way be willing to give proof that they detest duelling as contrary to reason, the public good, and the laws of the State, and as incompatible with salvation and the Christian religion, without, however, relinquishing the right to avenge in every legal way any insult offered them as far as position and birth make such action obligatory.

Louis XIV supported his nobles, and for a long time after this duelling became infrequent in France.

But in the German-speaking empires there seemed to be no remedy. As early as 1681, the Austrian Emperor Leopold I banned all duels. Maria Theresa went one further. She ordered not only the challenger and the challenged but also all who had played any part in a duel to be beheaded. Joseph II punished all duellists as murderers, whether the guilty or innocent party.

To the north, in the German Empire, arrested duellists were supposed to be incarcerated indefinitely in the nearest fortress. Frederick the Great refused to tolerate duellists in his army. But none of these measures actually worked; on the contrary, a form of legal privilege for the person who killed his adversary in a duel came to be commonplace. Imprisonment, in the case of officers, was not enforced. In fact, an officer who refused to fight a duel in Germany and Austria was in danger of being cashiered from the army.

Parliament despaired. In 1896 when, after yet another fatal duel, the Reichstag called on the Chancellor (von Bülow) to abolish duelling. The criminal code was clearly inadequate. Courts of Honour, established the next year, were supposed to deal with disputes in the army concerning questions of honour, but since they retained the option of permitting or even commanding a duel to take place the situation got worse. On 15 January 1906, General von Einem, the Prussian Minister of War, declared that the principle of the duel was still in force, and the Chancellor added that 'army officers can tolerate no member in its ranks who is not ready, should necessity arise, to defend his honour by force of arms'.

Leo XIII, in 1891, eloquently made the moral case.

> Divine law forbids a man as a private person to wound or kill another excepting when he is forced to it by self-defence. Both natural reason and the inspired Holy Scriptures proclaim this Divine law.

By this time, in England anyway, duelling had died out. No duel occurred, it is said, in the British army in the whole of the nineteenth or twentieth centuries. Indeed, English law contains no special rules against it, and the wounding or killing of another in a duel would be punishable according to common law.

Even the United States, where the tradition arrived with their German immigrants, saw a marked decline in Wild West shoot-outs.

How different it was in Germany! Despite being forbidden from on high, and despite Lowenstein's League, students and subalterns found any excuse to duel according to their ritualised rule book, where a face mask was carefully opened to allow a sword to slash a cheek. Occasionally, and as late as the Second World War, two people who should have known better would seek to kill or maim each other. These traditions die hard. Surprising how many nasty accidents a German student can have to his cheek, even today.

Lowenstein's League? A convention, held at Frankfurt in 1901, issued an appeal for support in its struggle against the duel, and in a few weeks a thousand influential signatures were received. A constitution was drawn up at Cassel in 1902, under Prince Carl zu Lowenstein, and by 1908 Lowenstein's committee, or League, had established a permanent bureau at Leipzig.

Its mandate reads:

> The undersigned herewith declare their rejection, on principle, of duelling as a custom repugnant to reason, conscience, the demands of civilisation, existing laws, and the common good of society and the State.

But banning something that is part of a nation's identity begs another question. Just what sort of government is it that seeks to banish or prohibit its own or its people's traditions? Only one that believes that voter apathy or even civil unrest happens only in other countries. It is a curious feature of 'democracy' that it will always strive to impose conformity to majority tastes, by force of law, and that minorities become progressively frustrated. Is this abuse of power inevitable?

The general 'triviality' of modern democracy – the urge to suck up to as many people as possible – seemed notably absent in Heidelberg. Perhaps it's because Germany is new to democracy. I am not talking about the hiatus of the Second World War, far from it. Hitler, it must always be remembered, was democratically elected. Taking a longer view, before Bismarck's unification, the German rulers were absolute monarchs, in the Palatinate and especially in Prussia. Heroes were less the windbags of popular oratory but were instead those gallant soldiers who could be ordered into certain death by their emperor and would not flinch at the prospect. For the Prussians, that Roman chap who held his hand in the fire to demonstrate his loyalty to his emperor was a role model from Valhalla itself.

As recently as (say) 1840, what we now call democracy had few champions in Germany. Of course, the wave of popular insurgence that was to herald the Risorgimento in Italy and elsewhere in Europe came that decade. Twenty-five years later, Bismarck, managing the unification of the German princely states after his victory in the Franco-Prussian War[7] was forced to use a parliamentary system to bind the princely states together.[8]

It was time for more tourism.

My first impression of the castle at Heidelberg was that despite a lot of bomb damage, and that much of it was roped off, it was imposing in the extreme.

---

[7] 1870–1871.

[8] The Declaration of the German Empire, or *Deutsches Reich*, was in 1870. The proclamation of King William I of Prussia as German Emperor came in 1871. The Imperial Constitution was declared in April 1871. Bismarck was appointed Imperial Chancellor at that time.

The oldest parts of the building date back to the fourteenth century.

Magnificence came with Prince Elector Philipp, who liberated some columns from a ruined palace of Charlemagne and installed them in the Fountain Hall.[9]

The later Prince Electors were not to be outranked. They turned the fortress into a superb castle. Ottheinrich[10] added a couple of important buildings, and so did Friedrich IV.[11] The following century Friedrich V[12] erected the 'English Building'. Why 'English' was not obvious to me, but I suppose there must be some Tudor detail. Not that I spotted it.

But this is Germany. The castle and its garden were destroyed during the Thirty Years' War, only to be rebuilt by Prince Elector Karl Ludwig.[13] And just as the dust settled, it was destroyed once again, this time by the French.

Prince Elector Karl Theodor tried to make the castle habitable again, but in vain: lightning struck it in 1764. This time it burned down.

Now the unfortunate castle became a quarry, its stones helping to build houses in the town below. The ruin would suffer this indignity until 1800, when Count Charles de Graimberg ordered it to stop.

And so it went on. One step forwards, another back. In 1934, and despite its Gothic interior, the King's Hall was added.

It will have looked pretty good for about ten years. Then the Americans bombed it.

But it still stands. The King's Hall, at least, is used these days for dinners, balls and banquets and, in summer, the great court is used for musicals, operas and concerts. American troops will have attended some of these. Heidelberg, in December 1972, was up to here in GIs.

Both the British and the Americans kept a considerable amount of soldiery in Western Germany at that time, ostensibly to prevent the Russians invading the West.

---

[9] c. 1490.
[10] 1556–1559.
[11] 1583–1610.
[12] 1613–1619.
[13] 1649–1680.

It was a curious arrangement. Whenever we, or the Americans, went on manoeuvres, the Russians sent their observers. And, naturally, we did the same, sending our best troops to watch the East Germans and the Russians strut their stuff.

A friend of mine, Charles Battye, had been with his regiment in East Germany the previous year. Everything had gone smoothly, and the men and their commanding officer waved goodbye to their communist counterparts and climbed on board their train, bound for 'civilisation'.

To the British officer's surprise, at the frontier they were greeted not by the usual member of the East German border guards, but by a Russian officer. Battye handed his papers over for inspection. The Russian glanced at them and at the young captain.

'Come with me,' he ordered. 'We will put these matters in order.'

So Battye followed the Russian into the station master's office.

'What's up? Have I left out something?'

'No, the papers are all in order. Please sit down.'

A puzzled British officer did as he was told.

'My name is Ivan Dmitrievitch Kasparov, Lieutenant in the People's Army. What is yours?'

'Charles Battye, Captain in Her Majesty's Irish Guards, at your service.'

'Good, Captain Battye. The world is changing and we should be friends. You will join me in a small vodka before you are on your way?'

Well, it would be churlish not to. The Russian produced a bottle of Okhotnichya Hunters' Vodka and a pair of shot glasses.

'Mother Russia,' he said.

'The Queen,' said Captain Battye. And they both drained their glasses.

The effect of this toast was to take any chill there might have been in the air clean away. A series of toasts followed, until the litre bottle was empty and the two were so friendly they might have been at school together.

'Wait there, Ivan Dmitrievitch,' said the Englishman. 'Don't move, whatever you do.' And Charles Battye returned to his train compartment, rummaged through a suitcase and returned to his lifelong friend with a litre bottle of Glenfiddich.

The two of them now repeated the previous series of toasts and invented some new ones for good measure. Night grew in and the troop-filled train hissed and sighed impatiently just outside their cosy drinking den.

But all good things must come to an end. With great gravity, given the circumstances, Battye struggled to his feet and saluted his opposite number, while the Russian insisted on a final bear hug and planted a kiss on Battye's two cheeks.

Battye made his way back to his train and gave the order for it to pull out. A few minutes later they were back in the West.

And a few days later, he found that an article had appeared in the *Daily Telegraph*. 'Tension mounts at border,' it read. 'Troop train held up for six hours by Russian border guard. Only the cool head of a British officer prevents a major diplomatic incident.'

I was thinking about the Allies in Germany as I wandered about Heidelberg that evening, seeing American soldiers everywhere I went.

Their base must have been nearby – the town was practically English-speaking. They were very noisy and a little intemperate, but I suppose it was just after Christmas and some revelry is surely acceptable.

I did notice that many of them were queuing, in a reasonably orderly way, to buy a hamburger at a particular outlet, and I was curious. The 'restaurant' had no tables, and its American customers ate their fare in the street, clearly considering more formal dining conventions irrelevant to their busy lives. They ate as they walked and talked. They ate their buns from dawn, through the day and into the night. Some of them may have taken their burgers to bed.

If you consider my tone too lofty, I beg you to remember that in 1972, most Europeans, including myself, had never eaten a meal except at a table, except for the occasional picnic. Well, I thought, there is only one way to learn about life, and that's to join in. I tagged on to the end of the queue.

This was a 'fast food outlet'. I had never even heard of such a thing. They were still unknown in Britain, I think. About a hundred people in front of me walked at the pace of a funeral procession into the shop. They were anything but gloomy, however, and the whole stately procession had a carnival air. Having entered, almost immediately they re-emerged into the Heidelberg night, cramming their smiling faces with bun.

In no time at all, it was my turn to order.

'Same as him,' I said, pointing to the happy American now leaving the place.

'One burger, fries, regular Coke, coming right up. Fifty cents, please, sir.'

And I was in trouble. It had not occurred to me that the place would only take American money.

I waved a five Deutschmark note around pathetically. The queue stopped moving. The GIs began to notice me in a way I didn't much care for.

'C'mon, son,' said a tremendously muscular chap behind me, 'we're in a hurry.'

I could see an incident coming up. They happened often enough. A small paragraph in *The Times* would read, a few days later, 'British tourist found floating in the Heidelberg river. Fifteen GIs confined to barracks.'

It was a little chap with spectacles, cast in the Sergeant Bilko mould, who rescued me after what seemed an eternity.

'I'll give you a dollar for that bill. No, for you, I'll make it a dollar ten.'

I agreed. This was no time to be casting the moneychangers from the temple.

And so I found myself in a narrow Heidelberg Street, eating this sweetened bun and its tasteless beef. I attempted to digest the things they called French fries that I had just watched being extruded into boiling oil. I ate one carefully. What exactly was this thin chopstick-like thing actually made of? Was it potato? It tasted too sweet. And can you extrude potato?

This cannot be called a scientific experiment. The sample is too small. And sadly, for posterity, I have never tried another.

With the odd taste of sweetened shirt cardboard still in my mouth, I began to hunger for Paris. I wandered off to the railway station to calculate the best route back.

Chapter the Twenty-first
1973: Job Interviews in Paris

In which the author experiences a couple of interviews for a 'serious' job, gets a nine-to-five job with a sensible salary and is suddenly a 'jeune professionel'. Sick of commuting on his borrowed vélosolex he takes a flat on the left bank overlooking the Louvre and embraces Parisian public transport.

What would have been for any sane Parisian another blasted windy early morning in January was for me my big, big day.

Only a few weeks before, I had wandered into the British Council in Paris where I had seen an ad on their board for an English teacher. Aérospatiale, the state-owned giant that produced the Concorde at their factory in Toulouse, had pinned it up. I had telephoned and had received a ten-page application form by return. I gazed at it in dismay. My French wasn't up to it. I would need some help with it from my old friend Charles-Henri – it required that curious bureauphilic language everyone everywhere has to use in forms.

Clement Freud, I think it was, complained on the radio about these forms. He claimed that in the box against the word 'Sex?' he would write 'Yes, please'. Apparently in the one about your age that habitually drove him nuts, he was once given the question 'Age? If over twenty-one, approximate age', to which he cheerfully inked in 'over twenty-one'.

Charles-Henri had considerably more patience than me and together we made a good fist of it. Even though I can truthfully say I expected nothing to come of it, I slipped our response into the little yellow postbox on my way to my private lesson in my glamorous pupil's apartment.

But something had come of it. There had been a telephone call – to Charles-Henri's number – and he, pretending to be me, had made an appointment for me to go to an interview at their northern factory, just south of Paris. They were going to be disappointed when they discovered I couldn't speak French like Charles-Henri. But then, nobody could.

'How much should I ask for?' I asked my old friend, before setting out for Chatillon-sous-Bagneux.

'Oh, I would ask for 3,000 francs a month, if I were you. That's the starting salary for a business school graduate here in Paris.'

It seemed an enormous amount of money.

'Are you sure?'

He was sure.

I had tried before to get a serious job. In London, it had been a non-starter. The country was heading into ruin. We were about to borrow a great pile of money from the IMF in order to be able to pay our civil servants. There would be strings attached, of course, but we would never learn what they would be. They would be protected under the ninety-year rule, 'in the public interest'. We would probably be required to fight in pointless wars alongside the Americans for ever. Frankly, we were being governed by the CIA, by idiots, the criminally insane, a number of antediluvian donkeys disguised as trade unionists and paid-up members of the KGB.

But France was another kettle of fish. The whole place radiated prosperity. I had tried my luck with a number of their banks. Start at the top, I told myself. I was a Cambridge graduate, after all.

One morning, in early December, I rang J P Morgan (the one American investment bank to make Paris its base in Europe), and asked the girl on the switchboard to put me through to 'le Président, s'il vous plaît.'

'C'est de la part' de qui?' she had replied with that Parisian voice that suggests that you are a pain in the neck for diverting her attention from that comparatively exciting piece of gum she was chewing.

'Tell him it's Jeremy Macdonogh. He'll want to speak to me,' I told her (in French).

'Putting you through now,' she said. I hadn't actually expected that.

But I was not put through to the President of J P Morgan. I was through to another secretary.

'May I ask your business with the President?' the new voice asked me, in exquisite French, naturally. It was an astonishing voice. It packed authority and charm in explosive combination. Nothing got past her without her knowing.

'It's about a particular position with the bank. I need about twenty minutes of your president's time. Is there a space in his agenda for, say, tomorrow?' It was obvious from the start that I would never get to see him, so I didn't mind pushing this hard. Actually, it seemed like fun.

'Normally these matters are dealt with by personnel. Are you a student?'

She had seen straight through me. Not for a single second had I deceived her into thinking that I was the deputy governor of the Bank of England, looking for a strategic move. Oh, well. At least she would tell me whom to write to.

'I am a graduate. Cambridge. I'm living in Paris. It's time for me to begin my career in earnest.'

'Please hold the line.' And I did. This was not what I had expected. Why on earth was I holding on? The whole business was undignified enough. I toyed with the idea of hanging up when the Voice came back to me.

'The President of J P Morgan, France, will see you tomorrow afternoon at 15.20 for twenty minutes. He has a meeting at 15.40. If you are late your meeting will be shorter. May I confirm that you will attend?'

Yo! as Americans say. 'Please tell the President that I very much look forward to making his acquaintance. I'll be very punctual, I promise.'

I told my student, Bulle Ogier, about this meeting later that day. She fussed about, telling me what sort of tie I should wear, but I could tell that she thought that either I was pulling her leg, or that the President of J P Morgan, France, was pulling mine.

But it was true.

The next day, in my new shoes and second-hand Charvet tie (of which I was inordinately proud) and sporting a newish suit, I entered the glass door of their august establishment in Place

Vendôme. I told reception that I had an appointment with the president of the bank, and I allowed myself to look at the liveried flunkey in a superior sort of way. He looked straight back at me, wholly unimpressed. I very much doubt it, I could hear him thinking. Not in a suit like that. And my dear, that tie!

He picked up a phone to check and his manner changed quite abruptly. He clicked his fingers and a smaller, younger lackey appeared by his side.

'Show Monsieur Macdonogh to the office of the President. Immediately.'

The sub-lackey ushered me into a gilded, art nouveau lift and placed his key into the control panel. A young French banker tried to join us, but he was peremptorily ordered out. We rose in silence to a floor that could only be accessed by the Holder of the Presidential Key. And then the twin doors of the lift opened to reveal the sort of arrangement the film-makers in Hollywood would build for God.

I stepped into a huge anteroom, hung with paintings by Ingres and Delacroix, mainly of Napoleon or his generals. Great vases of flowers and marble busts of famous French bankers (Which one is John Law? I asked myself) alternated with the Louis-Quinze furniture. In the distance I could see an immense door case, probably taken from some wrecked château after the Revolution, a full twelve feet tall and carved from the whitest Carrara marble. To either side sat a secretary, busy in their unknowable ways, guarding their master from contact with untouchables or alien life forms. Both of them were unutterably lovely.

As I walked towards them, unbidden, one of them looked up briefly. She managed to glance at her watch in the tiniest fraction of a second, but you could not miss it. Nor were you supposed to. This was a most practised way of keeping the unwashed humble in the Great Presence. I could tell beyond doubt that she was the Voice.

'I hope I'm not early,' I said, knowing full well that I was exactly on time.

'Monsieur le Président will see you now.' She stood up and went to the door. I half expected a pair of soldiers from the household cavalry to throw it open, but the Voice did this menial task herself, stepping slightly aside to let me pass.

'Monsieur Macdonogh,' she announced, 'as you requested.'

The President's office was designed to impress. OK, everyone has seen offices with two drop-dead gorgeous secretaries surrounded by works of art and with a carpet that pygmies are advised not to walk on. Or in. What not everyone has seen is this exquisitely panelled drawing room, hung with Aubusson tapestries. Extraordinary Renaissance bronzes rested idly around the room on the most delicate pieces of Louis-Quatorze furniture, obviously 'rescued' from Versailles. To either side, doors led who knows where. A gym? A cinema? A private flat? His helicopter?

'Come in, my dear fellow,' he said to me. My legs had momentarily refused to function.

He waved at the gilt armchair on my side of his vast uncluttered desk. The absence of files or paperwork allowed me to notice that its sixteenth-century marquetry described a royal hunt.

'Cigarette?' I accepted one from the silver box, itself a finely wrought replica of an eighteenth-century battleship.

'Now that you are here, tell me what job you want.'[1] As he perched on the edge of his desk and towered over me, I tried to assess him. He was greying a little, fifty or so years old, but the framed photographs on the desk, showing him playing polo, confirmed his fitness. Another showed him shaking hands with Nixon. Yet another, this time in private audience with Pope Paul VI.

I had prepared a little for this.

'Well, sir, it's actually your job that I want. But not necessarily immediately. I thought you might let me start in the post room and work my way up.'

He smiled.

'No, that won't happen. But it is quite another proposal I have for you. From what you told Madeleine, my secretary, you are single, have found a way of living in Paris and have a modest income. Is this true?'

I said it was.

'Then I would like to swap places with you. I am fifty-seven

---

[1] '...quel boulot tu cherches' He used the tu form, as if I were his son, perhaps. When I replied I scrupulously used the vous form.

years old. I work from eight in the morning to seven at night. I am married to a woman I know almost too well and have a young son I seldom see. True, I have a few trappings of high office, but I am bored with them. You want my job? I hate it. You are twenty-three years old I think? Single, with every girl in Paris weighing you up to see if you are marriageable. Or even game for a lighter commitment. You want my job? OK, it's yours. I brought you here to see if you could offer me a job.'

There was a knock at the door, and the president shouted, '*Venez!*'

Madeleine came in, smiled at me and approached her boss.

'Alan Greenspan is here, sir,' she said. 'He is waiting outside.'

I stood up and the great man offered me his hand.

'It goes without saying, what I really want is to be young, and have every door in the world still open to me. I brought you here to remind myself of what such a young man looks like. I was you once. Good luck.'

And so I thanked him and left. I passed the man who, fourteen years later, would become the chairman of the United States Federal Reserve Board. I knew his name even then, from his book *Capitalism: the Unknown Ideal*, which I had read at Cambridge. He was also reputed to be a great jazz musician and to be some sort of philosopher-king.

But, if true, that would only endear him to the man who, perhaps to amuse himself at my expense, or perhaps to teach me the value of what I already had, had given me such an odd but unforgettable twenty minutes of undiluted attention.

A month had passed since this strange encounter, and it had been at best a rum sort of preparation for the one I faced today.

I reread the instructions I had scribbled down and made my way by Métro to a bus station just south of Paris at Porte d'Orléans, on the *périphérique* ring road.

I arrived in good time, caught my bus and got off by a bar opposite Aérospatiale's factory gates. There was still time for a coffee. I didn't want to hang about too long in some awful waiting room.

Eventually the hour struck and I moved across the road, like some skinny fellow out of an L S Lowry painting. I remember wondering what Aérospatiale produced so close to Paris. I knew that they produced the Concorde at their factory in Toulouse.

I had put on my Charvet tie for luck. It was a fine item, bought at the flea market near St Denis. It was elegantly thin and rather short, as in the thirties (when it had been new) every man who could afford a genuine Charvet would have worn a waistcoat.

A bored and impatient general manager, who took to neither me nor my sense of elegance, conducted my interview.

'Why do you wear that ring?' he demanded, looking at my little finger. 'In France, only aristocrats wear those things.' Glancing at my signet ring, I vaguely understood my faux pas.

'It's just an old badge my clan is proud of. My father said you need to wear it in case you are killed in battle.'

We were off to a poor start. For many ordinary Frenchmen, the old upper class (from pre-Revolutionary times) enjoys a reputation for cruelty. Signet rings in France can make you as many enemies as friends.

'*Zut, j'suis plus sociale que socialiste.*[2] It's been a bit of a waste of time your coming in. We've decided to give the job to another chap. He is a serious fellow. He writes poetry. Ordinary working man. Doesn't wear a tie. He loves all things English, he told us. Spent years there. And he would do the job for next to nothing.'

'Well, I won't take up any more of your time,' I said, getting to my feet.

'Not so fast, young man. I have had to get our students together for a trial lesson, in any case. We made the other chap teach our staff for half an hour or so. We might as well be thorough. Go in there and teach them English.'

So I did. And I knocked their little Samaritaine socks off. I got them all to ask each other's names in English, to engage in a little small talk about the weather, to ask what was on for lunch, to tell me the names of their wives, husbands and children. Basically, everything you need at the bar in a holiday hotel where you have to make light conversation with a British tourist. And they loved it. I even got a little round of applause at the end of the ninety minutes I gave them. I knew my stuff. I had been doing it long enough in Rome and Pompeii.

---

[2] 'I'm more sociable than socialist.' The French love this sort of word play.

And so, the general manager felt obliged to offer me the job. 'Pity,' he said, quite openly. 'I feel you and I won't get on. How much money do you need?'

'Three thousand a month,' I said without hesitation. I was not there for philanthropic motives. I was there because I wanted to enjoy my time as a would-be Parisian.

If he had worn a monocle, this was the time for it to pop out of his face.

'Three thousand a month? We were planning to offer 1,500.'

I stood up again and offered my hand. It was not taken.

'Still, perhaps you are worth it. You had better be. All right, 3,000 a month it is. Be here on Monday morning at eight. I'll have your papers ready for you. You will need to register with the *mairie* and *préfecture* and obtain your work and residence permits before we can put you on the payroll.'

These were strange times for British 'Europeans'. Edward Heath had taken Britain into the Common Market, literally a few days before,[3] to the general irritation of the French and not a few English. The terms had been less than brilliant. The prime minister had thought that some of the details could be negotiated better from the inside. Nevertheless, under Heath's terms, many British people felt that our contribution to the Common Market budget imposed too heavy a burden on our way of life.

There was a perceived threat to employment in Britain, arising from the movement in the Common Market towards a projected economic and monetary union. For the British, this seemed to imply that we would be forced to accept a fixed exchange rate, seen as restricting industrial growth and putting jobs at risk.

This threat would eventually be 'removed', in 1974, in the Dublin Agreement with a 'rebate' of £125 million a year. In 1973, however, the Labour Party was threatening, if re-elected, to allow the British to reconfirm our membership in a referendum, which did indeed take place in 1975. To the chagrin of some, the country voted by a considerable margin to remain a member.

But that January, this was a newly born trading arrangement, not a political union. To work legally in France, we British still needed to have a written offer of employment before we could

---

[3] With effect from the 1 January 1973.

formally apply for a residence or a work permit. But the authorities had softened a very little and at least we no longer had to apply from our home addresses.

I had a week of mind-numbing bureaucracy with the town hall and the police until I finally had the papers I needed. I also opened a bank account with one of the smaller private banks. I had to have somewhere to pay in my princely salary, after all.

It all worked out in the end. I had a job, and a well-paid one at that. I took Charles-Henri out to dinner, to thank him for his help.

'How much are they paying you?' he asked. I was surprised by the question.

'3,000 francs a month, of course. Just as you said.'

Charles-Henri's face was a picture. I realised with a start that he had never expected me to get such a salary. I had, at long last, succeeded in impressing him.

As it turned out, the job was not just to teach English. It was to head up the language department.

Aérospatiale had a number of receptionists, senior secretaries, salesmen and engineers who needed to speak English, Spanish and some other languages. They were to be taught the language in-house, in what amounted to a little school.

This was an armaments factory. The pluton, a nuclear-armed aerial torpedo, was made here (though its warhead was made elsewhere). So too was the Exocet. Missiles of every kind, anti-tank grenade launchers, side arms and automatic rifles, were turned out at Chatillon-sous-Bagneux and could be sold to deserving and non-deserving causes alike. In fact, the factory produced everything a self-respecting army could ever want. France was then the biggest armaments-selling country in Europe – after the UK, that is.

I was warned that all my students would have sworn some form of official secrets oath and were not allowed to speak to me in any detail about their work. If they did, I would certainly be fired immediately. Probably imprisoned. Possibly guillotined. All things considered, it was best not to encourage any confidences.

English was easily the school's most important subject, and I had two British assistants, on a sandwich course from their degrees in modern languages, who were enthusiastic and ambitious. I envied their foresight. They were spending their year abroad deliberately, and not because they were unemployable in England. And what a great place to spend that year. Paris is hardly a hardship posting.

I looked through the materials my predecessors had used. They were worthy but dull. They would do for now, but my team and I could do better. We would evolve our own materials.

I could not justify staying any longer in Charles-Henri's *chambre de bonne* now that I had a salary. I spent a whole Saturday reading the small ads and making a number of calls. I wanted a studio flat, and it would have to be in an historic part of Paris. I was not going to live in some Pooterish suburb.

Eventually I found what I was looking for. It was hideously expensive at 1,000 francs a month which, after all the deductions for tax and so forth had come off my pay cheque, was almost half my take-home pay. But it was on the corner of the rue Bonaparte and the Quai Mazarin, on the Left Bank of the Seine. It was on the top floor of an eighteenth-century block of flats, had a bar on the ground floor – the Café aux Beaux Arts – and looked over the Seine and, across the river, to the Louvre itself. The flat itself lacked some of the prerequisites of true *grand luxe*, such as a lavatory, which was outside the flat a little way along a corridor. It also had the most revolting red flock wallpaper. As the months came and went, I became aware that it had been hung upside down. Funny how little things like that can annoy.

I had borrowed a vélosolex from Charles-Henri, to get around Paris on the surface, but now that I was commuting to Chatillon, seat of Aérospatiale, I decided to return it.

At first I had enjoyed this strange and very French invention. A vélosolex is basically a bicycle with a minute petrol engine clamped to the front wheel. It will manage twenty miles an hour if you really wind it up, and can weave in and out of the near stationary traffic on the *périphérique* like nobody's business.

But not only was it illegal to take it on to the ring road, it was very definitely bloody dangerous. It was also hell in the rain.

So I decided to get to my office by public transport, which in Paris is very effective and very cheap. On the Métro to Porte d'Orléans every morning, into the bus station for my first coffee of the day and to watch the workers drinking their cognacs, and then on to the bus until it stopped just outside my factory gates.

My lessons were always in the morning, and at lunchtime I would head for the staff canteen.

The food here was as good as it is in many English restaurants. There were two sections, one for workers and the other for management, but you could sit in either as you chose. In the workers' section, you queued at a self-service bar, and took your three-course meal and your sachet of wine to your table. This would cost you a luncheon voucher, which had a notional price of five francs, about fifty pence (or ten shillings as I still thought of it) in the money of that time. If you sat in the managers' section, you had a waiter do the queuing for you, and your wine appeared in a glass, freshly decanted from the sachet. And you would pay two luncheon vouchers. The food, however, was exactly the same either way.

Most of the local bistros would also accept these vouchers, but why bother? The food at Aérospatiale regularly won prizes for being the best canteen food in France.

'Do you know why it is called a "canteen"?' asked one of my young colleagues, as the three of us shared a table in the workers' sector.

'I have no idea,' I replied honestly.

'It's because, in all Roman military forts, the fifth avenue was always where the entertainment – restaurants, bars and brothels – was to be found. In Latin, "fifth" is *quintana*, and with the passage of centuries this word became "canteen".'[4]

Why does this matter? Bertrand Russell once wrote that he had been puzzled by the word 'apricot'. On checking its derivation he had discovered that 'pricot' comes from *praecox*, meaning 'prematurely ripe', and that the 'a' at the beginning was spurious. 'Ever since that day', he wrote, 'those fruit have tasted better.'[5]

After lunch, my colleagues would mark papers and plan the

---

[4] *Sed quaerere cantina*; the word had become the modern Italian for a cellar.

[5] But Lord Bertrand had not considered the passage of the word via Arabic, when it became *al barkuk*, and its rejoining the European mainstream as 'apricot' some centuries later – Ed.

lessons, and I would write the course materials, with an altogether spicier tone than the boring stuff we had inherited. Some of it was frankly bordering on salacious, but the students seemed to like it.

At the end of the day I would get home to my flat in the VIe *arrondissement*, stopping perhaps at Charrette in the rue des Beaux Arts for a crepuscular Ricard. Sometimes I would try and cook myself something to eat. Thank goodness I had a number of invitations to dinner. My cooking was not exactly brilliant. My speciality was *spaghetti alla carbonara*, which was more adapted *to la vie estudiantine* than *la vie parisienne*. My courteous neighbour, a Berber Arab, thought I would do better to learn to cook couscous, which would have been far more appropriate. He was right. The French would always eat African food rather than Italian.

Every time I walked past my Arabic friend's door I heard the most curious sound. I thought at first that he was torturing a cat. It seemed unlikely. He was a quiet soul and had simple tastes. Still, you never know...

It was some time before I discovered that he was listening to Moroccan music on a tinny gramophone. It pays not to leap to conclusions.

I would walk past Cardinal Mazarin's old palace on my way to the Boulevard St Germain, taking in a beer at La Pallette or a coffee at the Deux Magots, with my newspaper or some improving literature from the countless bookstalls in the Latin Quarter providing me with intelligent company.

I had a lot of acquaintances in Paris, and a good friend in Charles-Henri, but I was feeling a little lonely, some of the time. Particularly in the absence of a *petite amie*. I had even sent Arianna a wistful postcard.

Sometimes I would climb out of my window and scale the roof, where the view over Paris was unsurpassed. Paris is like no other city. At night she puts on her sparkling jewellery and lies beneath you like a harem girl, her tent lit with starry lanterns.

I just wished that on nights like that wretched Arab could have stopped murdering that pathetic cat and put on *Scheherazade*.

354

A Republican Sunday
1973: St Denis

In which the author advances his absurd ambition to visit every cathedral in France. This time he looks upon a royal mortuary.

I had been taking my time over seeing every cathedral in France and it was time for me to put my skates on.

In the 1830s, France was a mess. The Minister of Public Works, Prosper Mérimée, now sent the engineer and architect Viollet le Duc to the Royal Cathedral, once Abbey, at St Denis for a thorough reconstruction. I decided to follow in his footsteps.

The Abbey of Saint Denis lies four miles to the north of the cathedral of Notre Dame, effectively in Paris, though very slightly outside the modern *périphérique*. It sits in what has become an Arab quarter, dominated by a vast street market, larded with the most appetising food. There is also a flea market close at hand, similar to the famous one in London's Portobello Road, and which is an absolute must for any traveller to Paris.

St Denis was the first ever bishop of Paris. In his day, his friends knew him as Dionysius. Regrettably the Roman authorities were singularly unimpressed by his devotions and he was duly martyred in AD 270. A small chapel was built over his tomb and it was for the next two or three hundred years a modest place of veneration.

In 630 King Dagobert replaced the chapel with a basilica, the seed of a brand new Benedictine abbey. The shrine of St Denis gradually grew into one of the richest and most important shrines in France.

Unfortunately for the cause of humble prayer, Charlemagne stamped his feudal authority on France. He had no time for primitive sentiment and he swept his Merovingian predecessors' architectural legacies off the map. His new church, directly over the ancient chapel, was begun in 750. Christ himself assisted the Abbot at its consecration, it was later reported to the Emperor and posterity.

But that was a while ago. Work began on the present day church of St Denis as recently as AD 1140. Stylistically, the cathedral is the first 'Gothic' architecture anywhere in Europe. Further additions and refinements, continued by abbot after abbot, resulted in what was arguably the finest such building in the world.

One of these abbots, Matthieu de Vendôme, was Regent of France when St Louis went to the Crusades in 1269. His banner, the 'oriflamme', became the standard of the kings of France. Suspended above the high altar, it was only taken down when the king took the field of battle in person. Its last appearance outside the church, *en plein air*, was on the field of Agincourt in 1415.[1]

Fourteen years later the Maid of Orléans hung up her arms in the church.

But all good things must come to an end. In 1691 Louis XIV suppressed the abbacy[2] and united the monastery and its revenues with the 'Royal House of Noble Ladies' at St Cyr, founded by his mistress Madame de Maintenon. It must have been the ultimate in girls' schools. Something like St Trinian's on springs, I imagine.

At the Revolution the abbey was at last dissolved, and a philistine rabble was 'authorised' by a delinquent government to destroy the royal sepulchres. The Committee for Public Safety in August 1793, just a few short months after the execution of their king, was bent on doing its worst to the church and its tombs.

As I stood just inside the main door, my gaze fell slowly from

---

[1] The oriflamme was the sacred banner of the kings of France, and was brought out only in times of great danger. Distinct from the fleur-de-lys, it consisted of a gilded lance and a red silk banner with green fringes. The floating end of the banner split into several trailing strips. Hence its name, *aurea flamma*, linking the banner (*flamma*) and the colour of the lance. It is sometimes depicted as a flag, or (especially in the nineteenth century) as attached to a horizontal bar, itself suspended from the lance. It was kept in the Abbey of Saint Denis, next to the martyr's relics. On going to war, the French king would come to Saint Denis to 'raise the banner'. Like so much else, it was destroyed by Revolutionaries.

[2] The complex of abbey, dependent houses and subordinate churches, almshouses and other charitable holdings.

the magnificent roof, over the great rose window and settled on the entrance to the ancient tombs of the French royal house.

What the revolutionaries had done to these tombs was truly shocking.

Forerunners of Lazlo Toth had attacked the marble effigies of the illustrious cadavers. The effect was oddly reminiscent of a battlefield.

Lying on top of the tombs were body parts, a leg here, a severed arm there. Their marble whiteness had the pallor of death. It was as though I had stumbled into a regal palace a second or two after the murderous mob had departed, its machetes dripping with blood and gore, its members baying for another royal victim. The chill of the great cathedral penetrated my skin.

> The hatred that the revolutionaries had managed to instil in the people for King Louis XVI, and which his death on the scaffold on 21st January had not been sufficient to assuage, had now reached back to the kings of his race: they wished to harry the monarchy all the way back to its source, and the monarchs into their tombs, and scatter the ashes of sixty kings to the four winds. And then, perhaps, they were curious to see if the great treasures that it was claimed were hidden in some of those tombs had indeed been preserved intact. So the people rushed over to Saint Denis. From the 6th to the 8th of August, they destroyed fifty-one tombs – twelve centuries' worth of history… Then it became a matter of wiping out the very name, the very memory and the very bones of the kings; it had become a matter of eradicating fourteen centuries from history. Poor mad fools – they don't understand that men can change the future, but never the past![3]

Viollet le Duc's restoration, completed under Napoleon III, makes this sordid and loutish desecration even more startling, for the rest of the great church looks pristine.

Looking around this mocked and slighted cathedral, today so enchanting and seemingly unspoiled, you begin to realise how Viollet le Duc thought of Gothic architecture as wholly rational. And wandering around, you see that he was happy to use modern

---

[3] Alexandre Dumas, in *One Thousand and One Ghosts*, wrote about this awful time in 1848, drawing almost certainly on eyewitness accounts.

materials, such as cast iron. His purpose: to heal the wounds inflicted on a great civilisation by a people incited to violence by populist cynics interested in the exercise of absolute power.

Whenever possible and practicable, le Duc's practice was historically true and precise. Where not, he imposed his own remarkable and innovative designs. He got beneath the skin of the Gothic style but he was always a modern engineer. His appreciation of the Gothic achievement was wholly unsentimental.

In 1819, Louis XVIII ordered the relics of that paleo-Christian bishop and martyr, which had been transferred to the local parish church in 1795, to be brought back in triumph to their rightful place in the cathedral.

At least there was a happy ending.

Chapter the Twenty-second
1973: Normandy

In which the author decides to explore the D-Day beaches with an old friend and learns of their terrible cost. On the way home, he visits Fécamp, buys some Benedictine and endures a long and daunting drive across Normandy. He discovers a jewel of a Norman town at Honfleur and eats a memorable lunch.

My decision to visit Normandy was in no small part due to the French custom of having so many of their public holidays on a Thursday. Unsurprisingly, everyone takes the Friday off too – *on fait le pont*, they say – and it means that the French have a dozen long weekends every year. That is in addition to Europe's most easy-going working hours. No wonder that civilisation has risen to such heights in this country.

I had not yet been to Normandy (except as a child) and it was time to put this glaring shortcoming right.

I had a little background knowledge. I had recently discovered that my father had a flat in Veules-les-Roses, an astonishingly pretty little coastal town. I was long aware of the vast Anglo-Norman Empire, built by Norman kings, managed by Plantagenet ones before being lost by the Tudors. And from a dozen or more restaurants in Paris, I knew that it meant some permutation of cider and pork and apples and cream.

It also meant D-Day.

The Second World War started to end when our expeditionary force landed in Normandy – at dawn on 6 June 1944. Most of my friends' fathers, and my own, had fought in the war.

It seemed ungrateful not to have any insight into it other than that provided in the cinema, by films like *The Longest Day*.

That film had been made in 1962, and had starred a young Richard Burton and an even younger Sean Connery, among many others. It was Daryl Zanuck's last worthwhile film and, according to Johnnie FitzHerbert, my cine-addicted chum, it was the greatest war film ever.

I mean it. Johnnie and I had sat down together in Scotland, years before, and had compared notes on war films. Eventually we composed a list. Not in any particular order, they were: *All Quiet on the Western Front, In Which We Serve, Paths of Glory, Bridge over the River Kwai, The Wooden Horse, The Longest Day, The Dambusters, Reach for the Sky, The Life and Death of Colonel Blimp* and *The Cruel Sea*.

In our conclusion we differed. In my opinion, for what it's worth, the greatest of these is still Stanley Kubrick's 1957 masterpiece, *Paths of Glory*. We had both voted Powell and Pressburger's 1941 *Colonel Blimp* into second place.

All that was a while before. When I got to my office I rang Johnnie directly. I figured there was a real chance he would come. After all, he had joined me for a few days in Sicily and was still talking to me. My sales pitch was that we were going to check out a few of the locations in *The Longest Day*.

I was right; in the event he only wanted his marching orders.

I gave them to him. He was to take a couple of days off and bring his new car on the overnight ferry to Cherbourg, arriving on the Thursday morning. I would get there by train and then we would motor to the east. I wanted to stop at Omaha Beach and try to understand what went wrong there. After that I thought we might go to the Pegasus Bridge at Benouville. Definitely to Bayeux where, in my view, another cathedral and a tapestry were begging to be seen.

To my delight, he embraced my whole scheme enthusiastically, subject only to the provisos (1) that we would also go to Gold Beach, where the British landed, and (2) that I would try to persuade some girls to join us. Alternatively, proviso (3), failing (2), was that we might try to spring some cloistered virgin from her Norman fastness (or local nightclub) while we travelled. I readily assented. Gold was not a problem. But the girls might be. The truth is that girls are generally less interested in battlefields than boys. There is no accounting for taste.

I did my best to bone up a little in advance.

The English Channel, in that momentous summer of 1944, had been beset with unseasonable storms. Our troops were massed on our own shores ready for the invasion of France. Some of them were already on board their boats, impatiently waiting for the signal to go. Elsewhere, paratroopers were preparing for their inland drop, determined to secure key towns and bridges.

Planning for D-Day had begun as early as December 1943. President Roosevelt ordered Eisenhower, the Supreme Allied Commander, to 'enter the Continent of Europe, and in conjunction with other United Nations, undertake operations aimed at the heart of Germany and the destruction of her armed forces'. This became known as Operation Overlord.

At first, General Eisenhower had wanted the assault to land on just three beaches, under American command. The combined forces were to be flooded ashore, protected by our allied navies. Field Marshal Montgomery was to explain the danger in such a tight concentration. Not only did he increase the number of landing points, but he also segregated the armies so that they would have their own officers in charge.

The Britain of early 1944 was less an island, more a boot camp. Almost one inhabitant in ten – three and a half million soldiers, sailors and aircrew – were drafted into the operation. The south coast of England saw legions of Americans, Australians, Belgians, British, Canadians, Czechs, Dutch, French, New Zealanders, Norwegians and Poles. All of them had the same purpose: the Liberation of Europe from Hitler's evil clutches.

Montgomery had deduced that both flanks of the seaborne landing, planned for dawn, would need to be covered by airborne troops. These would be dropped at night to secure these positions. To do this we would need a full moon.

A date was needed. Astronomers (and the odd astrologer) saw that the only time the moon, tides and winds would be in the right phase for three whole days would start on Monday, 5 June. The British 6th Airborne would be dropped to the eastern flank, and the American 101st and 82nd Airborne would be dropped to the west.

On the other side of the Channel, Field Marshal Erwin Rommel, Monty's old adversary, was given command of Army

Group B in July 1943, and took over the defence of Belgium and Northern France. Thinking the likely invasion site would be somewhere in the Pas de Calais, he undertook the construction of an 'Atlantic Wall', designed to stop the Allied invasion in its tracks, before it could even get off the beaches of Normandy.

He thought that the Allies would arrive on the sandy coast of the Pas de Calais but he knew better than to put all his eggs in one basket. He realised that whenever and wherever the invasion force landed, the enemy would have to be slaughtered on the spot. He had huge concrete obstacles, invisible to landing craft, distributed in the shallow waters off the whole length of the Normandy coast. They were designed to rip the bottom out of any landing craft. As it turned out, many did.

The Allies would clearly try to discharge their troops at high tide. Rommel ordered mines to be attached to some of his 'obstacles'. This worked as planned. Men died horribly before they reached the beach.

And yet again, Rommel accurately predicted that an invasion of the beaches would be accompanied by a massive Allied airborne assault. He had vast areas of land flooded to hinder the paratroopers' progress. Many airborne troops were to drown in these man-made swamps, laden down as they were with heavy equipment – unaware, alas, of the fatal trap that had been set for them.

Rommel informed his officers that the Allied invasion would succeed or fail within the first twenty-four hours. He told his men that this would be 'the longest day'.

When I reached Cherbourg Station, wondering where I would find Johnnie, I wished I had decided on June and not February. It was perishing. Even my huge leather greatcoat was having some trouble keeping out the chill. And then I saw the fellow, knocking back a beer in the station bar, wearing a leather bomber jacket and white scarf. He had dressed the part.

'Good crossing?' I asked him.

'Sick as a parrot! The sea was about as smooth as my great-aunt's arse. And I thought it was supposed to be warm in France.'

'Did you bring your car?' I asked.

'There she is. Come and turn green. She's a little beauty.'

Which was undeniable. He had a bright red MGA, not exactly brand new, but it had a detachable hard top. This last point was fairly academic, as the weather looked set for snow. But Johnnie's car suited him down to the ground.

We decided to have a look around Cherbourg before setting about a good lunch. These days it's a pretty enough natural harbour, with a great port. And it was once a Plantagenet possession, though that didn't stop the French from trying to get control of it, which they first managed to do in 1204, when the King of France, Philippe-Auguste, made the most of some arcane feudal legal quibbles and got his hands on Normandy.

Franco-English relations became progressively worse during the thirteenth and fourteenth centuries. Towards the end of the thirteenth century the English raided Cherbourg, sacking the Abbey of the Vow and setting fire to the town. Only the citadel, or Fort du Roule, held firm.

When the Hundred Years' War began Cherbourg became strategic.[1] During that long drawn out conflict, the town changed nationality no less than six times. First the King of France awarded it to his future son-in-law, Charles de Navarre.[2] The King of Navarre then gave it to the English.[3] Charles de Navarre's son reconquered the town[4] and swapped it with the King of France for the Comté of Nemours. Then we English retook the town.[5] It stayed English for another thirty years[6] when, following a massive payment to (our) Henry V, it again submitted to the kings of France.

On 26 June 1944 Cherbourg briefly became American. General Lawton Collins, commander of the US Army VII Corps, was able to look over Cherbourg from the Fort du Roule with no small pride. After three exhausting weeks of mortal combat, he and his men had finally seized Cherbourg, one of the key objectives of the Normandy landings.

Cherbourg had always been the largest port in the Cotentin. In

---

[1] In 1337.
[2] In 1354.
[3] In 1378.
[4] In 1394.
[5] In 1418.
[6] Until 1450.

1944 none of its natives thought it would ever be again. When the German military commander realised that he would lose the town to the Americans, he gave orders for the place to be destroyed. Ships that would otherwise have been captured were scuttled in the port. All the railways and roads out of town were dynamited. Mark Clark called it 'the greatest demolition job in history'.[7] But the Germans eventually abandoned the port to the Allies, and once we had cleared the harbour of wrecks and mines, the Liberty Ships began to unload inside its vast and newly safe haven.

Allied vehicles and bivouacs – mostly British and American – were soon spread over Cherbourg's 4,000 acres, waiting for their orders to rid Normandy, France and conquered Europe of its German occupation.

As Johnnie and I strolled around, he talked non-stop about girls, cars and films, while I was looking out for relics of the Liberation. At first I couldn't find very much of anything that predated the war. The town had been repaired and modernised after its heady cocktail of German dynamite, American shelling and a soupçon of hand-to-hand fighting. There was a charming museum dedicated to the Liberation, on top of the hill that overlooks the city and which is still dominated by the old fort, but what struck my old friend most forcibly was the *Redoutable*, an enormous nuclear submarine, which was in port. Miraculously, thirty or more years later, it's still there. But today it is a museum. You can even go on board.

I was dead impressed by the art deco transatlantic harbour station, where the *Titanic* had briefly paused, stopping just one more time in Queenstown, Ireland, before her date with an iceberg. There was a sister departure station at Southampton, and I resolved that I would make the effort to see it. It was said to be even grander. Alas, I never got there. In 1999 the English transatlantic terminal in Southampton was destroyed in a moment of wanton vandalism, with the tacit support of the local council, who secretly wanted something nice and modern, and probably more 'relevant', 'multicultural' and 'vibrant', in its place.

As we explored we began to discover, here and there, private houses, statues and public buildings that had somehow survived

---

[7] General Mark Clark, *Calculated Risk*, 1950.

the conflict. They were largely built in the reign of Queen Matilda (the Conqueror's granddaughter) and Napoleon. There is also an especially magnificent Renaissance building, the Château de Ravalet, set in its own superb park.

There is a sad story of the Ravalets. In 1603, Marguerite and Julien de Ravalet, brother and sister, were tried for incest in Paris, convicted and beheaded. Their tombstone, long vanished, used to read, 'Here lie brother and sister. Do not enquire after the cause of their death. Continue on your way and pray to God for their souls.'

Queen Matilda's Abbey of the Vow manages to survive, and it's well worth a visit. Overall, however, Cherbourg has a rather breezy 1950s feel to it.

It was time for lunch and we found a place on the quay – Vauban, I think. According to my notes, I had Dover sole and Johnnie had steak. It must have made the choice of wine next to impossible. As a result, if I recall correctly, we compromised. He had a beer or two and I had a fine and young Muscadet Sur Lie, as crisp and dry as ever, just as it should be.

A coffee and an Armagnac inside us, and we were off to the landing sites – the Normandy Beaches. Johnnie seemed to drive like a maniac, but at least he hadn't downed a whole bottle of Muscadet. I let him have his head – as if I had any choice. It was his car and, like all young men everywhere, we were both immortal.

We screeched to a halt at Omaha Beach a few minutes before 3 p.m.

It turned out that Johnnie had a particular interest in military matters. The way he saw it, war's balance sheet was made of errors and miscalculations. Two things are always needed: courage and the ability to give orders. Not necessarily the right orders; any orders will do at a push, so long as there is no confusion. Confusion will kill more men than any enemy.[8]

I looked at the plaque in front of us and wondered what the men of the 16th Regimental Combat Team of the 1st Division and the 116th Regimental Combat team of the 29th Division would make of his theory.

---

[8] Napoleon said, to this effect, that one bad general was better than two good ones.

We were there, standing on Omaha Beach, so deceptively benign, our coats done up to our necks. At least it wasn't raining or snowing.

'By the way,' said Johnnie, 'how did you guess I would be so interested in the Normandy landings?'

'I had no idea at all. I just thought it would be interesting.'

'Rather more than that. My father was in the first wave at Gold Beach.'

He peered out to sea. The penetrating cold wind and low cloud did not really allow us to see much more that half a mile out. But it was all too easy to imagine the German troops exactly where we now were, dug in and well provisioned, their weapons trained on the beach, joking and playing *Bauernschnapsen* to pass the time.

'This is where the Americans landed,' he told me. 'A couple of our frigates had joined a couple of theirs, and began the day by shelling the beach. Unfortunately their shells and rockets fell over there, way short of any German defences. Similarly, the USAF bombers completely missed their targets.' He gestured to the steep hills that rose up from the shore. 'That left the German defenders ready for the kill. They could see everything and they were armed to the teeth. They put their cards away and waited for the Americans to land.'

I shivered and blew into my hands. The sea was rough. I could imagine myself wading ashore in that kind of water, laden with a huge backpack and heavy weapons.

'The truth is that it was the Americans and not the Germans who were completely taken by surprise,' he continued. 'The Yanks had expected to meet a demoralised and largely dead resistance. It was immediately obvious to even the dimmest officer that a major disaster was taking place. But what could they do? Americans have never been keen on plan B.'

'So they carried on regardless? They tried to land on a fully defended beach?'

'You've got it. And inevitably, it was a catastrophe. Dozens of their landing craft were sunk right out over there. Yet more hit Rommel's obstacles and were holed beneath the waterline, down there, only about a hundred yards out. Those concrete cradle thingies were waiting for them just beneath the surface of the water. Nearly half the Americans had drowned before they actually got to the shore.'

Half? That would be more than 10,000, I calculated. My mind boggled. I looked again at Johnnie, seeing in him for the first time his family's military tradition. He was twenty-three, a few months older than me. It occurred to me that he was already older than most of the fallen. What a sacrifice the Americans had made under their Freedom banner.

'But what about their floating tanks?' I asked. 'Didn't they build tanks which could float? I'm sure I remember that.'

'It was a sorry waste of time. Their much-vaunted floating tanks sank like stones, their crews trapped inside them. Almost everybody inside these death traps was drowned. Just six of them actually reached the beach, where they were promptly dispatched by German anti-tank grenades.'

'And the American heavy artillery? Was it landed?'

'Come on, get real! In those conditions? Most of the heavy stuff never reached the beach. It's probably still out there, under the sand, dragged under by the heavy tides.

'The first assault was at dawn, as planned.' Johnnie offered me a cigarette and lit up one of his own. 'It was completely over-whelmed. The American dead and wounded were everywhere, while the Germans were hardly touched. Wounded men were everywhere, crying for help, the medics or their mothers. No one knew what to do with them.'

'But they didn't give up?'

'They couldn't. As I said, there was no plan B. More and more troops were wading on to the beach, into a hail of machine-gun fire. The bodies were piling up, here and there as many as four or five deep. Even General Bradley, watching the massacre from the USS *Augusta*, about five miles off shore, was on the verge of cutting his losses.'

It was all a bit depressing. We turned and headed slowly back to the car.

'Before we go, tell me the end of the story at Omaha. How did the thing end?'

Johnnie took a deep draft on his cigarette and exhaled slowly into the miserable February air.

'Bradley was able to order some destroyers to go in closer to the shore. The idea was to obliterate the German fortifications. It might have worked, too, but the currents were so strong that many of the men were landing as much as two miles away, where the gunboats couldn't cover them. The soldiers were immediately killed or captured.'

'I don't get it,' I said. 'You make it sound as though we lost the whole thing. But we didn't. We got through, didn't we?'

'Yes, but not for another seven long hours. Until about half past twelve the Yanks were either drowning or were being shot by German artillerymen who must have thought themselves at a turkey shoot. Sometimes they had to stop firing simply because their gun barrels had turned red-hot.

'The hero of the day was a Colonel Max Schneider, ironically of German stock, who landed his Rangers and the 116th Infantry on the beach. These were experienced soldiers – the Americans had sent the babies in first like lambs to the slaughter.'

That would have been me, thirty years ago, I thought.

'General "Dutch" Cota led a division from the front, from one end of the beach. Colonel Canham brought his infantry from the other. When these guys appeared, their sheer courage was palpable. Small pockets of men started to make advances up the beach, supported by the Rangers.' He shoved his cold hands into his pockets, leaving his cigarette between his lips.

After a while he began again.

'A company of infantrymen were the first to break through. They fought their way to the top of the bluff, just behind you there, well to the east of the beach. At the same time another company climbed that steep hill at the other end, over there. Any Germans they fell upon were fought hand to hand, man to man. These soldiers were fit, well trained and very angry. The survivors of the first assault rallied and supported them. And by noon they had taken the bluff.'

'At a cost.'

'At an awful cost,' agreed Johnnie.

'How many died here?' I asked.

'We admit to 15,000. In truth, it's probably many more. Can you imagine 15,000 dead?'

'No. I don't believe I can,' I replied truthfully.

'Then let me help you.'

Johnnie waited for me to close my door before he switched on the ignition.

We drove no more than half a mile, and stopped by a couple of concrete blockhouses, once German field emplacements.

And there, at Colville-sur-Mer, stretching out as far as the eye could see, covering acre upon acre of ancient farmland, were 15,000 tombstones in tight military order; 15,000 Christian soldiers, marching on before.

We were in a sombre mood as we climbed back into the little red sports car and headed for Gold Beach. Had it not been for the fact that Johnnie had insisted we go there, I would have called it a day.

The enormity of it was breaking over me in waves. My university had 12,000 students. It was if we had arranged for all of them to die – to be machine-gunned or drowned – in just one morning. And then gone over to Oxford and repeated the exercise.

And all of these young people had parents, for whom they would remain twenty-three years old for ever, in fading sepia as they smiled out of silver photograph frames on countless upright pianos.

In some parallel universe, the war had not happened and they had grown old, had children and led happy lives. Or in yet another universe they had been ruled by Nazis, and had gone to work in grey neoclassical cities 'cleansed' of Jews and gypsies and decorated with huge paintings of an elderly Führer.

We were by now on the road to Gold Beach, where the 50th Northumberland Division had landed. This one was a British adventure.

Johnnie turned the car heater up a bit more.

We travelled for a while in silence. For once Johnnie was not in a hurry.

We got to Gold Beach half an hour later.

Johnnie broke the silence. 'Can you guess why I insisted on seeing Gold Beach?'

'Your father?'

369

'My father, a junior officer in the Green Howards, was among the first to land here. Happily for me, he survived.'

'Is that how you know so much about it? Did you get all this from him?' I asked, curious as to this side of an old friend I had never seen before.

'Lord, no!' laughed Johnnie. 'He never talks about it. You know the way he is. Mum says he was quite cheerful before the war.'

We got out at the east end of Gold Beach and went to the memorial. My little leaflet told me that our (British) objective for Gold was to take the beach and move directly inland over the seven miles to Bayeux. There we would meet up with our victorious American cousins, coming off Omaha with their German scalps.

'My father set foot here at half past seven on D-Day morning,' began Johnnie as we shivered on the concrete podium and looked out over the beach and the sea. 'The Americans up the road at Omaha had already been having the shit kicked out of them for almost two hours. We had prepared for, and we got, some very nasty German defence. Our plan was basically the same as the Yanks. The Royal Navy gave the Hun a terrible pounding and, confident that the Germans would be totally obliterated, we launched our landing craft from about seven miles out from shore.'

'Isn't that rather a long way?' I was slowly realising that the Navy would have almost been on the horizon. Maybe beyond.

Johnnie laughed. 'Well, it is a long way to go in a landing craft. It took them the best part of two hours to reach the beach, under constant fire. But it was a lot closer than the Yanks, who launched theirs from twelve miles out.'

Johnnie lit another cigarette. I wished I had thought to bring a hip flask. It was bitterly cold.

'Well, when our ships stopped shelling the Germans, the enemy started to strafe us. Due to the heavy seas, it was decided not to launch the so-called floating tanks from the landing craft but to run them straight up on to the beach. Thank God for that. Unlike Omaha, our infantry had the protection of heavy armour landing with them on the beach. I am certain that this is the only reason why my father and his men weren't cut down like the Americans.

'But despite this good decision, it was still a desperate struggle. The sand out there is depressingly shallow and the men had to wade on to the beach from much further out. They were sitting ducks, and the Huns opened up with their rifles and their pistols as well as with their heavy machine guns. The first wave came under especially heavy fire. It was the last thing we needed, and the last thing many of them ever knew.

'A company of the Hampshires lost its CO and second in command within minutes of landing, and the men had to fend for themselves. The Commandos were the next to land, but they too were to take terrible casualties. Just one of their landing craft actually reached the shore.

'Then came the Green Howards – my father's lot – and within a few minutes of setting foot on French soil, his Sergeant Major, a certain Stanley Hollis, cleared a German pillbox and captured twenty-five of their troops. He got himself a VC for that.

'In the end, we landed 25,000 men and their equipment on that beach with less than 1,000 killed or injured.'

It was growing dark. I could picture a thousand dead men, mere boys many of them, lying on the beach below us. It was a grotesque image.

When I had left university I was still a boy. So many of the experiences I had had since then seemed to conspire to force me to grow up, to find a man within me. But many of the lads who fell at Gold, and Utah and Sword and Juno and all of the other beaches, were as young as sixteen. More than half of them were younger than me. What chance had they had to travel, to develop, to read the masterpieces I had read, or even to sip a cold beer in Positano overlooking the Mediterranean Sea and the 'Arabic' dome of its cathedral? Some of them had yet to kiss a girl.

We stood in silence for a while. The wind whistled around us but I am not sure if that was why I shivered.

'C'mon,' said Johnnie, pulling his coat around him, 'I'll buy you a beer.'

We got back in his little car and drove into Bayeux, and found a café near the centre of town. I beat him to the bar and got the first round in.

I had the strong feeling that we, the Free World, had attempted something that had the very real risk that it wouldn't work. And yet it had. Force of will, perhaps. Or just possibly God really was on our side. Or maybe it was because once we got there, there was simply nowhere to run and hide.

The beers revived my spirits all right, but Johnnie had found a route into his father's unspoken past. In his mind he had waded ashore, the machine-gun rounds whistling like mosquitoes past his ears as they killed his friends, his kit weighing on his back like the Cross.

'What was your father up to on D-Day?' he asked me. I didn't know.

'Bombing Caen, I expect,' I said.

We left it there. We had both decided that the Pegasus Bridge, or the Falaise Pocket, could wait for another day.

Bayeux itself is a really pleasant little Normandy town. A little river runs through the heart of it in a very picturesque way. It was the perfect antidote to the horrors of the afternoon, and we began to let it work its healing magic.

We thought we would see the Tapestry. They call it Queen Matilda's Tapestry (*la Tapisserie de la Reine Mathilde*) over there, after the granddaughter of the Conqueror who commissioned it. They ought to give her her correct title, I thought: the Empress Matilda.[9]

---

[9] Matilda, or Maud, was the daughter of Henry I (aka 'Henry Longshanks' or 'Henry Beauclerc'), and married Henry V, the Holy Roman Emperor – hence 'Empress'. The emperor was much older than his wife, and there was plenty of time for her to marry again when he died; this time to Geoffrey of Anjou. Their son became Henry II, first of the Plantagenet kings, and commissioner of the death of Thomas à Becket. Henry II was known as Henry Fitzempress in recognition of his mother's title.

Matilda's grandfather was William the Conqueror, whose wife was also a Matilda (of Flanders). On her mother's side, she descended from Edmund II 'Ironside', Ethelred II 'the Unready', Edgar 'the Peaceable', Edmund I 'the Magnificent', Edward I 'the Elder' and Alfred 'the Great'.

After Henry I's death, his nephew, Stephen, quickly usurped the English throne. Despite their oath of allegiance to Matilda, many nobles supported Stephen because they did not believe a woman could or should hold the office of ruler of England. These kingmakers also assumed that Matilda's husband would be the true ruler – the idea that a queen could rule in her own right was not well established then, despite

I also planned to see the late Romanesque or early Gothic cathedral. Its choir stalls came highly recommended.

We discovered a pension called, appropriately enough, La Reine Mathilde, booked ourselves in and set off in search of a decent supper and, truthfully, some more to drink. I had half expected Johnnie to insist on trying a nightclub, but the sight of Gold Beach had drained him. His father was very definitely not a natural storyteller and Johnnie had only just understood what his father had been through. My historian friend had become very introspective – not at all the Johnnie I felt I knew so well.

In these peaceful times, Bayeux is a great town to explore on foot, and Johnnie and I strolled through quaint backstreets, passed pretty old houses with their well-kept gardens, stopping here and there to take in a beer or a glass of wine. The weather was cold, but my greatcoat did its stuff. And Johnnie began to recover from his brown study.

Bayeux was ancient even when the Tapestry was made. The Greek geographer Ptolemy mentioned it, in 120 BC, as being an important market town. The Romans were happy there too, some recent excavations suggest. At some point in the ninth century a number of marauding Norsemen, or Normans, decided to take it by force. Their leader married the daughter of the local chief and established a dynasty that in 150 years would lead to the birth of William the Conqueror and, thanks to Matilda's efforts, the future kings of England.

The town survived the Second World War practically unscathed. There are a still a good few authentic half-timbered houses intact in Bayeux. These medieval buildings have curious and quaint carvings on their timbers. One of them, the 'Grand'

Boadicea's earlier but valiant efforts – and the Count of Anjou's main interests were in France, which made him unpopular with the barons.

A vocal minority, however, including Matilda's illegitimate half-brother (Henry I had more than twenty illegitimate children), Robert Duke of Gloucester, supported Matilda's (and Henry II's) claim against Stephen (and his wife, also called Matilda) for most of the long civil war of succession which followed. The Empress's supporters held the west of England during her lifetime, giving Cornwall pre-eminence in royal titles, and her children, the Plantagenet line, were to win the day.

I hope it's all clear now.

Argouges', had marvellous carvings of the Virgin and assorted saints all over its largely wooden façade. Fine Renaissance buildings, too, were all over the place. Grand eighteenth-century mansions added tone to the better-heeled streets of Bayeux. Religion had done well under Louis XIV, when many churches and abbeys had been built or extended. By the time we headed back to our hotel Johnnie was talking about buying a house there.

The next morning we found the Bayeux Tapestry in an old seminary known as the *Centre Guillaume*, another of Louis XIV's civic improvements, built on the site of a former priory. It's actually a bit tattered but it is, after all, 900 years old. It's very, very long, in a glass case, and we slowly filed past. Anyone trying to follow in these footsteps today should know that it has been rehoused and made 'accessible', both to the physically and intellectually challenged. Behind it are a lot of very simple explanations, trying to make it 'relevant' to our modern, vibrant and multicultural community, explaining that the Normans were not really conquering, murderous and pillaging Vikings, some of whom had enormous genitalia, but were actually rather likeable immigrants seeking peaceful coexistence with the indigenous peoples they came into contact with.

Actually, there is plenty wrong with revisionism. It runs directly counter to the notion of truthfulness. And the somewhat political notes failed to mention the simple fact that the tapestry was a piece of self-congratulation and moralising one-upmanship centred on the Battle of Hastings.

But even in 1973, an era supposedly before political correctness, the pseudo-scholarly notes failed to admit that the embroidery – it's not a tapestry at all – was made for the cathedral. Its length was exactly what it had to be to stretch around the interior of the nave.

Nor did they confidently date it. I had to turn to a guidebook to discover that William the Conqueror's half brother, Odo of Conteville, who was Bishop of Bayeux at the time, dedicated the Tapestry on 14 July 1077. Even here there was a problem. The guidebook insisted that the dedication would have taken place on the day it was first unveiled. This can't be right, can it? It will have been on the day that work began.

'It must have been awesome in the cathedral,' said Johnnie. 'I wonder why they moved it?' Of course, there was no answer to this good question to be had in the seminary, which appeared to want us to think that the Tapestry had always been there.

It would take me more than thirty years to find out why. I have since discovered that Bayeux Cathedral was cajoled into offering it to a certain Guy de Boutrai, a Knight Hospitaller attached to the seminary, for military services rendered to the Conqueror. This man, who presumably charged a fee to the pilgrims who wanted to see it, was the ancestor of my neighbour John Bawtree, who solved this riddle for me as lately as 2005.

The cathedral was built just in time to house the Tapestry. As always, there had been a church there for much longer, and the remains of a Roman temple have been discovered under the crypt. Johnnie and I were able to see some spectacular stained glass, and the impressive frescoes had somehow survived the Revolution. That so much had survived was an especial joy as, when religion had been abolished, the cathedral had been 'reordered' into a temple of 'Reason' and later 'the Supreme Being'.

'Shall we go and see the British War Graves Cemetery, or the Battle of Normandy Museum?' I asked Johnnie over lunch.

'Let's skip the museum. But yes, I should like to see the graves,' he replied. 'A lot of my father's friends are there. Maybe most of them.'

There had been little actual fighting in Bayeux itself. The town was entered by the Sherwood Rangers late on the big day, 6 June 1944, and was formally liberated the next. In fact, it was the first French town of any importance to be liberated from the Germans. The returning commander of the Free French, General Charles de Gaulle, established his first seat of government here. In fact, he stayed in Bayeux until Paris was liberated. After that, this superb little town became the main staging post for the British Army in Normandy.

We located the cemetery in the outskirts of town, on the ring road, which we British had built towards the end of the war. The streets of Bayeux were far too narrow for military vehicles and so the Royal Engineers and Pioneer Corps constructed the ring road round Bayeux immediately after D-Day. There were signs for the cemetery everywhere, and attached to it was a huge war memorial and a museum.

I don't know why, but I had expected a more modest affair. Instead, we discovered the largest Commonwealth cemetery of the Second World War in France. Over 4,000 soldiers were buried there, mainly British but not a few from remoter parts of the Empire. There are over 300 graves whose inmates have never been definitively identified. To my even greater surprise, there were also about 500 German graves. It seems that after the war, graves were moved in from all over the Normandy battlefields, many of them having been makeshift or isolated burials.

The graveyard was well tended. Beside almost every grave were flowers. Their sacrifice had not been forgotten.

We didn't skip the museum, of course. In it we found a citation for a gallant man, Cpl Sidney Bates, VC, who lies here.

> In north-west Europe on 6 August 1944, the position held by a battalion of the Royal Norfolk Regiment near Sourdeval was heavily attacked. Corporal Bates was commanding a forward section of the left forward company which suffered some casualties, so he decided to move the remnants of his section to an alternative position from which he could better counter the enemy thrust. As the threat to this position became desperate, Corporal Bates seized a light machine gun and charged, firing from the hip. He was almost immediately wounded and fell, but he got up and advanced again, though mortar bombs were falling all round him. He was hit a second time and more seriously wounded, but he went forward undaunted, firing constantly till the enemy started to fall back before him. Hit for the third time, he fell, but continued firing until his strength failed him. By then the enemy had withdrawn and Corporal Bates, by his supreme gallantry and self-sacrifice, had personally saved a critical situation. He died shortly afterwards of the wounds he had received.

'I think that will do me for this trip,' said Johnnie. 'This sort of stuff does your head in. Got any other bright ideas? Don't forget, my ferry is booked for Sunday morning.'

It was now late afternoon on the Friday and it was growing dark. There was a hint of snow in the air, but Bayeux itself was rather pretty and I would have been happy to stay put. But Johnnie had other ideas.

'I'm going to buy some cider and take it home with me. This Norman stuff is amazing compared with the crap in my local pub. What else do they do here?'

'You could try the Calvados. Or the Benedictine.'

'Well, what are we waiting for?' asked this superannuated Ampleforth-educated schoolboy. 'Let's buy some Benedictine!'

'Would you like to see where it's made?' I asked. 'It's sometimes cheaper and it's always more fun.'

We had found another bar where we were drinking cider. I asked the barman if I might look at the label on his Benedictine bottle and he warily passed it to me.

I knew it was made somewhere in Normandy. The label gave me the missing information I needed: its origin was in Fécamp.

'Let's go there,' said Johnnie. He was his old self again. 'I'll just go and get the map. In the meantime I think you had better get a couple in.'

I did as I was told.

When he came back we opened the map and pored over it. Fécamp was the other side of Le Havre. It looked a very long way.

'Look, Jeremy, I can do London to Edinburgh in five hours in my turbocharged road machine. This distillery, or whatever it is, is in the same county we're in now. It can't take that long. What time is it now?'

'It's just turned half past four.'

'Assuming it's as far as Edinburgh is from London, which it isn't, we'll be there in time for a late supper and a glass of how's your father. C'mon, drink up! We're off on an adventure.'

It was gladdening to see Johnnie completely recovered.

I am afraid, however, that Fécamp was not the real motive for Johnnie's sudden enthusiasm. He was after the thrill of the country drive. He wanted to test his little car to its limit, and up the stakes a bit by carrying a passenger. Not that he normally drove especially dangerously. No more so than the average Frenchman, that is.

But how we drove that night! We hugged the coast, racing in the dark and icy roads along the north coast of Normandy. His MGA had no seat belts and despite myself I found myself looking for bits of the car to hold on to. We took corners at breathtaking speeds and I am not at all sure that all four wheels were always on the ground. At one roundabout, when some idiotic driver felt he had priority simply because he was coming in from our right, we stopped so suddenly that I nearly went through the windscreen.

At last we came to the Seine, where it empties into the Channel, and had to turn inland to find the bridge, the magnificent Pont de Tancarville. That detour took us another half an hour alone, before we could cross into Eastern Normandy. And then, Johnnie's foot flat on the accelerator pedal, we were in Le Havre and out again. At 11 p.m. we reached Fécamp.

Normandy is a bloody big place, and an MGA is a great car if you happen to be driving it. My stomach, however, was still somewhere near Deauville.

At least we had little trouble finding rooms. One of the wonders of France is that there are hotels and pensions everywhere, asking very little. We got the landlady of the first hotel we saw out of bed. She seemed less than grateful when we told her it was just for one night. There was no restaurant, and all the bars were shut, so we went to bed hungry. After that drive, the effects of the cider and Benedictine had worn off, and I for one was in need of a very stiff drink if I were to sleep at all.

My *Guide Michelin* told me that there was a *Palais Bénédictine* in Fécamp, and gave it two stars. Well, that was our agenda for the next day settled. And it was probably where I would find that drink. I settled into my little cell and climbed between the nylon sheets. I spent the night convinced I was at Le Mans, testing some roadster to extinction.

There are times when you long for a decent British breakfast, replete with kippers or kedgeree or poached smoked haddock. That was not our destiny. Two very hungry Englishmen had to make do with a coffee and a baguette's worth of bread and apricot jam. It's always apricot jam in France. Haven't they heard of marmalade?

After an early breakfast, we went in search of the palace where Benedictine is made. After getting slightly lost we finally arrived, faintly cross with each other's navigation skills. But we soon cheered up; it turned out to be glorious.

From the outside I thought for a moment that this fairy tale château must have been built in the Renaissance and mysteriously transported here from the banks of the Loire. In fact, in 1882, a certain Alexandre Le Grand built this 'Tudor' confection of towers and galleries, all in honey-coloured stone, and ranged around a cloister and *court d'honneur*. He had decided that a distillery didn't have to look like a factory and had this extraordinary building erected.

Alexandre Le Grand was alcohol's Mr Big. Not only did he build this tremendous palace, he built a huge scale model of it for the Paris World Fair of 1900.

He registered his trademark and drove brand awareness like a modern professional, earning the compliment of being widely copied. He commissioned such artists as Sem, Lopes and Silva to produce posters for his 'elixir', and they are collectors' items today. Inside his palace there is a great pyramid of counterfeit bottles, produced by his rivals, who imitated his label and even the shape of his bottle.

Alexandre Le Grand widely promoted a fabulous history of Benedictine. He had us all believe it all began during the Renaissance. To begin with, a Venetian monk at the Abbey of Fécamp, Dom Bernardo Vincelli, was supposed to have created an elixir from twenty-seven plants and spices, coming from all the corners of the globe. This elixir, it seems, was highly regarded by King François I, that same king who had wrestled our Henry VIII on the Field of the Cloth of Gold. Up to the end of the eighteenth century, Benedictine monks had produced the drink, which was by then very famous. The turmoil of the French Revolution, however, caused the recipe to be lost. Rescue came in 1791, when a Fécamp worthy bought a sixteenth-century manuscript containing the formula for the elixir. But in his ignorance of the secret held within, he put it away into his library and forgot about it.

This 'official' history must be true. You couldn't make all this stuff up.

In 1863, Alexandre Le Grand, a distant relation of the aforesaid Fécamp notable, came across the book of spells by chance and uncovered the secret recipe. Straight away, he decided to recreate the mysterious liqueur. Tenacity eventually enabled him to do so.

'Modernising' the recipe, and giving credit where it was due, he called it 'Bénédictine'.

Well, there you go.

It certainly went for Alexandre Le Grand. With a new and immense fortune, Le Grand began to collect *objets d'art*, statuettes, paintings and sculptures, mainly from the Middle Ages. The palace has dozens of sculptures depicting Christian martyrdom or scenes from the lives of the saints, in wood, marble or stone, alongside the pot stills and bottling machines that made the great man so rich. Johnnie and I found some fifteenth-century English alabaster sculptures of scenes from the New Testament, alongside a display in tiles of a marvellous advertisement, this time by Mucha, for Le Grand's silky liqueur.

There was a tasting bar and there was a shop. Johnnie was like a pig in clover. He bought three bottles. 'One for England, one for the road and one for the boat,' he explained. It seemed logical enough to me. English customs in those days disapproved of you bringing home much more than a single bottle.

It was beginning to dawn on me that we were far from Cherbourg and would have to get back there if Johnnie were going to catch his ferry to England the next morning.

'Let's find a spot about halfway back where we can put in for a late lunch,' said Johnnie. 'I'm famished.'

We spread the maps over the bonnet of the MGA and synchronised our watches. It would be Honfleur for lunch. We had bypassed it the day before, in the dark, at what must have been 200 mph, but I had heard that it was a handsome place. It meant going back across the Seine and over the remarkable bridge at Tancarville, with perhaps another hour along the coast. We'd just make it, if we hurried.

The drive was even more petrifying in daylight than it had been at night coming the other way. An MGA is a handsome little car, I readily concede, but it sits awfully low on the road, and some of these French *camionistes* do not appear to notice you at all. Johnnie's language was becoming rather colourful as he leant out of his window and hurled abuse at their retreating tailgates. It became progressively more so with every swig he took from his bottle.

Then there is the business of *priorité à droite*. France is probably the only nation on earth that wilfully sets out to kill its motorists.

It's not, as you thought, a political slogan. It's a rule for motorists entering a roundabout. Even the French seem at last to be aware of the imbecility of this law. So that in today's France half the roundabouts now have signs saying '*Vous n'avez pas la priorité*' and in the other half you do. It is an official version of the old Irish joke, where the government, switching driving from the left to the right-hand side of the roads to conform better with the European Union, announces that in the interests of safety and making a smooth transition, cars would switch with effect from 1 January, and lorries would switch a month later.

By the time we got to the Pont de Tancarville I was ready to jump ship, but then Johnnie sensibly slowed down a little, to take in the remarkable spectacle. Eiffel was the great engineer who had connected Porto and its sister city, Gaia Nova, with a bridge over the river Douro, or Duero, which had previously separated them. He had won the competition to build a bridge over the Seine and had chosen a spot where the river is forced to narrow on its way through a gorge, thus reducing both span and cost. The views are spectacular. We stopped halfway across and Johnnie got out of the car with his camera and snapped away at the hills and the cargo carriers so far beneath us. A queue of furious drivers started to build behind us, but he didn't mind. He just took his photos and then, without a care in the world, calmly got back into his little car to the sound of a hundred car horns. Had he left it a minute longer we could have been beaten to a pulp.

The bridge at Tancarville, these days, has had to give way to the magnificent Pont de Normandie over the Seine a little further downstream. This new bridge is the second longest motorway bridge in Europe, the longest being the one that connects Denmark with Sweden. But take my advice: take the old bridge. You will learn what the word 'exhilarating' really means.

We were on our way again, taking every corner at full tilt. I use this word advisedly.

'Do the tyres need changing often on this car?' I heard myself asking. Anything for light conversation.

Every so often, said tyres touched the kerb and jolted our little vehicle, threatening to overturn it. Momentum alone kept our direction true. At every corner the wheels whined like tortured cats. At last, safe and sound, we screeched to a halt in a scruffy little square just outside Honfleur's town centre and I shakily emerged from the cockpit of Johnnie's little car. My brilliant driver had liberated a precious hour for us to see the town before it would be too late to eat.

This jewel of a town is the most painted location anywhere in France. It is a city of artists. Just outside the town is the Ferme St Siméon, where the better-off Impressionists would stay on their regular excursions from Paris. Not just the French Impressionists. The marvellous but short-lived English painter, Bonington, brought Turner with him here. Practically everyone who has ever owned an easel seems to have stayed here at one time or another. St Siméon is today a very smart hotel with a panoramic view over the town and its restaurant has a Michelin rosette.

On the rue de la République there is a shop, selling the work of the resident artistic community. It is less of a gallery and more of a warehouse. The prices are very affordable. If you're going to visit Honfleur, take enough money to be able to return with a souvenir you can hang on a wall.

If you want detail, I must refer you elsewhere. This memoir is not intended to replace your guidebook. But national pride forces me to reveal that the French claim to the town is only slightly better than ours. Honfleur did not finally become French until the end of the Hundred Years' War, in 1450. That's scarcely 500 years ago.

That long war had led to a shipbuilding industry. When it ended, the shipwrights had nothing to do, so they set about building a church from naval timbers. It is still there, in the market square, and Johnnie and I nosed our way inside. It is very fine indeed. It has two parallel naves, which for me was a first. The roof sits on pillars carved in oak from the Touque Forest. Where the columns meet the ceiling there are primitively carved angels. After the Revolution, a Greek porch was added in the name of 'reason', but this was taken down in 1929. Johnnie was gratifyingly impressed.

'I have never really taken architecture that seriously, old boy. But this is rather good, isn't it?'

'This is the only wooden church in Normandy,' I told him, 'and one of just two in the whole of France. The other is in Champagne. If you want lots of wooden churches, go to Norway. Or, I am told, Romania.'

We found a café in the Vieux Bassin and ordered a cider or two. It was too early in the year to sit outside, which was a shame, as the old port is very fine. It was created in the seventeenth century under the orders of Jean-Baptiste Colbert. Colbert was, at the time, King Louis XIV's comptroller general of finances. The old man had had this job – roughly equivalent to our chancellor – since 1665. French historians now treat him as having been the greatest of their statesmen.

The port was enlarged over the next 400 years. In front of our café was a curious mixture of small yachts and fishing boats, and around the Basin tall, slate-topped houses were built on the slopes of a massive fortification ditch. The building plots were just eight metres – twenty-five feet – wide, which forced the locals to build very tall houses. Because they were built on a slope, their back doors are on the third floor. Don't take my word for it; this you have to see for yourself.

The grand fortifications were taken down in the seventeenth century and all that remains of them is the 'Lieutenancy' and the Caen Gate. The former is most definitely a very curious building by the entrance to the Basin. It is in total contrast to everything else and looks the odder for it.

We had tarried a while and Johnnie and I agreed that it was high time to test the local restaurants to check that they were up to the task.

We settled on a place called l'Assiette Gourmande, after some painstaking scientific research; i.e. we asked the bar keeper which was the best restaurant in town.

Just remembering that meal makes me feel hungry.

My cunning idea was to let the waiter choose for us. He accepted our orders with grace and reappeared with a *Kir à mûre* for us both and some exquisite miniature vol-au-vents, filled with smoked prawns, just to whet our appetites. It worked.

We began the meal in earnest with roast Coquilles St Jacques. We had a glass of a white wine to see this on its noble journey, chosen by the sommelier. It was a delectable white Burgundy; a 1966 Pernand-Vergelesses.

The roast turbot that followed was delivered in the form of a lasagne, layered with wild mushrooms. This demanded a light red wine, and our man brought us a fine Ménétou-Salon, slightly chilled, from the Loire.

Over this superb lunch, we talked about Canada. Johnnie had been there, though not to the French bit, but he had an opinion.

It was appropriate to talk about Canada in Honfleur. Samuel de Champlain sailed from here to found Quebec.[10] He founded trading posts and sent the young men who sailed with him to live with the Indians, to convert them and/or marry them. In 1660 half of the population of Canada was Norman. The Canadians take Honfleur very seriously, or at least the French ones do.

I had another reason for being interested in the connection. Champlain[11] was a brilliant explorer and navigator. He mapped much of north-eastern North America.

In 1609 Champlain discovered a lake, which has since been named after him. It is on the borders of New York State and Vermont.

It was on Lake Champlain that a certain young American commodore, named Thomas Macdonogh, defeated the Royal Navy in the war of 1812. He commanded the American fleet at the Battle of Plattsburgh Bay, and prevented a Canadian advance into New England and the possible return of the fledgling United States to a British administration.

'You must get out there and take a look. Even if he was on the wrong side,' suggested Johnnie.

I agreed with him. But in reality it would be a very long time before I could put his idea into action. It took until 2005 when finally, and with my wife and son, I was able to visit Lake Huron, north of Toronto, with its Georgian Bay and its 30,000 islands, some of which were discovered by Champlain. It was a very pleasant experience and I would highly recommend it.

---

[10] In 1608.
[11] 1567?–1635.

Honfleur was such a pretty port that we decided to hole up there for the night before getting back to Cherbourg, for Johnnie's ferry home and my three-hour train journey to Paris.

I have already described Johnnie's driving, and I will spare you most of the details of that petrifying early morning. Needless to say we had surfaced late and had lingered too long over our *café crème*. When we finally hit the road we had to shave half an hour off the time it had taken us the other way.

To this day I can see us on the wrong side of the road, overtaking vast lorries at incredible speed without any guarantee that another one was not coming our way.

We treated every traffic light with contempt. If the road were straight, the speedo never dropped below three figures. Where it curved, we relaxed. To about ninety.

Twice, maybe three times, over the course of an hour or two, I had that near-death experience that we are all supposed to have once in a lifetime.

I had started my trip to Normandy a young twenty-three-year-old, with dark hair and an untroubled countenance.

By the time we slowed and stopped at Cherbourg my hands had turned to claws, seeking to find something to hold on to in Johnnie's MGA. My hair had turned grey, or it should have done. Unbridled fear had etched its way on to my brow, causing the natives to back away, muttering, 'Poor man. You can see how he has suffered…' Girls with that nursing gene began to notice me as a suitable case for treatment.

Johnnie was unaffected by the whole thing.

'There, I told you so. Masses of time to spare.'

He took the cork from the Benedictine bottle and took a hefty swig. He passed it to me. I looked at it for a moment. There was very little in it. Then I gave it a hefty swig of my own. I believe I drained it.

To this day I cannot imagine Johnnie without thinking of Benedictine. Unfortunately, I have a minor aversion to the bloody stuff.

Chapter the Twenty-third
1973: Le Mans

In which the author goes to a smart but distressing wedding, discovers anglophilia, learns of the loss of a friend, gets tested to exhaustion at the Twenty-four Hours of Le Mans, and is arrested for vagrancy.

I had finally had a message from Arianna and I was thrilled. She had always promised me that she would call me in Paris, but even though I had sent her a couple of postcards, with my office number underlined, she never had. But in the event, and when I returned her call, it was not good news. In fact it was terrible news. She had found a suitable match, a Frenchman no less, and was to be married in his village in France.

She bubbled over the phone. He was a brilliant banker, and he was not a Catholic – this was why they would not be spliced in the Eternal City – but they would still have a church wedding, and what's more his church was the prettiest little place in the whole wide world.

Tutta Roma would descend on northern France for the event. Arianna assured me that *al minimo* half my old Roman friends, whom I had so rudely ignored for almost a year, would be there. There would be a magnificent breakfast that her fiancé's chef would prepare. He was thought to be the best chef in France still in private service, and all I had to do was get there.

The French are a little odd about their wedding breakfasts. As in England it is generally a huge feast, as the bride and groom have supposedly been fasting before the wedding. But in France, there has to be a civil service, so in fact a registrar usually marries the couple several days before the event. France, unlike England or Italy, is a secular state.

A good woman's chastity is supposed to remain in no-man's-land for this long interval.

My first impulse was to say 'no', but I suppressed it. I rather missed my old crowd and I wanted to see Arianna again, despite her heartless treachery with some loutish French money-maker. I said, of course, that I was as pleased as Punch and would certainly be there. After a minute or so of gossip, I was able to put the phone down politely and of course my mind dwelt upon our every encounter. Just why I thought I had any right to a say in the matter escapes me. But I went back to my classroom at Aérospatiale that afternoon in a sombre mood.

The more I thought about the matter the sadder I felt. Yes, it was true that I been pathetic in my efforts to hold on to her. In fact I had never staked a claim to her in public. *Au contraire*, I had taken great care that our exciting and passionate liaisons were well out of the public eye. At the time this had seemed a gentlemanly thing to do. Now it seemed plain idiotic.

'Rally,' I said out loud. I hadn't been out of Paris for a while, and the country air would do me good. I had no other plans. There were bound to be plenty of country walks, old churches, fine restaurants and other good stuff like that. There would be glamour and stunning women. And yet...

I looked up Reux in my atlas. I found it easily enough, about forty miles inland from Deauville, in the heart of Calvados. Rather a pleasant part of France, in fact.

To justify the trip as merely an excuse to stand about in an overdressed sort of a way in a country church watching one's first major love getting hitched was obviously foolish. I looked at the map to see if there were something else in the area that I could also do, wanting to turn what was obviously destined to be a distressing event for me into an adventure.

I had a calendar of sporting events and, wondering whether there might be any racing at Deauville, perhaps, I checked against the date. The only thing that was happening in the whole north-west of France, as far as I could tell, was the Vingt-quatre Heures du Mans.

I could hear myself, full of faux bonhomie while my heart was breaking...

'I decided to combine my dropping in at your gorgeous wedding, darlings, because I just had to stop by and see you all on my way to the Twenty-four Hours at Le Mans.' But this cunning plan contained a major flaw. France is a huge country and on a map, even a French one, everywhere looks much closer to anywhere else than it actually is.

Mine showed Le Mans to be about halfway between Deauville and Paris. To my stupid mind that meant that it would be easy to get to. The wedding was at 11 a.m. I could be in Le Mans in time to see the famous running start. Follow that with a comfortable night in some little dive in the town and I could be back in my office refreshed for the Monday morning. Ah, the innocence of youth.

France is rightly famous for many fine things, and according to the *Gentleman's Dictionary*[1] they are wine, food, cancan girls, disagreeing with America, the Resistance and the twenty-four-hour race at Le Mans.

One of my earliest memories, from when I was only six, was of sitting with my father by the wireless, listening to the start of the race. Everyone in Britain was rooting for the Coventry team and a BBC Outside Broadcast Unit had decided to drop in on the race from time to time during the twenty-four hours.

In accordance with tradition, the drivers had run out on foot to leap into their cars and drive off, and our two British Jaguars were favourites to win yet again. The legendary team of Lance Macklin and Mike Hawthorn were our drivers. My father's heart swelled with British pride as we prepared to hear them outclass the Ferraris and Mercedes for yet another year.

But this was not a year like any other. Not too long after the race had started, Macklin had swerved to avoid Mike Hawthorn's Jaguar as he headed for the pit. This put him right in the path of Pierre Levegh's Mercedes, who pulled hard on his wheel, desperate to avoid a collision. But Levegh lost control. His Merc went clean over the outside wall and, at 150 mph, sailed straight into the crowd, decapitating many before bursting into flames. Levegh and eighty spectators lost their lives.

From that moment, racing cars were associated in my mind with danger.

So I had dreamed up a weekend of fast women and faster cars.

---

[1] www.twochapstalking.com.

Always a heady cocktail. How could it fail?

I quickly discovered that a girl I knew, Diane, had also received an invitation to the bash, and I asked her for a lift to the wedding. She agreed happily enough but she was unimpressed by my logic.

'Just how will you get from Reux to Le Mans without a car?' she asked.

But I had already prepared for this. A telephone call to Rome had supplied the essential ingredient for my 'perfect' weekend. My old friend and flatmate, Sandro, had agreed to come to my rescue.

'An old chum from Rome is coming to the wedding. He also wants to go to Le Mans. In fact he's a motor racing nut. He'll drive me there.'

'You do know the wedding's tails and all the works? You'll stand out a bit at the racetrack dressed like that.'

'Don't worry. I'll have a change of clothes. It's all taken care of.'

And so the great day began to close in on me.

The wedding itself was a fairy tale. It was just as weddings should be, and always are in our imaginations. It was a perfect June day, cloudless and dry, and the heat (it must have been over 30 °C) was perfectly bearable. An anxious groom, perfectly dressed and carrying a pair of white kid gloves in his black silk hat, paced nervously outside the church, hoping that his bride – my Arianna – would condescend to turn up. Unusually, perhaps, for a simple country wedding, dozens of black limousines were parked near the church, and some of the guests seemed to have walkie-talkies and bulges under their tailcoats. Not tails but arms, I thought. Perhaps they were expecting trouble.

And then, at the perfect moment, and when the suspense was almost too much to bear, an open caleche appeared, drawn by four grey horses, which danced rather than walked their precious cargo to the church door. Arianna, looking like a priestess of Vesta on day release from her vows, sat shyly against the bulk of her father. Behind their carriage, driving at a stately *lenteur*, a fleet of landaulets and open tourers bore the remaining members of her tribe.

When the applause died down, I joined Sandro and the two of

us went into the church. Going in at the last minute meant that we were at the back, but it also allowed us to chat a bit during the noisier bits of the rite. As Arianna was led to the altar, an orchestra played the grand march from *Aida*. A little bit of Rome had found its way to northern France.

'*Non è mica male, quella femina tua,*'[2] volunteered my old friend. She certainly wasn't. 'You knew her quite well, didn't you?'

'She was one of the first people I met in Rome. And yes, you're right. Doesn't she look exquisite in her gold-trimmed toga. I particularly love the laurel-leaf tiara.'

'She's certainly better looking than he is. He looks totally out of his depth. He's Jewish, isn't he? He must be a bit puzzled by all this Latin.'

'He'll cope. He's a Jewish Frenchman. That means he can call this theatre and just enjoy it.'

'That's true. He is already married to her, after all.'

'First thing this morning, I was told,' I said. 'By the mayor in person. A nice little secular service.'

'Are you on for the reception?'

I was.

The wedding was a great success. The music was heavenly, most of it, though the bits that weren't were so sickeningly sentimental that it felt like being smothered in sugared almonds. The local school choir did their best, and the congregation loved them for it, but I found it nauseatingly cute.

We watched the happy couple endure an agonising three-quarters of an hour being photographed for magazines like *Point de Vue* and *Tatler*, and I mingled happily with the crowd, before I got in Sandro's car and headed for the château.

I remember realising that, overall, the French had a better dress sense than the Italians. Or maybe I simply preferred their little pillbox hats and veils to the overblown numbers the Roman girls seemed to like more. And perhaps, just perhaps (and then only by a whisker), the French have the better figures.

There were a number of English people there. I didn't know any of them. To my eye their manner was the grandest of all the countries represented and frankly they were rather daunting. I

---

[2] 'Your bird's not all that bad.'

was happy that by speaking French and Italian I was invisible to them.

And then I saw Peter Townend.

Peter recognised me immediately, but that was always his great gift. His amazing ability to remember a face and its accompanying pedigree had long been his fortune. His services were in expensive demand by every serious hostess in Britain. In particular, his gift was to provide a list of suitable young men – dress extras, really – for the coming-out balls of our debutantes. The poor chicks had been at all-girl schools in remote and inaccessible parts of the country and they had scarcely ever seen, let alone met, a man they weren't related to. Without Peter's help they would have had very queer dances indeed.

'What are you doing here?' asked the great man in his faintly northern voice.

'Much the same as you, with a few refinements,' I answered. Luckily he laughed.

'Ah, excuse me, dear boy. Lady Badingham, have you met Jeremy Macdonogh?'

But Lady Badingham was less interested in her own social circle and more in that of her daughter. She paid me the briefest courtesy of a slight nod, but little Harriet had to be brought out, as the task was called, and I watched Peter set about his trade and take her gently aside with his expert blend of unction and snobbery.

There was one very great difference between this wedding and a British one. It was the dogs.

Half the congregation seemed to have brought their dogs into the church. Others had left their pooches with their drivers. But as we all milled about, waiting to go into the château, it was like being at Crufts.

Irish breeds did superbly. There must have been dozens of wolf-hounds, plus not a few red setters. England too fared well, with a mixed pack of Old English sheepdogs, golden retrievers and black Labradors. The Germans had their schnauzers and dachshunds, and the French, naturally, had brought to the nuptials an essay on poodles, from Miniatures through Toys to Standards, all cropped like topiary and beribboned like bridesmaids. Everywhere, at ankle level, were Pekineses, Jack Russells, King Charles spaniels and the usual assortment of little barking pestilences. The nearest cat must have been in Brittany.

What a racket these dogs made, but no one appeared to notice. The French are definitely odd about dogs.

I must say, they were on the whole obedient. The curious thing was that they, the dogs that is, all spoke English.

'Sit!' I heard one *grand' dame* tell her water spaniel. And the dog sat. Diane came up at this point and I introduced her to Sandro.

'Do all French dogs speak English?' I asked her.

She smiled. 'It is a little pretentious of us, isn't it?' she said. 'But on the whole they do. Do you not consider that "sit" is easier to say that "*asseyez-vous*"?'

'It would be quite odd to *vouvoyer* your dog,' I agreed. The French are quite unpredictable as to whom they call *vous* and who gets the *tu*. But I would have thought that dogs, at least, were a dead cert for the *tu*. I was taught at school that children are generally *tu*, and their elders and betters are generally *vous*. Still, Charles-Henri called his mother *vous* and his father *tu*, so there really is no accounting for it.

Peter Townend was back.

'I suppose your services are no longer available. You're getting a bit too old for my lists. Shall I take you off?'

I had first met Peter Townend with Johnnie FitzHerbert, three years before. Johnnie was at a loose end and had wanted to get about a bit more. Peter was keen to add a young Catholic gent – Ampleforth, son of a war hero, all the trimmings – to his all-important 'lists'. He had taken down my details too.

Now he looked at me with an odd look of great sadness. It was obvious he was remembering something troubling.

'You have heard about Johnnie Fitz?' he asked.

'What about him? I haven't seen him since February. We did the Normandy Beaches together.' I felt a chill in the June heat.

'Jeremy, he is dead. He died last winter. In February, in fact. A terrible car accident. Killed outright. He was just twenty-three. His parents are completely inconsolable.'

The ice formed into crystals in my veins. I thought of him in his MGA, driving so fearlessly, so outrageously, on the Norman roads.

And then I remembered the Benedictine.

'One for England, one for the road and one for the boat,' he had said. It had been funny at the time. My God, had he crashed on the way home?

'I had absolutely no idea,' I said to Peter. 'How appalling! I must speak to his mother. Have you got her number?' And of course he had.

The thrill of the perfect wedding had totally receded. Left to myself I would have gone from there on the spot, but there was Sandro, whom I had promised company at Le Mans, and upon whom I depended for transport.

I remember through a haze of sadness the cavalryman riding his grey horse through the marquee and cutting the cork from a Nebuchadnezzar of Dom Pérignon with his sabre.

I remember the re-emergence of the bride and groom, she now with her veil raised, with clusters of bridesmaids at her feet.

I also remember how Anglophile the whole scene seemed. Half the guests could lapse into English as easily as they quickly reverted to French or Italian. These were 'well-dressed and well-bred' men and women – 'BCBG'[3] as the Parisians would have it – and at their most elegant. I felt again confirmed in my theory that the French, who have far more in common with the English than they do with the Americans, have not really forgotten the helping hand we lent them during the Nazi years. If there is any hostility in France towards 'perfidious Albion', it is mainly from the politicians and only a little from the masses. Unfortunately, the benign disposition of the French towards the sort of Englishmen who wear ties may end. Their historians, having to pay for material and illustrations from the Imperial War Museum, prefer in these money-conscious days to go to the American Library of Congress, where such stuff comes free. Our government, ever penny-pinching, insists on financial rewards for access to its archive, and these trivial, greedy and inflated demands have resulted in our being airbrushed out of the world's collective memory.

---

[3] *Bon chic, bon genre*, the acronym pronounced 'bay-say-bay-jay'.

Even so, in 1973, at this level anyway, we were so close that, with the exception of the dogs in church, we could almost have been in West Sussex.

Breakfast was concluded, and while it had been a compendium of every delicacy known to man, my mind was elsewhere. The last of the speeches and the toasts was over, and Sandro was now tugging at my sleeve. He wasn't in France to enjoy himself. He was here to go to the races.

Sandro was fanatic about Ferraris. Out of some contrariness, he actually drove an Alfa-Romeo. But an Alfa was not wholly inappropriate. Their team was hot favourite to win the twenty-four-hour endurance test at Le Mans.

Sandro's encyclopedic knowledge of racing cars strongly reminded me of Johnnie FitzHerbert, who had been similarly addicted. I felt a rush of sadness.

We climbed into his Alfa Romeo Berlina, me with the atlas on my knee, and headed for Argentan, Alençon and finally Le Mans itself.

Les Vingt-quatre Heures du Mans is arguably the best-known motor race in the world.

By 1973 it had been running for fifty years. It was not just the Italians who had won the prizes there. We British had acquitted ourselves with great distinction over the years. Every time the Jaguar team competed they actually drove their cars there from Coventry. Sometimes they would stop off en route (so to speak) to win in Monte Carlo or over the Mille Miglia.

The drivers, whose names were in my schoolboy Valhalla, were Stirling Moss and Graham Hill. They were already veterans of the Vingt-quatre Heures.

'Do you know how it began?' asked Sandro.

I did not. Not that I really cared. This was absolutely the wrong time for me to be going to a motor race.

'The first ever great European race, the French Grand Prix of 1906, was run at Le Mans,' began Sandro, delighted to have a pupil.

'Georges Durand of the Automobile Club de l'Ouest and Charles Faroux of *La Vie Automobile* thought a sporting event would galvanise the motor industry. Specifically, it would beef up reliability. Emile Coquille, the French distributor for Rudge-Whitworth Wire Wheels, joined in. He suggested that racing at night could test and develop the fledgling industry's new lighting systems. Basically, this is still its raison d'être.'

'When was the first endurance test?' I asked, mainly to keep the conversation going.

'In 1923, when a two man team, Lagache and Leonard, won it in their Chenard-Walckers. Since then there has been a race every year except in 1936, when crippling strikes and the Spanish Civil War got rather in the way. The race was also suspended between 1940 and 1948, when the British, the Germans and the Americans used the racetrack as an airfield in some sort of roster. After the war the track was rebuilt.'

'It's not the original course, then?'

'Actually, it pretty much is. After the 1955 tragedy, some of the Le Mans circuit needed improvement. A new grandstand was built and the straight was widened, mainly to protect the spectators from any future disaster.'

'It's slower and safer, then?'

'The track is a little shorter, at just thirteen kilometres, and it's a lot wider. But the speeds are the stuff of rocketry compared with earlier days, and they get faster every year. The changes were not about safety. This is not a game.'

Sandro's feathers were ruffled.

'In fact, the track is even more twisted than the one Durand and Faroux laid out in 1923. And the Mulsanne, the great straight section of the track, is infinitely more dangerous to the drivers than ever before.'

I said that I thought the quirky rules of Le Mans lent the event a lot of charm.

'You're right,' said Sandro, his enthusiasm now returned. 'When the thing started, every repair had to be done by the drivers. Two "passengers", made of ballast, had to be carried in every car. At first, the rules required the car's top to be raised after the first five laps, and left up for at least for two more laps.'

'Next you'll tell me about red flags,' I said, trying to be light-hearted.

'No, there were never red flags, Jeremy. It's a race, you see.

But drivers did have to hang side curtains before even starting their cars. The rule was only abolished in '28.'

'Will we get there in time to see the famous start, when the racing drivers run across the track to their waiting cars?' I asked Sandro, who was leaning on the wheel and trying to overtake a large lorry.

'I don't imagine so. But it doesn't really matter. The authorities decided a couple of years ago that it was a bad idea to have the drivers buckling their seat belts while already on the first lap. It's a rolling start these days.'

'God, Sandro, you do know your stuff! Which of us was the greatest ever? You and your Ferraris? Or us with our Bentleys?'

'I believe we all take it pretty much in turn,' he replied diplomatically. 'Certainly, before the Second World War we Italians and you British pretty much owned the place.'

He went on. 'In fact, your Bentleys won the endurance test five times between 1923 and 1930. In '29 they took all four top places. But our Alfas were finally a match for you, and we won it between 1931 and 1934. Apart from Bugatti and Delahaye no one else got a look in.'

'But what about those Ferraris of yours?' I asked him.

'Eventually, yes. They stole the show after the war. Chinetti gave Ferrari the first of their nine Le Mans titles so far. Chinetti drove all but one hour of the twenty-four. This was so impressive that Ferrari could launch in the US. After that Ferrari lost only once over the next six years.' He glanced at me for a moment. 'To Aston Martin, if you must know.'

'The Ferrari drivers were thought to be the greatest drivers of their time. Ferrari also produced the last front-engined car to win the Le Mans Twenty-four Hours, the 330LM in 1962.'

'No Americans at Le Mans, then?'

'On the contrary. True to their national character, they were just a little late in arriving in Europe. The first American to risk his luck here was the oil millionaire Briggs Cunningham, who brought two 5.5 litre Cadillac V8 racers to the event in 1950. He came away with a respectable tenth and eleventh place.'

'I expect you know which models his team drove?'

Sandro smiled. 'A Sedan and a rebodied *Le Monstre* special.'

We laughed. Thank God, I could still laugh.

'Go on,' I said. 'Tell me about Cunningham.'

'Well, Cunningham began to compete regularly. He ran Corvettes there from 1960 onwards. You know, if Henry Ford had bought Ferrari in the early '60s, before Gian Agnelli got it, the GT40 would never have been born.'

'The Ford GT40? That was a tractor, not a car.'

'OK, it was a bit of a turkey at first. But a little respect is in order. In 1966, Ford finally got it right. The Mk IIs, powered with those enormous 7 litre V8s, took all three top places.'

'And what about Jaguar?'

'Ah yes, the Jags. The 1950s were their era. C-types, and later D-types, driven by heroes like Ron Flockhart, Mike Hawthorn and Tony Rolt. The big cats' aerodynamics and superb disc brakes made their name.'

'So who else do we have to look out for?' I wondered if a ghostly MGA would appear from nowhere and take the chequered flag to a standing ovation from the crowd.

'Porsches, obviously.' Sandro looked at me as if I were a complete idiot. 'Porsche will turn out to be the most successful car of all time, mark my words.'

Porsche had already won three times, and as he and I drove south through the French countryside, Sandro speculated whether they could bring off a fourth. The car that could outrun all the others was the 911/917.

'I'm going to buy a Porsche. What do you think?' Sandro took his eyes off the road and looked straight at me.

'Nice cars.' I still hadn't taken my test. Nobody has a right to an opinion on motor cars until they've driven one. And in some (female) cases, not even then.

As predicted, we had already missed the start by the time we pulled into the parking enclosure inside the Circuit at Le Mans.

'Not to worry,' said Sandro. 'Let's go and get a coffee and explore the track. I've got pit tickets for Ferrari, so we can watch the boys in action. I want to check out the Mulsanne.'

So we wandered about. The temperature had reached 37° and I was finding it stifling. The noise was unbelievable. It is appallingly loud, which is only to be expected, and it sweeps by you from right to left like a gale, almost spinning you round. Porsche and Ferrari appeared to be slogging it out, but it was early yet.

We went to the Ferrari pit, which was a great privilege, but it had that slightly nauseating smell of kerosene or whatever the fuel is, and the noise seemed to be even louder. After watching a rapid change of tyres to one of the Ferraris, I shouted to Sandro (he was six inches away) that I would find him later and headed off in search of a quieter spot and a beer.

The truth is that the news of Johnnie's death, coupled with the sight of Arianna hitched to someone else, had depressed me more than I cared to admit. But Arianna had merely betrayed me. Johnnie had died.

I kept remembering him at lunch in Corleone, or in his dinner jacket in some Scottish country house. Or maybe seeing his father through him on the Normandy beaches.

What made it perhaps worse was that Johnnie would so much have liked to have been here at Le Mans. In fact, he would have infinitely preferred Sandro's company to mine. He and Sandro would have been able to swap stories on synchromesh and gravity-fed fuel systems until Hades froze over.

And had I contributed to his end? That trip to Fécamp, and the Benedictine. What had he said? Did he drink the third bottle on the way home and then try to drive?

I could hear his voice. 'One for England, one for the road and one for the boat.'

It was no good. The wind was out of my sails. The French have a saying: '*Manger bien, ça remonte la morale*'.[4] I looked at my watch. It was six o'clock in the evening. Very early, it's true, but there were Americans at Le Mans, so somewhere had to be open for dinner. First find Sandro and tell him what I was up to.

But I couldn't find him. The place was absolutely packed with people, and when I got to the Ferrari pit the lads had no idea where he was.

These were days before mobile phones and the problem might not arise today, but in 1973, if you lost a friend at an event on this scale your only hope was an announcement over the tannoy, or the police. But with the noise of the race the public address system was unintelligible, and the police had crowd control to

---

[4] 'Eating well will cheer you up.'

deal with. And anyway, how were they going to find someone from a description I gave them any better than I could?

By seven o'clock I was beaten. The food on the trackside was of the hot dog variety, and I needed some peace and quiet. I slipped out of the grounds on foot and headed for the centre of town, about three miles away – an hour's walk in the still intense heat.

Eventually I found a restaurant. It was called St Lô, I believe. As far as I can remember, the food was excellent. I do recall tucking in with a purpose and ordering far too much to drink. And I imagine I may have even felt a little better before I realised that I had not just lost Johnnie FitzHerbert. I had also lost Sandro and my suitcase – in the back of his car – and that I had nowhere to sleep that night.

I paid my bill. The waiter looked at me sadly when I asked him about rooms in Le Mans.

'You would do better to look for a virgin in Perpignan,' he told me enigmatically. I suppose this unhappy bachelor must have come from there.

It had turned midnight before I got back to the Circuit de Vingt-quatre Heures and I went at first to the pit to see if Sandro had returned. Neither hide nor hair of the chap had been seen. So I decided to leave a message for him on his car, and set off for the car park. He might even have left it unlocked, in which case I would take a few winks in it. Maybe all forty.

But his car was not there. Had I mistaken the pound? There were several of them. So I tried them all. It was nearly three in the morning when I came to the conclusion that he had disappeared. Despite the stamina of the drivers, driving non-stop for a whole day and night at a speed that never fell below a hundred, I was flagging visibly.

The temperature had fallen to a more bearable 28 °C, but it was still far too hot for me. I supposed Sandro had needed a room himself and had gone into town to find one. Well, what difference would it make now? I reconciled myself to my fate and headed back on foot into town, hoping that I would spot his car outside a pension somewhere and could cadge a place on a sofa.

The first lights of dawn were warming the horizon when I got back to the Avenue Leclerc in the centre of town. It goes without saying that everywhere was shut. I wandered around morosely, looking for a red Alfa with Roman number plates. I even found one outside the Concorde Hotel and my spirits soared, only to peer in through the window and realise that this Alfa was not the one I had arrived in.

At least it wasn't raining.

I went to the river, the Sarthe that runs through the centre of Le Mans, and saw a bridge. There was no one about, and I clambered down to the water's edge and sat down out of sight under an arch, where I fell asleep.

I dreamt I was back in Johnnie's car, his co-driver, and staring through his windscreen at a blurred and foreshortened Mulsanne. The indicator on the speedo was parked against its upper limit and the rev counter firmly in the red. Johnnie was trying to tell me something but the roar of the car made it impossible for me to hear him. Johnnie, desperate to make me understand, let the wheel go. He turned to me, reached out and shook me by the shoulders.

I awoke with a start. A gendarme with a mean streak where the milk of human kindness should have run was rudely pulling me to and fro.

'You are under arrest,' he told me. 'Get up.'

'What have I done?' I asked, naturally.

'You are a vagrant. Vagrancy is not permitted in Le Mans.'

Without very much in the way of ado, I was thrown in the back of a van with a number of fellow vagrants and taken off to a police station about fifteen kilometres outside the city limits. I suppose I looked pretty rough, though I hoped not quite as much as my companions of the road. They may have thought the same about me. One of them looked at me with pity and produced a half-full bottle of red wine.

'Go on, son, have a swig. This will kill or cure you.'

I was tempted, either way.

At the police station we were made to wait to be charged in a sort of pen, from where we were brought out one at a time. The gendarme at the desk asked for identity papers, which none of the vagrants seemed to own. And one by one they were taken down to the cells.

I was the last one let out, and I had my papers on me. I was a 'young professional', salaried, working for a major government-owned corporation near Paris. I had residence papers, work permit, passport, you name it. I also had some fifty francs on me.

'Well, you are obviously not a vagrant.' My pride returned a little to hear the good news. I was beginning to entertain some reservations about myself. 'What were you doing under that bridge? Taking drugs? Fornicating?'

Despite my reflections on marriage, I thought fornication would have been highly appropriate. I considered telling the officer that the word derived from the Latin for 'arch', and that it related to the practice of the girls who plied their trade by the Colosseum in Rome. But I decided not to.

'I'd only been there a few minutes. I had been looking for a room for the night.'

'A room for the night while the race is on?' he asked rhetorically. He was clearly talking to an idiot. 'Go on, get out of here.'

'I don't suppose a lift to the station is at all possible?' I asked in my best French.

'No it bloody isn't!' he replied with that famous Gallic spirit of *fraternité*.

It had turned midday when I finally reached Le Mans railway station and bought myself a single for Paris. I had been in Le Mans for a shade under twenty-four hours. My electrical systems had pretty much failed but at least my tyres had held out. I resolved, as I stretched out in my bath very much later that afternoon, to tell Charles-Henri that he had been right all along to send me to Weston's to buy my shoes. They had certainly earned their keep.

I did bring myself to speak to Johnnie's mother, a few days later. He had not died on the way home from Normandy, thank God, but a few days later, on his way to a dance in Cheshire, in fact. His car was estimated to have been travelling at over 120 mph when it left the road. There was no suggestion that he had been drinking.

I told her about our time in Normandy together, leaving nothing out, not even his toast to the road. And in return she told me how he had sat down with his father, a notoriously taciturn old Irishman, and had recounted his time on Gold Beach in Normandy. And how his father had looked at him, gratefully she said, for having discovered what he had been through without making him tell his heartbreaking soldier's tale.

His mother made me promise to keep the stuff about the Benedictine to myself while she and her husband were still alive. A promise I have kept.

Another Magical Sunday
1973: Notre Dame de Senlis

In which the author visits an unspoilt Senlis, an undiscovered jewel of a cathedral city just outside Paris, and wonders if he has died and gone to heaven.

The next cathedral on my list was at Senlis, an ancient city that managed to sidestep the industrial revolution. It's essentially a Parisian cathedral, only slightly north of Charles de Gaulle airport at Roissy. It's not too far from Chantilly, but without a car it's a devil of a place to find.

It took me some time to get there. For some reason, the good burghers of nineteenth-century Senlis thought railway stations an unnecessary self-indulgence and I was obliged to take a train from the Gare du Nord to Chantilly and finish the journey by bus.

But it was well worth it. Senlis, the ancient *Civitas Sylvanectensium* of the Romans, is a minor rural town, and yet it brims with a very intense charm. The town is veined with narrow alleys and overhung medieval streets, studded with merchant palaces and Renaissance mansions.

There are no new buildings. The town's prosperity of a couple of centuries ago was put into suspended animation when an Englishman invented the spinning jenny and undermined Senlis' textile industry. It only returned with the motorcar, when the town was revived as a dormitory for Paris.

Right at the heart of the town, the spires of the ancient cathedral and its neighbouring church of St Pierre tower over the low-lying roofs. Even quite close up, the first impression is of a confused jumble of towers and turrets, and it takes a moment or two to separate the vast mass of the cathedral from the stonework of its smaller neighbour.

Notre Dame de Senlis was begun in 1153, just sixteen years

after St Denis and ten after its Parisian namesake. The cult of the Virgin was taking off about this time, and the tympanum over the main portal shows the end of her life on earth, with her ascension into heaven carried by angels, to her coronation as queen of Heaven, *Regina Coeli*.

The cult is most obvious when inside. Above the altar, where perhaps should be seen a sombre crucifixion, hangs instead the loveliest sculpture of the Virgin's ascent into paradise. Two angels carry her aloft on a marble throne. The effect is magical.

The cathedral endured all manner of refinements until a big blaze in 1560, and when the royal architects 'repaired' the church they raised the original vault an astonishing further six metres. This alone would make the church majestic. Significant parts of the older Romanesque cathedral are still standing, but it is the Gothic element that ravishes you. It is in that style known only in France, called 'flamboyant'. Stylistically, most of the church belongs to the sixteenth century, a period when in England we were abandoning our magnificent perpendicular for the simpler Tudor style of our own early Renaissance. But for a student of architecture, the cathedral at Senlis could prove a valuable short cut, as it has examples of almost every style in France.

The oldest part is the choir, dating from 1180, of elegant if dainty proportions. Around it, five radiating chapels flank an ambulatory, and the rostra over the large arcades are the most gorgeous I have ever seen.

The astonishing thirteenth-century steeple is sculpted in the purest radiating Gothic. It's taller than a twenty-storey skyscraper and can be seen for miles around. Picardy is a fairly flat region, which is useful for steeples and airports alike.

The cathedral is still surrounded by old houses, some of which existed before the cathedral was built and have been consistently inhabited for nigh on a thousand years.

The ancient episcopal palace nearby is a thirteenth-century town house and a museum, so I wandered in, as I haven't really seen enough thirteenth-century town houses.

I saw a collection of Gallo-Roman bits and pieces. In fact, in the basement there is a trace of a Gallo-Roman rampart dating from the tail end of the Low Empire. Above, a great Gothic hall is filled with medieval sculptures. By now I was getting hungry, but I made it to the floor above and saw some paintings by Corot, Philippe de Campaigne and Boudin. I was never really a great Corot fan, but Boudin is rather fine. Trouble is, he always makes me think about lunch.

I found a rather nice little *créperie* and ordered some cider to restore my feet. I propped up my *Baedeker* and read what it had to say about the town.

It turns out that one of those big historical moments happened here. In AD 987 in the now abandoned and ruined castle that still dominates the town, an archbishop of Rheims had asked the assembly to name Hugues Capet as King of France. Presumably the Capets were drawn here by a superabundance of venison. It seems to be the underlying reason for a great deal of French history.

The royal connection was not to last. As the pages of France's *événements* turned in the wind, the monarchy upped sticks and headed first for Compiègne and then for Fontainebleau. As for the cathedral, the sees of Beauvais, Amiens and Paris itself are all too close. Senlis began its early drift towards a noble obscurity. What a blessing! The town is an antique jewel, set in northern stone.

As I headed for the bus station I thought it would be the spire that would provide my lasting memory. Church architects have always found it difficult not to create a visual break between the base of the tower and its gently dwindling spire above, but here one seamlessly melds into the other. I doubt if even the twin spires of Chartres are as enchanting as the relatively small and single example to be seen here, especially in the context of its sublime environment. If anyone today should want a model for a spire for a moderate-sized Gothic church, they could hardly do better than to make a replica of this graceful example. But what am I saying? We should be so lucky. We'd probably get some modernist Lego block in primary colours.

Senlis is a little bit of paradise on earth. By car it's only half an hour from Paris and about the same from the airport. If I ever made any money, I thought to myself, I would buy myself a little house here. Umbria has competition!

Chapter the Twenty-fourth
1973: Paris – Arms for Sale

In which the author starts a lifetime's research into the greatest restaurants on earth, meets up with a French friend on the latter's return from an English hospital, learns more about the legacy of the Revolution, and discovers that his company is involved in some very risky political games in South America.

The summer of 1973 progressed very well. At work I had had a brilliant idea, though I say it myself. It turned my teaching job at Aérospatiale from a very good one into the best job in the world.

Naturally enough, most of my pupils – they were mainly sales guys – had expense accounts. These are priceless things anywhere, but for a 'foodie' in France they are the closest things on earth to paradise itself. My students had to indulge their clients with lunch from time to time, which meant that they would frequently cancel their appearance for the late morning sessions in my little language school to have time to get to Paris. The solution seemed to me to be obvious. I would take the ball to them.

'Do you have to talk English over lunch?' I asked my class one morning. All of them nodded enthusiastically.

'And are you all confident that your small talk is up to it?' They all shook their heads with unanimous *tristesse*.

'Well, here's my idea. Once a week, one or two of you will take me to lunch in Paris. I will keep your conversation in English and give you the small talk you need. Cinema, current events, British politics, the three-day week, the Common Market – you name it.'

I omitted to include football as, oddly enough, when predilections were being handed out, that one passed me by.

About a week later, one of my students rang me up to invite me to lunch at Le Train Bleu and my scheme was up and running.

If you ever go anywhere in Paris I recommend this curious little restaurant. You'll find it up a flight of wrought iron stairs in the main concourse at the grand *deuxième empire* Gare de Lyon, the railway station that serves the south-east of France.

The story of this little jewel of an eatery began in 1900 with the Universal Exhibition. This was Paris's golden age, or one of them, and many superb buildings went up at this time – the Grand Palais, the Petit Palais, and the Pont Alexandre III to name a few. The Gare de Lyon, something like Paddington Station but less chaotic, was born then and was baptised by an elderly Empress Eugénie.

The station needed a buffet for weary travellers, naturally, and at that time money seems to have been no object, anywhere in Europe. We had yet to burn it by the cartload in a full-scale European war.

In 1973 Le Train Bleu had already been a striking restaurant for many years. It's the epitome of Second Empire style. The very second you step through its revolving doors, it quite takes your breath away.

'Well, what do you think of this?' said my student Jean Froissart, one of our senior arms dealers. He was gratified to see the amazement on my face. 'Monsieur Malraux, our Minister of Culture, has just declared the whole restaurant to be an historic monument. It's quite something, don't you think?'

I certainly did. Why didn't we British have a Minister of Culture, doing useful things like listing restaurants? But the odds were shorter on a Minister for Leisure. Or Football. Or Tracksuits.

The bar, the tables and the furnishings in general were typical of the belle époque, an extravagant confection of dark panelling with gilded beading, crystal chandeliers and an incredible stuccoed ceiling. Figures of slaves in both the purest white marble and the blackest of ebonies held torches aloft and deep purple curtains fell languidly across the windows.

There were four rooms in all, each one with the same astounding attention to detail. The Réjane and Dorée dining rooms were simply beyond belief. The Tunisian and Algerian lounges were unforgettable. Put the whole thing together and it spelt masterpiece.

What Jean Froissart had really wanted me to admire were the immense and brilliant frescos. They showed, like picture windows on a train, the rolling countryside and cathedral cities the passengers from the Gare de Lyon pass through on their way to the Côte d'Azur.

As for the food, it was everything I could possibly have imagined. Most of the recipes came from the south of France, and I can remember vividly ordering a *moelleux d'anchois frais marinés aux épices* – a sort of spicy anchovy *velouté* (it's so difficult to translate French menus) – which I followed with *caneton de Challans en cocotte* – a superior sort of duck stew, in other words. Jean ordered a bottle of Condrieu to help it on its way. The white Rhône wines are brilliant yet almost unknown in the UK. Let's keep it that way: it can be our little secret.

I had simply never in my life eaten anything like it.

Anyone's first experience of a Michelin-starred restaurant is unquestionably a life-changing experience. And, I thought as I hovered between this world and Elysium, I was getting paid to eat this. That, and to talk a whole load of English nonsense about any subject that came into my head. I felt as if I had won the *Loterie Nationale*. If the world had gone mad, I was happy to be included in the general lunacy. I ordered a bowl of alpine strawberries, dusted with a very little freshly ground black pepper and with a drizzle of lemon juice. A marc de Gewürztraminer brought our 'light' lunch to a close.

When I finally got back to my office I beamed amiably at my assistants. They told me later that I had beamed at them all afternoon. It was actually a bit scary, they said.

Still in great form, later that evening, I set off for rather an odd gathering.

Some of the guys were throwing a little 'welcome home' party for their friend, Thierry Grivaud, who had been away for ages. We had made up a sign saying *'Rentrée de Thierry'*, hung it over the door to the school hall we had hired, and had decided to go in fancy dress. I went as a *clochard*, the friendly French tramp of Chaplinesque sentimentality.

I recognised Thierry immediately, even though his costume could easily have thrown me; he was dressed as an eighteenth-century admiral, complete with dress sword.

Thierry was a brilliant physicist. When I first met him, he had talked to me for what seemed like hours about some amazing secret project he was working on that tested Cerenkov radiation against high velocity particulate re-entry in planetary atmospheres other than our own. I confess that a lot of what he had said had gone straight over my head, but I could understand why NASA was so keen to work with him.

He had been in hospital in England for six months, but I had never found out why. Six months is a long time, and when I had last seen him he had seemed as healthy as I was. It had been an unresolved mystery, but anyway, here he was, right as rain, and back in Paris, looking, well, great, if somewhat nautical.

The French health system has its demerits, but on the whole it is roughly the equal of ours. Their doctors are dedicated, possibly slightly less stressed than ours, and they generally enjoy a public esteem far greater than their English counterparts.

The main problem for French doctors is that the whole French nation is utterly hypochondriac, down to its last inhabitant. French doctors steer their way round this is by prescribing every known medication to their patients and then leave it to the suffering pharmacist to decide what is actually the best cure for the malady in question.

When I saw Thierry I naturally asked him why he had chosen to go to England.

'Oh,' he replied nonchalantly, 'your hospital in Northampton is simply the best in the world for my condition.'

I was very pleased to see him again. But of what ailment had he been cured? It's not easy to ask, particularly in France where the French take such a poor view of disease of any kind, in anyone other than themselves.

'He was in for delusions,' Olivier told me, baldly. 'He had thought himself a laureate scientist and had been speaking nonsense to everyone. His parents were deeply ashamed and sent him to one of your British funny farms, telling everyone he had gone to bone up on his English.'

'I see.' There was a brief pause. 'So he is completely cured?'

'So we understand.'

I found myself in conversation with Thierry a little later.

'Did you enjoy your stay in England?' I asked him.

'I certainly did. I particularly enjoyed meeting your Queen.'

'Oh, you met the Queen?'

'We spent many days together, chatting about this and that. She speaks faultless French, you know. No trace of an accent.'

'I'd heard that,' I said. 'Where did you meet her?'

'Oh, in Northampton. She came to visit me, regularly.'

'Well, I'm very impressed. She knows your people, probably?'

'I believe so. But sadly my family couldn't come to the investiture.'

'What a disappointment. Whose investiture?'

'Why, mine, of course. She conferred upon me the dignity of the dukedom of Northampton. I am now an English duke.'

'That's wonderful,' I said. 'Welcome home, sir.'

I shook his hand solemnly. It would not be long before he was back in England, I felt. In all likelihood he'd be there before me. The British economy was still in free fall. But I didn't really mind that much. After all, I had the best job in France, possibly the world.

My tour of great restaurants was now starting in earnest, and I was very pleased with the way my students had embraced my idea. In my diary were dates to go to lunch at Clovis, a fashionable *endroit* in the VIIIe *arrondissement*, and another at the restaurant under l'Hôtel, the ultra-chic seventeenth-century palace in the rue des Beaux Arts, just around the corner from my flat.

The latter was where Oscar Wilde had stayed – so I suppose some extravagance was forgivable. Indeed, if the staff were a little camp, the hotel made up for it by being excessively over-decorated. Though perhaps having peacocks freely roaming around the restaurant may have been too much for some.

My diary also had a dance in it a few pages later; what we in England would call a coming-out ball, and for one of the most elegant and sensational girls in Paris. This was Laurence de Vergennes,[1] a descendant of Louis XIV's famous foreign minister, who had taken over an ultra-smart nightclub to introduce herself to the world.

I was greatly looking forward to this and, despite my intro-

---

[1] Laurence is a girl's name in France. The male equivalent is Laurent.

duction to those superb restaurants, the week seemed to drag.

Laurence's invitation card was pretty much the same as it would have been in England, except for three subtle differences.

Her father's coronet was at the top of the card, which is not really standard practice in the UK. Even above that, in small letters, there was the expression *Rallye de la Duchesse de Crillon*. And at the bottom was written *Tenue de Soirée de Rigueur*, which was heavily underscored.

Many French families subscribe to the *rallye* system. The idea is that you join a social circle, which takes its name from its grandest member. Once signed up, you give a cocktail party for the *rallye* every two or three years and a dance every ten. In this way the French of a certain outlook all know each other, which in the absence of our public school system or perhaps our House of Lords would not otherwise happen. The *rallyes* are in every part of France and some are very large, others small. And once a year, there is a great ball in Paris, the *Bal Interrallié*, which is something like Queen Charlotte's, except without that weird presentation to a cake, and which takes place in Gabriel's exquisite Crillon Hotel in Place de la Concorde.

As for 'black tie', or *tenue de soirée*, the French have an ambivalent outlook. If those three words are put on the invitation, perhaps half your guests will put on the relevant kit. If you are really serious, you add the words *de rigueur*, and now three quarters of the invitees will oblige. If you really, really, mean it, you underline the phrase. That way some 90 per cent of your guests will be properly attired.

Emmanuel rang me up and suggested a glass at his place before going to Laurence's nightclub. I duly pitched up at his apartment to find him wearing jeans and an old pullover. Yet again I felt overdressed.

'Emmanuel,' I remonstrated, 'it says "black tie" on the invite.'

'Jeremy, you just haven't grasped that we have had the benefit of a Revolution in France. My "smoking" is in this bag.' He pointed at a beaten-up carrier bag marked 'Champion'.

And so I, Jeremy Macdonogh, resplendent in my crumpled dinner jacket, and Emmanuel de Bodard de la Jacobière, scion of one of the oldest families in France and clad as a student, travelled on the Métro together – a butler and his eccentric young master, perhaps. And, as I had predicted, no one paid the slightest attention to us.

But we both paid attention, even homage, to Laurence who, with her perfect figure so enchantingly highlighted with her fantastic red hair and leopard-skin print dress, was the loveliest sight I had yet seen in Paris.

A few days later I had a very different but very curious evening.

One of my students at Aérospatiale had invited me to dinner at his house in Le Vésinet, a western suburb of Paris.

Hervé Gamel, an Algerian *pied noir* (the nickname the French give to their returning colonials) had been describing North African tagines to me. They were a curry-like dish served with couscous and cooked in a huge ceramic pot. His enthusiasm had infected a young and willing dinner guest. His wife (whom I hadn't yet met) rang me up to invite me over for a supper party.

'Come early,' she commanded, 'and we will eat in the garden. When it gets dark we will put on a film.'

'It sounds perfect. I'll be there at seven o'clock, then?'

'I'm so looking forward to meeting you. I've heard all about you.'

Again, that scary phrase. What could it mean?

Le Vésinet had been laid out in the late nineteenth century as a garden suburb and was still lived in by its target market, i.e. Parisians who like mowing large lawns and who keep large English dogs. Here the true bourgeois spirit of France was allowed if not forcibly encouraged to flourish in an untrammelled way, and to blossom on a rich diet of tennis clubs and framing shops, of Poggenpöhl kitchen suppliers and of beauty parlours that cannot accept any new clients.

The Gamels had gathered a dozen of their friends to their supper party, and Hervé had somewhat theatrically put on a brilliantly coloured cotton *kéfir*[2] from his native city of Sidi Bel Abbès. In fact, with his pair of Turkish slippers, the only thing Hervé lacked was his fez.

His birthplace, now the centre of an important agricultural

---

[2] A *kéfir* is an overshirt in bold and striking stripes, which is worn over a cotton undershirt and black trousers.

region, had been the headquarters of the French Foreign Legion for many years. I wondered if he had seen my fellow countryman Trevor John wandering about, looking for a fight?

His wife, Marie-Françoise, was much more obviously of Berber stock. She greeted us all with an effusive charm that had grown out of her Bedouin sense of hospitality, and gave us all a flower for a corsage or a buttonhole. She had put on a record of rai music so that we could have the sounds of Algeria as well as its smells; the latter coming from the barbecue, where she was preparing a lamb and apricot tagine.

'Rai', Marie-Françoise explained to the infidels around her, 'literally means "to state an opinion".' The music, she said, was particularly popular in urban Algeria and Morocco, and especially appealed 'to those young people who wanted to modernise traditional Islamic values and attitudes'. What we were listening to, it seemed, was 'a *pot pourri* of secular and religious music played on a frame drum (a *bendir*), with a backing melody provided by a flute and perhaps a violin'. The lyrics apparently spoke of a new national identity.

It was rather interesting, seeing this side of France. Most of the guests were a little more soberly dressed than our host, but all entered into the spirit of the thing with enormous vim.

Moroccan wine had been decanted into great North African jugs, placed at intervals on a table already groaning under mountains of fruit, sweetmeats and pastries. Bowls of olives and dips for the unleavened bread – hummus and tahini, mainly – completed an almost Rabelaisian board.

The tagine was heating on the barbecue, and Marie-Françoise deployed a little coriander in order to transmute a great dish into a masterpiece. Algeria, which up to then I had not really considered as a holiday destination, suddenly became rather appealing. The wine flowed freely, and Hervé was as much a partaker as the thirstiest of his guests.

These French people were a great deal less starchy than some others I had met on my travels. Dozens of travellers' tales were rewarded with gales of laughter as we celebrated the bizarre customs of so many far-flung francophone kingdoms and dictatorships. None of the banter was unkind in any way – I should say straight away – though there was definitely a discernible delight in the indecorous and the absurd.

After the inevitable cheese board, the light faded as if by prior arrangement with God,[3] and we moved indoors to where Hervé (or possibly Marie-Françoise) had set up an 8mm projector and a screen.

The film turned out to be a holiday movie and I prepared myself for another twenty-four-hour endurance test, but I was unduly pessimistic. They had made themselves a thoroughly professional twenty-minute documentary about voodoo in Haiti, which included the mandatory beheading of a chicken. Hervé's droll and clever commentary had been dubbed on to the soundtrack. It was all a resounding success, and he and his wife got a well-deserved round of applause at the end. The lights came back up and some of our party began to disband. There was the usual long-drawn-out kissing ceremony that the French so adore. I was also going to go myself, but Hervé winked at me and indicated a chair. He wanted me to stay.

It was still reasonably early, and when he appeared with a family-size bottle of a venerable cognac in his hand I was delighted.

'I insist,' he said, to the three or four of us who remained. 'I think you will like this.' For my part, I don't remember objecting.

Hervé had recently been on a business trip to Chile. Chile was the preoccupation of the newspapers at the time and we all wanted him to tell us what was going on down there.

With twenty-twenty hindsight I can see that he was a little refreshed with all that fine Moroccan wine. So too was I. Well, that's my excuse.

Marie-Françoise had shown out the early leavers. Declining the offer of a *digestif*, she went into the salon, to tidy up I suppose. I can't remember which of us actually put the question, but it will have been preying on all our minds.

'You've just got back, Hervé. What do you make of the situation in Santiago?'

And Hervé began to talk.

The more astute of us had seen things beginning to go wrong

---

[3] Nowadays the weather is brought to us by Powergen.

in Chile at the end of the 1960s. Before then, a centrist compromise had prevailed. True, the American Central Intelligence Agency had covertly influenced elections in Chile from the '50s but it was not until 1970, when a radical socialist doctor named Salvador Allende was elected president that the outside world noticed, sat up and began to fret.

Allende got in on 36 per cent of the vote. The left, centre, and right had been unable or unwilling to form coalitions and they had all nominated their own candidates in the mistaken hope of obtaining an outright majority. Together they might have staggered, but divided they fell.

'The Americans are totally freaked out by this guy,' explained Hervé. 'When Allende got elected, Nixon ordered the CIA to stage a coup. They even assassinated one of the opponents of their coup, the Chilean Army Chief of Staff, General René Schneider, but it came to nothing. Allende took office as scheduled.'

There was a sharp and collective gasp. What was this? As calmly as a seasoned general might report a massacre, Hervé had just told us that the Americans had had a general executed.

When I first joined Aérospatiale I had been warned that some confidential information might come my way, but I hardly expected to be told of an assassination. I could barely believe my ears.

One of the guests glanced at me and at Hervé in a meaningful sort of way, but our host either didn't notice or didn't care. Either way, he paid no attention. Hervé was on a roll. He refilled our glasses and carried on.

'Allende's first year worked out pretty well, all things considered. It has been the last two years that have threatened to bring down the whole house of cards.'

Like everybody else, I had been watching the Chilean drama unfold in the press. It was the best political story in town. Many of my friends were left-leaning and believed that the Marxist president could walk on water, if they stopped short of predicting his second coming. I was less convinced. It was not and still is not clear to me why a government should always make a better taskmaster than a 'private' enterprise. Indeed, state or 'social' ownership only really seemed to guarantee underinvestment.

Profits were diverted from shareholders and employees' salaries into the administration – and ended paying countless freeloading civil servants. In Britain we had more functionaries in the Ministry of Defence than soldiers in all three armed forces together. British Railways,[4] with its expensive tickets and low standards, had cured me of socialism from an early age.

Allende claimed and seemed to believe that parasitic foreign imperialists and domestic capitalists were exploiting his fine country. By the end of 1971 he had taken over, in the name of the people, naturally, the Kennecott and Anaconda copper mines, both US-owned. He didn't stop there. Foreign firms, oligopolistic industries, banks and large estates, all of these were confiscated (or 'nationalised') by the minority government. He had a unanimous vote in the Chilean parliament that same year which, as it turned out, proved to be one of the few bills Allende ever got through the opposition-controlled legislature.

'It's not working, is it?' I asked.

'You're not wrong, *mon ami*.' The cognac communicated again with our glasses. 'Under Allende the country's economy has been in even worse shape than yours, and that's going some.' I laughed. The British economy was indeed in dire condition. 'Allende has "socialised" the means of production. He has taken over virtually all the great country estates and turned the land over to the resident workers. And, as night is preordained to follow day, food production has fallen and food imports have risen.'

'How has he got away with it, if he can't get his bills through parliament?'

'Surprisingly easily. Eighteen months ago, his government unearthed some emergency legislation from the 1932 Socialist Republic that allowed him to confiscate industries without congressional approval. He uses this as *carte blanche* to turn the factories over to their workers, in what he calls a "joint venture" with the state.'

'So,' I said, realising that stories of a socialist utopia might be over-egging the custard, 'the workers now work to support a host of government functionaries and a ragbag of fellow-travellers – is it another Cuba?'

---

[4] As it was then called.

'It does rather look that way now,' Hervé sighed. 'At first, Allende used Keynesian measures to raise salaries and wages but, more recently, he has started to roll the presses. He prints more and more money to fuel a consumer-led boom. He uses laws to hold down prices. A first-year economics student could have told him that unemployment would rocket. But politically, to keep control of the country, he needs support from the Far Left, who believe he is not moving fast enough. They want nothing less than total socialism.'

'Five year plans, that sort of thing?'

'The Latin Left sees the Cuban revolution as their blueprint. They want the peasants and workers to take industry, property and the revolutionary process into their own hands.'

'What about the Right? Don't they have any influence?'

'The Christian Democrats have formed an anti-Allende bloc in combination with the National Party and the landowners. And way out on the margin is the fascist *Patria y Libertad*,[5] who are ready to use force to sabotage *Unidad Popular*.'

'How is Allende getting on with the Americans?' one of the guests asked our host.

'Ah, the Americans. Not well, I have to tell you. It particularly galls them that Allende bangs on about developing nations and socialist causes everywhere. He has actually opened embassies in Cuba, China, North Korea, North Vietnam and Albania. And he has persuaded the Soviet Union to send him aid.'

'So what are the Americans going to do? Allende seems to be picking a fight.'

'Well, Washington has a twin-track policy. On the surface, the US is frosty. They are still smarting from Allende's confiscation of their copper mines. Nixon has launched an economic blockade, with the help of the IMF and the World Bank.'

'Do I detect the footprint of "Herr" Kissinger?' asked one of the guests.

'Spot on! Mr Kissinger said, "I don't see why we need to stand by and watch a country go communist due to the irresponsibility of its people".'

'Will Nixon go for the military option?' I asked.

---

[5] 'Fatherland and Liberty'.

Again the remaining guests looked at each other, and I had the curious sensation that I was not supposed to hear any of this.

But Hervé just leant forward conspiratorially and poured a little more cognac into our glasses. The house was very quiet, there was no passing traffic, and all I could hear was Marie-Françoise patiently loading her Poggenpöhl dishwasher in the kitchen.

'For the last eighteen months or so the US has been increasing its financial aid to the Chilean military, where Allende has few admirers. They are also training some carefully chosen Chilean soldiers in the US and in Panama.'

'Everyone knows that already. It's even been in the newspapers. What's the CIA up to?'

'They've been told to "make the economy scream".[6] They are using every clever trick in their book to spawn discontent. They want a home-grown military coup d'état. The Agency is in bed with *Patria y Libertad*. There are secret training camps where *PyL* is being taught guerrilla warfare and bombing, and the fascists are already waging a hideous but effective campaign of arson on economic targets. The CIA has covert funds from ITT and other interested US corporations and, via corrupt union officials, is bribing officials to strike and demonstrate. They also exploit their massive influence in the media, particularly in the country's largest newspaper, to fan the blaze.'

'What were you doing there, exactly, Hervé?' I asked. 'France is hardly popular with the CIA.' I was flattered to be in this conversation and I found it exciting.

'Jeremy, have you never even heard of the *Rive Droite*?[7] What do you imagine your company does? The Chilean military has fistfuls of American dollars but cannot buy arms from the US because of the blockade. I would have thought you especially would have put two and two together.'

'All right, I read you. So when do we expect Allende to fall?'

'We are talking of a country where demand outstrips supply, the economy is shrinking, deficit spending is spiralling, new

---

[6] These very words are confirmed in the minutes of a 1970 meeting in the Oval Office, now in the public domain. CIA director Richard Helms spoke them.

[7] A secretive inner circle of the CIA.

investments and foreign exchange are as rare as hen's teeth, copper sales have all but ended, food shortages are rife and inflation is running at 500 per cent. Any supposed gains for the working class have gone into reverse and the only way to get sugar or petrol or whatever is on the black market. Never mind that the government has started to bus staples and other supplies into working-class areas, or even that worker-management of enterprises has actually worked in some rare cases. The cash-strapped government can't stop the economy from going into free fall. Its hands are tied. It can't impose austerity measures on its own working-class supporters. It can't get new taxes approved by Congress, nor can it borrow enough money abroad to cover the deficit.'

'So, civil war or a coup?'

'We prefer a coup. A civil war is not out of the question. The Right is now on the offensive and has allied itself with the Centre. All *Unidad Popular* initiatives in Santiago are effectively blocked. The newspapers are denouncing the administration as illegitimate and unconstitutional, and all it needs is for Congress to endorse this view and the military can take over.'

'But Allende is no fool. He will have seen all this. He has his spies, I suppose, and the CIA is hardly the master of discretion,' I offered.

'You are too hard on them. They can be heavy-handed, but here they are just pushing where it is most likely to give. Allende has made the mistake of trying to stabilise the situation by appointing military officers to cabinet posts. Unfortunately this stratagem has helped politicise the armed forces.'

'Couldn't Allende do a deal? With the Right, I mean?'

'Perhaps he could, but he is more convinced than ever that socialism is the way forward. His more gung-ho supporters are still taking over businesses and land.'

One of the guests looked thoughtful. 'So if there are constitutional grounds for opposition, why doesn't the Right impeach him? Why is a military coup the best way?'

'We all hoped or expected that Allende would lose support in the mid-term elections, this March. The prediction of the Quai d'Orsay was that the National Party and PDC[8] would win two-thirds of the seats, enough indeed to impeach Allende. But in the event they only netted 55 per cent of the votes, which wasn't enough of a majority to end the stalemate. Moreover, *Unidad Popular*'s 43 per cent share actually increased, giving Allende's coalition six more seats. The socialist cause has effectively strengthened.'

'I still don't get it,' said one of our number. 'You're telling us that Allende has increased his support. Militant workers are forming committees in their workplaces to press for faster social change and to defend their gains. Meanwhile Allende seems to imagine that a national plebiscite could resolve the impasse between his party and the opposition. All this talk of a popular uprising seems to be a CIA fantasy. Allende has outwitted everyone.'

'I don't think so. I saw with my own eyes the riots and demonstrations, and they are more and more violent with each new day. The opposition is almost openly knocking on the doors of the barracks in the hope of bringing out the military. But it is true that the attempted coup a couple of months ago was a failure.'

'So why are you betting on that horse a second time?'

'Just think about it. Timing and opportunism, as always. The president's legitimacy has been undermined with the accusations that he is systematically violating the constitution. Educated Chileans want the military to intervene.'

I glanced at my watch and put down my empty cognac glass. It was time to go.

'Thank you, Hervé, for your superb hospitality. Please thank Marie-Françoise for me, too. You have certainly given me something to consider.'

And he had. I had been told, I reflected, that the CIA had a strategy that included assassination, perverting news reporting, and training the fascist paramilitary in economic sabotage. I had been told that the French were supplying a blockaded country with the tools of a coup. And that the army was being besought to save their country by the majority of Chilean congressmen.

But was he right? Was Chile about to be taken over by the

---

[8] Partido Democratico Chileño.

420

army? And even if it were, what on earth should I do about it?

As I travelled back into Paris on the RER, the suburban Métro network, I thought about repeating Hervé's claims to our ambassador, or even to *Private Eye*. I wrote down our conversation as best I could remember it.

But in the event I did nothing with it. All's well that ends Allende, I thought to myself in a pseudo-Shakespearean way as I went to sleep.

I spent the next morning nursing a terrible headache. My one hope was that neither Hervé nor his guests would tell anyone else that we had discussed these sensitive matters. Both he and I would be in breach of our terms and conditions of employment; we'd both end up in the nick – probably the Château d'If.

An Incendiary Sunday

1973: The Church of the Holy Cross, Orléans

What is the difference between Noah's Ark and Joan of Arc? One is made of wood and the other is maid of Orléans.[1]

Now it was the turn of the cathedral at Orléans to benefit from my curiosity. Its star attraction was its most famous inhabitant, 'Jehanne La Pucelle' – Joan of Arc – who in 1429 had relieved the long siege of that city by the English.

Orléans has, moreover, the benefit of a railway station.

Orléans is to the French what Agincourt is to the English, the site of an extraordinary victory of one over the other, and a huge source of national pride. It is not possible to overestimate the importance of the saint to the national psyche – she was so brave, so holy, so feminine and well, so French. If I were going to understand what made the country tick, it all added up to a visit.

The vast Church of the Holy Cross, in the centre of Orléans, was constructed in two phases, the first in the late thirteenth century by devoted Christians and the second in the early seventeenth, under the suspicious and watchful eye of Henri IV – the king who became a Catholic – and his frightening queen dowager, Catherine de Médicis.

I had found in a book of old photographs a plate by William Henry Fox Talbot, which he had taken in the June of 1843. I adore old photographs. They have an uncanny immediacy that is akin to time travel. Old snaps have a way of realising the past. In 1843, the chapter house of Orléans cathedral was decorated with filigree stone tracery, creating a paper chain of tears and what looked like the letter 'w'. I had to see if it had survived so many wars and revolutions between then and now.

---

[1] Courtesy of John Molony.

Fox Talbot's photograph was taken just as the Gothic revival was working up a head of steam. I'll wager our great revivalists, Waterhouse, Street, Gilbert Scott, even Barry and Pugin, studied his photographs. In some mysterious way an echo of this striking masonry will be found in some humble English parish church somewhere. Gavin Stamp would know.

But what did I already know about Orléans?

I knew where it was, at least. It is on the River Loire, just where it curves south on its long climb upstream towards its source in the Massif Central.

Doing my homework, I also discovered that a great number of Protestants had been murdered somewhere in the city in the massacres following St Bartholomew's Day in 1572.

My pre-war *Baedeker* went so far as to describe the Cathedral of the Holy Cross as dominating a Renaissance city.

When the time came, I was appalled to alight in a post-war city, at first utterly devoid of charm. It had evidently been very badly damaged in the Second World War.

I got there on a Saturday in the summer of 1973. I found a nondescript city on a great wild river. I was cheered by the cathedral, which can still be seen from everywhere. It is the largest Gothic cathedral in France[2] and what remains of the devastated Renaissance city in which it is set seldom rises to half its height.

Mass was being celebrated in the cathedral when I put my head round the door. Considering it rude to interrupt, I backed off and sought out the tangible remains of the Maid of Orléans elsewhere in town. Joan of Arc is all around you in Orléans, especially in the sixteenth-century Hôtel Groslot, close by, and in the great Tower of Bourges, where on two occasions Joan stopped on her extraordinary military campaign.

The Renaissance city, so eulogised in my ancient *Baedeker*, met its nemesis first with the Wehrmacht and later with the USAF, who set out to destroy the German aerodromes that were the base for squadrons of Stukas. Between the two of them they almost razed the town to the ground. German Panzers and American Shermans completed the destruction. As Operation Overlord

---

[2] Beauvais would have been larger, had it been completed.

made its relentless way north, in August 1944 the town became the ground for a pitched land battle. American tank destroyers fired their long-range shells along the planned and ancient Orléans streets as they sought to destroy the German tanks on the other bank of the Loire, and successfully caused the Germans to retreat. But it didn't do the remaining ancient buildings much good. Today it is a modern town.

The first cathedral here was built in the fourth century, when the known world was ruled by a quadrumvirate of late emperors. A little earlier, Constantine had ordered the Empire to embrace Christianity and his edict slowly spread through France from the sea, gently colonising the shores of the Loire. The precise location of the very first cathedral is uncertain, but the records show that one existed on the site of the present building from at the latest the seventh century – very probably a lot earlier. The church was known as the Cathedral of the Holy Cross, after its principal relic – a large chunk of the cross that Constantine's mother had discovered in Jerusalem.

The Holy Cross had been located by Empress Helena in a cave under a paleo-Christian church near Golgotha. There were, as you will have predicted, three old crosses in that cave, together with a *Titulus* – a piece of wood on which was painted the painfully ironic legend 'Jesus of Nazareth, King of the Jews' (INRI). The imperial party sent for a leper, and the unfortunate fellow wandered about and touched the first of the crosses without any discernible effect. He then touched the second, but still no reaction came from the man. And then, to the delight and amazement of the Empress, he touched the third cross, and his infirmity fell away. The poor afflicted man stood straight, his illness gone, his sores now vanished. And so it was that Helena knew she had found the real thing.

She ordered the True Cross, together with the *Titulus*, to be cut into three parts. One third went to her palace in Rome, the second went to the imperial seat at Constantinople, and the last was carved into miniature copies of the original and was distributed, with great ceremony, to the leading churches of the known world. It was said to cure all ills if you could 'touch wood', but for fear of it being brought into contact with the ungodly, no one was ever again allowed to test this theory.

424

That early church, whose appearance we can only guess at, burned to the ground in AD 989. It was replaced by a Romanesque one, apparently generously and amply proportioned, and which itself was the largest such building in France. But, very probably due to an earthquake, it partially collapsed in 1278 and the burghers and burgesses elected to build a new one from scratch. Work began that year, and the scaffolding remained in place for the next 200 years.

Joan of Arc dominates the cathedral I saw that afternoon. All the way around the interior of the church are renaissance frescoes depicting the childhood of the saint, the siege and the infamy of the Burgundians and particularly the perfidious English. The Joan of Arc Festival (which implausibly claimed to be having its 544th 'anniversary'), and the sheer numbers of schoolchildren pressed into studying the scenes, cause the story of the saint to speak to the present day.

I followed a party of school kids around.

The general background I already knew. After all, we had done Bernard Shaw's *St Joan* at school – a set text for the English Literature O level – and I had seen Ingrid Bergman's moving performance on the subject. I was aware of the dukes of Burgundy's war with France and that the former had called on their English allies for assistance. The French in turn had invoked their 'auld alliance' and several enthusiastic and bloodthirsty Highland regiments had joined the fray on the other side. There are Sholto Douglases buried with some pomp under the nave of the great church. The war was about the ancient dukedom, which at its peak had spread from Geneva to Bruges. There was a question over whether the Burgundian dominions should remain an independent country or be ruled by France.

The first of the frescoes tells the faithful of Orléans about the maid's birth. We see her prosperous farming folk and the infant Joan in their farm at nearby Domrémy, shortly after her birth in January 1412.

The series of huge frescoes explains in pictures how the saint had had from her earliest girlhood a mandate from God to drive the English not just out of Orléans but out of all of 'France'. This divine commission was confirmed in the affidavits she would later give to Charles de Ponthieu, the future King Charles VII. From her earliest days she had heard angelic voices telling her that this was her purpose.

Even now, no one questions that everyone who knew her – her family, and the workers on her father's farm – believed her completely. So much so that her reputation as a saint of some kind preceded her. It was only a matter of time (and the subject of the following fresco) before she was brought to the attention of the Dauphin. Charles wanted verification of her 'conduit to God' before he would take her seriously, and sent her to the clerics and scholars at Poitiers, that March of 1429. The following fresco shows their great astonishment, and not a little awe, as they too confirmed that her voices were not in her imagination, but were from God Himself.

The next fresco shows how the French thought themselves equipped with the ultimate ally in their fight with the English. No less than God in person, through the medium of this worryingly weird waif of a woman. Clearly protected by the Almighty, Joan was given an army that, under her guidance and command, actually raised the siege of Orléans on 8 May 1429.

The fourth of the series shows her invincible, her army going on to capture Jargeau, Meung-sur-Loire and Beaugency. By mid-June that year she had defeated a massively superior English force at Patay.

And then she turned her attention to Troyes, at that time occupied by the Anglo-Burgundian alliance. After some very ingenious stratagems and manoeuvres she accepted its surrender. Her nostrils flaring with the sweet scent of victory, she sent her army to bring Charles de Ponthieu to Rheims, which was already in French hands. He was crowned, there, King of France. The maid is said to have looked on modestly from the back of the cathedral.

The next fresco crowns her with nobility. As a reward for her service, the new King Charles VII granted her noble status, along with her father, on 29 December 1429. She returned to them in triumph. There are still those who suggest that Joan of Arc was of royal blood. In my humble opinion, this is unlikely. Most probably some royalist historians had failed to realise that her father's noble titles were created at the same time as hers.

But the story turns sour. The following year she returned to the field, despite having foreseen her own defeat. She was captured by the Burgundians at Compiègne on 23 May 1430, and handed to the English for trial as a heretic. Her accusers, in English-held Rouen, were a carefully selected group of pro-English clergy. Even so, coercion was necessary to obtain the necessary guilty verdict.

The penultimate fresco, scarcely visible through the dense hordes of grimly fascinated schoolchildren, tells the terrible result of that trial. As everyone knows, she was convicted and burnt at the stake on 30 May 1431.

No sooner had the embers cooled than her appeal began, albeit posthumously. The Holy Inquisition, after twenty-five years of debate, found her innocent. Her retrial began shortly after the English had been driven from Rouen, and after the French were able to gain access to the court documents and some rather less biased (or simply more Francophile) witnesses.

The last fresco shows the presiding inquisitor, Jean Bréhal, ruling that there had been outright fraud, illegal procedures and real intimidation of both the defendant and many of the clergy. This had tainted the original trial, and the Inquisitor therefore described her as a martyr.

What the final chapter in her long story would have depicted, if it could, was that she was beatified on 11 April 1909 and canonised as a saint on 16 May 1920. As usual, the Church took its time to make up its mind, despite 500 years of French pressure. The Church is not the servant of France in these matters.

These days there is the Joan of Arc Festival. Every year the town elects a new Joan of Arc, usually a second-year high school literature student. To date, the choice has always been a girl. Despite the trends of our times, let's hope it stays that way. A couple of local lads are also elected as her pages. They already even things out enough.

The new Joan makes her first appearance every January. A procession of knights accompany a beautiful teenager in a carriage through the streets and she waves regally to cheering crowds.

By the time I arrived she had made her pilgrimages to

Domrémy, Vaucouleurs, Rheims, Compiègne and Rouen. She had been given riding lessons, probably from the 6th Cavalry, and further coaching in deportment on how to carry her standard and how to wear her armour with feminine allure.

The real fun had already begun. In early May, a full costume procession had kicked off a whole day of medieval events, such as jousting and spit roasting an ox. Joan of Arc, reincarnated, had accepted the homage of her knights and the submission of her prince, whom she would later crown King of France.

A good thing I got there late. I cannot stand that sort of thing.

Chapter the Twenty-fifth
1973: The Loire Valley

In which the author revisits the Latin Quarter that had originally drawn him to Paris, revisits the Paris Panthéon, is invited to stay at a great French château and begins to understand why there was a Revolution. He gains some insight into the bizarre relationship the French have with their royal family, goes out to shoot partridge, and is nearly killed.

The autumn of 1973 started well in France. The trees had had enough of being green. That colour was just so much last summer. It was time to put on evening dress, a soupçon of finery, perhaps. Bring out the reds and golds.

Personally, I was beginning to ache for the country, and I was thrilled when one of my grander and more recent Parisian acquaintances rang me early one Saturday morning to invite me for a long weekend at his vast pile in the Loire Valley.

'If you get bored, I'll lend you a gun. You'll bring back a couple of red-leg partridges for the pot, I promise you. And we'll try not to bore you with endless country matters.'

It didn't take me long to decide to accept. Possibly half a second.

Caroline Swan, whom I had met in Rome a year before, and who like me had also moved to Paris, decided to give me a call.

'I hear you've been invited to stay with the Pompierres. Are you going?'

I said I was.

'Oh good,' she said. 'They've asked me to shoot some partridge. I've always wanted to shoot.'

I thought about her lethal driving and hoped she would be better with something as harmless as a shotgun. Yet again my mind was prompting me to think about the insurance industry.

Still, all that was a week away. Right now, another weekend in Paris was upon me, with yet another chance to explore its byways.

How I had grown to love this place, and especially the Left Bank where I now lived.

I had stopped briefly to take a coffee and an *orange pressée* at the Café aux Beaux Arts, underneath my flat, and I took my usual stool by the *zinc*. Breakfast in Paris has quite a lot to say for it, even if their coffee is not a patch on the Italians'. The fact that you can ask for a freshly squeezed orange juice at almost any bar in France is a definite plus. Happy with my modest intake, I scanned the previous day's *Times*, freshly bought, for news of Blighty, and idly plucked a hard-boiled egg from the little rack.

I had begun to read the hatch, match and dispatch columns but without any great purpose. My friend's parents were too young to die, my friends too young to marry, and their future children not yet a lecherous suggestion.

I remembered my first walk through the Latin Quarter a year or so before and suddenly felt the need to retrace my steps. I was more used to Paris now and my eyes were sharper. Yes, let's have the bill.

In the eighteenth century one of my forebears had lodged in the rue de Seine in an *hôtel particulier*, the private Paris mansion of the Count de Luvin. The house was called the Hotel Mirabeau. The rue de Seine was just around the corner from where I was sitting on the Quai Mazarin. My forebear, Felix Macdonogh, had been trapped there during the Terror, before becoming a contributor to the *Spectator*. He always wrote under his *nom de plume*, 'The Hermit'. I have a letter from him, given to me by Felix Pryor of the manuscripts department at Sotheby's. In the letter he begs for money – £100 no less – so that he could get well clear of Paris. His problem was that, unless he could satisfy the relevant Revolutionary Committee that he had no debts to any tradesman, he couldn't get the relevant passport to go home.

Very soon I was in the rue de Seine. I decided to walk its full length. The road is not too long. I thought I stood a reasonable chance of discovering his house and wondered if, when I did, it might jog some inherited memory.

I walked the entire length of the street twice. It was lined with chic galleries and clothes shops and, it being Paris, a good half-dozen restaurants that conspired between them to remind me of lunch. Of the Hotel Mirabeau there was no trace. It was a disappointed amateur historian who sat down in La Palette and beckoned a waiter.

Felix the Hermit must have sat in this very place, the ancient café about halfway along the street. I could imagine him chewing his nails and hoping that his correspondent, a banker called Mr Grey, would respond with the relevant draft. At the height of the Reign of Terror, as the tumbrels rattled by with their noble cargo, he must have wondered just how long it would be before he was arrested as a spy.

Felix had been educated at Oriel College, Oxford. He would have spoken Latin to a passable if not brilliant level. I wondered if he belonged to an intellectual coterie where they kept the old language alive. After all, the Revolutionaries had only just forbidden its use, ironically perhaps, in their Latin Quarter.

La Palette is terribly well known these days, so much so that the Café Rouge chain has used it as their model. But in September 1973 it was still possible to find a seat outside on a Saturday lunchtime and idly watch the crowds pass by. I found an unoccupied table and ordered a *demi pression*, or a quarter-litre of draft lager, and a *marmite de lapin* – a rabbit casserole.

As I ate this excellent (and very cheap) meal, I thought about the old schools of the Sorbonne that were so painfully 'rationalised' by the revolutionary Committee for Education, after the colleges themselves had been plundered by Louis XV.

It was curious to realise that the university that so dominates the Left Bank of the Seine, the Sorbonne, was the creation of just one man, the brilliant but ill-fated Peter Abélard.[1] Before him, most theology and philosophy students had studied at the Notre Dame cloister school on the Île de la Cité. After a famous dispute on some recondite matter of theology, Abélard told the church authorities where to go and he set up a rival camp on the south side of the river. A thousand students went with him.

He coined the word 'university' to demonstrate the range of subjects to be taught – initially law, philosophy and theology – covering between them the whole contemporary gamut of worthwhile learning. It was a tremendous success from its

---

[1] 1079–1142.

conception, and students began to arrive from all over France, sometimes from even further away. One such early student was the Englishman Roger Bacon.[2]

Bacon had demonstrated his analytical skills at Oxford, and was duly recognised by Adam de Marisco and Roger Grosseteste, the modestly named Bishop of Lincoln. He entered the Franciscan order in 1233, though probably only as a lay brother. With the support of his order – his own estates having been despoiled and confiscated by Henry III – he arrived at the Sorbonne, then the greatest of a vast number of colleges of which Cambridge and Louvain remain the best examples of the ancient style still around today. Oh yes... and Oxford.

The hot theological issue of Bacon's time was between Alexander of Hales (for the Franciscans) and Thomas Aquinas (for the Dominicans).

Bacon had studied what we now call 'science' (then, 'philosophy') directly from Arabic texts newly translated into Latin. The Arab writers allowed him a new insight which revealed the defects of the Dominican model – mainly that their awareness of the original Aristotle was patchy, to say the least. Not only were the earlier translations deeply flawed, but none of the professors could actually read the fragments of the original that had come down to them. Neither Arabic nor Ancient Greek were yet academic disciplines.

When the debate concluded in Bacon's favour, the holy scholar turned to ancient languages and to scientific research, principally optics, though he is credited with the invention of gunpowder – in the West, that is. It had long been known in the East.

He may have been Abélard's greatest successor; there is no doubt that the old Sorbonne considered him to have the same status as Aristotle, Averroes or Avicenna, to start with the 'a' list. And, as a lay brother, he would have eventually been allowed to marry. My mother is a Bacon by descent. It would be gratifying to know she and I descended directly from him. Though what's left of his blood would have worn pretty thin by now, after 800 years and some twenty-five generations.

[2] 1214–1294.

Bacon had been a member of a college, of course, but the university's founder, Abélard, had been forced by circumstance to teach in the open air. Within a generation, however, the first of a great number of colleges had been built by monastic orders to accommodate homeless students. By the Renaissance there were more than thirty of them.

Over the centuries, the various and competing holy orders created a whole series of colleges and faculties. Sadly, Louis XV dismantled them all in 1763. This was a terrible year for France. The King, having lost the Seven Years' War and most of France's colonial empire, was desperate for cash. The Sorbonne was systematically pillaged for its saleable property. It was a low point for France's prestige in Europe. Possibly its lowest point, excepting the day they executed their queen and proved for all time that France was never quite a gentleman.[3]

What remains of the old University of Paris is largely the work of Napoleon, though in 1973 another serious reorganisation had just taken place. The authorities, determined to minimise the chances of another uprising like that of 1968, had been persuaded to inject a little long-overdue cash and to give a little thought to the students' well-being.

The university had long remained jealously independent of the Crown or the Doctors of the Faith. It relied much more on bequests and patronage; until the Revolution, that is. All lessons were given in Latin. By way of contrast, the English had already been teaching some subjects in English for upwards of a hundred years, although until 1792, at Cambridge, students still had to produce their dissertations and arguments in the ancient and noble tongue before proceeding to their degree. The present examination system, the 'tripos', was introduced that year (and similar tests in rival universities elsewhere a little later).

I decided to see if there were any traces of these ancient colleges still to be seen and, when I had finished my lunch and paid the waiter, I set off purposefully towards the rue des Écoles.

After no great distance, I turned into a narrow little street, the rue Laplace, and almost immediately found a fine doorway that once had led into the Collège des Grassins. In my mind I

---

[3] A paraphrase of Edmund Burke's famous observation.

assembled a great Oxbridge college around it. Now that would be something.

Walking more or less at random, I turned into the seventeenth- and eighteenth-century rue Valette, lined with its handsome houses. Standing there for a moment, my eyes luxuriated in a spectacular view of the Panthéon in one direction and the towers of Notre Dame in the other.

In this very street had once stood the fourteenth-century Collège de Fortet, where the proto-Protestant Calvin[4] had once been a student. It was odd to imagine that he had still been a Catholic while an undergraduate. I also found a working remnant of the old days. It was the Collège Sainte Barbe, which had been founded in 1460 and is today the oldest surviving school in France. It was 'renovated' in the nineteenth century, but it is sobering to realise that its most famous pupil, Ignatius de Loyola,[5] the founder of the Jesuits and just twelve years older than the schismatic Jean Calvin, may have walked past the latter.

Very close is the rue d'Écosse, where another three ancient colleges have their doors, and I passed along it thoughtfully (and carefully, as it's very narrow) until I emerged into the Place Marcelin-Berthelot, dominated by the Collège de France. This truly venerable institution is still going strong, giving free tuition and public lectures, just as it has since its foundation by François I, in 1530.

I arrived at Place de la Sorbonne and took a seat at one of the many cafés there. The bustle of the students, all in a hurry or volubly debating some academic point in the bar, conspired to make me feel aged. I was twenty-four and an old man by their standards. When I graduated I had still been only twenty-one. It felt as though a lifetime had passed between then and now. I felt I should be treated with respect. Deference is owed to age.

As a student I had been as insouciant as the rest, without the remotest idea of what my career might be. But over those three years that had followed I had seen some of the better bits of Europe and had learned two modern languages, rather well, if I say so myself. I gazed over the Panthéon in front of me, the

---

[4] 1509–1564.
[5] 1491–1556.

symbol of the great and good, les *Grands Hommes de la Patrie*. I couldn't spend the rest of my days teaching English to a whole lot of armaments salesmen. There had to be a bigger game in town.

I remembered the Panthéon in Rome and an empty space, perhaps a void, which was waiting for the deposed monarch to return posthumously from exile. I could see my little sister, cheerful and impatient, as keen as I was to have an adventure. The rather earnest neo-classicism of the façade conspired to make the comparison more apposite.

I had been there before. Rather better informed than then, this time I decided to wander inside the noble building.

The Panthéon was built as a 'Roman' church to replace the decrepit Église Sainte Geneviève. Louis XV had sworn he would rebuild the ancient church if he were to recover from some frightful ailment he had contracted. He did, and work duly began in 1755. His architect, a certain Soufflot, immediately discovered that the Romans had systematically quarried the site for its perfect clay, used for terracotta, and their excavations were so extensive that ten years would pass before the first stone could be laid. Soufflot couldn't wait that long. He died a disappointed man, leaving the construction to his deputy, Rondelet, who finished it a month or two before the Revolution. The new Assemblée Constituante (the successor to the Parlement) took one look at it and decided it should not be a church at all but a Panthéon, like the one in Rome, and should be dedicated by a thankful nation to its great men.

Once inside you are immediately struck by Foucault's pendulum; not literally, of course and nor is the pendulum the real one, but a modern replica. But it was here, in 1851, where the self-same scientist had demonstrated beyond contradiction the rotation of the earth.

Around the walls is a collection of tombs, including Voltaire's, Jean-Jacques Rousseau's and Victor Hugo's. The Resistance fighter Jean Moulin is there, too, with rather a touching inscription. He lies not far from Émile Zola.

There are frescoes by Antoine Gros, one of Napoleon's official painters, which depict the apotheosis of St Geneviève, surrounded by kings of France. At first it's surprising to see them in a building that was held so long hostage to revolutionary fervour, but of course these works were commissioned after the madness had abated.

The best bit of the Panthéon is the view from the top. You have to climb 250 steps, but it well worth it. The panorama is superb. Almost every building you associate with Paris is visible from here, from Notre Dame de Montmartre to the Sainte Chapelle, from the roofs of the Gare St Lazare to the gilded dome of the Invalides.

It was such a magnificent sight that my good humour began to return. Tellingly, I began to think about an early supper.

Half an hour later, while tucking into a *salade de gesiers* in the 'Boul Mich' (the boulevard St Michel has been called the Boul Mich by countless generations of students), I remembered a story I had heard about my father.

He had been at a café somewhere in Paris a few years before, nursing a cold beer on a hot afternoon, when a lost American intruded into his reverie.

The American was going from table to table, saying 'Métro?' in the hope that someone would have the decency to direct him to the Parisian underground.

The Parisians do not care for this unceremonial means of address and all but ignored the hapless fellow, and so it was a furious and baffled American that arrived at my father's table, pathetically repeating the word 'Métro?'

My father elected to help the poor man.

'Take this road here, and then the first on the right, and you can't miss it,' he said in English.

A greatly relieved American smiled gratefully at him.

'Thank God you speak my language,' he said.

'I think you will find,' said my father, 'that it is you who speak mine.'

In no time at all the weekend was over and another enjoyable week at Aérospatiale took me to another sequence of unforgettable restaurants. Teaching these sales guys to speak English over the lunch table had been my most inspired idea yet. They were desperately keen to show off what their master chefs could do, and I was their most obliging witness.

But at last it was Friday again and I hurried back to my flat to wait for the gang to pick me up and whisk me off to the Loire on what promised to be an exceptional house party.

My host, Luc-Eduard de Pompierre, lived – at least some of the time – with his extended family near Saumur.

Sure enough, at six o'clock, my bell rang and the team had arrived, in a huge open Citroën DS. It had to be big because, with me on board, we were six cheering and happy young people on our way to three days of merrymaking.

Halfway to the Loire we stopped to put more petrol in the car's capacious petrol tank. A drunk in the filling station took against us, abusing us all with a string of invective derived from classwarfare.

'*Vous êtes tous de la merde,*' he declared, apropos nothing in particular.

To my surprise, no retaliation was offered. The party simply froze him out. No one said anything at all. We simply refilled the car, paid up and were on our way.

We had travelled a mile or so before one of us began to laugh, and then we all did, me included. Laughter is infectious.

But in England it would have happened differently. We would have given as good as we had got. In France, however, the long memories of the populace stretch back to a time when they had the law on their side and could pull you out of your carriage and rough you up with impunity. The long shadow of the Revolution had for a moment or two eclipsed the bright afternoon sun.

We arrived in Saumur an hour or so later, and the girls wanted to freshen up before making their grand entrance at the great house at Pompierre. We stopped in an ancient and irregular square replete with half-timbered buildings and sat ourselves in a café in front of a splendid church.

In our bar, in that picturesque 'square', or trapezoid, in Saumur, we were all comfortable after our long drive. We mostly had a coffee but I had broken with custom and had taken a Ricard, topped up with iced cold water. My companions did not approve of drinking too much in public, especially in a café such as this, but being English I was of course allowed to do as I pleased. A couple of the fellows followed my example, 'simply so he does not drink alone, you understand'.

And now we were off again.

The Château de Pompierre is a few miles to the north-east of Saumur, and is set in its own deer-filled park some way back from the river. It is a majestic affair, not on the scale of Blois perhaps, but an imposing and dignified palace of a place.

The family had owned the château for a very long time, but were evicted during the Revolution and had for a time lived in England, as guests of either the Sackville-Wests, or the FitzAlan-Howards. The detail escapes me.

When Napoleon had taken over, they thought the coast clear for their return to France. Not that the Emperor had that much time for them. The Emperor was no particular friend to the ancien régime.

The industrial revolution, when it came to France, had been kind to this family. Their forests, which they had planted in the reign of Louis XIV, were now filled with mature and sometimes seasoned oak. Even more important was coal, which they had discovered in the 1720s at one of their estates near the eastern town of Creutzwald, near the border with Germany. It was ripe for massive exploitation. It would not be until 2005 that France would close its last coal mine, saying goodbye to an industry that endured for nearly 300 years and helped turn France into an industrial power. As everyone knows, 80 per cent of the country's power is now nuclear.

In the meantime, Luc-Eduard's people had grown very rich.

As we drew up by the front door, the scale of their fortune became evident. This family could buy or sell Croesus.

Luc-Eduard de Pompierre met us and initiated the usual happy round of handshaking and kissing. He then brought us into the house, up a great flight of stairs and into a vast saloon, where his family required another round of the same. The French habit of shaking hands and kissing all the time is quite exhausting.

There was champagne, as there always is in France, and this time there was no restraint. We were among friends, so to speak.

But dinner was a demanding business, that's for sure. There was a dress code – the blue suit for us chaps. This, in France and Italy anyway, is the level just below dinner jacket and is considered (in these palatial circumstances at least) informal. The trouble was that I did not own one, so I had compromised with my black tie. Better overdressed than under.

The dining room was opulence itself. We were perhaps twenty for dinner, and being the only foreigner there I was sat uncomfortably close to the business end of the table. I was on my hostess's right.

At the other end of the room, hanging above a magnificent fireplace, was a terrific oil of a young and dashing King Louis XVI, the one who had met his end with Dr Guillotin's merciful invention.

'*Quel bel image*,' I said cheerfully to my hostess, indicating the painting with an aristocratic nod of my head.

'*Je rejouis que ça vous plaise*,'[6] replied my hostess, exploiting her exquisite French subjunctive.

'Been there long?' I asked.

'We commissioned it in 1775, when the King was just twenty-one years old. This was when he had recently become King of France and Navarre. He was very popular then.'

'You were obviously monarchists,' I said.

'Then, yes, of course. France was a monarchy. We were loyal and patriotic. And our monarchy was appointed directly by God.'

'Many French houses have a portrait of a king in their dining rooms, I've noticed. This one is one of the most exquisite I have seen.'

'We French have long hung a royal portrait in our dining rooms. It means that the King is present at all our meals. It's both a prayer and a practical means of raising a glass to him. Ours was painted in time for the King himself to sit under it in person, when he stayed here in 1776.'

Somewhere at this point I began to go wrong.

'So you are still monarchists?' I asked. I wish I hadn't.

'*Monsieur*,' said my hostess, '*il n'y a qu'une personne qui est digne d'être Roi de France. C'est le Roi Jésu Christ.*'[7]

This rather threw me. A certain froideur descended on my side of the table. If you are in a hole, it is best to stop digging. But what was I getting wrong?

'But perhaps you would support the claims of the Count of

---

[6] 'Fine picture, that.' – 'I'm so glad you like it.'

[7] 'Sir, there is but one person fit to be King of France. That is the King Jesus Christ.'

Paris?' I asked, my voice sounding loud in the sudden silence. I had just read in the *Nouvel Observateur* that it had been estimated that any party advocating a revival of the monarchy might achieve 25 per cent of the vote in a plebiscite. Henri, Compte de Paris[8] was pretender to the French throne and head of the Orléanist faction of the royal family. He clearly thought he was in with a chance.

'*Monsieur, il est de la branche régicide.*'[9]

And that was that. For the rest of the weekend she treated me as an ignorant excrescence. Not the nicest sensation. And it was wildly unfair. Just because the Count's ancestor, Louis-Phillipe, duc de Chartres et d'Orléans,[10] had voted for the execution of Louis XVI during the Revolution. But this careless vote had given the fanatics a majority of one, and the 'people' duly sanctioned the King's decapitation.

The next day was the Saturday, and after breakfast I wandered around the house and into the stables. I found Luc-Eduard in a cobbled courtyard. He had a huge revolver in his hand. I had no idea that my faux pas had been that serious.

'Morning, Jeremy,' he said, holding out an unarmed hand for me to shake. 'Fancy a go?'

Why not? I took the gun and the sheer weight of it almost made my arm drop to my side.

'That is a Colt 45,' he said. 'It weighs around three kilos. It's the sort of weapon that John Wayne would want. Go on, take a potshot at that water barrel over there.'

I raised the gun at arm's length and pointed it at the barrel.

'Both hands,' said Luc-Eduard.

So I steadied the gun and squeezed the trigger.

There was the most enormous explosion. My arm shot up in the air and a round flew through a window on the first floor, shards of glass falling on to the cobbles.

'Good thing nanny's not in,' said Luc-Eduard, calmly. 'Perhaps it does take a bit of practice.'

I thought, all things being equal, it would probably be better if

---

[8] 1908–1999.

[9] 'Sir, he is from the regicide branch of that family.'

[10] Also known as Philippe Egalité.

I made myself scarce. I made my excuses, found Caroline Swan and suggested a leg-stretching trip into Saumur. She was happy to play truant with me and we eloped together into Saumur, on the banks of the Loire itself. Saumur I had long wanted to see; it is famous for its *Cadre Noir*, the annual horse show given by the École Nationale d'Équitation in its wonderful Plantagenet castle atop the town. In the eighteenth century, the castle had been a royal cavalry school. It is now a humble prep school for apprentice tank commanders.

The area is justifiably renowned for its wines and, oddly enough, for its mushroom caves. Only the French would have a *Musée du Champignon*, and that too is in Saumur. The city is also celebrated for a great factory where carnival masks are made. Its museum, the *Musée du Masque*, is full of waxworks, elaborately clad and wearing the most preposterous masks. It is an eccentric jewel.

In the surrounding hills, from some time in the twelfth century, the French peasantry began to dig villages into the soft stone hillsides of the river banks between Saumur and Montsoreau. They created hundreds of kilometres of underground passageways.

Before the Revocation of the Edict of Nantes, the town's university was the academic centre of French Protestantism. Later, during the religious wars, the Huguenots hid in these ancient caves. Mostly, they died there.

We explored the troglodyte houses, some of which had been rebuilt and were open to visitors. Others had been restored and were privately lived in. We found them surprisingly spacious. We tasted the local wines and over lunch we discussed the whole French monarchy thing.

'You know, I can't think why you went there,' she said helpfully. 'You must know that the French have a long list of taboo subjects. Italian wines, the execution of their queen, the American military, the Revolution, the Antichrist...'

'The Antichrist?'

'Yes. Monsignor Lefebvre. He said that a Catholic should only speak to a Protestant if he is trying to convert him. Rather a testing sentiment in a secular society.'

'My goodness, Caroline, it's easier in England. All we have to do over there is keep off money, politics and religion.'

At dinner that night I was placed mid-table, and there I found rather less difficult company. And Caroline proved a deft and loyal ally.

But I still needed rescuing when the conversation slipped on to the relative barbarity of our two cultures.

'It is you French who are Europe's barbarians,' I said, provoked but unwisely. 'Drinking port before dinner. It's indefensible.'

'*Mais non!* It is you the English who do not know how to behave. Sending your women out after dinner, just when they are ready for gallantry and manliness…'

A Holy Day of Obligation
Château de Pompierres

In which the author learns a little more about why the French are what they are, this time in a private chapel.

If I thought things would lighten up on Sunday, I was overoptimistic. After breakfast we were all to go to church. I suppose I was expecting a trip to the local cathedral, which I would have enjoyed, but instead we all set off, in order of precedence, through a whole enfilade of double doors the whole length of the palace. Eventually we emerged into the gallery of a chapel, the front of which was carved in marble and painted to resemble nothing so much as a box at the opera.

At the front were two gilded armchairs, where my host and hostess sat. Behind were placed a number of canvas chairs for our party. Down below I could watch a swarm of leathery farmhands and gnarled retainers take their places.

The Mass was simple and short, in the execrable vernacular that Vatican II has made of the language of Christendom. And then it was time for us to take Holy Communion and we clambered down a corkscrew staircase to pass through the villagers, who seemed to me to ogle us in a deeply sinister way. When we had taken the Body and Blood, we returned via the stair to our lofty positions and beneath us, the peasantry now took their turn to experience the Eucharist.

I found it all quite extraordinary. After we had returned to the salon for even more champagne before yet another superb lunch, I (having no longer anything to lose) cornered Luc-Eduard and told him I now knew why France had had a Reign of Terror.

'But Jeremy, you still don't get it, do you? We built the gallery *after* the Revolution.'

After a gentle lunch it was time to murder a few unfortunate partridges. True to form, Caroline was determined to wield a gun, and I thought I would have a go as well. I had tried rough grouse shooting in Scotland and had thoroughly enjoyed it.

Luc-Eduard, Caroline and I wandered through the park, our guns broken and over our arms, heading for the rougher stubble fields that were supposedly packed with game birds. As we walked we came across a fairy tale cottage, curiously established in some miniature but formal parterres.

'It's our *trianon minuscule*,' said Luc-Eduard, answering my unspoken question. 'Once it allowed my ancestors to play at being peasants. Now it houses our head gardener and his wife.'

And sure enough, leaning on the garden gate were the fortunate couple. All they lacked were smocks and a piece of hay between their teeth to have been a tourist attraction in their own right. I thought I recognised them from the chapel a little earlier.

'Bonjour, Monsieur Roulet, Madame Roulet,' beamed a delighted Luc-Eduard.

'Bonjour M'sieur le Compte, m'sieur-dame,' chorused the happy pair.

We walked on for a while.

'She curtsied,' I said. 'Isn't that a little old-fashioned?'

'It is a bit. I'm certain they don't do that when we're out of sight.'

I too was sure they didn't.

'Where are these so-called partridges?' said Caroline, bringing us back to earth. 'Only in France can you shoot on a Sunday, and all you two do is rabbit.'

'We're almost there,' said Luc-Eduard.

We climbed a stile into a field of stubble and began to walk around the edge.

'If you see one, just aim and fire,' said Luc-Eduard.

And suddenly Caroline did just that. Except that she didn't fire. Furiously pulling at the trigger, nothing happened and a fat red-leg partridge took leisurely to flight, sounding like a helicopter.

'This bloody gun doesn't work!' she snapped, turning around furiously, the barrels now pointing at Luc-Eduard and me. And Luc-Eduard threw himself to the ground.

'You may have the safety catch still on,' I said nervously.

'Bloody hell, I have! You can get up, Luc-Eduard. I'm not going to shoot you.'

Now both the English guests had made fools of themselves. Thank goodness it was Sunday, and Caroline and I could discreetly return together to the relative sanity of Paris.

Chapter the Twenty-sixth
1973: Parisian Dinners

In which the author gives a small and disgusting dinner and is consequently invited to an even smaller but very considerably grander one. He goes to the races (again) but gets pneumonia. During his convalescence, he finds a bar where he can drink in pyjamas. While celebrating his survival he reflects on French children and dogs in restaurants.

The intense summer heat had begun to subside by the end of September and I felt ready to give a dinner party of my own. It was high time. I had been to dozens but had never reciprocated. I rang around seeing who could come the following Friday.

Paris shares some of its social codes with London. To invite someone to dinner the same week means either that what you are doing is highly informal or that you are replacing someone who has fallen out.

In my case it was certainly informal. When I had got to five people who said they were free, I called it a day. Including me, that meant six. With six people there is just one conversation. Eight guests will break a theme in two. The next good number is ten, or even twelve.

It was to be as smart as I could plausibly make it in my tiny flat and I thought long and hard about the food. My problem was that I had not the faintest idea how to cook, apart from my legendary *spaghetti alla carbonara*, that is.

I spent a couple of days agonising about what I could serve, mooching about the Latin Quarter, when I stumbled on an Indian restaurant. On its menu was tandoori quail. I couldn't resist and in I went. It was an epicurean triumph.

Indian food, ironically, is the major part of our British contribution to world cuisine, and I determined there and then to give my Parisian friends their first curry evening.

Prawn vindaloo seemed wholly appropriate. *Aloo* is a Hindi word for 'potato', and most of us (British) believe that the word 'vindaloo' means 'cooked with potatoes'. The French have other ideas. The *immortels* of the Academie Française would have us believe it means *viande à l'ail*, or meat with garlic. According to the Indians (who should know best) the dish originated with the Konkani-speaking Christians of Western India. Whatever the truth, most French people have never eaten a curry the way we like it.[1] Vindaloo is a remarkable dish and it was the perfect answer to my conundrum. Naturally I would not serve it *à l'anglaise*, i.e. with five pints of lager per head. I would present it with a fine Gewürztraminer from Hugel. A marriage made in heaven.

Finding the wine was easy. There was a surfeit of Alsatian wines in Paris that year and I could hardly avoid the stuff. But the next stage was rather harder. I had to buy the relevant spices – cumin, ginger, red chillies, peppercorns, cardamom seeds, cinnamon, black mustard seeds and fenugreek.

The simpler ingredients were easy enough, but the fenugreek and black mustard seeds were causing me a lot of problems.

There is a grocer, called Fauchon, just north of the Madeleine. This is not your average outlet. This is the very acme of food shops.

Some years ago, with a Russian winter approaching, the Kremlin spin doctors sent their photographers to find a scene in the West that would show that even under capitalism things were pretty desperate.

It is a French custom to greet the New Year with fois gras d'oie, preferably the raw lobes of the goose liver that are flash-fried and served unimaginably rare. To obtain this most sought-after treat in perfect condition it is vital to leave the purchase to the last possible minute and only to buy from the most reliable source.

Every year, therefore, there is one thing that can be safely predicted in Paris. On the last day of the year there will be a queue of Parisian ladies patiently forming a line outside the great

---

[1] Resolving this issue, perhaps, the *OED* says it means 'cooked with wine and garlic'.

food hall, shuffling through the cold at a steady pace, and protecting themselves from the icy winds with their sables and arctic-fox coats and hats.

It was this well-mannered and stoical line that the Soviet paparazzi discovered, and their photograph, the next day in both *Pravda* and *Izvestia*, had the memorable caption, 'Capitalism Continues to Fail; Food Queues in Paris Grow Ever Longer.'

Pravda means 'News', *Izvestia* means 'Truth'. Not for nothing did the world-weary Russians say that there was no truth in the news and no news in the truth.

I should have gone there for my fenugreek.

On the appointed day I still had only half the vital bits and pieces necessary for a great curry and, rather than ruin it, I went for plan B. I bought a pre-assembled curry that (according to the label) only needed rehydrating and it would represent the subcontinent like a maharajah. The labelling told me reassuringly that 'Shiva Ready-Curries are the nearest on earth to the true taste of the Punjab'. No mention here of Western India, I noticed, but who was I to disagree? A Shiva Ready-Curry it was going to be.

Friday passed charmingly – a little pedagogy at Aérospatiale in the morning, and then a light but heavenly lunch with two of the sales guys at Le Pré Catalan. Back to the office on a post-prandial cloud to write some more teaching materials and then back to the flat to prepare dinner and await my guests.

I arrived home in due course and poured myself a stiff gin and tonic to get myself in party mood. There is something about a gin and tonic. It seemed unfair to stop at one, and so I had the second. Umm, that was good. Now I was ready for anything, including the kitchen.

The rice came in transparent paper packets that had to be dropped into boiling water. I got a saucepan up to speed and duly immersed the 'pure Basmati rice' that had been included in the idiot-proof kit.

Now I looked at the desiccated prawn vindaloo. 'Just add water and bring to the boil', said the instructions.

I did as I was told, pouring a jug of cold water on to the reddish powder and putting the pan on to the hot ring. I stirred the horrible mess pensively. The problem is, I said to myself, that these curries are never hot enough. If I add a little spice it will be more genuine. And I can more reasonably claim to have cooked it myself...

I took a clove of garlic and squeezed it into the larval mass through my little press. The French like garlic. Next I tipped in a tablespoon of red chillies. It needs to be authentically hot.

I took stock of the spices I had successfully acquired. Let's not be timid, I said to myself. A pinch of cumin here, a teaspoon of peppercorns there, a good dusting with the cardamom seeds and cinnamon. That should do it.

Onions. It needed onions.

I turned the heat right down and ran down the stairs on to the street. You could always find fresh vegetables in the Boulevard St Germain, even at this late hour. I made my way through the early evening crowds to the main square in front of the old abbey and paused for breath. Onions were over there. Supper was on a safe slow burn. Yes, there was easily time for a quick beer.

When I got back to my flat, at five to eight, a thin smoke had pervaded my kitchen. It was coming from the rice pan, but no real harm had been done. The bottom of the rice was a little blackened, but I could still spoon away the vast majority of the rice into a bowl. I threw the burnt saucepan into the rubbish bin.

The French take food very seriously, as everyone knows. I had elected to play by their rules and was in grave danger of being found wanting.

I was troubled by the unarguable fact that the curry had an ominous look to it and was emitting an acrid smell. Good thing I had some onions to sharpen it up.

The doorbell rang. It was the first of my guests, Caroline Swan.

'What on earth are you cooking?' she asked amiably, forcing me aside and diving straight into my kitchen.

'Prawn vindaloo,' I replied, affecting a jaunty air of self-confidence.

'That means potatoes. Hold on, you'll need some to go with this. Leave this to me.'

I had some adolescent new potatoes, and Caroline had already discovered them and was giving them a turn in the sink.

'Your curry smells a bit potent,' she observed.

The doorbell rang a second time and I opened the door to a pair of my Parisian *copains*.

'Welcome to my house,' I said like an old Irish chief. Antoine looked around the little flat and took in the upside-down wallpaper immediately.

'It looks better that way up,' he said charitably. Meanwhile Elizabeth tried to wander into the kitchen but was ushered out by Caroline, who had rather taken over.

'Jeremy,' said Caroline in a hushed voice, 'the rice is a little overcooked. In fact, it has set solid and needed to be carved rather than served.'

'They won't even know it's not supposed to be like that. None of them has ever eaten a curry before.'

I offered my guests a drink – a very chilled Chambéry. Even in France this is not as widely known an apéritif as it deserves to be. It is in fact my favourite. Chambéry comes from near Annecy, just south of Geneva, in French Savoy. The town is well worth a visit, but you won't learn the secret of its recipe – it's a closely guarded secret. Alpine herbs and spices have something to do with it. The French sometimes mix it with tonic, lemonade or mineral water. Fools, all of them.

With the arrival of Olivier and Laurence it was time to eat.

I poured the Grand Cru Gewürztraminer with a bit of a flourish and made a speech of sorts.

'Welcome to England,' I said. 'This is what we eat on Friday nights.' I then sat down. There as here there is a preference for short speeches.

Caroline, brave old mate that she is, helped me dish out the plates in front of my guests, and she and I tucked in, the French looking at us for encouragement and an example.

It was absolutely vile.

I had bought some mango chutney and some other bits and pieces.

'It needs a bit of help,' I said truthfully. 'I recommend some of these sauces.'

The French do not lack good manners and dutifully they picked up their forks and took a mouthful. They smiled agreeably, nodded approval and put their forks back down. Silence reigned for a little while.

'I have some cheese,' I said, at last.

I may be the only person in Paris's long history to have given a dinner party that was over by ten o'clock. Maybe this is a cause for celebration, but as I ushered my guests into the street, all of whom were still saying how delicious the food was, only that they had an allergy to chillies, or that their doctors had made them promise to avoid fenugreek, I felt I was facing social ruin. I had reinforced their unnatural prejudice against English food in general and had made myself and Caroline look like idiots.

When I came back into the flat Caroline was waiting for me.

'I believe they appreciated that,' she said, implausibly.

'How do you work that out?' I asked, pouring myself a stiff whisky and passing the bottle over to her.

'Well, they never expected the meal to be a success in the first place. Everyone likes to be proved right. Next, they thoroughly appreciated your wine. And it was thoughtful of you to have had some cheese. The banter was civilised and occasionally amusing. What more can they want?'

Caroline was right, as always.

News of my dinner party talents circulated like wildfire. I had a dozen calls from various people I hardly knew who cheerfully volunteered that they would not be available for dinner anytime over the next six months.

I tried to persuade them to change their minds, offering Kurdish and Uzbek delights if they could see fit to give me one last chance, but they declined even these temptations.

And over the next two days postcards came from everyone who was there, thanking me in terms of outright and sometimes indelicate irony for my delicious dinner.

Antoine's note was different from the others.

'Come over to us on Thursday,' it read. 'Come and try some simple French food.'

It felt like a lifeline. I rang the number and gratefully accepted.

I kept a low profile for most of the week before turning up at the appointed hour at Antoine's *hôtel particulier*, or private house, in the XVIIe arrondisement.

I love this part of Paris, so central but somehow off the tourist map. Even Parisians seem not to know this dense accumulation of urbanity and *haute bourgeoisie*. A few Russians have found their way here – their faux Byzantine cathedral, something like our Catholic one in Westminster but filled with icons and frescoes, is here. So is À La Ville De Petrograd, the Russian diaspora's flagship restaurant, where they continue to plot for the return of the Romanovs.

I had discovered this *quartier* searching for the ghost of Marcel Proust, who had once lived in the rue des Courcelles. Proust had been visited here by Oscar Wilde who, to the great annoyance of the Frenchman, had devoted a significant part of his conversation to a critical assault on the novelist's furniture.

Another spirit, rather more troubled, haunts this area. The Park Monceau was laid out on the site of the *Folie de Chartres*, the urban estate of Louis-Philippe, Duc de Chartres et Orléans, who had so enthusiastically embraced the spirit of *égalité* during the Revolution. Notoriously, he had cast his vote for the beheading of Louis XVI. Philippe Egalité, as he became known, was himself guillotined in 1793, and not too many aristocratic tears were shed for him.

Antoine's home was an august mansion, separated from the superb park by a road and some gilded railings. Two small pavilions flanked a courtyard, and behind them an early nine-teenth-century town house stood a little back from the street.

The front door was not through the courtyard as I had expected, but through one of the pavilions, where I was let in by a chap in a white jacket and ushered at some speed up a flight of marble stairs into an elegant reception room, quite oval in shape, with a shallow domed ceiling. Furnished with gilded bronze statues and fitted panels, it was the very essence of Bourgeois-Imperial opulence.

I stood in Antoine's window, looking out over the park and musing on Proust's taste in furniture. I was trying to guess who the statue in the park below might be[2] when my host came into the room, with a breathtakingly elegant and soberly dressed lady on his arm. The double doors framed Antoine and his mother and their two perfectly groomed shih-tzus.

---

[2] It is of Alfred de Musset.

'Maman,' said Antoine in his almost over-perfect English, 'this is Jeremy, of whom I have told you so much.'

Even now, I am not totally at ease with being introduced like this, but then it was totally paranoia-inducing. What could Antoine have told her? That I worked for an armaments factory? That I had taken to enjoying an occasional heart-starting Calvados first thing in the morning? That I had recently been arrested for vagrancy in Le Mans?

I shook hands with my hostess and her son.

'You have the advantage on me, madame,' I said in my most formal French, 'but this room is an essay on your elegance and style.'

'I'm glad you like it, monsieur. Some people find it, well, a little old-fashioned. May we offer you a small glass of something?'

At this point I noticed the waiter who had let me in. He had put an ice bucket on an occasional table and was opening a bottle of champagne.

'How thoughtful of you,' I said. Antoine beamed at me. I suddenly suspected that all his friends were Spartacists or active members of Baader-Meinhof and that he never let his mother meet them. Personally I was glad that I had had the foresight to put on my Charvet tie.

Antoine's mother sat on the end of a small sofa and patted the space next to her for me to sit upon.

'We have such admiration for the British,' she said. 'Though your name is Irish, I believe.'

But it's not Barry Lyndon, I thought to myself. Out loud, I tried to unspin her comment. 'Not all Irishmen are Republicans. We chose to fight with Britain in the two wars, while their own men were conscripted.'

'Very commendable,' she said. She no longer looked quite so benign as I had first thought.

She pressed on.

'Don't you Irish envy the English their country houses? I have always felt that English houses are very pretty.'

I thought I would dodge this one. 'Not perhaps as exquisite as the villas of the Veneto. Those would be my favourites.'

'But I don't believe the Italians can afford to live in their houses, can they?'

This was getting tricky.

'I rather like the way they compromise with economic reality. I would hate to see Venice turned into some state-maintained film set, like St Petersburg.'

'St Petersburg?' queried the countess.

'I mean of course Leningrad. I'm so sorry, a slip of the tongue.'

'No, no, don't apologise. Please. It is charming to hear that enchanting city addressed by her maiden name. I only reacted because Sergei here' – she indicated the waiter – 'is the only person I have heard call it St Petersburg in some thirty years. Sergei's father came to us from there some years ago. His people once knew better times.'

She smiled at me warmly, and I looked across to Sergei, who was smiling at me too. I took a moment to take in the portraits. Among the countless severe grandees on the walls, how many were Russian? A pity I had not asked Antoine for a proper briefing. But then perhaps he was paying me back for a Shiva Ready-Curry and my upside-down wallpaper.

Sergei coughed discreetly and my hostess stood up. 'Will you take me in to dinner, monsieur?'

'With pleasure, madame,' I said, jumping to my feet. My God, was I the only guest?

Antoine said hardly a word throughout dinner and I felt about as relaxed as Jack did when interrogated by Lady Bracknell.

At least Sergei made a fuss of me, and while I took a spoonful or two of chopped egg and onion to add to my sevruga caviar, he made sure my champagne glass was never empty.

The main course was a *magret de pigeon* simply decorated with chantarelle mushrooms. It was memorable. Pigeon is a much underestimated bird. I had been wondering whether Antoine was going to offer a curry after my dubious efforts, but I had again underestimated his charity.

The red wine was fabulous, too, but it had been decanted and I never saw the label. It was certainly a Bordeaux and too complex to have been a Merlot. I resolved to ask Antoine at a later date, but I never did. I do so prefer to see the label. Otherwise it is only half an education.

'*On prendra du café au salon,*' Antoine's mother told Sergei, after we had eaten some fresh strawberries that had been dipped in dark chocolate, and we upped sticks and decamped into the oval drawing room.

Antoine managed a chance to say to me quietly, 'Maman has really taken to you. She is completely captivated.'

I couldn't see why, but it was good to know. However, I still felt that a job interview would have made for an easier conversation.

'Now you must tell me something, Jeremy,' she began. I nodded at her encouragingly and sipped at my coffee.

'Is it really true, that in England the upper classes are waited on by female servants in the manner of the French *petite bourgeoisie?*'

I nearly lost a mouthful of coffee over the pale lawn of the sofa.

'I'm not sure my own experience is a large enough sample,' I said, hoping to duck the subject.

'Well, is your family's staff male or female?'

I stammered that we did our best to manage without domestic staff. It was not a good enough answer. Whatever progress I had made was lost and a look of impatience flashed across her face.

Antoine showed me out. As we went down the stairs to the front door, an answer came to me. I should have said, 'In England we consider it rude to look too carefully.'

The French have an expression for only realising what you should have said when you are on the stairs, going home. They call it, most appropriately, *ésprit de l'escalier.*

The next day, after yet another unbeatable lunch, this time at the Ciel de Paris restaurant, on the fifty-sixth floor of the Montparnasse Tower, I took the afternoon off. I had to find a morning coat as my old one was probably still in the back of Sandro's Alfa Romeo Berlina, following our adventures at Le Mans. I didn't need it for a wedding, this time. It was for the races. If I was going to the Prix de l'Arc de Triomphe at Longchamp, I was going to be properly dressed.

My old friend Emmanuel had invited me to go in his party and he had tickets to the 'royal' enclosure.

I had loved racing since my university days, when I would frequently get to Newmarket. Having fluked a sizable win at the

Curragh, my interest in the 'sport of kings' had redoubled.

The Prix itself was inaugurated in 1920, to celebrate the Allies' victory in the Great War, and from those days the Arc de Triomphe Weekend has been the highlight of the French racing calendar. Something like 45,000 spectators pack the stands, and perhaps another 33 million television viewers, in 126 countries, sit glued to it every year.

The 'Arc', as it is affectionately known, takes place annually every first weekend in October at the Hippodrome de Longchamp in the Bois de Boulogne, right in the heart of Paris. The big race, the Prix de l'Arc de Triomphe, is run on 'Arc Sunday' and attracts the best middle-distance thoroughbreds from all over the world, especially Ireland, Italy and Germany, and the English delegation will include the winner of the Derby. The prize money is huge – it is in fact the largest purse in Europe.

The Prix is run over a mile and four furlongs of flat turf. Any three-year-olds or over may apply, except geldings. I have never found out why geldings are singled out for exclusion.

The racecourse is right-handed. It's been laid out in a giant horseshoe loop that rises gently to begin with before gradually descending to the long right-hand bend, where it leads into a 500 metres (or two and a half furlongs) finishing straight.

I found a tailcoat for hire in a wedding shop near the Opéra and, at the allotted hour on Sunday morning, I arrived in it at Emmanuel's flat, from where his party was gathering prior to setting off.

I was certainly well dressed. No other male in our party had seen fit to wear tails.

'Perhaps I am a bit overdressed?' I asked anxiously.

'No, no, not at all,' replied Emmanuel, in his immaculate blue suit, looking me up and down. 'That rig-out used to be obligatory. These days it's optional, but it's still rather stylish.'

'Of course it's not what it used to be,' Emmanuel told me in the car, as we set off for the track, 'Napoleon III wanted a French Royal Ascot here. He leaned on the *Loterie Nationale* to fund it.'

'Napoleon III had lived in England, hadn't he?'

'He had. We had locked him up after his second botched

coup[3] and he spent nearly six years inside before he managed to escape to England. We only let him back after the 1848 revolution, and then the wily old villain immediately stood for election.'

'As a member of the Assemblée?'

'No!' Emmanuel laughed. 'Napoleon was rather more ambitious. He stood for president.'

'What can he possibly have promised the French?'

'Oh, the usual right-of-centre platitudes: strong government, social consolidation and national greatness. President Bonaparte, as he became, waited another three years before he overthrew the Second Republic and seized total power. Then he was crowned Napoleon III.'

'He had style.'

'He certainly did. He had Longchamp sorted within a year of declaring the Second Empire, and he turned up at Longchamp with his young bride, Eugénie, at the first ever racing Sunday, back in 1857. Eugénie was quite a girl. Even before she married, Eugenia de Montijo, Countess of Teba, was the doyenne of European society. She was born in Spain and was of both Scottish and Spanish descent. The Emperor and his gorgeous young Empress, with their infant son the Prince Imperial, sailed down the Seine on their private yacht and arrived in the Royal Enclosure in time for the third race, where they joined Prince Jerome Bonaparte, his son Prince Napoleon, the Prince of Nassau, Prince Murat and the Duke de Mornay, the famous gourmet and racegoer.'

'You had recovered from your Revolution, then?'

'We certainly had. Non-aristocratic members of the upper classes were not allowed into the Royal Enclosure and had to content themselves with watching from their barouches and calèches on the lawn. But it was still a day out for the whole of Paris, and thousands of ordinary Parisians caught the steamboat at the Pont de Suresnes and cruised and drank for an hour before they got to the track.'

'Wasn't that infant boy to make his way in England?'

'I rather think he was. God knows why. Whoops!' He realised

---

[3] The future Napoleon III's attempts to seize power by force were in October 1836 and August 1840.

he had been tactless. 'I should tell you that he actually fought with the British in South Africa. Very sadly, the prince imperial, Eugène Bonaparte, was tragically killed down there. At Rorke's Drift, I believe. A shocked British people shipped his body home and he was buried with all appropriate pomp in the imperial crypt at Saint Michael's Abbey in Farnborough, Hampshire. His father, a committed Anglophile, saw to it.'

We pulled into the car park, and when we got to the Enclosure I looked around to see just how overdressed I actually was. As it turned out, there were a few others in tails at the meeting. I imagine they were all British.

But something more sinister was beginning to happen. I thought at first that I had had too much champagne, which was probably true, but it doesn't normally make me feel faint.

I wanted to ask my host about how I might put on a bet when I was overtaken by a great paroxysm of coughing. I seemed unable to stop or draw breath, and the spasm was becoming very painful.

I sat down for a while, but even though I managed to stop barking, I still felt very weak. Every time I tried to stand, I felt I would keel over. Shuddering waves of coughing racked my chest and I couldn't breathe in. I was in danger of running out of oxygen. Eventually, and with enormous force of will, I found Emmanuel and made my excuses.

'I am so sorry, old chap,' I told him. 'Not feeling too good. I'm going home.'

Which is what I did.

I spent most of the Métro ride with my head between my knees. At least the furious coughing had died away a bit. Nevertheless I was completely exhausted when I reached St Germain-des-Prés and it took me an age to walk the last stretch home and another age to climb the Himalayan staircase up to my flat. Once in, I threw off my tailcoat and fell on to my bed, either falling asleep or passing out.

It was not even 4 p.m. when I had gone to bed, but it was my alarm clock that woke me at 6 a.m. the next morning. It was time to get to my office.

Having slept in my shoes, I felt generally a bit vile, but at least the faintness seemed to have passed. I had a shower and put on something more appropriate for a day at the workface.

I couldn't face even the idea of breakfast, so I made my way to the Métro station on an empty stomach. I would have been in very good time if, halfway there, another wave of giddiness had not overtaken me. I sat down on some steps until I was better. Minutes later, on the Métro platform, another great coughing fit stopped me in my tracks. I concentrated on trying not to hack or faint, letting the trains go by until I recovered.

I was beginning to suspect I might be in worse condition that I had first thought.

Eventually I was able to board a train, but I only managed a few stops before I had to get off and recover again. This was going to be a very long journey.

It was almost midday when I finally arrived at Aérospatiale and made my way unsteadily to my office. My secretary, Michelle, took one look at me and told me I wasn't well. Tell me something I don't know, I thought.

I picked up my phone and started the series of apologies I had to make to all the people I had let down. I also cancelled my lunch. A pity, this last one, as I had been looking forward to getting to the Truffe Noire in Neuilly.

It was no good. I really wasn't well. I told Michelle that I was going home to bed and stood up. I lost consciousness immediately and fell down where I stood, as if a sniper had taken me out.

The next thing I knew was coming to in the factory's infirmary. After I had collapsed Michelle had sent for help and a nurse and my assistants had carried me there. My trousers were soaking and the doctor was trying to take my shirt off.

I caught his eye.

'You relieved yourself when you passed out,' he told me, a tone of disgust in his voice. 'Now we must get your shirt off for an X-ray.' I tried to unbutton it for him but he pulled it impatiently over my head. I had trouble walking to the X-ray machine, but I eventually made it, with help.

'All right,' the doctor said a few minutes later. 'You have pneumonia. We will get you to a hospital immediately.'

'Is it serious?' I asked.

'It used to be. You will be prescribed a course of antibiotics and you'll be on your feet again in, say, two weeks.'

I ended up in a private room at a nearby Parisian hospital. Aérospatiale generously took care of my costs. I was prescribed penicillin. It was extremely effective. Just forty-eight hours later I felt well and keen to get out of hospital and get on with my life. There were two reasons why I didn't: (a) The doctors ordered me not to; and (b) I had no clothes.

On the Thursday there came a knock at the door. It was Emmanuel and his mother.

'Good heavens!' I said. 'How marvellous to see you. How on earth did you know where to find me?'

It seemed they had worried for me when I left Longchamp and that as they discussed my sudden exit they became more rather than less anxious. They had telephoned my flat all Sunday night and had had no reply. On Monday they had rung my office, which had told them that I had been taken ill and was in the infirmary. They persisted, got hold of the infirmary nurse, who told them I had been taken to a hospital. No, she didn't know which one.

They had then started ringing all the Parisian hospitals, until, after being told to 'bear with us' (or its French equivalent) by countless receptionists for long periods of time, they had located me. And now, here they were, with fruit and a bottle of wine ('We have checked, and yes, you are allowed to have a glass with your meals') and a great bunch of flowers.

'Do you want us to ring your family?' asked Mme de Bodard, helpfully.

'No, that would only worry my mother. I'll be out of here in a few days. I'll ring her then.'

'Well, we'll come back and see you at the weekend,' Mme de Bodard promised.

They were as good as their word. At the weekend I was able to receive them with a little more style. Emmanuel took my keys and promised to return with some clothes (and to have the ones I arrived in laundered).

It was true. I had been burning the candle at both ends and a period of enforced rest was fine by me. But I was quickly becoming very bored.

There was a smoking room on my floor and I met an old boy

there who had served in Algeria. He was a diehard cynic, and hated politicians, his relations and doctors with equal enthusiasm. Happily, he had a mordant and irreverent sense of humour.

'What do you think of the coffee in this place?' he asked me one day.

'It's execrable,' I said.

'I know where we can get some decent stuff.'

And so the two of us, in hospital issue pyjamas and slippers, and sporting regulation dressing gowns, walked self-confidently out of the hospital and across the main road to a little café.

The owner did not bat an eyelid as we came in and sat at the bar. Obviously, patients came in this sort of attire all the time.

'Bugger the coffee,' said my *pied noir* friend. 'What I want is a cognac.'

And so, ignored by the other customers and with our elbows on the *zinc*, the two of us demolished the best part of a bottle of cognac and discussed the OAS, the war in Algeria and the miscalculations (even treason) of General de Gaulle.

Emmanuel brought me something to wear a few days later. He tried to explain something that was troubling him.

'The thing is, there is an association in France between illness and sin. My mother has concluded that you are ill because you stay up too late, get up too early, don't eat enough and drink far too much. Your illness was caused by your lifestyle.'

'Well, you can put her right, please, Emmanuel. My illness was caused by a bacterium. Penicillin, a British discovery, cured what would have been fatal thirty years ago in a couple of days. As for sleep, I take what I need. You can't believe how much food I eat, or even imagine its quality. And as for drink, there is no such thing as too much.'

Emmanuel laughed nervously.

'Perhaps when you come out, you will take life more easily.'

'I doubt it, old man. I intend to live it to the full.'

'Oh well, I'll tell my mother we spoke. See you in a few days.'

And he was gone.

I went along the corridor to see if I could discover my drinking companion. I was feeling rebellious.

I found him all right, but he glanced at my jeans and pullover and declined my offer. 'Where's the joy in going to the café dressed like everybody else? You don't find people basing their memoirs on people in jeans they saw once in a café quietly having a coffee. Either you go in uniform or you drink alone.'

My health was now completely returned to me and I saw the doctor in order to discharge myself. He did one last check of my blood pressure ('You have the tension of a little girl. At least you will never have a heart attack!') and signed the release.

I was free to return to civilisation.

There was one last task. I had endured a week of very basic hospital food and I wanted to celebrate my liberty. I collected my belongings in the little case that Emmanuel had considerately brought with him and went to the Grand Véfour for lunch, stopping only to put on a jacket and tie. After all, I had had my first near-death experience, and I wanted to sample life at its best.

Le Grand Véfour was awe-inspiring.

It is an eighteenth-century survivor, situated in the Palais Royal. It is just possible to get in without booking at lunch, though it never is in the evening. It is decorated in a Pompeian style. In fact, it claims to be the oldest restaurant in France, probably in the world.

It had fewer pretensions at the time of the Revolution. Then it was a superior kind of coffee house. What changed it was the influx into the capital of quondam private chefs, who suddenly found their households literally headless. These great chefs had grown up in private kitchens and now needed to earn a living, and the new masters of France needed places to scheme and plot. The concept of the restaurant was born.

Murat and Lamartine combined and agitated within these walls, and from their sinister dialogue was born the revolutionary Committee for Public Safety. Plans to encourage people to spy on their neighbours were hatched here, and rewards for good citizens who denounced petty criminals or hidden aristocrats were drawn up over the almond sorbet. The pacification of the Vendée was also dreamed up in these majestic rooms.

Already at their table was an elegant couple with their two children, going through the menu. I like the way the French habituate their young to restaurants from their earliest years.

French children are the best-behaved in Europe – in public, anyway.

Next to me, to my right and dining alone, was a woman in her middle years. Under her table her young little dog lay obediently and peaceably.

An American couple took the table to my left. The menu did not impress them. The waiter promised them that the chef would prepare whatever they liked, within reason of course, but to no avail. In the end they ordered, in English, a bottle of water and a couple of plain omelettes, complaining noisily about the prices and the fact that there were no vegetarian options.

Both my dog-owning neighbour and I had observed this strange little scene. And when the waiter reappeared, she called him over.

'*Quoi qu'ils mangent, s'il vous plaît, pour mon petit chiot.*'[4]

And the waiter duly brought the dog a plain omelette and a bowl of water and placed them under her table. As he did so, and with some ceremony, I heard him say, '*Monsieur le Chien est servi.*'[5]

It is good to know that in great French restaurants you will always be served, no matter how eccentric your order.

---

[4] 'What they're having, please, for my little puppy.'
[5] 'Master Dog is served.'

Epiphany
1973: Chartres

In which the author finally gets to Chartres, the greatest cathedral in Christendom, and is ravished by it as he should be. He also discovers chilled red wines from the Loire. They are very good with duck.

A little divine assistance would do me no harm. God was not immediately available, so I asked Charles-Henri. Which was the most striking cathedral in France – not the largest, which I had just visited, or the most practical, which was Notre Dame in Paris? Charles-Henri, such a devout Catholic, was bound to know the answer.

It took him several days before he came back to me with his answer.

It was Chartres.

Charles-Henri's dictum was that it was magnificent on account of its location, its architecture and its stained glass. But it was also beautiful because every man in Chartres, from the utterly unskilled gentry to the most highly skilled stone masons, had pulled the wagons up the steep hill to its site, regardless of their earthly rank and in the humble recognition that they were all equal (or equally guilty) in the eyes of God.

I liked his reasoning. I pictured a princess with her white skin, silk dress and conical hat, pushing a cart loaded with twenty tons of cut stone, next to a weather-beaten horny-handed son of toil.

John Julius Norwich wrote about this cathedral in one of his books.

> In 1194, the master-builder of Chartres outlined new principles which would inspire all the great architects of the 13th century. The elevation was in three tiers as it had no gallery (the relationship between the three levels should be noted), and the vaulting

was quadripartite, which eliminated the need for alternating sup-ports. Externally, an important change was introduced by abandoning the five towers initially planned over the transepts.[1]

I tried to picture quadripartite vaulting unsuccessfully. And any ability I might conceivably have had was rudely compromised by a vision of a tattooed workman gallantly passing a huge piece of carved stone to the princess on the ladder above him.

Chartres is reasonably close to Paris, at least by train, and I had set aside a perfect winter's day to see the cathedral and the town. I arrived earlyish one Saturday morning in November 1973. I was equipped with a guide and a pair of Charles-Henri's field glasses.

When you come to Chartres from any little distance, your first impression may be that it hovers in mid air above waving fields of corn. It is only when you draw close that the city that built it comes into view, clustering around the hill on which the cathedral stands. The cathedral soars over its town, its flying buttresses hardly obscured by the buildings that surround it. Its two grandiloquent but very different spires – one twelfth-century Romanesque, the other sixteenth-century flamboyant – rise majestically from its pale green roof. They have to be visible from thirty miles away and I dare say, on a still day, 10,000 Christians can still hear their bells.

This building is widely described as the prototypical Gothic building, but even from a distance you can tell from the spires alone that the cathedral is actually an anthology of different styles. When you get up close and go inside this is confirmed in spades. For all that the guidebooks may call it 'unified', there are count-less subtle variations of style in the detail.

Most of what you can see today was built incredibly quickly; in just twenty-six years, in fact. Rather better than the usual 200.

Charles-Henri's story of the whole community doing their bit is of course repeated in all the guidebooks.

One of them, which I had been poring over on the train, told me about the oak timbers used in its construction.

The cathedral I was visiting was based on the foundations of the Romanesque one that had been there before. Chartres

---

[1] John Julius Norwich, *The World Atlas of Architecture*.

cathedral is yet another French Gothic masterpiece built because a fire had destroyed its predecessor. A series of churches had been built on the site since Roman times, all of which seem to have had ended their careers in flames. In 1020, a certain Bishop Fulbert set out to build the most breathtaking basilica, over a massive crypt. When, in 1134, yet another conflagration burned the city to the ground, the cathedral was miraculously spared. But not for long. Unfortunately, the very height of the church combined with its metal roof in a conspiracy to attract lightning during the menacing thunderstorm of 1194. Only the western towers, the rose window, the crypt and the royal portal could be salvaged from the smouldering earlier work. It was decided to do the whole job again, this time on an even more epic scale.

The church's principal relic is the *Sancta Camisia*, the tunic worn by the Blessed Virgin Mary. Charles the Bald had given it to the cathedral in 876, having inherited it from Charlemagne who, in turn, had liberated it from Jerusalem during a crusade. As a result, Chartres became one of the earliest places of Marian pilgrimage in the Latin Church.

At first it was thought that the robe had been destroyed in the 1194 fire, but as the rubble was cleared it was discovered to be safe in the cathedral treasury. It was taken as a sign, and it was agreed by all that a new and even more awe-inspiring cathedral should rise from the ashes of the old.

Donations both of money and of human muscle power came from all over France. The townsmen, so the story goes, hauled the stones to the site from the quarry five miles away. The nave came first. By 1220 the main structure was complete. The old crypt and the ancient royal portal, having escaped the worst of the fire, were incorporated into the new building. On 24 October 1260, King Louis IX was present to watch the founding dedication of the church to Our Lady.

The crypt would henceforward serve as a foundation to the 'modern' cathedral, saving much time in the legendary team effort, where all the townspeople took part in the rebuilding and when the vast Gothic masterpiece was erected in a single generation.

Almost thirty years before reconstruction actually started, a very large number of oak trees had been felled to create a supply of seasoned wood for the reconstruction of the church, and for some of the city's greatest buildings.

The sawn timbers, cut from these massive trees, had been carried down to the river and submerged. There they stayed, as oak seasons itself underwater as much or possibly more than it does in air. The clear waters of the Loire slowly washed the sap from the trunks and made the oaks immortal.

My train slowed as if to give me a better view. I admired the green copper roof and its mismatched towers. I tried to visualise the church without the larger tower and in my mind I replaced the green copper roof with the dull grey of its original lead roof, trying for a better sense of the building's original appearance.

From the station I chose to ignore the attractions of the town and went directly up the pilgrims' hill. Eventually I found myself in the cathedral square, in front of the west front. I found its curious asymmetry oddly unsatisfactory, though the triple portal was, even from a distance, most impressive. So too was the famous rose window, a survivor from the earlier church. The window seemed as though it had been stamped into the solid stone, as a jeweller might do on our silver. It was interesting to read that it was a hundred years older than the rest of the church. I stared at the filigree stonework for a while.

My spiritual journey to Chartres really began when I got up close to that so-called royal portal on the western front of the church, and continued as I went through directly into the nave.

The west portal had also belonged to the earlier church. It was probably carved in the 1140s. It was carefully reordered to fit into its new space between the towers, and this has made the composition even more intense. The capitals and Old Testament kings and queens seem to wind continuously along the façade.

Above them, a great tympanum shows Christ in Majesty. As in most Romanesque churches, scenes from the Day of Judgement surround Our Lord, but here He is flanked by the symbols of the evangelists, while the Elders of the Apocalypse have been pushed out into the archorders. In the lintel the twelve apostles, along with a pair of prophets, complete the composition.

The portal is called 'royal' after its Hebrew kings and queens. Christians need maybe ten seconds to realise that this is who they are. Which makes it all the more reprehensible is that some vandalistic members of the revolutionary rabble took them for the kings and queens of France and attempted to guillotine them with their garden spades. But the damage they caused was slight and, despite the scars left by the 'age of reason', and perhaps thanks to the only light restoration they sustained in the 1850s, one is transported by the breathtaking elegance of these elongated figures, deliberately distorted to make them comprehensible to a head upturned in wonder, carved only a little less than 1,000 years ago.

Charles-Henri's view, that Chartres is the greatest of all Gothic cathedrals, is a view I took on trust when he shared it with me, and which over the intervening years I have done my best to test. I have ended by believing it absolutely.

The soaring aisles, the labyrinth, the intricate delicacy of stonework, the elegance of the exterior – the church is an encyclopedia of wonders, inside and out. There are not enough superlatives in the dictionary to pay homage to this building, or its stained glass.

I was ready to 'do' the windows, and Charles-Henri's field glasses were ready to serve.

Everywhere you go inside this glorious church, patterns of coloured light splash on to the floor. The undimmed cobalt blue, used so widely and to so much effect in the windows, was for a long time exclusive to Chartres.

The windows represent the most complete collection of medieval glass in the world, including our greatest English windows in King's College Cambridge, York Minster, Long Melford in Suffolk and St Peter Mancroft in Norwich.

Twice were they nearly lost to us. The religious wars of the sixteenth century did a lot of damage to such glass everywhere, and a well-intended but typically misguided 'modernisation' of 1753 removed a number of fine pieces. Saying that, out of the original 186 stained glass windows, 152 have survived. And the light shines through them in indeterminable complexity, a firework display of art created with the aim of creating in imitation of God's own creation.

All that was missing, I thought to myself in my English way, was the music of the young Thomas Tallis, with his searing treble lines and hymn-like bass.

Even without such music, Chartres is a dazzling display of stone and glass, and a lexicon of the medieval universe. Its wood and stone are in concert. An immense iconography fuses soul, spirit and body with nature and the stars. Tourists and faithful inside the cathedral are forcibly wedded into a congregation and together, willy-nilly, they share God's creation in its moment of conception. Once through the portal, the materialist 'enlightenment' has not yet happened, nor yet the 'reason' of the Revolution. The lives of Jesus and Mary predominate the galaxy of carvings and images everywhere you look, but so too do sundials and the signs of the zodiac. Surrounding you are vices and virtues, animals and flowers, and hosts of angelic seraphim and cherubim. The seasons are reunited with their labourers, all busy at their appointed tasks.

The philosophers and alchemists pore over the seven liberal arts. Aristotle, Ptolemy and Pythagoras are all a part of this catholic, or universal, vision. So too, in a humbler way, are the members of Chartres' ancient guilds, hobnobbing with earthly royalty, countless ecclesiastics, and hundreds of unidentifiable men and women of every station in life.

This celestial city above your head, carved into the choir stalls, populates the very stone columns that sprout like an avenue of trees. This heavenly city is peopled with numberless saints, martyrs and confessors, and all the ancient kings and queens of Judah. And the cathedral unites this quarrelling mass of peoples as One.

> The One remains, the many change and pass;
> Heaven's light forever shines, Earth's shadows flay;
> Life, like a dome of many-coloured glass, stains the white
>   radiance of eternity,
> Until Death tramples it to fragments.[2]

It was time to cool my head. I found a bar in the cathedral square. One of the great truths concerns 'thirst after righteousness'.

I asked for a glass of red wine as I looked through the lunchtime menu. A chilled red wine was immediately passed across the bar.

---

[2] Percy Bysshe Shelley, *Adonais*, LII.

A chilled red wine? I called the waiter and complained.

He looked at me in a tired but not unkind way.

'*Vous consommez un Chinon, monsieur. Vaut mieux le boire frais,*' he said.[3]

I ordered a *magret de canard* for my lunch that day, and took a half bottle of a red Sancerre – chilled, naturally – to help it on its way.

Nothing, but nothing, goes better with duck than a chilled Loire red.

I was going to put my plan to visit every cathedral in France on hold for a little while. If you have already seen the best there is nothing to look forward to.

And on my way home, in a Damascene gesture, I threw my well-thumbed copy of *The Origin of Species* out of the train window.

---

[3] 'You are drinking a "Chinon", sir. It's better to drink it chilled.'

Chapter the Twenty-seventh
1974: Coming Home (Part II)

In which the author invites his brother to join him and spend some of his gap year in Paris, entertains a British friend in an unusual way, learns at bit more about the Chilean coup, gets sacked from his super job and returns to England, to find the recession is showing early signs of ending. He lands a serious position in the City.

My clever eighteen-year-old younger brother, Giles, greeted the 1974 New Year with a spring in his step. He had won his place at Balliol and he now had a 'gap' of his own until October, when he would go up to Oxford. It was time for him to stretch his legs, and after the briefest of telephone calls he decided to accept my invitation and to come to Paris.

I was about to set off to explore the estate agencies, wanting to find a bedsit suitable for my little brother, when my new telephone rang again.

It was George, possibly my oldest friend. His career was working out better than mine. After graduating from Christ Church, Oxford, a year before I had from Cambridge, the City had still been recruiting and he had sailed into a stockbroking firm on a graduate entry scheme. He had taken to the City like a duck to water. He was, or should have been, proud of his tremendous achievement, as he had managed to remain employed during the power cuts and three-day weeks when nobody at all had been recruiting, and half the last in were the first out. Particularly clever of him was to have been recruited by one of the boutique brokers that were springing up with bear market specialists who could make money when all the indices were falling.

'So how do I find you, old scout?' he asked me.

'No use grumbling, dear boy. Nobody listens. I've asked Giles to come over and now I have to find a room for him. What are you up to?'

'Just got my first serious bonus. I thought I might come over and blow it all in Paris. You could show me the sights, if you know what I mean.'

I will admit I didn't immediately understand that telling 'you know what I mean'.

'The Eiffel Tower, the Jeu de Paume; they're all very worth-while,' I suggested.

'Certainly, old scout. If there's time we'll see those places too. Then it's all fixed. Meet me after work at the Bristol Hotel next Friday. We'll start from there.'

The Bristol is one of Paris's many grand hotels and is much favoured by businessmen, especially those with taste. Despite its undoubted style, if my expense account could take the weight, I'd rather stay at the Ritz or the Plaza Athenée. Or even the Meurice, as the Nazis did some years ago.

Finding a bedsit for Giles was no labour of Hercules. The agent told me he had just the place. So perfect was it, he told me, that there was no need for me even to see it. It was a little studio with its own entrance and a little stove for a cooked breakfast. Ideal student stuff. In truth it sounded rather better than my old *chambre de bonne*.

I signed on the dotted line and handed over the deposit. That hadn't been too hard.

What now? Into the Café Flore for a late breakfast, I thought. I checked my pockets – force of habit – for *jetons de téléphone*, the telephone tokens we all carried about in those days. I had rather a lot of them. They were redundant, more or less, now that my own phone had finally been installed, but I could get rid of some of them when I broke the good news to my bright little brother. He would find a job just as easily as I had. And it didn't really matter if he didn't. I had money enough for two.

I felt very happy when I hung up the phone in the basement of the Café Flore. Giles was coming over to Paris, just as his sister had once come to Rome. It made sense to me to get your travelling done before going to university – not mooching about aimlessly afterwards, as I was doing. As for Giles, he had a string of parties to go to in London and would join me early the following week.

The telephone kiosk was at the entrance to the unisex lavatory and just outside sat a large harridan of a gatekeeper at her desk, with her little wicker basket of small coins. Her relieved customers would toss her a *pourboire* to thank her for keeping the place immaculate. What a way to earn a living, I thought. I couldn't really see Giles doing that. I made a mental note to check to see if any language schools were advertising for a teacher.

I had another great week at Aérospatiale, which included an epic lunch at Pétrossian with my two assistants. Pétrossian (then) had only one Michelin star. I felt it best for them to have a gentle introduction to haute cuisine.

Then as now, Friday is the only day for heroic lunchtimes. It was almost five when we stumbled out into the sunlight and sobering fresh air. I had completely forgotten that I had agreed to meet George at the Bristol Hotel, but in my pocket, trying to present their case to my pickled brain, were two tickets to the opera – a modern piece by a young Polish composer, having its Parisian stage début. From memory, it was called *Here, There and Everywhere*.

It's not every day that an up-and-coming young stockbroker determines to blow his bonus on a weekend in Paris, and as principal beneficiary, I didn't want to let him down. I wished my Aérospatiale colleagues a good weekend and hailed a passing taxi. The car screeched to a halt in American fashion and the driver wound down his window.

'*L'hôtel Bristol, s'il vous plaît, et allons-y au plus vite possible, j'suis déjà énormément en retard,*' I ordered.

'*Je ferai de mon mieux,*' he replied, helpfully.[1]

From Pétrossian to the Bristol you have to cross the river, and the early evening rush hour was upon us. We seemed to be going nowhere. The only thing that moved was the taximeter.

'You must know a faster route,' I told my driver, in French.

'A faster route, perhaps, but it's not the shortest,' he said.

'Just take it.'

---

[1] 'The Bristol, please, and go as fast as you can, I'm already very late.' – 'I'll do my best.'

It certainly wasn't the most direct, but at least we were moving again. We passed near the Eiffel Tower and crossed the bridge into the XVIe *arrondisement*, heading for Place d'Etoile and the Champs-Élysées. And there, going round the Arc de Triomphe, my driver drove straight into the side of another car that was trying to carve him up.

Immediately, both drivers were out in the road, squaring up to each other.

'Please,' I said to them both, 'I am on an important mission. I saw the accident. No one was at fault.'

'Well, monsieur,' said the driver of the other car, 'if you say so. Here are my details.'

We got back in our cab and the driver gave me a claims form, saying, 'You couldn't help me with this? I'm not good at forms.'

It was obvious that without my help we were going to be stuck in the traffic, being hooted at by a very great number of irate Parisians. I told him I would trade a favour. He would now go to the Bristol and I would fill in his form while he drove. I duly got all his details from him – his name, his address, his driving licence details, his social security number, his insurance policy reference, and all the bureaucratic shenanigans that the French were able to dream up. And then we were there.

I gave him back the form, complete with a description of the incident, needing only his signature.

The driver was suitably grateful and refused to accept a fare. I was just about to get out when he said, 'Are you from Tours?'

'From Tours? Why on earth from Tours?'

'It is only that you speak so well, and everybody knows that the best French is spoken in Tours.'

This wonderful compliment from a Parisian taxi driver put me in a good mood for many years.

George was already at the bar when I came in, beaming with pride.

'Sorry I'm late,' I said.

'You don't exactly look it,' said George.

'Anyway, it's great to see you. I've managed to get us two tickets to the opera. I hope that's OK with you?'

I will admit he didn't actually look overjoyed, but he put a brave face on it.

'That's very thoughtful of you. Will this suit be all right?'

'It'll be fine. After this drink, let's go to Harry's Bar. It's a brilliant little place.'

We did go to Harry's Bar, where we sank a couple of Bloody Marys, as tradition dictates. We then walked the hundred yards or so to Garnier's Opera House, arguably the most extraordinary opera house in Europe. It has the unusual distinction of having been Hitler's favourite building, but it is not in the stern neoclassicism promoted by Albert Speer. On the contrary, the building is entirely feminine, all curves and sumptuousness, an essay in spirals of deeply coloured marble and monumental chandeliers, of ornate statuary, grand staircases and deep carpets, patrolled by bewigged footmen.

I had found us a box. In reality, it hadn't been difficult to get one, even at the last minute. Tickets for this new production had been on sale at the box office for days, and were going for half the usual price. Outside, the touts were selling them at a discount to the discount. On the way to our box, a flunkey sold George a programme and took his order for some champagne. He also showed George where he could hire some opera glasses.

As soon as we took our seats at the front of our box, George was immediately in the spirit of the thing and trained his mother-of-pearl binoculars on the other opera goers.

'Not a vast crowd here tonight,' he observed. Quite correctly. The opera house was about half full.

Despite the champagne and the box, the lasting memory I have of *Here, There and Everywhere* was its mind-numbing tedium.

The audience loved it, of course. They must have been friends of the composer, or have come from the Drummond School of Music-through-pain.

Every cliché of our times was there, the spikiness, the strict absence of melody, a structure based around some modernist theory – atonal or serial composition, I suppose. The orchestration, largely achieved via tape recorders, reminded one forcibly of the sound of two factories mating. The young singers, performing their octave leaps and being forced to sing outside any known human vocal range, sounded alternately like saws in a timber yard or copulating cats on Beecham's tin roof. All it lacked was a Peter

Sellars *mise en scène*. I took refuge in the champagne.

George, bless him, pretended to be amused by all this affectation.

After a while I wandered into the back of our box, where the management had installed a chaise longue, totally out of sight of any other opera lover. I remember thinking that a box at the Garnier would be the perfect place for an assignation. The staff was discretion itself. But if seduction were the object, perhaps this dreadful cacophony could be bettered. Delibes' *Lakme*, for example, would provide a better background for romance.

I felt obliged to let George off the hook and I whispered to him that we might leave at the interval.

'Really?' he said, raising an eyebrow. 'I'm rather enjoying it.'

Whoops...

George, who has many great qualities, will not be too put out if I say that being a music lover is not one of them. At this time, he only had one record, or at least, he only played one record. That was 'I Get a Kick out of You', in a cover version by Gary Shearstone.

Yet, there he was, plainly engrossed. *'De gustibus non est disputandum'* is the old saying. There's no accounting for it.

We emerged at around 10.30 p.m. and George wanted to know where the action was.

'What sort of action?' I asked him.

'Oh, you know, a black man playing jazz blues on his piano, ladies of the night making a fuss of a tourist, a svelte blonde singer doing the whole Mistinguett number...'

'That's 1930s Hollywood. This is Paris, forty years and a world war later.' Still, I thought, there must be cosy *endroits* of this type in Paris. A pity it wasn't Marseilles, where I, man of the world, knew my way around.

Madame Claude had famously run just such a place somewhere off the Champs-Élysées for many years. Sadly she had just been shut down after a series of scandals involving half M Pompidou's cabinet.

'I've heard there's fun to be found around the rue St Denis,' said George. 'Is that too far to walk? Shall we take a cab?'

'I do know a suitable bar there, as it happens. Let's get there and see what the form is.'

This was ridiculous. My old friend wanted me to play *boulevardier* to his purse warden, but I had yet to pay any attention to the seamier side of Paris.

I decided to wing it. Our taxi dropped us at the Pigalle end of the rue St Denis and we headed for a little wine bar, certainly *louche* but not nearly as decadent as George seemed to want.

Once armed with a glass and seated at the bar, I told George that I just had to make a phone call and would be right back. I stepped into the street.

Almost immediately I saw a *péripatétienne* in the full costume of her ancient profession.

'*Excusez-moi, madame,*' I said politely, '*mais je cherche une maison de tolérance, et comme préférence, une telle avec un peu de classe.*'[2]

'*Ah, m'sieur, vous voulez grignotter les lorettes?*' At least, I believe that is what she said. *Lorettes* made a little sense, at least. They were the young girls who thronged from the provinces in the nineteenth century to seek jobs in the capital and who then often lurched into prostitution.

'*Allez par-là,*' she told me, '*et frappez à numéro douze. Amusez-vous bien, donc, monsieur. Et vive le sport!*'

I rejoined George. When I told him that I knew where to go, he threw back his drink and stood up. He didn't want to waste any more time.

Number twelve turned out to be an ancient town house and boasted some rather useful-looking North Africans standing around outside. We ignored them and went straight in.

The oval hall had a sensational staircase that wound its way tightly around the wall from the floor to a gallery, where a number of doors led off.

Below, milling about, were a number of girls who looked at George and me with the whole gamut of emotions between indifference and faint curiosity. Most continued to paint their nails or chew gum, and some were intelligent enough to do both simultaneously. There was no pianist, however, and the whole place needed a lick of paint and some softer lighting. The girls definitely needed a couturier to bring out their better points.

George turned to me.

---

[2] 'I'm looking for a brothel with a touch of class.'

'This is more like it,' he said, helping himself to a blonde. 'I'm going up there.' And with that, he and a giggling lady made their way up the cantilevered stairs.

I found myself below, talking idly to some of the girls. They were mainly talking about their children, Montessori schools, the better supermarkets, discounts on make-up, and Robert Redford. As everybody in 1974 could talk about these subjects, I confidently added my two cents' worth.

But I felt no urge to help myself. Even now I would still have to get into a certain mood to contemplate what George was doing, or at least to have a reasonable chance of delivering. As far as I am concerned, unless a number of romantic bases are touched first, the whole erotic thing just falls apart. These days, of course, I speak academically. I am about to celebrate my silver wedding.

In due course, the enthusiastic noises from George's room died down and the man emerged, beaming like a Cheshire cat.

'Do you suppose, *vieux scout*,' he said, as we left the august establishment, 'there are any late night operas on in this perfect city?'

We headed off for the Moulin Rouge. These days the august institution is merely a cinema and cabaret theatre and nothing is left of the original except the wings. Don't expect the ghosts of Manet or Lautrec. Nevertheless, it was nearly four in the morning when we parted company and headed for our respective beds. George's gratitude was effusive. Marvellous, really.

The following weekend my brother Giles arrived in Paris, brimming over with excitement.

I had been dutiful, and had found him a job, or at least, the opportunity to get a job, at one of the many Parisian language schools, and now we went shopping to stock his fridge and wine rack.

I was relieved to discover that his bedsit was fairly comfortable. It had its own front door, in any case. True, the bed looked fairly ropey and a spring had surfaced somewhere, but if you found the right position it was adequate. And it was very affordable and centrally located. He should be all right.

'I should be all right, here,' he agreed. 'Mainly because I'll be at your place most of the time.'

'Ah,' I said. But, anxious to prove him right, I took him over to my place where we talked about home, university and the future well into the night.

From then on, Giles and I met every evening, after I got back from Aérospatiale. This made my current girlfriend, a secretary at Aérospatiale, a little grumpy, but I would have none of it. I delighted in introducing the young fellow to Paris. Winter brought dark evenings, so he did the big tourist stuff without me during the day. As far as work was concerned, at first he only netted a few hours, and he didn't really enjoy it. It really didn't matter. What mattered was Paris, and what it would make of him.

I introduced him to some of my friends and he got on with them very well indeed. I was confident that I had done the right thing, even if (truth be told) he did cramp my style a little. I had rather forgotten just how young eighteen actually is.

But things at work, where I was coming up to my first anniversary, had taken a new and dangerous turn.

In Chile, in September, the political situation had turned from charged to explosive.

Allende had been preparing to call for a referendum to unblock the impasse between his coalition of the Left and his Rightist opposition. Who knows whether his plan would ever have worked? My opinion, for what it's worth, is that even if successful it would have done no more than postpone the inevitable.

In any case, the military made such speculation futile. On the morning of 11 September 1973 they launched an attack on their government.

This time they would take no chances. Just prior to the assault, the army commanders, headed by the newly appointed commander-in-chief, General Augusto Pinochet Ugarte, purged those officers who were thought to be sympathetic to either the president or the constitution.

The last time anyone saw Allende alive was when he was glimpsed defending his palace, or his family, or both, with an assault rifle. But as the presidential palace fell to the army he, together with several cabinet ministers, was either assassinated or committed suicide.

Within minutes the universities were put under military control and all opposition parties were banned. Over the weeks that followed, thousands of Chileans were tortured and killed. The Left was dismantled. The CIA provided Pinochet's hit squads with the names of 'insurgents'. As a consequence the opposition, real and potential, 'disappeared'.

Even so, here and there, resistance to the coup broke out. The military, having had time to plan, managed to consolidate control much more quickly than commentators had believed possible. And the protracted civil war that everyone had feared was prevented by the sheer speed and pitilessness of the coup.

Hervé Gamel and I, discussing the matter over countless coffees, had come to the conclusion that all the players in the Chilean landscape were to blame. They were all too ideological and too stubborn. A minority president facing adamant domestic and foreign opposition was never going to be able to uphold democracy and create socialism at the same time.

As for the involvement of the CIA, leaked secret materials were already appearing in the press.[3]

In mid-January, it was time for me to renew my *carnet de séjour* and the other documents I needed to work in a classified establishment and, slightly hung-over from an evening with my office mates celebrating a great first year, I turned up at the *préfecture*, armed with all my papers.

I was received with courtesy and a smile and all seemed to be going like clockwork – as much as French bureaucracy ever can.

My residence permit, my work permit, all these things, all had the same renewal date, as I had officially been a tourist up to the time I had got my job with my factory. The Prefect of Police could and should renew them all.

---

[3] Michael J Harrington (D-MA) leaked details of secret Congressional testimony by William Colby. Later, in late 1975, the Senate Committee headed by Frank Church released the report on 'Covert Action in Chile, 1963–1973'. And later still, in 1982, Costa-Gavras directed *Missing*, which starred Jack Lemmon and Sissy Spacek, providing a dramatised account of the true story of Charles Horman, a thirty-year-old American freelance journalist, who 'disappeared' during the coup. See also 'Covert Action in Chile, 1963–1973: a Staff Report of the Select Committee to Study Governmental Operations with Respect to Intelligence Activities (US Senate)', which was published on 18 December 1975.

He smiled at me amiably enough, took out an official-looking stamp and duly banged it down on my completed applications.

He then passed them back across his desk to me.

In large red letters was the single word. '*Refusé*'. Withheld.

'*D'ici vous avez juste au fin du mois de quitter la France.*'[4] With the same friendly and helpful expression on his face, he added, '*Bonne chance et bon courage.*'

I remonstrated, but to no avail. He couldn't, or wouldn't, say why my application to remain had been declined. There was no obvious line of appeal. With my work permit cancelled, I could not even draw a salary any more.

I had not seen this coming and I panicked a bit.

When Giles came over that evening, I told him what had happened.

'Oh well,' he said, '*tant pis*. So you're going back home, then. Good thing the economy seems to be recovering a little. I might stay on here for a bit. You know, I bet it's all that stuff about Chile. The CIA has given your name to the Deuxième Bureau, or vice versa. They've probably been listening to your phone calls. Why don't you ring up your friend Hervé and see if he's all right?'

I did ring up Hervé in the office but he was away on business, they told me. No one seemed to know when he would be back, or where he had gone. I toyed with ringing Marie-Françoise but I lacked the courage.

Giles and I decided that the old French expression, '*manger bien, ça remonte la morale*', was worth testing in a scientific way, and we set off for dinner. We went to the restaurant simply called 'Paris', around the corner from my flat.

We didn't hold back.

After we had eaten like lions, it seemed a good idea to finish off my cognac.

We talked 'exit strategy'. I had paid my rent until the end of January. There was a deposit, too, that needed reclaiming. Giles could do that – the money would be useful to him.

I must say my younger brother was very practical about the whole catastrophe. 'You speak two European languages like a native. You have got beneath the skin of the French and the

---

[4] 'You have until the end of the month to get out of France.'

Italians. How many people can say that? Your maths is strong and you have always had an interest in economics. Ring up the people you know in the City. After three years of employing nobody, I bet they are on the lookout for talent now the Americans have paid our debts. I feel you have done a very clever thing, being abroad all this time, while the dead weren't being buried and there were rats all over London. I believe I will try and do the same when my time comes, though perhaps I'll try Germany rather than France or Italy. I always did prefer Wagner to Rossini.'

We drank until dawn, as you do when you are twenty-four years old, and then Giles decided he would have to go to his bedsit. He went to the door, waved farewell and headed unsteadily for the stairs.

I threw off my clothes into a corner and climbed clumsily into bed. I wasn't planning on going to work the next day.

But when I woke I began to realise that a feeble rapping was coming from my door. I opened it carefully. It was Giles. His face was covered in blood.

'Jesus Christ! What on earth happened to you?' I asked, appalled at the sight.

'I fell down your stairs on the way out. Quite concussed myself. After a bit I made it back to your landing, but nothing I did, until now, could raise you. So I slept there.'

The wound to his face was not as bad as it had first appeared under the dried blood, and I patched him up as best I could. I felt very guilty about letting an eighteen-year-old get into that condition, and I still do.

My office rang me, to say that (a) they had heard that I was leaving France (b) I would not be reappearing in the office, and (c) my belongings would be delivered to my home address at a time to suit me. Oh yes, and that (d) they would pay me until the end of the month. No, they had no idea why all this had happened, except that the decision seemed to have been taken at a very high level. '*Bonne chance et bon courage.*'

My last days in Paris were a whirl of social activity. I had a lot of friends to say goodbye to, after all. But there was to be no great party as there had been in Rome. For one reason, there just wasn't time. And I knew that as the Pope is a Catholic, and how bears do what they must in the woods, the security services would be on my case from midnight on 31 January.

I rang George, and Piers de la Force, and some others in London. They all seemed to share my brother's opinion that I would have few problems. Piers' encouragement came with some practical suggestions. I should have lunch with him the very minute I was back.

He had a friend, called Monneret de Villard, who also spoke French and Italian and who was something rather important at Lloyd's of London.

Piers would set up a date. Monneret would give me the once-over, and then – providing all went well – would take up my cause.

A few days after that, I was back in London, where it all worked out as everybody had said it would. On 1 April 1974, after a string of interviews, I was a graduate trainee at Piers's company, C T Bowring, the giant reinsurance broker in the heart of the City of London. I bought myself a new suit, bravely put on my Charvet tie, and took my seat in a vast and very modern office overlooking the Thames and the Tower of London. I was told I would have to spend a year or so learning how it all worked. After that, they promised, my languages might just come in useful.

'So how should I describe my adventures in Europe?' I had asked Piers while completing my CV for the people at Bowring's.

'Oh, that,' he replied. 'Just put it down as a gap year or two.'

Printed in the United Kingdom
by Lightning Source UK Ltd.
119166UK00002B/31-213